CHRISTOPHER HITCHENS AND HIS CRITICS

Christopher Hitchens and His Critics

TERROR, IRAQ, AND THE LEFT

◈

Edited by

SIMON COTTEE *and* THOMAS CUSHMAN

With an Afterword by

CHRISTOPHER HITCHENS

NEW YORK UNIVERSITY PRESS
New York and London

NEW YORK UNIVERSITY PRESS
New York and London
www.nyupress.org

Library of Congress Cataloging-in-Publication Data
Christopher Hitchens and his critics : terror, Iraq, and the left / edited by Simon Cottee
and Thomas Cushman ; with an afterword by Christopher Hitchens.
p. cm. Includes bibliographical references and index.
ISBN–13: 978-0-8147-1686-1 (cl : alk. paper)
ISBN–10: 0-8147-1686-5 (cl : alk. paper)
ISBN–13: 978-0-8147-1687-8 (pb : alk. paper)
ISBN–10: 0-8147-1687-3 (pb : alk. paper)
1. War and society. 2. Terrorism. 3. Liberalism. 4. Hitchens, Christopher.
I. Cottee, Simon. II. Cushman, Thomas, 1959–
HM554.C475 2008
303.6'6—dc22 2007049414

New York University Press books are printed on acid-free paper,
and their binding materials are chosen for strength and durability.

Manufactured in the United States of America

c 10 9 8 7 6 5 4 3 2 1

p 10 9 8 7 6 5 4 3 2

The real test of a radical or a revolutionary is not the willingness to confront the orthodoxy and arrogance of the rulers but the readiness to contest illusions and falsehoods among close friends and allies.

—CHRISTOPHER HITCHENS,
For the Sake of Argument, 325–26

CONTENTS

Contents

PART II: HITCHENS ON IRAQ

Contents

Contents

Contents

Contents

ACKNOWLEDGMENTS

We thank, first and foremost, Christopher Hitchens for generously providing free and unfettered access to his work and for graciously agreeing to write a response to his critics. For granting us the permission to use their work, we also thank the contributors to the Critical Responses and Exchanges section.

For personal and professional support during the preparation of this book, Simon Cottee is grateful to Terry Bartholomew, Howard Davis, Stephen Hester, Roy King, Ian Loader, John Palmoski, and Francesca Salinari. Thomas Cushman thanks all those who have helped him in this project and other work over the past six years; they are too numerous to mention, but they will know who they are. We owe a special thanks to Wellesley College, which supported this project through research funds from its Committee on Faculty Awards. We thank Reed Malcolm from the University of California Press, who enthusiastically supported this project from its inception to its completion but could not prevail over an editorial board that delayed the project for reasons that readers can surmise for themselves. We also thank Eric Zinner and Despina Papazoglou Gimbel at New York University Press for their dogged support and assistance.

Beyond his generous permission to reprint the articles which the editors selected and writing the afterword, Christopher Hitchens played no part in the conceptualization or production of this volume. His distance from the project was a necessary condition for the success of this book.

Simon Cottee, Bangor, Wales, UK
Thomas Cushman, Wellesley, Massachusetts

Introduction

Terror, Iraq, and the Left

SIMON COTTEE AND THOMAS CUSHMAN

I am prepared for this war to go on for a very long time.
I will never become tired of waging it, because it is a
fight over essentials.

—CHRISTOPHER HITCHENS[1]

Christopher Hitchens—political journalist, cultural critic, and public intellectual—is one of the most controversial and prolific writers in the English-speaking world.[2] A contributor to a daunting variety of newspapers, magazines, and periodicals and the author of sixteen books, Hitchens has written on an extraordinarily wide range of subjects: Leon Trotsky, Kingsley Amis, Route 66, Saul Bellow, Bob Dylan, the death penalty, holocaust denial, Michael Moore, Bosnia, Mother Teresa, Mel Gibson, the Kurds, North Korea, and the Taliban.[3] On these and countless other subjects, Hitchens brings to bear a thrillingly volatile combination of analytical rigor, an exceptional breadth of reading and historical knowledge, a savage wit, and an acute feel for irony and contradiction.

Hitchens writes not just to illuminate the world but to roundly demystify it: to question and to repudiate the litany of clichés and prejudices that contentedly inhabits our everyday discourse. By exposing their contradictions and inadequacies, Hitchens's aim is to weaken their demotic appeal. Of the various literary genres to which he applies himself, it is the polemic at which he best excels. As a polemicist, Hitchens is combative, elegant, and ruthless.[4] Nothing excites him more than the prospect of an argument. The British novelist Martin Amis recalls that when he went to Cyprus to be best man at Hitchens's first wedding in 1980, he spent his mornings lazing by the pool, whereas Hitchens would appear midmorning in a suit and go straight to the bar to find someone to argue with.[5] Hitchens is never happier than when arguing, and arguing is what he is best at.

In argument, Hitchens cuts a formidable and intimidating figure. He never lets a cliché or a euphemism pass uncontested, and he never gives so much as a millimeter, nor does he back down—ever.[6] Above all, he is daring and morally courageous: Hitchens will take on anybody or any subject.[7] For the sake of argument or point of principle, he will antagonize and infuriate and, if need be, unmake friends and allies. The great merit of Hitchens's work is its honesty. Hitchens can be relied on to say exactly what he thinks, whomever it offends.

Hitchens is a vivid example of what the great German sociologist Georg Simmel described as the "antagonist," a social type who thrives on conflict and disputation. Guided by the "spirit of contradiction," the "antagonist" sees himself (to quote Simmel) as the "defender of threatened rights," as a "fighter for what is objectively correct," a "knightly protector of the minority."[8] He is best represented "in the person of Robert Ferguson: his hostility was not to Popery or to Protestantism, to monarchical government or to republican government, to the house of Stewarts or to the house of Nassau, *but to whatever was at the time established.*"[9]

Like the "antagonist" of whom Simmel speaks, Hitchens is instinctively skeptical of the conformist mentality, believing that it undermines progress and freedom. Cliché and stock response are his principal enemies, since they exemplify an unquestioning mind and a willingness to capitulate to the social and ideological status quo. Conversely, what he most admires are the qualities of critical skepticism, ironic distance, and originality of voice.

Allied to Hitchens's distrust of convention is what sociologists would call his moral and intellectual "absolutism." Not only is he strongly committed to a rationalist defense of Enlightenment values; he also believes, in the tradition of Marx and the Frankfurt School,[10] that truth is an essential tool for unmasking the relations of domination that stand in their path. To put this in less grandiose terms, Hitchens believes that some principles—like freedom of expression or gender equality—are simply universal and must be defended without compromise. He also believes, furthermore, that there is such a thing as "truth" and that it can be wielded at the expense of those who threaten or undermine universal values. This clearly places Hitchens at a vast distance from the world of academe, where Foucauldian perspectivism and Rortyian antiuniversalism tend to predominate.[11] From this rarefied setting, Hitchens's moral certitude and epistemological naturalism (to say nothing of his colossal appetite for alcohol and cigarettes)[12] will seem terribly atavistic or "inappropriate." What also serves to antagonize many of Hitchens's critics, and those not remotely susceptible to anti-Enlightenment themes, is what might be called his epistemological arrogance or the firmness of his belief that he is "telling it like it is." As Stefan Collini explains, "As always with Hitchens's work, one gets the strongest possible sense of how much it matters to prove that one is and always has been right: right about which side to be on, right that there are sides and one has to be on one of them; right about which way the world is going, right about which policies will work and which regimes are wicked; right about the accuracy of one's facts and one's stories; and right when so many others, especially well-regarded or well-placed others, are demonstrably wrong. There is a palpably macho tone to all of this, as of alpha males competing for dominance and display."[13]

As a combatant, Hitchens can certainly be aggressive and domineering (and the cause of despair among his friends),[14] yet he can also be intelligent, funny, and delicately skilful. What is impressive about Hitchens's best work is how fully it combines all these different elements, fusing steely contempt with intellectual nuance and literary flair. In our judgment, Hitchens's work represents a template for polemical excellence: the writing is deadly, even vicious, yet somehow charming, refined, and intelligent.[15]

Of Hitchens's recent battles, it is those with the Western Left—the very political family from which he himself descended—that have been the most memorable and vitriolic. In the aftermath of the September 11 attacks, Hitchens very publicly estranged himself from this quarter, castigating many of his former comrades for what he saw as their abject accommodations with all kinds of religious barbarism and political tyranny, and their failure to take seriously the global threat of militant Islam. It is our belief that in Hitchens's recent political writings it is possible to discern one of the most powerful self-critiques of the Western Left today. Hitchens is therefore an essential reference point for the Left, and his criticisms demand to be engaged with if it is to combat the corrosive relativism, fatalism, and cultural pessimism to which it at present seems to be succumbing. Indeed, Hitchens's writings can be seen as part of a wider historical tradition of leftist self-criticism, drawing inspiration from the work and example of Rosa Luxemburg, Victor Serge, Boris Souvarine, Arthur Koestler, C. L. R. James, and George Orwell. In his book on Orwell, *Orwell's Victory*, Hitchens praises his subject for his uncompromising opposition to both capitalist imperialism *and* Soviet Communism, and for his "power of facing unpleasant facts"[16]—especially those that served to question his own beliefs. In an encomium to C. L. R. James, Hitchens writes that the true mark of a radical lies not in "the willingness to confront the orthodoxy and arrogance of the rulers" but in "the readiness to contest illusions and falsehoods among close friends and allies."[17] Although he does not explicitly say so, Hitchens clearly sees himself as a member of this elite group of dissident progressive intellectuals.

By challenging the Left from within, by pointing out its contradictions, Hitchens's intention is not to destroy it but, as he sees it, to honor the great traditions to which it owes its birth. He wants to reawaken a spirit of reflexivity and critical self-examination among those who now profess its mantle, as well as to thoroughly demoralize those among them who have aligned themselves with reactionary Islam and state tyranny. Not surprisingly, given that disputes within families are always hotter than those among strangers, Hitchens's criticisms have been met with a storm of protest from those at the receiving end. The critiques included in this volume boldly set out the core lines of dispute.

This book is predicated on the belief that conflict is an essential—indeed eminently desirable—feature of social, political, and intellectual life. In the therapeutic culture of the modern West, the idea that conflict is *good*—is humanly valuable and something actually to be desired—will strike a somewhat discrepant note. Conflict, we are taught, is not good but *bad*: uncivilized, destructive, polarizing. Yet conflict, as Karl Marx brilliantly testifies, is the very life force of social change; without conflict there can be no progress and no path out of error and unfreedom. In the world of ideas, conflict is what makes intellectual development possible.

Conflict is a great clarifier; in a conflict, the opposing antagonists not only come to a better understanding of each other's arguments but are forced to reflect on the cogency and clarity of their own beliefs. Conflict prevents one from becoming bewitched into thinking that there is only one truth. It also serves as a powerful antidote against intellectual sterility and decline, since it encourages the dialectical adjustment and refinement of competing positions.

Hence, the aim of this book is to pit Christopher Hitchens directly against a representative group of his leftist critics. The contest that we have orchestrated is, as it must be, bruising and lacerating. Yet it is also, we believe, profoundly illuminating and instructive. To witness the entanglements that ensue is to gain a fascinating insight into the world-view of the contemporary Western Left; it is also, more broadly, to gain an appreciation of the centrality of language and rhetoric in public intellectual and political debate.

Our broader aim is to use the example of Hitchens to reinstate a model of vigorous debate, argument, and conflict among those—Left intellectuals—who all too often seek the comfort of ideological conformity, fearing (not without reason) that dissent among ideological comrades will lead to ostracism, banishment, and a kind of social death.

What follows in this introduction is a three-part summary of Hitchens's key positions on the "war on terror," the war in Iraq, and the state of the contemporary Left. Our aim is to set Hitchens's arguments into context and to spell out exactly why Hitchens deserves to be taken seriously as a unique kind of intellectual and why his thinking is indispensable for strengthening the project of secular, democratic, cosmopolitan humanism. But it is categorically *not* our intention to proselytize, and we leave it strictly up to the reader to decide how Hitchens fares against his various foes.

Terror, Islamic Fascism, and the Left

Of all the human emotions, hatred is perhaps the most undervalued; hatred, argue its enemies, is coarsening and dangerous. Yet, for all its pathological manifestations, hate is the primary motivating force behind all radical social criticism: without it, criticism lacks the trenchancy and doggedness that its calling necessarily demands. When Hitchens confesses to waking up to "a sensation of pervading disgust and annoyance,"[18] it is the energizing properties of hate to which he is paying tribute. For Hitchens, there is nothing quite like hate to focus the mind or sharpen the sword.

In the context of polite modern public discourse, Hitchens's respect for hatred will seem odd, gratuitous even. Today, the term *hate* is commonly used to denigrate the action, speech, or disposition of others. In studies of criminal behavior, *hate* is used interchangeably as a synonym for racism, anti-Semitism, or sexism. But from the perspective of Greek antiquity, there was nothing remotely odd or morally dubious about praising the merits of hatred.

This is Aristotle:

> There are two chief motives which induce men to attack tyrannies—hatred and contempt. Hatred of tyrants is inevitable, and contempt is also a frequent cause of their destruction. Thus we see that most of those who have acquired, have retained their power, but those who have inherited, have lost it, almost at once; for, living in luxurious ease, they have become contemptible, and offer many opportunities to their assailants. Anger, too, must be included under hatred, and produces the same effects. It is often times even more ready to strike—the angry are more impetuous in making an attack, for they do not follow rational principle. And men are very apt to give way to their passions when they are insulted. To this cause is to be attributed the fall of the Peisistratidae and of many others. Hatred is more reasonable, for anger is accompanied by pain, which is an impediment to reason, whereas hatred is painless.[19]

When Hitchens fondly remembers not his first love but his first hate, far from being merely "provocative," he is placing himself firmly within the intellectual tradition of Aristotle.

Among the common objects of Hitchens's hate are the following: religious absolutism,[20] political and ideological dogma, cruelty, superstition, and teleological utopianism. This list is by no means exhaustive; nevertheless, it provides a convenient summary of what inspires

Hitchens to get up in the morning. It also serves to explain, even more accurately, why on the morning of September 11, 2001, Hitchens was convulsed with a sense not only of disgust and rage but also of, as he put it, "exhilaration." For here, in plain view, was the summa of everything that he most intimately hated: theocratic barbarism. The enemy had unmistakably revealed itself and declared its intentions. Positions would now have to be taken, lines drawn, and battles fought. One can imagine Hitchens trembling in anticipation of what was to come.

For Hitchens, the meaning of the September 11 attacks was, as he put it in an interview, a "no-brainer": the intention was to murder as many American civilians as possible, for the purposes of rejuvenating the forces of jihad in the Muslim world. It was an attack on "the ethics of the multicultural, the secular, the skeptical and the cosmopolitan," carried out by "theocratic fascists"[21]—an attack for which there could be no possible excuse or justification. Yet within just days of the attacks, it became glaringly apparent to Hitchens that the vast majority of his comrades on the Left did not share his sense of moral revulsion, much less his interpretation of why the attacks occurred and who was to blame. Among the more prominent members of his circle, Susan Sontag demanded to know, "Where is the acknowledgment that this was not a 'cowardly' attack on 'civilization' or 'liberty' or 'humanity' or 'the free world' but an attack on the world's self-proclaimed superpower, undertaken as a consequence of specific American alliances and actions?"[22] Noam Chomsky asserted, "Nothing can justify crimes such as those of September 11. But we can think of the United States as an 'innocent victim' only if we adopt the convenient path of ignoring the record of its actions and those of its allies, which are, after all, hardly a secret."[23] Gore Vidal wanted to "meditate upon the unremitting violence of the United States against the rest of the world," in an effort to understand "why Osama struck at us from abroad in the name of 1 billion Muslims."[24] Andrew Arato, professor of politics and social theory at the New School for Social Research, mockingly distilled these responses into the following formulation: "*Yes*, it was terrible what happened downtown . . . *but* US foreign policy (or the capitalist world economy, take your pick) is (ultimately) responsible. Do not therefore call the perpetrators terrorists; they are the last ones speaking in the name of the victims, hoping to call the beneficiaries to account. Call those who respond the aggressors, because it is they who continue aggression against the wretched of the earth."[25]

In typically Hegelian fashion, the most forceful and penetrating criticism of this mode of thinking came not from the Right but from within the ranks of the Left itself. Paul Berman, for example, argued that the protagonists of jihad are inspired by an irrational, totalitarian hatred of the idea of liberal democratic secularism.[26] Jihadist terror, he insisted, is a reaction against not the vices of the liberal democracies but their virtues—pluralism, democracy, female emancipation, and rational scientific inquiry. Michael Walzer similarly wrote that bin Ladenism "is not, even unintentionally, unconsciously, or 'objectively,' a left politics."[27] The aim of the new jihadis, he observed, is not freedom but the resurrection of the lost Islamic empire.[28] Norman Geras was even more forthright: "They are the enemies of democracy and the enemies of all humankind. They must be fought till they have been defeated."[29]

But of all the liberal-leftist detractors from the Sontag-Chomsky-Vidal position, none was more unrelenting and incisive than Christopher Hitchens. Observe, for example, the following:

The people who destroyed the World Trade Center, and used civilians as accessories, are not fighting to free Gaza. They are fighting for the right to throw acid in the faces of unveiled women in Kabul and Karachi. They didn't just destroy the temple of modernity, they used heavy artillery to shatter ancient Buddha statues in Bamiyan earlier this year, and in Egypt have plotted to demolish the Pyramids and the Sphinx because they are un-Islamic and profane.[30]

The bombers of Manhattan represent fascism with an Islamic face. . . . What they abominate about "the West," to put it in a phrase, is not what Western liberals don't like and can't defend about their own system, but what they *do* like about it and must defend: its emancipated women, its scientific inquiry, its separation of religion from the state.[31]

[They] calmly rehearsed their own deaths, and the deaths of strangers, for years. They are not even "terrorists" so much as nihilists:

at war with the very idea of modernity and the related practices of pluralism and toleration. In order to comprehend them we need the images not of Beirut in the 1980s or of Palestine today but of the crusades or the Thirty Years War. These are people who are seen by the Taliban as extreme. No settlement for the Palestinians or the Chechens or the Kashmiris or the Bosnians would have appeased their barbarous piety.[32]

In just three short paragraphs Hitchens sharply conveys the essence of the enemy with which secular modernity is currently at war. The enemy, Hitchens contends, is not Western imperialism but an astonishingly venomous strain of reactionary Islam: in Hitchens's phrase, "fascism with an Islamic face."[33]

When bin Laden declares that death is "something we wish for"[34] or that Muslims "have the right to kill 4 million Americans—2 million of them children—and to exile twice as many and wound and cripple hundreds of thousands,"[35] it is imperative, says Hitchens, that we take him seriously. In particular, he says, we must pay extremely close attention to the grievances of which he makes explicit mention:

The grievance of seeing unveiled women. The grievance of the existence, not of the State of Israel, but of the Jewish people. The grievance of the heresy of democracy, which impedes the imposition of Sharia law. The grievance of a work of fiction written by an Indian living in London. The grievance of the existence of black African Muslim farmers, who won't abandon lands in Darfur. The grievance of the existence of homosexuals. The grievance of music, and of most representational art. The grievance of the existence of Hinduism. The grievance of East Timor's liberation from Indonesian rule.[36]

Hitchens implores us to recognize that the new jihadis *really do mean what they say*. And what they say, he adds, informs—with perfect consistency—what they do: they throw acid in the faces of unveiled women, they bomb synagogues, they threaten to kill voters, they incite the murder of novelists, they kill the wrong kind of Muslim in Darfur, they torture and murder gay men, they blow up night clubs, they destroy ancient Hindu monuments, and they murder Catholics in East Timor.

Let us therefore acknowledge, Hitchens concludes, that "we have met an enemy and that he is not us, but someone else," someone "with whom coexistence is, fortunately I think, not possible."[37]

It of course remains unclear whether September 11 "changed everything." But it undoubtedly lit up the global political landscape. For Hitchens, it was clarifying in precisely two senses: first, it dramatically exposed the threat and sheer menace of theocratic barbarism, and second, and more delicately, it exposed what he saw as the intellectual, moral, and political bankruptcy of the contemporary Western Left.

Surveying the post-9/11 reactions of Sontag, Chomsky, and many other leftists, Hitchens was appalled by the robotic, unresponsive quality of the prose and thinking. It prompted him to recall an observation from the opening pages of Karl Marx's *Eighteenth Brumaire of Louis Bonaparte*: "when people are learning a new language, they habitually translate it back into the one they already know."[38] Thus, Walzer says,

> Any group that attacks the imperial power must be a representative of the oppressed, and its agenda must be the agenda of the left. It isn't necessary to listen to its spokesmen. What else can they want except . . . the redistribution of resources across the globe, the withdrawal of American soldiers from wherever they are, the closing down of aid programs for repressive governments, the end of the blockade of Iraq, and the establishment of a Palestinian state alongside Israel?[39]

For Hitchens, to conceptualize 9/11 in the terms evoked by Walzer was merely to substitute "tired slogans for thought."[40] As a result, the Left catastrophically failed to understand what desperately needed to be understood: namely, that the September 11 atrocity was a product of an extremely toxic, fundamentalist belief system that celebrates and sanctifies death and the mass murder of the innocent and that, more centrally, it signified, in the most graphic way possible, the evolution of a new tactic in the civil war between secularizing Muslims on the one side and the Islamic reactionaries (Hitchens pointedly refuses to call them *radicals*, *radical*, in his view, being a term of honor) on the

other—the tactic, employed by the reactionaries, of striking prominent Western targets.[41]

September 11, Hitchens argues, should be seen not as a reaction
against any specific Western-inflicted "grievance" but primarily as an
act of jihadist propaganda, manufactured largely for the consumption
of the Muslim world. By attacking the world's leading superpower, Al
Qaeda's intention, says Hitchens, was to demoralize and intimidate
the domestic infidel/renegade enemy, as well as to rejuvenate the true
believers.[42] In this analysis, 9/11 signified a civilizational clash to be
sure, but one that was occurring *within* a single civilizational bloc, and
not, contra Samuel Huntington,[43] between two opposing ones.

Hitchens forcefully insists that the real object of Islamist contempt
is not in fact "the West" as such but very precisely Muslims of a secular, modernizing temperament. Reactionary Islam, he says, promises
loudly to cleanse the Muslim world of the poison of unbelief and heresy, to create a society based entirely on the unbending rules of Ko-
ranic law—a utopia of compulsory, endless servitude to Allah. The
project, therefore, is not greater social justice but further Muslim enslavement, as Hitchens testifies:

> In Nigeria a young woman sits holding a baby and awaiting a sen-
> tence of death. The baby is the main, if not indeed the sole, evi-
> dence against her. The baby is proof positive that the young woman
> has engaged in sexual intercourse. The form that the appointed
> death sentence will take is by stoning, death in public, death that
> will make a crowd of participants into killers and the baby into a
> motherless child.
>
> Why is this happening? It is happening because the Islamic
> forces in the northern regions of Nigeria want to impose Sharia
> law, the primitive Muslim code of mutilation and retribution. Do
> the religious authorities propose to inflict this code only on mem-
> bers of their own congregation, who share the supposed values
> and taboos? No they do not. They wish to have it imposed also on
> Christians and unbelievers. This they already do in the regions of
> Nigeria that have fallen under their control.
>
> But they also want to extend Sharia law to the whole of Nigeria,
> where Islam is still a minority religion. . . .

Now perhaps somebody will tell me how this—the stoning, the disregard of pluralism, the stupidity and the viciousness—connects to the situation in Gaza, or would help alleviate the plight of the Palestinians.[44]

For Hitchens, the origins of 9/11 lie in the regional conflicts within the Arab-Muslim world itself, not in the dynamics of US foreign policy.

In a more general sociological sense, what Hitchens had pointed out, and what most Western leftists could not or would not acknowledge, is that the culture of reactionary, nihilistic Islamism is an independent causal force in the world and that those who identify or sympathize with this culture, are *active agents* rather than simply reflexes of structural political, economic, or other social forces.[45] Hence, Hitchens casts serious doubt on the assumption that economic and political change alone will limit or placate the threat of Islamist terror.

Equally catastrophic, Hitchens argues, was the Left's failure to absorb the terrifying political-historical significance of the 9/11 attacks. The death toll in the World Trade Center attack was just under three thousand. But had the planes hit the towers half an hour later and hit them lower than they did and had the columns fallen differently, the number of dead could well have exceeded twenty thousand: "it was clearly meant to be much, much worse than it was."[46] Now, if tens of thousands can be countenanced, then why not seventy, eighty, or a hundred thousand? The attacks of 9/11 brutally confirmed the emergence of an entirely new kind of threat: a disparate, unappeasable terror network with the will and technological knowledge to inflict vast death and destruction upon the civilian citadels of the modern West. For Hitchens, it was astonishing just how profoundly the Left had failed to grasp this terrible fact.

Perhaps even more dismaying for Hitchens was what he identified as the Left's "moral cretinism." In his view, the September 11 atrocity was an act of spectacular inhumanity, carried out by a group of "woman-stoning, gay-burning, Jew-hating medieval theocrats."[47] Here, said Hitchens, was a clear chance to reaffirm some very important Enlightenment principles, to declare one's allegiance to the ideas of liberal internationalism and universal human rights—and the Left, as he put it, went "AWOL."[48]

In her by-now-infamous *New Yorker* piece on the 9/11 attacks, Susan Sontag mentioned the decade-long ravaging of Iraqi civil society by sustained US aerial bombardment.[49] Gore Vidal produced a twenty-page chart of US imperial aggression.[50] Noam Chomsky reflected that 9/11 was "a terrible atrocity, but unless you're in Europe or the United States or Japan, I guess, you know it's nothing new."[51] Alexander Cockburn seethed at Madeleine Albright's appalling suggestion that the death of half a million Iraqi children was a just price for the "containment" of the Saddam Hussein regime.[52] Howard Zinn contemplated "the resentment all over the world felt by people who have been the victims of American military action—in Vietnam, in Latin America, in Iraq."[53] Charles Glass made reference to US crimes against Libya, Iraq, Lebanon, Somalia, and Palestine.[54] Fredric Jameson alluded to "the wholesale massacres of the Left systematically encouraged and directed by the Americans."[55] For Alan Singer, 9/11 brought to mind even greater atrocities, like the US bombing of Hiroshima and Nagasaki.[56]

Hitchens is aghast that in all these responses to 9/11 not even the faintest glimmer of moral compassion or sorrow for the dead and bereaved is to be found. He was also stunned that in the face of an utterly repulsive foe—and one radically antithetical to every ideal of its own—the instinctive response of the Left was to change the subject, and to do so in a way that suggested a moral equivalence between the Muslim fundamentalists and the custodians of the Western liberal democracies.[57]

From Hitchens's perspective, the rhetorical strategy of "subject-change" was not only a shameful abdication of critical thinking; it was also a betrayal of secular Muslims the world over. Hitchens never tires of reminding his Western audience that the chief victims of jihadist violence and slaughter are Muslims.[58] To suggest that Islamic terror is no big problem, he thinks, is therefore a grotesque insult to the very constituency on whose behalf the Left ought to be fighting. To ridicule or "deconstruct" the so-called war on terror is, in Hitchens's mind, to abandon to clerical fascism the very people who are most at risk from its menace. This perhaps explains why Hitchens is so impatient with the tone of self-righteous indignation that can be detected in so many leftist critiques of Bush's "war on terror."

Hitchens is no less scathing about what he regards as the Left's failure to seriously engage the post-9/11 policy debate. The Left, he says, failed to address the absolutely crucial question of how, in the wake of 9/11, the United States and its allies should best protect themselves from future terrorist atrocities. Hitchens finds it depressing that by focusing almost exclusively on the constitutional dangers of Bush's new security measures, the Left could find little or nothing to say about how the terror threat should be countered. Richard Rorty's confession that "I have spent more time worrying about what my Government will do than about what the terrorists will do"[59] was emblematic of the mentality against which Hitchens was fighting. Rorty, presumably, is the kind of progressive that Hitchens had in mind when he made scornful reference to "the sort who, upon discovering a viper in the bed of their child, would place the first call to People for the Ethical Treatment of Animals."[60]

Hitchens, by contrast, advocated a military response to the 9/11 attacks. The United States, he argued, was entitled, under international law, to defend itself against the aggression of Al Qaeda and the regime to which it was wedded: the Taliban of Afghanistan. Not only was this a legal imperative; it was a moral one too: "Did we not aid the grisly Taliban to achieve and hold power? Yes indeed 'we' did."[61] Well then, Hitchens urged, "let us now cancel this crime" by ending their tyrannical regime.[62]

After the fall of Kabul, Hitchens triumphantly declared, "The United States of America has just succeeded in bombing a country back out of the Stone Age." "We are rid," he went on, "of one of the foulest regimes on earth, while one of the most vicious crime families in history has been crippled and scattered."[63] Against the opponents of the war, he wrote,

> I can remember a time when the peace movement was not an auxiliary to dictators and aggressors in trouble. Looking at some of the mind-rotting tripe that comes my way from much of today's Left, I get the impression that they go to bed saying: what have

I done for Saddam Hussein or good old Slobodan or the Taliban today? Well, ha ha ha, and yah, boo. It was obvious from the very start that the United States had no alternative but to do what it has done. It was also obvious that defeat was impossible. The Taliban will soon be history.[64]

In the light of this quotation, it is not difficult to see why Hitchens inspires such fierce contempt in his former leftist comrades: he seems to take inordinate, almost sadistic, delight in ridiculing what he sees as their illusions and inanities. Rarely does he miss an opportunity to antagonize them. His aim is not just to point out their misconceptions but to rhetorically *destroy* them. When they fail, he wants nothing less than to see them crash and burn. And then he wants to rub it in and then rub it in some more. Occasionally, this leads him into excess and error. To respond to the concerns of those who stood in opposition to the war in Afghanistan by saying "Well, ha ha ha, and yah, boo" was ill judged. Even more gratuitous was his view that the war was prosecuted on the basis of "an almost pedantic policy of avoiding 'collateral damage.'"[65] Both proclamations offer clear examples of Hitchens's desire to antagonize getting the better of him.

As it turned out, Hitchens's expectation that "the Taliban will soon be history" was unduly premature, and, as Richard Seymour correctly points out in this volume,[66] Hitchens's view that the war resulted in "no serious loss of civilian life"[67] cannot survive critical scrutiny. Yet despite these (and other) exaggerations and miscalculations, we feel that Hitchens is right on the essential question of reactionary Islam and what ought—indeed must—be done about it. Although it is arguable just how illuminating the term *Islamic fascism* really is,[68] few writers better understand, and are better able to articulate, the nature and seriousness of the menace of militant political Islam. And Hitchens is fundamentally right, it seems to us, in his assessment that a large part of the contemporary Left has failed—intellectually, morally, and politically—the test of taking that menace seriously.

In the following section we set out Hitchens's case for the 2003 military intervention in Iraq, focusing in particular on his critique of the liberal-Left antiwar position.

Iraq, Antifascism, and the Left

Here, briefly enumerated, was the liberal-leftist case against the war in Iraq:

1. War against Saddam Hussein is an act of capitalist imperialism.
2. The occupation and invasion of Iraq will inflame Muslim anger against the West; far from disrupting the terrorists, it will only serve to strengthen them, attracting new recruits and supporters to their cause.
3. Concentration on Iraq is a distraction from the war against Al Qaeda.
4. The war will perilously weaken the authority of the United Nations Security Council.
5. War against Saddam Hussein is unnecessary: sufficient tightening of sanctions and surveillance is capable of defanging the Baath regime, while sparing innocent lives and preserving the unity of the international community.
6. A preemptive strike against Iraq will undermine respect for international law.
7. Occupation of Iraq will be too hazardous and costly; in all likelihood it will result in a long and bloody quagmire.

It is exaggerating only very slightly to say that since the early days of 2003, when it became obvious that the Bush administration was going to depose Hussein, Hitchens has spent, often to his dismay,[69] virtually every conscious living moment resisting these conventional wisdoms.

Hitchens's critique of the antiwar position was based on a single, irrefutable logical fact: *the case against the war would, if politically successful, leave the Baathist regime in power.* For Hitchens, such an outcome would have been morally and politically inconceivable: morally, because of the exceptionally brutal and murderous nature of the Baathist regime, and politically, because of the regime's uniquely pathological and dangerous character.

On the matter of the moral argument, Hitchens was emphatic: the Saddam Hussein regime was cruel and depraved *in the extreme*:

◈ Between 1987 and 1988 Iraqi armed forces gassed and "cleansed"— *fouled*—over two hundred Kurdish villages and towns and organized the deportation and execution of 182,000 Kurdish civilians.

◈ In the 1990s, Hussein's regime drained the marshes of southern Iraq, displacing five hundred thousand people, half of whom fled to Iran, and killing some forty thousand. In addition to destroying the five-thousand-year-old Marsh Arab civilization, draining the marches inflicted vast ecological damage on one of the most important wetlands systems on the planet.

◈ In the six months following the collapse of the March 1991 Shiite uprising, Baathist forces slaughtered upward of three hundred thousand Shiites.

With the exception of North Korea, no other regime in recent decades matched Hussein's record for inhumanity.[70] This *alone*, Hitchens argued, warranted "regime change" in Iraq.

On the matter of the political argument, Hitchens observed that Hussein was deeply irrational and untrustworthy, especially when it came to weapons of mass destruction (WMDs). "It is very obvious" he wrote, "that Saddam Hussein has tried to acquire the only real WMD—the thermonuclear type—and it's fairly apparent what he wants them for."[71] "The best evidence," he continued, "is that he has failed in this enterprise, while a good intuition would suggest that having sacrificed so much in the quest he is unlikely to give it up."[72] Even as late as December 2002, an Iraq-bound cargo of North Korean Scud missiles was intercepted as it neared the Yemeni port of Aden. "What," Hitchens inquired, "might the next secret cargo from Pyongyang to the Gulf be carrying?"[73] To persevere with further inspections, he warned, was to flatter Hussein with the very presumption to which he was least entitled: the presumption of innocence. "'More time'" was really "a plea to give Saddam the chance to join the North Korean madman-plus-WMD club."[74] In any case, Hitchens added, intervention in Iraq was "inescapably in our future."[75] It was wiser, then, to intervene at a time of our own choosing and under infinitely better terms and conditions.[76] A broken, imploded Iraq was too frightening a prospect to contemplate: civil war, opportunistic interventions from rival and neighboring powers, the possible sabotage of the oil fields, and the proliferation of terrorist groups. Regime change, counseled Hitchens, was the only possible means by which Hussein could effectively be disarmed and the ghastly scenario of state failure averted.

Hitchens's case for intervention in Iraq can thus be said to rest on considerations of *principle* and considerations of *prudence*. Regarding the latter, Hitchens concedes that he—like almost everyone else—was mistaken in his assumption that Saddam Hussein was in possession of WMDs. Yet, he argues, there can be absolutely no doubt that Hussein had every intention of acquiring them and that given the chance he undoubtedly *would* have acquired them. It is one of the great merits of "regime change," Hitchens says, that Hussein's nuclear aspirations have been put to an abrupt, permanent end.

On the question of the morality of the war, Hitchens reflected:

For twelve years of compromise and dither, those inside Iraq have been kept by a cowardly international statecraft as hostages in a country used by a madman as his own laboratory and torture chamber. In the face of a modern Caligula, many of them continually risked everything to try and free their people from a system of atrocity and aggression. I feel that they were fighting all this time on my behalf. Only after a long train of blunders and hesitations and betrayals did the United States decide that it was, at long last, in the same trench as the resistance. No matter how it comes out, or how this alliance may fray, I shall never have the least serious doubt that it was the right side to have been on.[77]

For Hitchens, of all the possible rationales for the war in Iraq, the most powerful was the moral one: in his mind, the removal of the Baath Party from power was—beyond any doubt—simply the right thing to do. It was a question of elementary justice, a matter of punishing and ending an exorbitantly brutal dictatorship. Moreover, says Hitchens, because the United States had previously supported and indulged the Hussein regime, it was morally incumbent on the United States to lead the job of removing the regime. In this sense, Hitchens's pro-war position is indistinguishable from that of the Iraqi dissident Kanan Makiya. Makiya writes,

I support a war on the grounds that the current regime of the Baath Party in Iraq is a criminal state that has gone beyond the pale even as judged by the very low standards of the Middle East region, and certainly of the international community. My position rests on the exceptional nature of Baathi totalitarianism in Iraq (and is therefore not extendable to all the nasty states that exist in the world). Moreover, it derives from the particular historical experience—dating back to the 1991 Gulf War—that binds the United States to Iraq. The outcome of that war, which left the dictator in place and precipitated one of the harshest sanction regimes of recent times, places an extraordinary moral responsibility upon the shoulders of the United States to finish that which it in a very important sense left unfinished. Such a responsibility might not exist were it not for that particular historical experience. One does not transport half a million men halfway across the world and then leave the people of a country, who were not responsible for their state's outrage, broken and bleeding for ten years with no end in sight to the torment that they are going through.[78]

In Hitchens's eyes, Bush's readiness for regime change was therefore fortuitous indeed, for it furnished the United States with a rare and precious opportunity to redeem itself after years of shameful collusion with Baathist fascism. Like Makiya, Hitchens says that it was bad enough to have betrayed the Iraqi uprisings at the end of the first Gulf War in 1991. But to have opposed the war this time around would have entailed prolonging *even further* the hegemony of the Baath Party: not content with betraying the Iraqis once before, we would have betrayed them all over again. To Hitchens, the prospect of such a double betrayal was morally unthinkable.

Hitchens was therefore appalled to find not even a tincture of moral doubt or uneasiness among the "radical" contingent of the antiwar movement. Since, he says, they were effectively marching to keep Saddam in power, one would have expected a certain degree of humility, maybe even a sign that the weight of an interminable dilemma had been shouldered. Humility, however, was absent. In Hitchens's view, the entire edifice of the liberal Left case against the war was thus built on a denial: on a failure or refusal to acknowledge that the alternative to war was not peace but the continued repression and immiseration of the Iraqi people.

For twenty-three years, the Saddam Hussein regime murdered and tortured and terrorized hundreds of thousands of Iraqis. Prominent among the victims were the Kurds and the Iraqi communists and trade unionists. For twenty-three long, arduous years, this group of brave and tireless dissidents had been fighting, and risking everything, to effect a regime change of their own. In view of this, Hitchens says that the case for demolishing the Baathist tyranny ought to have found strong support among the international Left. "When I first became a socialist," remarked Hitchens in October 2002, "the imperative of international solidarity was the essential if not the defining thing, whether the cause was popular or risky or not."[79] And yet:

> I haven't seen an anti-war meeting all this year at which you could even guess at the existence of the Iraqi and Kurdish opposition to Saddam, an opposition that was fighting for "regime change" when both Republicans and Democrats were fawning over Baghdad as a profitable client and geopolitical ally. Not only does the "peace" movement ignore the anti-Saddam civilian opposition, it sends missions to console the Baathists in their isolation, and speaks of the invader of Kuwait and Iran and the butcher of Kurdistan as if he were the victim and George W. Bush the aggressor.[80]

From Hitchens's viewpoint, this masking of Hussein's atrocities and the cognitive inversion of perpetrator and aggressor was a betrayal of staggering proportions. At one time, he recalls, the Left used to be resolutely firm and courageous and absolutist in its opposition to fascists.[81] But now, he says, it has degenerated into a relativistic, "neutralist, smirking isolationism."[82] What we are now witnessing, he laments, is nothing less then the eclipse of a durable tradition of antifascism in the twentieth century on the Left.

We address some of the shortcomings of Hitchens's pro-war position in the next section, but whatever the weight one wishes to assign to them, there are two essential points with which no serious person could reasonably quarrel. The first is that Hitchens shows us, better than anyone else does, that the antiwar position was not itself a neutral one but functioned to keep Hussein and his hideous regime in power. Correspondingly, being serious about the war requires consideration not just of the moral and political costs of going to war but also of the moral and political costs of *not* going to war. The second point is that of all the auditors of the latter costs, Hitchens was undoubtedly the most impassioned and rhetorically effective.

Apostasy, Socialism, and the Left

In 1990, Robert Conquest—author of *The Great Terror* and numerous other works on the crimes of Soviet Communism[83]—was bestowed, at a plenum of the Central Committee in Moscow, with the title of "anti-Sovietchik number one."[84] It is not too dramatic to say that Hitchens enjoys a comparable status among his left-leaning critics, except to add that in Hitchens's case the animus directed against him is even greater, since he was once a deeply admired traveler among them. At the hands of his former comrades, Hitchens has been subjected not just to criticism but to actual *disparagement*. He has been denounced and excommunicated, purged from the orbit of the Left, and subjected to a plethora of what the sociologist Harold Garfinkel has referred to as "degradation ceremonies."[85] The main accusation is that he has become a rank ideologist of imperialism and a fanatical "cheerleader" for the Bush administration and American expansionism.[86] Thus, he is a "turn-coat," a defector, a traitor. And since being a "turn-coat" seems always to be indicative of a far wider moral decline, Hitchens is accused, variously, of being a racist,[87] an alcoholic[88] (a "drink-soaked former Trotskyist popinjay," as the British Member of Parliament George Galloway famously phrased it),[89] a snob,[90] dishonest,[91] venal,[92] overweight,[93] unkempt,[94] psychopathic,[95] and a closeted homosexual. Hitchens has thus been, to paraphrase Garfinkel, reconstituted into a deviant, into someone lower in the local scheme of social types; he has been "ritually separated" from the Left, his former identity defamed as a sham. Marc Cooper is perhaps right: "Leaving the left can be a bit like trying to quit the Mafia. You can't get out without getting assassinated—literally or figuratively."[96]

In the eyes of the Left, Hitchens has metamorphosed from a brave, eloquent critic of state power into a crude apologist for capitalist militarism. According to Stefan Collini, the post-9/11 Hitchens reminds him less of Leon Trotsky than of the "pop-eyed, spluttering and splenetic" English reactionary novelist Kingsley Amis.[97] Gary Malone writes that "anyone familiar with Hitchens's previous incarnation as an arch-muckraker will know that his full-throated support for George W. Bush is a true metamorphosis, and nothing beautiful has emerged from the chrysalis."[98] Or as Studs Terkel puts it, "Christopher Hitchens, poor boy, since his conversion, has been transmogrified from a witty observer of the human comedy to a bloody bore, seated at the far-right end of the bar."[99]

Trawling through the endless critical commentary directed at Hitchens, one is struck not just by the outstanding ferocity of it all but also by the fact that the focal point of critical interest is virtually always the same: the all-too-human Christopher Hitchens, and not his actual arguments. The central line of criticism seems to be this: Hitchens is no longer a leftist. Thus, Edward S. Herman writes that "Hitchens has abandoned the Left and is rushing toward the vital center, maybe further to the right, with termination point still to be determined."[100] Dennis Perrin materializes the same point when he observes that Hitchens is "becoming a coarser version of Norman Podhoretz."[101] In a similar vein, Tariq Ali warns that Hitchens will "soon find himself addressing the same gatherings as his sparring partner, Henry Kissinger."[102]

Now, it is disputable just how far to the Right Hitchens has gravitated. But what cannot be disputed is that there has been a movement away from the Left. It is indeed true to say that Hitchens, as he himself freely admits, is no longer a socialist.[103] This, he says, is because the emancipatory promise of socialism has now elapsed. As a politics, it can no longer be taken seriously because it lacks any clear practical conception of how to firmly inscribe its principles into the material setting of the societies in which we now live. As he put it in a 2001 interview (reprinted in this volume):

There is no longer a general socialist critique of capitalism—certainly not the sort of critique that proposes an alternative or a replacement. There just is not and one has to face the fact. Though I don't think that the contradictions, as we used to say, of the system are by any means all resolved.[104]

Hitchens explains that in the aftermath of the historical collapse of socialism, his politics henceforth must be "à la carte,"[105] by which he means that his thoughts and convictions are no longer rooted in a single ideological vision.

Despite his ideological disillusionment, Hitchens remains deeply affectionate toward the socialist project, observing that it "enabled universal suffrage, the imposition of limits upon exploitation, and the independence of colonial and subject populations."[106] Indeed: "I don't think I would ever change my view that socialism is the best political moment humans have ever come up with."[107]

However, no such affection is extended to his former comrades on the contemporary Anglo-American Left,[108] toward whom he feels nothing but contempt. At the root of his disillusionment with them is his belief that they have abandoned their intellectual and moral bearings: first, by succumbing to the "creepy concept" of moral equivalence,[109] and second, by adopting the all-embracing ideology of "anti-Americanism." On the question of "moral equivalence," Hitchens says the following: I absolutely refuse to associate myself with anyone who cannot discern the essential night-and-day difference between theocratic fascism and liberal secular democracy;[110] even less do I want to engage with those who are incapable of recognizing the basic moral distinction between premeditated mass murder and unintentional killing.[111] On the question of "anti-Americanism," Hitchens is similarly trenchant: I am through, he declares, with those who think that America is the cause of all evil in the world—through with those whose masochistic contempt for their own societies prevents them from siding against Islamic fascists and genocidal one-party dictatorships.[112]

Hitchens is also scathing about what he sees as the contemporary Left's growing tendency to conservatism. It has degenerated, he claims, into a status quo force, fighting not to destabilize but to *preserve* corrupt and repressive regimes. From an interview with Danny Postel:

One's task in the 1970s and 1980s was reasonably simple—you could say that the Cold War was a danger in and of itself without taking a side in it; and that the arms race was a danger in and of itself, as a counterpart to the Cold War, and needed to be criticized; and that, in the meantime, certain important causes, such as the Polish Workers Movement, or the African National Congress, or the people of El Salvador, were good causes in their own right. There were some on the left who took a pro–Warsaw Pact view. But essentially you were with or on the left. What you were doing was with the left. Once the Cold War was over, there was a recrudescence of one-party totalitarianism and of one-god authoritarianism—the decision by Saddam Hussein to abolish the existence of a neighboring state, and of Slobodan Milosevic to go from Yugo-Communism to National Socialism, an ethnically pure Serbo-nationalist fascist state with Christian Orthodox support. Then you found that, oddly enough, what you were doing was without the left. On the whole, the left wanted to sit that out. Let's not get involved. These could be quagmires. Another Vietnam. I didn't think we could really have the Muslim population of Europe put to the sword in public. Many felt, if you do that, you're getting involved in the Balkans, and who knows what that might entail?[113]

For Hitchens, the malady of what he calls "neutralist and conservative isolationism"[114] is now so acute among his former comrades that he can no longer remain part of their family.

Hitchens's leftist critics in one sense are therefore right: Hitchens is no longer a fellow comrade-in-arms. And, as Hitchens himself is willing to concede, *some* of the *ad hominem* remarks about him might well be true.[115] But none of this actually matters. Whether or not Hitchens remains a leftist (whatever that really means) is intellectually irrelevant. So too is his legendary enthusiasm for cigarettes and alcohol.[116] None of it has the slightest bearing on whether he is right on the essential questions with which he is concerned. For example, Hitchens's case for the war in Iraq is either convincing or it is not. And it certainly does not cease to be convincing because he no longer chooses to define himself as a socialist or because his recreational pursuits do not meet the exacting moral standards of the *bien pensants.*

Hitchens's critics are also right to point out that Hitchens has not been nearly critical and trenchant enough, at least in print, about the many failings of the Bush administration. George Scialabba sets out the indictment in this way:

> From its first days in office, the Bush Administration made clear its determination to reverse as much as possible of the modest progress made in the 20th century toward public provision for the unfortunate; public encouragement of worker, consumer, and neighborhood self-organization; public influence on the daily operation of government and access to the record of its activities; public protection of the commons; and public restraint of concentrated financial and corporate power—not only at home but also, to the (considerable, given American influence) extent feasible, abroad. And from the first weeks after 9/11 ... the Administration has found ways to take advantage of that atrocity to achieve its fundamental goals. The results ... have been a vast amount of suffering. Enough, one would think, to be worth mentioning in the second or third place, after the dangers of clerical barbarism. Not a word from Hitchens, however, at least in print.... The Bush Administration is the most ambitiously and skillfully dishonest pack of liars in American history, probably by a large margin. And since 9/11, Hitchens has never said a mumbling word about it.[117]

Scialabba is definitely onto something here. Hitchens, it is true, has not been as vociferous in his skepticism of the Bush administration as his former leftist admirers would have liked. But it is unfair to say that on its all-too-evident shortcomings he has been silent. Hitchens, for example, has written passionately about the crimes of Abu Ghraib[118] and has strongly criticized the Bush administration for not doing nearly enough in the postwar reconstruction of Iraq.

Nor is it true to say that Hitchens's relative inattention to the failures of the Bush administration is emblematic of something sinister, like venality[119] or the onset of alcoholism.[120] Hitchens has not been endlessly preoccupied with the failures of the Bush administration because he has been endlessly preoccupied with exposing and discrediting what he sees as a far more menacing axis of foes: reactionary Islam, international terrorism, and one-party dictatorship.

Even less true is the assertion that Hitchens is an apologist for American imperialism. Hitchens, certainly, was an enthusiastic and unflinching supporter of both the wars in Afghanistan and Iraq. But he was so not out of any loyalty to the US "military-industrial complex" but because both interventions served to remove two uniquely repressive and dangerous regimes from power. Hitchens remains a liberal internationalist, and it was his liberal internationalism that overdetermined his decision to support Bush's wars in Afghanistan and Iraq. Reflecting on the war in Iraq, Hitchens writes, "I became involved in this argument before the Bush administration had been elected, and for me it always was (and still is) a matter of solidarity with the democratic forces in Iraq and Iraqi Kurdistan and of the need for the United States to change its policy and be on their side."[121] Hitchens is adamant that in supporting the Iraqi and Kurdish resistance, he was in fact being truer to his "left self" than had he opposed the war.[122] It is the liberal-Left antiwar contingent, he says, and not he, who owes the explanation for making excuses for terrorists of the most reactionary kind and for marching against the removal of repression and enslavement in Iraq. It is they, he says, and not he, who are defaming the great tradition of leftist resistance to tyranny and fascism.[123] It is a nice paradox that at the exact moment at which Hitchens feels most disillusioned by the socialist project, he finds himself defending—*against* its self-appointed custodians—the principles that historically came to define it: democracy, pluralism, secularism, and the idea that everyone should live a secure and fulfilled existence, free from egregious assault and violations of human rights.

Among the more creditable lines of criticism aimed at Hitchens is that in setting out his case for the war in Iraq he did not properly register or "compute" the potential costs of the war. In a grimly prescient article on the war in early 2003, Juan Cole, after extensively detailing the "risks of peace," observed that the "regional costs of a US war on Iraq are potentially great":

The war will inevitably be seen in the Arab world as a neo-colonial war. . . . The Sunnis of Iraq could well turn to groups like Al Qaeda, having lost the ideals of the Baath. Iraqi Shiites might become easier to recruit into Khomeinism of the Iranian sort, and become a bulwark for the shaky regime in Shiite Iran. . . . A post-war Iraq may well be riven with factionalism that impedes the development of a well-ensconced new government. . . . Commentators often note the possibility for Sunni-Shiite divisions or Arab-Kurdish ones. These are very real. If Islamic law is the basis of the new state, that begs the question of whether its Sunni or Shiite version will be implemented. It is seldom realized that the Kurds themselves fought a mini–civil war in 1994–1997 between two major political and tribal factions. Likewise the Shiites are deeply divided, by tribe, region and political ideology. Many lower-level Baath Party members are Shiite, but tens of thousands of Iraqi Shiites are in exile in Iran and want to come back under the banner of ayatollahs. . . . there could be a good deal of trouble in the country, and as the case of Afghanistan shows, the US cannot always stop faction fighting. . . . Shiite Iran will certainly attempt to increase its influence among Iraqi Shiites once the Baath is defeated. . . . A US-occupied country where the Iranian ayatollahs have substantial influence is a disaster waiting to happen.[124]

It is difficult to avoid the impression that Hitchens was too glib or perfunctory in his approach to weighing up these devastatingly important practical concerns, invidiously associating them with the thinking of reactionary and unprincipled conservative realists.[125] Although Hitchens was correct to insist that the majority of those who opposed the war, or at least the majority of its most vocal opponents, opposed it in a far from creditable way, he was quite mistaken in his belief that there could be *no* creditable reasons for opposing it. But, as Cole's reflections show, there *were* such reasons. The best case against the war was that it would actually *worsen* the position of the Iraqis. It is an occasion for regret that Hitchens did not fully engage with this line of argument, choosing instead to focus most of his fire on the wholly unserious and unscrupulous elements in the antiwar movement.

A no less serious criticism of Hitchens's pro-war position, expressed by Gary Malone,[126] is that it gave few or no compelling reasons as to why the Bush administration could be trusted to create effectively a secure and democratic Iraq. Hitchens, it seems, merely *assumed* that it could be trusted to do so. Given the administration's catastrophic and well-documented[127] mishandling of the intervention, it is now clear that such an epic assumption had no firm foundation in empirical reality. It is striking that Hitchens, who is able to exercise his skeptical intelligence so vigorously and penetratingly on other key issues, should have so readily surrendered it in regard to the Bush administration's competence in dealing with Iraq.

Despite the force of these criticisms, Hitchens's case for the war in Iraq was—and remains—a compelling one, strongly informed as it was by the view that the moral cost of keeping the Baathist regime in power was simply too high. As Norman Geras powerfully puts it,

> The Saddam Hussein regime had been responsible for, it was daily adding to, and for all that anyone could reasonably expect, it would go on for the foreseeable future adding to, an immensity of pain and grief, killing, torture and mutilation. . . . This was not merely an unpleasant tyranny amongst many others—it was one of the very worst of recent times, with the blood of *hundreds of thousands* of people on its hands, to say nothing of the lives torn and wrecked by it. Other things equal, there is no other moral option than to support the removal of such a regime if a removal is in the offing.[128]

On matters of principle, Hitchens remains stoically and obstinately unchanged. He is still a tireless, unapologetic, and vital supporter of the idea of secular democratic cosmopolitanism. But he is no longer prepared to fight for it from within the confines of the Left. Politically, Hitchens finds himself in new territory: he can no longer believe that democratic socialism is a practical possibility, and he is convinced, as he once was not, that American power can be used as a force for good in the world.[129] More strikingly, he is convinced that America, for all its ills, offers the best possible political model available for achieving progressive political goals. Hitchens's leftist critics believe that his optimism in this regard is fundamentally mistaken and long for the Hitchens who raged against the contradictions and injustices of American capitalism. Hitchens, they argue, is wrong about jihad, wrong about Iraq, and wrong about America. It is our belief that by pitting Hitchens directly against some of his former comrades, our consideration of these urgently important issues can be greatly illuminated.

A Note on the Text

Our vision for this book was to bring together a diversity of critical responses to, and exchanges between, Christopher Hitchens and his critics. Unfortunately, that vision could not be fully realized, since the following authors—all of them towering figures on the intellectual Western Left—refused to grant us permission to reprint their work in this volume: Tariq Ali, Noam Chomsky, Stefan Collini, Edward Herman, Steven Lukes, and Katha Pollitt.

Even though we could not reproduce the originals, we consider the ideas and critiques raised by Chomsky and Herman to be particularly crucial, so we briefly summarized their pieces to give the reader as clear a sense of their core arguments as we could. It would have been unfair to both authors to have reprinted Hitchens's replies to them without conveying what they wrote. However, it was not possible, and would have been ridiculous, to summarize all the articles that we could not reprint. We urge readers to seek out the originals of all these pieces. It is a disheartening irony that all the authors who refused permission are, or have been, robust defenders of free expression and the dialectical interchange of ideas.

NOTES

1. Christopher Hitchens, "It's a Good Time for War," *Boston Globe* (online), September 8, 2002; reprinted in this volume, 62.

2. In a recent readers poll taken by *Foreign Policy* and *Prospect*, Hitchens was voted fifth out of the world's "Top 100 Public Intellectuals" (http://www.foreign-policy.com/story/cms.php?story_id=3260). Noam Chomsky placed first in the poll.

3. These are just some of the subjects that Hitchens takes on in his most recent collection of journalism, *Love, Poverty, and War: Journeys and Essays* (New York: Nation Books, 2004).

4. Referring to Frank Kermode's preferred mode of criticism, Stefan Collini writes that "he mostly contents himself with a saddened shake of the head, a devastating weapon in its way, but one that doesn't leave any mess on the carpet." By contrast, says Collini, Hitchens "*loves* mess on the carpet" (Stefan

Collini, "'No Bullshit' Bullshit," *London Review of Books*, January 23, 2003, http://www.lrb.co.uk/v25/no2/collo1_.html, emphasis in original).

5. This anecdote appears in Lynn Barber's profile of Hitchens, "Look Who's Talking," published in the *Observer*, April 14, 2002.

6. In his brilliant memoir *Experience*, Amis recounts the following incident with Hitchens:

When in 1978 he left the *New Statesman* [the leftist British weekly] for the bourgeois broadsheet the *Daily Express*, I went *mano a mano* with him among the sawdust and fagsmoke and bumcrack of an infernal Irish pub in a basement off Piccadilly Circus. I was in the unwonted position of attacking Christopher from the left: for defection, for betrayal, for taking the rich man's shilling. Sadly watched by James Fenton, our wills, my will and the will of the Hitch, became concentrated in the glass we were both holding with our right hands. It was a wine glass, and it contained a single whisky. We were squeezing it, while looking implacably into each other's eyes, squeezing it till it began to creak. . . . I desisted. I climbed down. Because I suddenly knew that he would not desist, not in a million years, and when we went off to Casualty together, the Hitch would have no regrets, no regrets about that gashed palm, that missing finger, lost in the sawdust: none.

Martin Amis, *Experience* (London: Jonathan Cape, 2000), 258–59.

7. The latest object of Hitchens's polemical scorn is God; see *God Is Not Great: How Religion Poisons Everything* (London: Atlantic Books, 2007).

8. Georg Simmel, *Conflict and the Web of Group Affiliations* (New York: Free Press, 1955), 28–29.

9. Ibid., emphasis added.

10. See esp. Raymond Geuss, *The Idea of a Critical Theory: Habermas and the Frankfurt School* (Cambridge: Cambridge University Press, 1981).

11. See esp. Peter Dews's excellent introduction to his edited collection *Autonomy and Solidarity: Interviews with Jürgen Habermas* (London: Verso, 1986).

12. It is rare to read a review of Hitchens's work or a profile that *does not* make mention of these twin enthusiasms of his.

13. Collini, "'No Bullshit' Bullshit."

14. Here is how Martin Amis evokes the smoldering aftermath of an evening spent in the company of Hitchens and Saul Bellow: "Then it was over, and we faced the silence. My right foot throbbed from the warm work it had done beneath the table on the shins of the Hitch, availing me nothing. . . . The silence still felt like a gnat in my ear" (Amis, *Experience,* 261). With his unfailing sense of timing and tact, Hitchens had decided that dinner at the Bellows residence would be an apt occasion on which to attack Bellow's views on Edward Said and the state of Israel.

15. For an especially illuminating discussion of "the art of the attack," see Mark Grueter, "Offensive Art," *Canon* (spring 2003).

16. See also Christopher Hitchens, "Don't. Be. Silly. An Open Letter to Martin Amis," *Guardian*, September 4, 2002; reprinted in this volume, 177.

17. Christopher Hitchens, *For the Sake of Argument: Essays and Minority Reports* (London: Verso, 1993), 325–26.

18. Hitchens, introduction to *Love, Poverty, and War*, xiii.

19. Aristotle, *Politics*, Book V, Part X, Internet Classics Archive, http://classics.mit.edu/Aristotle/politics.5.five.html.

20. Hitchens tellingly writes that "cold, steady hatred for this, especially in its loathsome jihad shape, has been as sustaining to me as any love" (introduction to *Love, Poverty, and War*, xiii).

21. Hitchens, "It's a Good Time for War," this volume, 62.

22. Susan Sontag, "First Reactions," *New Yorker*, September 24, 2001.

23. Noam Chomsky, *9-11* (New York: Seven Stories, 2001), 35.

24. Gore Vidal, *Perpetual War for Perpetual Peace: How We Got to Be So Hated* (New York: Thunder's Mouth/Nation Books, 2002), 45.

25. Andrew Arato, "*Minima Politica* after September 11," *Constellations* 9, no. 1 (2002): 48, emphasis in original.

26. See Paul Berman, *Terror and Liberalism* (New York: Norton, 2003).

27. Michael Walzer, "Can There Be a Decent Left?" *Dissent* 49 (2002), http://www2.kenyon.edu/Depts/Religion/Fac/Adler/Politics/Waltzer.htm.

28. Michael Walzer, *Arguing about War* (New Haven, CT: Yale University Press, 2004), 133.

29. Norman Geras, "Against the Criminals," *Normblog*, posted July 7, 2005.

30. Christopher Hitchens, "The Pursuit of Happiness Is at an End," *London Evening Standard*, September 19, 2001; reprinted in this volume, 42.

31. Christopher Hitchens, "Against Rationalization," *Nation*, September 20, 2001; reprinted in this volume, 44.

32. Christopher Hitchens, "American Society Can Outlast or Absorb Practically Anything," *Independent*, September 16, 2001; reprinted in this volume, 39.

33. This is a conscious echo of Susan Sontag's formulation "fascism with a human face," referring to the declaration of martial law in Poland in 1981. See Christopher Hitchens, "Susan Sontag: An Obituary," *Slate*, December 29, 2004; reprinted in this volume, 197. Although Hitchens is frequently credited with coining the expression *Islamo-fascism*, he has never in fact used it, preferring instead *Islamic fascism*.

34. From bin Laden's March 1997 interview with Peter Arnett of CNN; see http://www.anusha.com/osamaint.htm.

35. See the Middle East Media Research Institute Web page, Special Dispatch Series No. 388, http://memri.org/bin/articles.cgi?Page=archives&Area=sd&ID=SP38802.

36. Christopher Hitchens, "We Cannot Surrender," *The Mirror*, July 8, 2005; reprinted in this volume, 87.

37. Christopher Hitchens, "Of Sin, the Left, and Islamic Fascism," *Nation* (online), October 8, 2001; reprinted in this volume, 47.

38. Hitchens, "Stranger in a Strange Land," *Atlantic Monthly*, December 2001; reprinted in this volume, 54.

39. Walzer, "Can There Be a Decent Left?"

40. Hitchens, "Stranger in a Strange Land," this volume, 54.

41. This point is brought vividly into focus by Hitchens in "Saving Islam from bin Laden," *The Age*, September 5, 2002; reprinted in this volume, 59.

42. Ibid.

43. Samuel Huntington, *The Clash of Civilizations and the Remaking of World Order* (London: Simon and Schuster, 1997).

44. Hitchens, "Saving Islam from bin Laden," this volume, 59.

45. This is a conception that is at the center of what sociologists call the "strong program" of the sociology of culture. This concept, developed by the prominent social theorists Jeffrey Alexander and Philip Smith, is outlined on the Web page of the Center for Cultural Sociology at Yale University, http://research.yale.edu/ccs/about/strong-program/.

46. Hitchens, "Of Sin, the Left, and Islamic Fascism," this volume, 47.

47. Christopher Hitchens, "Interview with Hitchens: Love, Poverty and War," by Jamie Glazov, *Frontpage*, December 29, 2004, available online at http://www.lastsuperpower.net/newsitems/hitch-love-poverty-war/.

48. Hitchens, "Bush's Secularist Triumph," *Slate*, November 9, 2004; reprinted in this volume, 82.

49. Sontag, "First Reactions."

50. Vidal, *Perpetual War for Perpetual Peace*, 22–41.

51. Noam Chomsky, *Power and Terror: Post-9/11 Talks and Interviews* (New York: Seven Stories, 2003), 13.

52. Alexander Cockburn, "The Price," *New York Press*, September 26, 2001.

53. Howard Zinn, "The Old Way of Thinking," *Progressive* (November 2001).

54. Charles Glass, "11 September," *London Review of Books*, October 4, 2001.

55. Fredric Jameson, "11 September," *London Review of Books*, October 4, 2001.

56. Alan Singer, "Now Is the Time to Teach Democracy," *Newsletter of the Organization of American Historians* 30 (2002).

57. See esp. the closing paragraph of Hitchens, "Don't. Be. Silly," this volume, 177; and Hitchens, "Taking Sides," *Nation*, October 14, 2002; reprinted in this volume, chap. 19.

58. See esp. Christopher Hitchens, "Al Qaeda's Latest Target," *Slate*, November 18, 2003; reprinted in this volume, chap. 10; and Christopher Hitchens, "Jihad in the Netherlands," *Free Inquiry*, February/March 2005; reprinted in this volume, chap. 14.

59. Richard Rorty, "Post-Democracy," *London Review of Books*, April 1, 2004.

60. Hitchens, "Stranger in a Strange Land," this volume, 54.

61. Hitchens, "Of Sin, the Left, and Islamic Fascism," this volume, 47.

62. For a riposte to this argument, see Edward S. Herman, "For Rationalization—Of Imperial Violence," *Z Magazine Online*, October 25, 2001.

63. Christopher Hitchens, "The Ends of War," *Nation*, November 29, 2001; see also Hitchens, "It's a Good Time for War."

64. Christopher Hitchens, "Ha Ha Ha to the Pacifists," *Guardian*, November 14, 2001; reprinted in this volume, 52.

65. Hitchens, "The Ends of War." See esp. Richard Seymour, "The Genocidal Imagination of Christopher Hitchens," *Monthly Review*, November 26, 2005; reprinted in this volume, chap. 52.

66. Seymour, "The Genocidal Imagination of Christopher Hitchens," this volume, 312.

67. Hitchens, "The Ends of War."

68. Richard Webster points out that as a term of demonization, *Islamic fascism* obstructs, rather than aids, conceptual understanding; see Richard Webster, "Israel, Palestine and the Tiger of Terrorism: Anti-Semitism and History," *New Statesman*, November 29, 2002, available online at http://www.richardwebster. net/israelpalestine.html.

69. Immediately prior to 9/11, Hitchens had resolved to "withdraw from 'politics' as such, and spend more time with the sort of words that hold their value" (introduction to *Love, Poverty, and War*, xiv). Hitchens's refuge was, of course, short-lived and, thanks to Osama bin Laden and his emulators, seems unlikely to be resumed any time soon.

70. See esp. Norman Geras, "Pages from a Daily Journal of Argument," in *A Matter of Principle: Humanitarian Arguments for War in Iraq*, ed. Thomas Cushman (Berkeley: University of California Press, 2005), 201.

71. Christopher Hitchens, *A Long Short War: The Postponed Liberation of Iraq* (New York: Plume, 2003), 38.

72. Ibid.

73. Ibid., 10.

74. Ibid.

75. This reflected his long-standing belief that "totalitarian regimes are innately and inherently aggressive and unstable, and that if there is to be a fight with them, which there must needs be, then it is ill-advised to let them choose the time or the place of the engagement" (ibid., 4).

76. See ibid., 4, 11, 12–13, 18. And see, more recently, Christopher Hitchens, "Fallujah," *Wall Street Journal*, April 2, 2004; reprinted in this volume, chap. 26; and Christopher Hitchens, "The Case for Regime Change," in Cushman, *A Matter of Principle*, 29–38.

77. Hitchens, *A Long Short War*, 15–16.

78. Kanan Makiya, "Kanan Makiya Responds," *Dissent* (winter 2003).

79. Christopher Hitchens, "So Long, Fellow Travelers," *Washington Post*, October 20, 2002; reprinted in this volume, 104.

80. Ibid.

81. For a similar judgment, see Thomas Cushman and Stjepan Mestrovic, introduction to *This Time We Knew: Western Responses to Genocide in Bosnia*, ed. Thomas Cushman and Stjepan Mestrovic (New York: NYU Press, 1996), 5–6; and, more recently, Nick Cohen, *What's Left* (London: Fourth Estate, 2007).

82. Hitchens, "So Long, Fellow Travelers," this volume, 104.

83. Conquest was also the dedicatee of Hitchens's book *Orwell's Victory* (London: Allen Lane, 2002).

84. See Martin Amis, *Koba the Dread: Laughter and the Twenty Million* (New York: Talk Miramax, 2002), 9–10.

85. Harold Garfinkel, "Conditions of Successful Degradation Ceremonies," *American Journal of Sociology* 61, (1956): 420–24.

86. See Michael Kazin, "The Passion of Christopher Hitchens," *Dissent* (summer 2005); reprinted in this volume, chap. 49.

87. See, for example, Edward Said, "The Imperial Bluster of Tom Delay," *Counter Punch*, August 20, 2003; Herman, "For Rationalization"; and Noam Chomsky's letter to the *Nation*, October 1, 2001.

88. See esp. Jack McCarthy, "Letter to a Lying, Self-Serving, Fat-Assed, Chain Smoking, Drunken, Opportunistic, Cynical Contrarian," *Counter Punch*, October 22, 2002; and Studs Terkel's letter to the *Nation*, January 6, 2003, reprinted in this volume, chap. 45.

89. See "Galloway and the Mother of All Invective," *Guardian*, May 18, 2005.

90. See Gary Malone, "Christopher Hitchens: Flickering Firebrand," *Arena Journal*, July 7, 2005; reprinted in this volume, chap. 50.

91. See McCarthy, "Letter to a Lying . . . Contrarian."

92. Ibid.; and see Norman Finkelstein, "Hitchens as Model Apostate," *Counter Punch*, September 10, 2003; reprinted in this volume, chap. 46.

93. McCarthy, "Letter to a Lying . . . Contrarian."

94. Richard Harth, for example, makes reference to Hitchens's "signature bedraggled appearance" on American television; see Harth, "Adieu Christopher, Adieu," *Counter Punch*, October 1, 2002.

95. See Finkelstein, "Hitchens as Model Apostate," this volume, 242.

96. Marc Cooper, "Hari to Hitchens: 'Come Home,'" September 27, 2004, marccooper.com.

97. See Collini, "'No Bullshit' Bullshit."

98. Malone, "Christopher Hitchens: Flickering Firebrand," this volume, 279.

99. See Terkel's letter to the *Nation*, January 6, 2003, this volume, 237.

100. Herman, "For Rationalization."

101. Dennis Perrin, "Obituary for a Former Contrarian," *Minnesota City Pages*, July 9, 2003; reprinted in this volume, 257.

102. Tariq Ali, "Hitchens at War," *Counter Punch*, September 26, 2001.

103. See esp. Christopher Hitchens, *Letters to a Young Contrarian* (Oxford: Perseus, 2001), 97.

104. See "Free Radical," *Reason Online* (November 2001); reprinted in this volume as "An Interview with Christopher Hitchens, Part I: Radicalism, Liberty, and the Post-Socialist World," 167.

105. See Barber, "Look Who's Talking."

106. Hitchens, *Letters to a Young Contrarian*, 97.

107. Interview with Hitchens, Web page for PBS film *Heaven and Earth: The Rise and Fall of Socialism,* www.pbs.org/heavenonearth/interviews_hitchens. html.

108. According to David Herman, Hitchens's estrangement from the Left began well before September 11, 2001: "Many people assume that Hitchens's break with the Left came over 9/11. That was a bitter falling out, part of a larger split within the Anglo-American Left intelligentsia. But signs of the break are apparent earlier: over Salman Rushdie and the fatwa in 1989, then Bosnia and Kosovo in the 1990s" (David Herman, "'The English Hitchens,'" *Prospect* 110 [May 2005]). This point is worth stressing, if only because so many commentators falsely suggest that prior to 9/11 Hitchens's relationship with the Left was a close and harmonious one. Johann Hari, for example, says that on September 10, 2001, Hitchens "was sailing along the slow, certain route from being the Left's belligerent bad boy to being one of its most revered old men" (Johann Hari, "In Enemy Territory? An Interview with Christopher Hitchens," *Independent*, September 23, 2004). In truth, Hitchens's relationship with the Left has *always* been fraught and complicated—over the Soviet Union, George Orwell, Rushdie, Kosovo, President Clinton . . .

109. See Hitchens, "Don't. Be. Silly," this volume, 177.

110. See ibid.

111. See esp. Hitchens, "Of Sin, the Left, and Islamic Fascism."

112. See esp. Hitchens, "Stranger in a Strange Land."

113. "Interview: 'Don't Cross Over If You Have Any Intention of Going Back': Politics and Literature in the Mind of Christopher Hitchens," *Common Review* 4/1 (2005).

114. See Christopher Hitchens, "Restating the Case for War," *Slate*, November 5, 2003; reprinted in this volume, 114.

115. See Hitchens's letter to Katha Pollitt, published in the *Nation*, December 16, 2002.

116. See Christopher Hitchens, "Booze and Fags," in *For the Sake of Argument*, 233–39.

117. George Scialabba, "Farewell Hitch," *Evatt Foundation News Letter* (April/May 2005); reprinted in this volume, 264. And see also Malone, "Christopher Hitchens: Flickering Firebrand."

118. See esp. Christopher Hitchens, "Prison Mutiny," *Slate*, May 4, 2004.

119. Hitchens notes with regret that there is "a general tendency—not by any means confined to radicals but in some way specially associated with them—to believe that once the lowest motive for a dissenting position has been found,

it must in some way be the real one" ("Left-Leaving, Left-Leaning," *Los Angeles Times*, November 16, 2003; reprinted in this volume, 189).

120. Responding to the accusation that he is an incoherent drunk, Hitchens says that his tolerance for alcohol was not a critical issue when he was on "the right side of the Left" (see his riposte to Terkel, this volume, chap. 45).

121. Christopher Hitchens, "My Ideal War," *Slate*, March 20, 2006.

122. See the exchange with Pollitt in the *Nation*, December 16, 2002.

123. See Hari, "In Enemy Territory?; and "Interview: 'Don't Cross Over.'"

124. Juan Cole, "The Risks of Peace and the Costs of War," *Journal of the International Institute* 10, no. 2 (winter 2003): 3.

125. See esp. Hitchens, "Restating the Case for War."

126. See Malone, "Christopher Hitchens: Flickering Firebrand," this volume, 279.

127. See esp. Peter W. Galbraith, *The End of Iraq: How American Incompetence Created a War without End* (New York: Simon and Schuster, 2006).

128. Norman Geras, "The Last Word on the Iraq War," *Normblog*, posted October 22, 2004, emphasis in original.

129. See "Frontpage Interview: Christopher Hitchens," by Jamie Glazov, *Frontpage*, December 10, 2003; reprinted in this volume as "An Interview with Christopher Hitchens, Part II: Anti-Fascism, Reactionary Conservatism, and the Post–September 11 World," chap. 41.

Hitchens on Terror

◀(1)▶

American Society Can Outlast or
Absorb Practically Anything

Any attempt at a forward look is still compromised by the dreadful, fascinated glance over the shoulder. A week when the United States itself was a "no-fly zone" from coast to coast. The wolfish parting of the lips as the second of the evil twins hastened towards New York, and saw that its sibling had already smashed and burnt the first of the harmless twins. (Truly, God must be great.) Then the scything of the second innocent twin. The weird void. The faint echoes of heroism from the fuselage of a United Airlines jet over Pennsylvania, as its condemned passengers decided they had nothing to lose, but would not be "collateral damage" in the blaspheming of another national landmark. America is the greatest of all subjects for a writer, in the first place because of its infinite space and depth and variety, and also because it is ultimately founded upon an idea. The idea, originally phrased in some noble document drawn up by a few rather conservative English gentleman-farmers, is that on this continent there might arise the world's first successful multinational and secular democracy. Profiting by the stupidity of European monarchs, its early leaders were able to buy the Midwest from the French and then Alaska from the Russians, both at knockdown prices. Profiting from the stupidity of later European statesmen, the United States did very well indeed out of two world wars and emerged as the only serious global and imperial power in human history. Even the least superstitious American often has a smidgen of belief in the idea of providence; the notion that this is a lucky country, if not a divinely favored one. The trauma of last Tuesday morning is quite unlike all previous tests of the American proposition, because it is humiliating and in some ways meaningless. Pearl Harbor—the most readily available comparison—was also subject to analysis and criticism as an outcome of American foreign policy in the Pacific. But the conversion of civilian airliners into missiles gives no such work for the heart or the mind to do. It is simultaneously sordid and scary: more as if all the gold in Fort Knox had turned to lead, or all the blood-banks in the country had been found to be infected with some filthy virus. This is why the very pathos of the public ceremonies—flag displays, floral tributes, candle-lightings—seems so tawdry and inadequate. It is also why the grounds for vengeance sound so hollow and unconvincing. President Bush has been criticized, quite rightly, for contriving to combine the utterly tame with the emptily bombastic. But it is difficult to imagine what even a Roosevelt could have usefully pronounced. What do you do when there's nothing to do? What do you say when there's nothing to say? (The answer of Congress to this pressing question: let's all assemble on the Capitol steps and sing "God Bless America" out of tune, was universally agreed to be the wince-making superfluous gesture of the week.) I am writing this in the temporary mental atmosphere of a one-party state. For the moment, every article and bulletin emphasizes the need for unity behind our leader and for close attention to national security. This culture of conformism and fear is the precise opposite of American optimism. Somewhere, there must be cackles of wicked mirth at the ease with which an American herd can be cowed or stampeded. But then the attack on American optimism is the whole point. The perpetrators have calmly rehearsed their own deaths, and the deaths of strangers, for years. They are not even "terrorists" so much as nihilists: at war with the very idea of modernity and the related practices of pluralism and toleration. In order to comprehend them we need the images not of Beirut in the 1980s or of Palestine today but of the crusades or the Thirty Years War. These are people who are seen by the Taliban as extreme. No settlement for the Palestinians or the Chechens or the Kashmiris or the Bosnians would have appeased such barbarous piety. As a result, we are all hostages for now to the security-mad, the anonymous "expert," the unsmiling professional. The very people who have served us so badly for so long. But these are the praetorians who inevitably inherit such situations. There is a uniquely American expression that usually surfaces at moments such as this. It is called "the loss of innocence." I was rather interested to see that it didn't come up last week. But then there was probably a surplus of innocence in the form of the families who had happily boarded those flights on a bright Tuesday morning, heading for the West Coast and a bigger sky.

In any case, the proper term would be "loss of American confidence." The whole idea that tomorrow will be better than today, and that each successive generation will be happier and more prosperous and more hopeful, has taken an enormous body-slam. It is absurd and upsetting to see schools closed in cities as far away as California. The TV and the web can spread panic as rapidly as any rumor of witchcraft. Yet, even as people were partially retreating into a bunker mentality, they were nonetheless managing to act as if they had learnt from previous panics. The single most impressive fact about the past few days has been the general refusal to adopt an ugly or chauvinistic attitude towards America's most recent and most conspicuous immigrants: the Middle Eastern ones. The response of public opinion has been uniformly grown-up and considerate. As if by unspoken agreement, everyone seems to know that any outrage to multiculturalism and community would be an act of complicity with the assassins. And in rather the same way, no one chooses to be very raucously in favor of hitting just anyone in "retaliation" overseas. This is an undemonstrative strength of the sort that will be decisive from now on. After all, a sober look at the odds discloses an obvious truth. American society cannot be destroyed even by the most horrifying nihilist attacks. It can outlast or absorb practically anything (of course, it could not entirely survive an attack by WMDs, but then neither can any society, and the greatest single political casualty of the week is undoubtedly the fantasy of the "missile defense" option as the front-line posture against "rogue" elements). A few months ago, a friend of mine was introduced to George Bush at a reception for aid workers in the Third World: "Tell me," said Bush. "What's the worst country in the world?" "Congo, Mr President." "OK, what's the second worst?" "Afghanistan, Mr President." "Oh yeah—that's where them loonies blew up those statues." Bush did better than perhaps he realized in this trivial exchange. Recall the Taliban's desecration of the Buddhas at Bamiyan, and you will see that the nihilists are at war with culture as a whole. They are capable of impressive vandalism and callousness, but that's the limit of their attainment. Last week, an entire population withstood an attempted rape and murder of its core and identity. It did so while the President was off the radar screen. But everyone, in an important sense, knew what to do, as well as what not to do. The whole point of a multinational democracy is that it should be able to run on its own power. In other words, if short-term foolishness can be minimized at home and abroad, then people will surely appreciate that, in the words of an old slogan worn out by repetition, the only thing we have to fear is fear itself.

Independent, September 16, 2001

⊰(2)⊱

The Pursuit of Happiness Is at an End

This is what a missing limb must feel like. I don't just mean the amputated feeling one gets when contemplating the New York skyline, which is what I'm doing at the moment. Nor the bizarre and weird emotions that occur at the realization that while I still live in Washington DC—the capital of the free world—it is now the only capital on the planet whose airport is indefinitely closed.

I spent some of last week stranded in a time and space-warp, caught in the first-ever American no-fly zone. And much of the time I couldn't get a phone call on the first or second or third dial, even to my home in Washington.

The light, space, air and freedom of the United States depend on two things working well all the time—the airline network and the phone system. To be deprived of both, as well as of the US Mail and all the wonderful overnight delivery services, was to experience a hellish feeling of powerlessness.

But these are merely the material symptoms of the dismemberment. I searched my cortex all week for the right phrase, which I knew was in there somewhere. I didn't locate it, prod and tug and probe as I might, until late in the weekend. Here's what's gone: the pursuit of happiness. Four words, which are to be found in only one audacious document of human ambition and aspiration—the American Declaration of Independence.

Nobody knows quite who inserted the phrase, or what was precisely intended by it. There's a learned dispute about whether "pursuit" means the search for happiness, or happiness itself as a pursuit. No matter: one knows the concept to be somehow indispensable. After the first Kennedy assassination, Senator Patrick Moynihan was talking to the columnist Mary McGrory. She said to him: "Pat, we'll never laugh again." "No, Mary," was his reply, "we'll laugh again. We'll just never be young again." How banal that sad exchange now seems. For the first time ever, I can feel grief at a public event and its dire and limitless consequences, and reflect that at my age I might never again feel entirely carefree. The absent limb may stop hurting, but it will not grow back.

Past US Crimes Are No Excuse

Ex-Ministers and ex-diplomats are the bane of the screen at times like this, clogging the airwaves with conventional unwisdom. Dust flies from the Rolodex as networks search out the has-beens with which to fight the last war. Still, I could not repress a twinge of sympathy for the former United States ambassador to Britain, Philip Lader, when I read about BBC's *Question Time* and the way he cracked under pressure.

One needs to be unambivalent here. I have written more criticisms of American foreign policy than most people. I have no time for the way in which the Sharons and Pinochets of the world profit from their Washington connection. (It was only four months ago that the Bush administration handed the Taliban a $43 million subsidy for its kind and fundamentalist help in the war on drugs.)

When Clinton rocketed a pharmaceutical factory in Sudan, to give himself a bounce in the opinion polls, I wrote in this newspaper that it was a war crime, and I found the applause as sickening as last week's footage of destitute refugees making a fiesta out of the news from New York.

But the mass murder of last Tuesday is in no sense a reprisal or a revenge for past crimes such as that. The people who destroyed the World Trade Center, and used civilians as accessories, are not fighting to free Gaza. They are fighting for the right to throw acid in the faces of unveiled women in Kabul and Karachi. They didn't just destroy the temple of modernity, they used heavy artillery to shatter ancient Buddha statues in Bamiyan earlier this year, and in Egypt have plotted to demolish the Pyramids and the Sphinx because they are un-Islamic and profane.

Look at what they do to their own societies, from Algeria to Afghanistan, and then wonder what they might have in mind for ours.

Liberal masochism is of no use to us at a time like this, and Muslim self-pity even less so. Self-preservation and self-respect make it necessary to recognize and name a lethal enemy when one sees one.

London Evening Standard, September 19, 2001

◃(3)▹

Against Rationalization

It was in Peshawar, on the Pakistan-Afghanistan frontier, as the Red Army was falling apart and falling back. I badly needed a guide to get me to the Khyber Pass, and I decided that what I required was the most farouche-looking guy with the best command of English and the toughest modern automobile. Such a combination was obtainable, for a price. My new friend rather wolfishly offered me a tour of the nearby British military cemetery (a well-filled site from the Victorian era) before we began. Then he slammed a cassette into the dashboard. I braced myself for the ululations of some mullah but received instead a dose of "So Far Away." From under the turban and behind the beard came the gruff observation, "I thought you might like Dire Straits."

This was my induction into the now-familiar symbiosis of tribal piety and high-tech; a symbiosis consummated on September 11 with the conversion of the southern tip of the capital of the modern world into a charred and suppurating mass grave. Not that it necessarily has to be a symbol of modernism and innovation that is targeted for immolation. As recently as this year, the same ideology employed heavy artillery to destroy the Buddha statues at Bamiyan, and the co-thinkers of bin Laden in Egypt have been heard to express the view that the Pyramids and the Sphinx should be turned into shards as punishment for their profanely un-Islamic character.

Since my moment in Peshawar I have met this faction again. In one form or another, the people who leveled the World Trade Center are the same people who threw acid in the faces of unveiled women in Kabul and Karachi, who maimed and eviscerated two of the translators of *The Satanic Verses* and who machine-gunned architectural tourists at Luxor. Even as we worry what they may intend for our society, we can see very plainly what they have in mind for their own: a bleak and sterile theocracy enforced by advanced techniques. Just a few months ago Bosnia surrendered to the international court at The Hague the only accused war criminals detained on Muslim-Croat federation territory. The butchers had almost all been unwanted "volunteers" from the Chechen, Afghan and Kashmiri fronts; it is as an unapologetic defender of the Muslims of Bosnia (whose cause was generally unstained by the sort of atrocity committed by Catholic and Orthodox Christians) that one can and must say that bin Ladenism poisons everything that it touches.

I was apprehensive from the first moment about the sort of masochistic e-mail traffic that might start circulating from the Chomsky-Zinn-Finkelstein quarter, and I was not to be disappointed. With all due thanks to these worthy comrades, I know already that the people of Palestine and Iraq are victims of a depraved and callous Western statecraft. And I think I can claim to have been among the first to point out that Clinton's rocketing of Khartoum—supported by most liberals—was a gross war crime, which would certainly have entitled the Sudanese government to mount reprisals under international law. (Indeed, the sight of Clintonoids on TV, applauding the "bounce in the polls" achieved by their man that day, was even more repulsive than the sight of destitute refugee children making a wretched holiday over the nightmare on Chambers Street.) But there is no sense in which the events of September 11 can be held to constitute such a reprisal, either legally or morally.

It is worse than idle to propose the very trade-offs that may have been lodged somewhere in the closed-off minds of the mass murderers. The people of Gaza live under curfew and humiliation and expropriation. This is notorious. Very well: Does anyone suppose that an Israeli withdrawal from Gaza would have forestalled the slaughter in Manhattan? It would take a moral cretin to suggest anything of the sort; the cadres of the new *jihad* make it very apparent that their quarrel is with Judaism and secularism on principle, not with (or not just

with) Zionism. They regard the Saudi regime not as the extreme authoritarian theocracy that it is, but as something too soft and lenient.
The Taliban forces viciously persecute the Shiite minority in Afghanistan. The Muslim fanatics in Indonesia try to extirpate the infidel minorities there; civil society in Algeria is barely breathing after the fundamentalist assault.

Now is as good a time as ever to revisit the history of the Crusades,
or the sorry history of partition in Kashmir, or the woes of the Chechens and Kosovars. But the bombers of Manhattan represent fascism
with an Islamic face, and there's no point in any euphemism about it.
What they abominate about "the West," to put it in a phrase, is not
what Western liberals don't like and can't defend about their own system, but what they *do* like about it and must defend: its emancipated
women, its scientific inquiry, its separation of religion from the state.
Loose talk about chickens coming home to roost is the moral equivalent of the hateful garbage emitted by Falwell and Robertson, and exhibits about the same intellectual content. Indiscriminate murder is
not a judgment, even obliquely, on the victims or their way of life, or
ours. Any decent and concerned reader of this magazine could have
been on one of those planes, or in one of those buildings—yes, even in
the Pentagon.

The new talk is all of "human intelligence": the very faculty in which
our ruling class is most deficient. A few months ago, the Bush Administration handed the Taliban a subsidy of $43 million in abject
gratitude for the assistance of fundamentalism in the "war on drugs."
Next up is the renewed "missile defense" fantasy recently endorsed by
even more craven Democrats who seek to occupy the void "behind
the President." There is sure to be further opportunity to emphasize
the failings of our supposed leaders, whose costly mantra is "national
security" and who could not protect us. And yes indeed, my guide in
Peshawar was a shadow thrown by William Casey's CIA, which first
connected the unstoppable Stinger missile to the infallible Koran. But
that's only one way of stating the obvious, which is that this is an enemy for life, as well as an enemy of life.

Nation, September 20, 2001

⁂(4)⁂

Of Sin, the Left, and Islamic Fascism

Not all readers liked my attack on the liberal/left tendency to "rationalize" the aggression of September 11, or my use of the term "fascism with an Islamic face," and I'll select a representative example of the sort of "thinking" that I continue to receive on my screen, even now. This jewel comes from Sam Husseini, who runs the Institute for Public Accuracy in Washington, DC: "The fascists like Bid-Laden could not get volunteers to stuff envelopes if Israel had withdrawn from Jerusalem like it was supposed to—and the US stopped the sanctions and the bombing on Iraq."

You've heard this "thought" expressed in one way or another, dear reader, have you not? I don't think I took enough time in my last column to point out just what is so utterly rotten at the very core of it. So, just to clean up a corner or two: (1) If Husseini knows what was in the minds of the murderers, it is his solemn responsibility to inform us of the source of his information, and also to share it with the authorities. (2) If he does not know what was in their minds—as seems enormously more probable—then why does he rush to appoint himself the ventriloquist's dummy for such a faction? Who volunteers for such a task at such a time?

Not only is it indecent to act as self-appointed interpreter for the killers, but it is rash in the highest degree. The death squads have not favored us with a posthumous manifesto of their grievances, or a statement of claim about Palestine or Iraq, but we are nonetheless able to surmise or deduce or induct a fair amount about the ideological or theological "root" of their act (Husseini doesn't seem to demand "proof" of bin Laden's involvement any more than the Bush Administration is willing to supply it) and if we are correct in this, then we have considerable knowledge of two things: their ideas and their actions.

First the actions. The central plan was to maximize civilian casualties in a very dense area of downtown Manhattan. We know that the killers had studied the physics and ecology of the buildings and the neighborhood, and we know that they were limited only by the flight schedules and bookings of civil aviation. They must therefore have been quite prepared to convert fully loaded planes into missiles, instead of the mercifully unpopulated aircraft that were actually commandeered, and they could have hoped by a combination of luck and tactics to have at least doubled the kill-rate on the ground. They spent some time in the company of the families they had kidnapped for the purpose of mass homicide. It was clearly meant to be much, much worse than it was. And it was designed and incubated long before the mutual-masturbation of the Clinton-Arafat-Barak "process." The Talibanis have in any case not distinguished themselves very much by an interest in the Palestinian plight. They have been busier trying to bring their own societies under the reign of the most inflexible and pitiless declension of Sharia law. This is known to anyone with the least acquaintance with the subject.

The ancillary plan was to hit the Department of Defense and (on the best evidence we have available) either the Capitol Dome or the White House. The Pentagon, for all its symbolism, is actually more the civil-service bit of the American "war-machine," and is set in a crowded Virginia neighborhood. You could certainly call it a military target if you were that way inclined, though the bin Ladenists did not attempt anything against a guarded airbase or a nuclear power station in Pennsylvania (and even if they had, we would now doubtless be reading that the glow from Three Mile Island was a revenge for globalization). The Capitol is where the voters send their elected representatives—poor things, to be sure, but our own. The White House is where the elected President and his family and staff are to be found. It survived the attempt of British imperialism to burn it down, and the attempt of the Confederacy to take Washington DC, and this has hallowed even its most mediocre occupants. I might, from where I am sitting, be a short walk from a gutted Capitol or a shattered White House. I am quite certain that in such a case Husseini and his rabble of sympathizers would still be telling me that my chickens were coming home to roost. (The image of bin Laden's men "stuffing envelopes" is the perfected essence of such brainless verbiage.) Only the stoicism of men like Jeremy Glick and Thomas Burnett prevented some such outcome; only those who chose to die fighting rather than allow such a profanity, and such a further toll in lives, stood between us and the fourth death squad. One iota of such innate fortitude is worth all the writings of Noam Chomsky, who coldly compared the plan of September 11 to a stupid and cruel and cynical raid by Bill Clinton on Khartoum in August 1998.

I speak with some feeling about that latter event, because I wrote three *Nation* columns about it at the time, pointing out (with evidence that goes unrebutted to this day) that it was a war crime, and a war crime opposed by the majority of the military and intelligence establishment. The crime was directly and sordidly linked to the effort by a crooked President to avoid impeachment (a conclusion sedulously avoided by the Chomskys and Husseinis of the time). The Al-Shifa pharmaceutical plant was well-known to be a civilian target, and its "selection" was opposed by most of the Joint Chiefs and many CIA personnel for just this reason (see, for additional corroboration, Seymour Hersh's *New Yorker* essay "The Missiles of August," October 12, 1998). To mention this banana-republic degradation of the United States in the same breath as a plan, deliberated for months, to inflict maximum horror upon the innocent is to abandon every standard that makes intellectual and moral discrimination possible. To put it at its very lowest, and most elementary, at least the missiles launched by Clinton were not full of passengers. (How are you doing, Sam? Noam, wazzup?)

So much for what the methods and targets tell us about the true anti-human and anti-democratic motivation. By their deeds shall we know them. What about the animating ideas? There were perhaps seven hundred observant followers of the Prophet Muhammad burned alive in New York on September 11. Nobody who had studied the target zone could have been in any doubt that some such figure was at the very least a likely one. And, since Islam makes no discrimination between the color and shade of its adherents, there was good reason to think that any planeload of civilians might include some Muslims as well. I don't myself make this point with any more emphasis than I would give to the several hundred of my fellow Englishmen (some of them doubtless Muslims also) who perished. I stress it only because it makes my point about fascism. To the Wahhabi-indoctrinated sectarians of Al Qaeda, only the purest and most fanatical are worthy of consideration. The teachings and published proclamations of this cult have initiated us to the idea that the tolerant, the open-minded, the apostate or the followers of different branches of The Faith are fit only for slaughter and contempt. And that's before Christians and Jews, let alone atheists and secularists, have even been factored in. As before, the deed announces and exposes its "root cause." The grievance and animosity predate even the Balfour Declaration, let alone the occupation of the West Bank. They predate the creation of Iraq as a state. The gates of Vienna would have had to fall to the Ottoman *jihad* before any balm could begin to be applied to these psychic wounds. And this is precisely, now, our problem. The Taliban and its surrogates are not content to immiserate their own societies in beggary and serfdom. They are condemned, and they deludedly believe that they are commanded, to spread the contagion and to visit hell upon the unrighteous. The very first step that we must take, therefore, is the acquisition of enough self-respect and self-confidence to say that we have met an enemy and that he is not us, but someone else. Someone with whom coexistence is, fortunately I think, not possible. (I say "fortunately" because I am also convinced that such coexistence is not desirable.)

But straight away, we meet people who complain at once that this enemy is us, really. Did we not aid the grisly Taliban to achieve and hold power? Yes indeed "we" did. Well, does this not double or triple our responsibility to remove them from power? A sudden sheep-like silence, broken by a bleat. Would that not be "over-reaction"? All I want to say for now is that the under-reaction to the Taliban by three successive United States administrations is one of the great resounding disgraces of our time. There is good reason to think that a Taliban defeat would fill the streets of Kabul with joy. But for the moment, the Bush Administration seems a hostage to the Pakistani and Saudi clients who are the sponsors and "harborers" the President claims publicly to be looking for! Yet the mainstream Left, ever shuffling its feet, fears only the discomfort that might result from repudiating such an indefensible and humiliating posture. Very well then, comrades. Do not pretend that you wish to make up for America's past crimes in the region. Here is one such crime that can be admitted and undone— the sponsorship of the Taliban could be redeemed by the demolition of its regime and the liberation of its victims. But I detect no stomach for any such project. Better, then—more decent and reticent—not to affect such concern for "our" past offenses. This is not an article about grand strategy, but it seems to me to go without saying that a sincere commitment to the secular or reformist elements in the Muslim world would automatically shift the balance of America's up-to-now very questionable engagement. Every day, the wretched Arafat is told by Washington, as a favor to the Israelis, that he must police and repress the forces of Hamas and Islamic Jihad. When did Washington last demand that Saudi Arabia cease its heavy financing of these primitive and unscrupulous organizations? We let the Algerians fight the Islamic-fascist wave without saying a word or lending a hand. And this is an effort in which civic and social organizations can become involved without official permission. We should be building such internationalism whether it serves the short-term needs of the current Administration or not: I signed an anti-Taliban statement several months ago and was appalled by the eerie silence with which the initiative was greeted in Washington. (It ought to go without saying that the demand for Palestinian self-determination is, as before, a good cause in its own right. Not now more than ever, but now as ever. There are millions of Palestinians who do not want the future that the pious of all three monotheisms have in store for them.)

Ultimately, this is another but uniquely toxic version of an old story, whereby former clients like Noriega and Saddam Hussein and Slobodan Milosevic and the Taliban cease to be our monsters and become monstrous in their own right. At such a point, a moral and political crisis occurs. Do "our" past crimes and sins make it impossible to expiate the offense by determined action? Those of us who were not consulted about, and are not bound by, the previous covert compromises have a special responsibility to say a decisive "no" to this. The figure of six and a half thousand murders in New York is almost the exact equivalent to the total uncovered in the death-pits of Srebrenica.[1] (Even at Srebrenica, the demented General Ratko Mladic agreed to release all the women, all the children, all the old people and all the males above and below military age before ordering his squads to fall to work.) On that occasion, US satellites flew serenely overhead recording the scene, and Milosevic earned himself an invitation to Dayton, Ohio. But in the end, after appalling false starts and delays, it was found that Mr Milosevic was too much. He wasn't just too nasty. He was also too irrational and dangerous. He didn't even save himself by lyingly claiming, as he several times did, that Osama bin Laden was hiding in Bosnia. It must be said that by this, and by other lies and numberless other atrocities, Milosevic distinguished himself as an enemy of Islam. His national-socialist regime took the line on the towel-heads that the Bush Administration is only accused, by fools and knaves, of taking. Yet when a stand was eventually mounted against Milosevic, it was Noam Chomsky and Sam Husseini, among many others, who described the whole business as a bullying persecution of—the Serbs! I have no hesitation in describing this mentality, carefully and without heat, as soft on crime and soft on fascism. No political coalition is possible with such people and, I'm thankful to say, no political coalition with them is now necessary. It no longer matters what they think.

Nation (Online), October 8, 2001

NOTE

1. At the time at which Hitchens was writing, the number of dead in the World Trade Center attack was generally thought to be much higher than it actually was (2,602 murdered).

◄(5)►

Ha Ha Ha to the Pacifists

There was a time in my life when I did a fair bit of work for the tempestuous Lucretia Stewart, then editor of the American Express travel magazine, *Departures*. Together, we evolved a harmless satire of the slightly driveling style employed by the journalists of tourism. "Land of Contrasts" was our shorthand for it. ("Jerusalem: an enthralling blend of old and new." "South Africa: a harmony in black and white." "Belfast, where ancient meets modern.") It was as you can see, no difficult task. I began to notice a few weeks ago that my enemies in the "peace" movement had decided to borrow from this tattered style book. The mantra, especially in the letters to this newspaper, was: "Afghanistan, where the world's richest country rains bombs on the world's poorest country."

Poor fools. They should never have tried to beat me at this game. What about, "Afghanistan, where the world's most open society confronts the world's most closed one"? "Where American women pilots kill the men who enslave women." "Where the world's most indiscriminate bombers are bombed by the world's most accurate ones." "Where the largest number of poor people applaud the bombing of their own regime." I could go on. (I think number four may need a little work.) But there are some suggested contrasts for the "doves" to paste into their scrapbook. Incidentally, when they look at their scrapbooks they will be able to re-read themselves saying things like, "The bombing of Kosovo is driving the Serbs into the arms of Milosevic."

If the silly policy of a Ramadan pause had been adopted, the citizens of Kabul would have still been under a regime of medieval cruelty, and their oppressors would have been busily regrouping, not praying. Anyhow, what a damn-fool proposal to start with. I don't stop insulting the Christian coalition at Easter time. Come Yom Kippur I tend to step up my scornful remarks about Zionism. Whatever happened to the robust secularism that used to help characterize the Left? And why is it suddenly only the injured feelings of Muslims that count? A couple of years ago, the same people were striking pompous attitudes about the need to avoid offending Serbian and therefore Russian Orthodox sensitivities. Except that those sensitive people, or their leaders, were engaged in putting the Muslims of Europe to the sword. . . .

There's no pleasing some people, but as a charter supporter of CND [Campaign for Nuclear Disarmament] I can remember a time when the peace movement was not an auxiliary to dictators and aggressors in trouble. Looking at some of the mind-rotting tripe that comes my way from much of today's Left, I get the impression that they go to bed saying: what have I done for Saddam Hussein or good old Slobodan or the Taliban today?

Well, ha ha ha, and yah, boo. It was obvious from the very start that the United States had no alternative but to do what it has done. It was also obvious that defeat was impossible. The Taliban will soon be history. Al Qaeda will take longer. There will be other mutants to fight.

But if, as the peaceniks like to moan, more bin Ladens will spring up to take his place, I can offer this assurance: should that be the case, there are many many more who will also spring up to kill him all over again. And there are more of us and we are both smarter and nicer, as well as surprisingly insistent that our culture demands respect, too.

Guardian, November 14, 2001

⑥

Stranger in a Strange Land

October 6, the day immediately preceding the first US counterstroke against the Taliban and Osama bin Laden, found me on a panel at the New York Film Festival. The discussion, on the art of political cinema, had been arranged many months before. But as the chairman announced, the events of September 11 would now provide the atmospheric conditioning for our deliberations. I thus sat on a stage with Oliver Stone, who spoke with feeling about something he termed "the revolt of September 11," and with bell hooks, who informed a well-filled auditorium of the Lincoln Center that those who had experienced Spike Lee's movie about the bombing of a Birmingham, Alabama, church in 1963 would understand that "state terrorism" was nothing new in America.

These were not off-the-cuff observations. I challenged Stone to reconsider his view of the immolation of the World Trade Center as a "revolt." He ignored me. Later he added that this rebellion would soon be joined by the anti-globalization forces of the Seattle protesters. When he was asked by a member of the audience to comment on the applause for the September 11 massacres in Arab streets and camps, he responded that the French Revolution, too, had been greeted by popular enthusiasm.

Although those who don't read the *Nation*, the *New Statesman*, and the *London Review of Books*, and who haven't come across Susan Sontag's disdainful geopolitical analysis in the pages of *The New*

Yorker, may not be aware of it, these views are, sadly, not uncommon on the political Left. Indeed, I would surmise that audience approval of Stone's and hooks's propositions was something near fifty-fifty. Clapping and hissing are feeble and fickle indicators, true. At different times, in combating both Stone and hooks, I got my own fair share of each. But let's say that three weeks after a mass murder had devastated the downtown district, and at a moment when the miasma from the site could still be felt and smelled, a ticket-buying audience of liberal New Yorkers awarded blame more or less evenhandedly between the members of Al Qaeda and the directors of US foreign policy. (And not just of foreign policy: Stone drew applause for his assertion that there was an intimate tie between the New York, Pennsylvania, and Washington attacks and the Florida ballot recount, which was, he asserted, "a complete vindication of the fact that capitalism has destroyed democracy.")

By this time I was entering my twenty-sixth day of active and engaged antagonism toward this sort of talk, or thought, and was impressed despite myself by the realization that I was the first person Stone and hooks and some audience members appeared to have met who did not agree with them. Or perhaps I should rephrase that: I was the first person on the political Left they had met who did not echo or ratify their view. As it happens, I know enough about Marxism, for example, to state without overmuch reservation that capitalism, for all its contradictions, is superior to feudalism and serfdom, which is what bin Laden and the Taliban stand for. (Stone, when I put this to him after the event, retorted that his father had spent many years on Wall Street, and thus he knew the topic quite well.)

Having paged through the combined reactions of Sontag, Noam Chomsky, and many others, I am put very much in mind of something from the opening of Marx's *The Eighteenth Brumaire of Louis Bonaparte*. It's not the sentence about the historical relation between tragedy and farce. It's the observation that when people are learning a new language, they habitually translate it back into the one they already know. This work of self-reassurance and of hectic, hasty assimilation to the familiar is most marked in the case of Chomsky, whose prose now manifests that symptom first captured in, I recall, words by Dr. Charcot—*"le beau calme de l'hysterique."* For Chomsky, everything these days is a "truism"; for him it verges on the platitudinous to be obliged to state, once again for those who may have missed it, that the September 11 crime is a mere bagatelle when set beside the offenses of the Empire. From this it's not a very big step to the conclusion that we must change the subject, and change it at once, to Palestine or East Timor or Angola or Iraq. All radical polemic may now proceed as it did before the rude interruption. "Nothing new," as the spin doctors have taught us to say. There's a distinct similarity between this world view and that of the religious dogmatists who regard September 11 in the light of a divine judgment on a sinful society. But to know even what a newspaper reader knows about the Taliban and its zealous destruction of all culture and all science and all human emancipation, and to compare its most noteworthy if not its most awful atrocity to the fall of the Bastille. . . .

I take a trawl through my e-mail and my mailbag. "Why sing the 'Battle Hymn of the Republic'? Don't they know John Brown was the first terrorist?" "What about the civilian casualties in Vietnam, Guatemala, Gaza [fill in as necessary] . . . ?" This goes on all day, and it goes on while I sleep, so that I open a new batch each morning. Everyone writes to me as if he or she were bravely making a point for the very first time it had ever been made. And so I ask myself, in the spirit of self-criticism that I am enjoining upon these reflexive correspondents, whether I have any responsibility for this dismal tide of dreary traffic, this mob of pseudo-refugees taking shelter in half-baked moral equivalence. Professor Chomsky's preferred comparative case study is Bill Clinton's rocketing of a pharmaceutical factory in Sudan in 1998—a piece of promiscuous violence that took an uncounted number of African lives as part of Clinton's effort to "look presidential" (and also one of many fainthearted earlier attempts to "target" Osama bin Laden). At the time, I wrote several columns denouncing the atrocity, and the racism and cynicism that lay behind it. I also denounced the vileness of the public enthusiasm for the raid, which I think was at least comparable to the gloating of the dispossessed and the stateless over September 11. Now I get all this thrown back at me by people who didn't read it on the first occasion and who appear to believe that only Chomsky has the civic courage to bring the raid up. (He didn't bring it up at the time.) Kipling is back in fashion these days, because of the North-West Frontier, so when I ask myself the question, I also allow myself this couplet from *If*, in which we are asked, "If you can bear to hear the truth you've spoken, / Twisted by knaves to make a trap for fools . . ."

It is perfectly true that most Americans were somewhat indifferent to the outside world as it was before September 11, and also highly ignorant of it—a point on which the self-blaming faction insists. While attention was elsewhere, a deadly and irreconcilable enemy was laying plans and training recruits. This enemy—unless we are to flatter him by crediting his own propaganda—cares no more for the wretched of the West Bank than did Saddam Hussein when he announced that the road to Palestine and Jerusalem led through Kuwait and Kurdistan. But a lethal and remorseless foe is a troubling thing in more than one way. Not only may he wish you harm; he may force you to think and to act. And these responsibilities—because thinking and acting are responsibilities—may be disconcerting. The ancient Greeks were so impressed and terrified by the Furies that they re-baptized them the Eumenides—"the Kindly Ones"—the better to adjust to them. Members of the Left, along with the far larger number of squishy "progressives," have grossly failed to live up to their responsibility to think; rather, they are merely reacting, substituting tired slogans for thought. The majority of those "progressives" who take comfort from Stone and Chomsky are not committed, militant anti-imperialists or anti-capitalists. Nothing so muscular. They are of the sort who, discovering a viper in the bed of their child, would place the first call to People for the Ethical Treatment of Animals.

I believe I can prove this by means of a brief rhetorical experiment. It runs as follows. Very well, I will stipulate that September 11 was revenge for past American crimes. Specifically, and with supporting detail, I will agree that it was revenge for the crime of past indifference to, and collusion with, the Taliban. May we now agree to cancel this crime by removing from the Taliban the power of enslavement that it exerts over Afghans, and which it hopes to extend? Dead silence from progressives. Couldn't we talk about the ozone layer instead? In other words, all the learned and conscientious objections, as well as all the silly or sinister ones, boil down to this: Nothing will make us fight against an evil if that fight forces us to go to the same corner as our own government. (The words "our own" should of course be appropriately ironized, with the necessary quotation marks.) To do so would be a betrayal of the Cherokees.

Some part of this is at least intelligible. My daughter goes to school just across the river from the Pentagon; her good-hearted teachers proposed an "Amity Walk" for children of all nations, to culminate at the statue of Mahatma Gandhi on Massachusetts Avenue. The event would demonstrate that children had no quarrel with anybody. It would not stress the fact that a death squad had just hit a target a few hundred yards away, and would have liked to crash another planeload of hostages anywhere in downtown Washington, and was thwarted in this only by civilians willing to use desperate force. But I had my own reasons, which were no less internationalist, for opposing anything so dismal, and for keeping my child away from anything so inane. I didn't like General Westmoreland or Colonel North or General Pinochet, and I have said more about this than some people. (I did not, like Oliver Stone, become rich or famous by romancing Camelot or by making an unwatchable three-hour movie showing Nixon's and Kissinger's human and vulnerable sides.) I detest General Sharon, and have done so for many years. My face is set against religious and racial demagogues. I believe I know an enemy when I see one. My chief concern when faced with such an antagonist is not that there will be "over-reaction" on the part of those who will fight the adversary—which seems to be the only thing about the recent attacks and the civilized world's response to them that makes the Left anxious.

At his best, Noam Chomsky used to insist that there was a distinction to be drawn between state crimes and insurgent crimes, or between the violence of the emperor and the violence of the pirate. The Taliban–bin Laden alliance is a horrific and novel blend of the two. It employs the methods of the anarchist and the rebel in one declension, being surreptitious and covert and relying on the drama of the individual "martyr." But it also draws on the support of police and military and financial systems, and on the base indulgence of certain established and well-funded religious and theocratic leaderships. It throws acid in the faces of unveiled women. It destroys and burns museums and libraries. (Do we need to submit to our own guilt to "understand" this?) It is an elemental challenge, still terrifying even when one appreciates the appalling fact that its program of medieval stultification cannot actually be realized but will nevertheless be fought for. How contemptible it is, and how lowering to the spirit, that America's liberals should have cried so loudly before they had even been hurt, and that they should have been able to be so stoic only when ignoring the cries of others.

Atlantic Monthly (December 2001)

⋈(7)⋈

Saving Islam from bin Laden

In Nigeria a young woman sits holding a baby and awaiting a sentence of death. The baby is the main, if not indeed the sole, evidence against her. The baby is proof positive that the young woman has engaged in sexual intercourse. The form that the appointed death sentence will take is death by stoning, death in public, death that will make a crowd of participants into killers and the baby into a motherless child.

Why is this happening? It is happening because the Islamic forces in the northern regions of Nigeria want to impose Sharia law, the primitive Muslim code of mutilation and retribution. Do the religious authorities propose to inflict this code only on members of their own congregation, who share the supposed values and taboos? No they do not. They wish to have it imposed also on Christians and unbelievers. This they already do in the regions of Nigeria that have fallen under their control.

But they also want to extend Sharia to the whole of Nigeria, where Islam is still a minority religion and where the society is emerging with some difficulty from a lousy period of military dictatorship. In the sanguinary sectarian rioting that has resulted, portraits of Osama bin Laden have been flourished by the Muslim militants.

Now perhaps somebody will tell me how this—the stoning, the disregard of pluralism, the stupidity and the viciousness—connects to the situation in Gaza, or would help alleviate the plight of the Palestinians. Quite obviously, the clerical bullies in Nigeria are doing this because they think they can. Their counterparts in Malaysia and Indonesia, who want to declare absolutist Islamic republics in countries celebrated for their confessional and ethnic diversity, are not reacting to any "grievance" or suffering from any oppression. They simply think it obvious that the true word of god is contained in one book, and that further reflection is not only unnecessary but profane.

Why should this be our business? Well, a year ago I would have said without expecting to be contradicted that the answer to that was self-evident. There is a civil war raging within the Muslim world, where many believers do not wish to live under Sharia any more than I do. This war has been at an incandescent pitch in Algeria, for example, for more than a decade. It is smoldering but still toxic in Iran, in Egypt, among the Palestinians and now in some of the major cities of "the West."

But the extremist and fundamentalist side in that war has evolved a new tactic. By exporting the conflict and staging it in Europe and America, it hopes both to intimidate and impress those who are wavering. This simple point was made, you may remember, in New York and Washington and Pennsylvania about 12 months ago, and we can be entirely certain that it will be rammed home to us again.

The most notorious manifestation of the other side in this two-front war is of course Al Qaeda, which combines all the worst features of a crime family, a corrupt multinational corporation and a fascist gangster operation. I personally think we owe its demented militants a favor: by doing what they did last year they alerted the whole world to something that was hitherto only dimly understood.

And by taking their own insane ideology seriously, they ruined the chance for some more cautious and tactical fanatics to take over the Pakistani state, including its thermonuclear capacity, from within. They also embarrassed and isolated the equivalent faction within the oligarchy of Saudi Arabia.

Paradoxically, I think the world is a less dangerous place as a consequence of September 11, 2001. Until that day, we had been suffering severely from "under-reaction" to the most lethal threat to our civilization.

This does not mean that a danger of "over-reaction," or mistaken diagnosis, does not exist. We are on the "right" side of this civil war in one way, because we have no choice. It is impossible to compromise with the proponents of sacrificial killing of civilians, the disseminators of anti-Semitic filth, the violators of women and the cheerful murderers of children.

It is also impossible to compromise with the stone-faced propagandists for Bronze Age morality: morons and philistines who hate Darwin and Einstein and who managed, during their brief rule in Afghanistan, to ban and to erase music and art while cultivating the skills of germ warfare. If they would do that to Afghans, what might they not have in mind for us? In confronting such people, the crucial thing is to be willing and able, if not in fact eager, to kill them without pity before they can get started.

But can we be sure we are on the "right" side of the Islamic civil war in the second sense? The holy writ on public stoning for sexual "offences" actually occurs often in the Bible and nowhere in the Koran, and much of the Islamic world is now in the position that "Christian" society occupied a few centuries ago. It has been widely discovered that you cannot run anything but a primeval and cruel and stupid society out of the precepts of one rather mediocre "revelation." Muslims want to travel, to engage with others, and to have access to information and enlightenment (to which they have already made quite majestic contributions).

I am sure many people make the assumption that the United States—which is actually the world's only truly secular state as well as in some ways the world's most religious one—is on the side of those Muslims who want to practice their religion but otherwise neither to impose it nor to be stifled by it.

However, the two regimes that did most to incubate and protect Al Qaeda and the Taliban—the Saudi feudalists and the Pakistani military—were and still are on the official "friends and allies" list of the American establishment. The obscurantists and fanatics were nurtured in the bosom of the same "national security" apparatus that so grotesquely, if not criminally, failed to protect our civil society a year ago. And this is to say nothing about the central question of Palestine, where our military and political elite cannot with any honesty state to this day whether it has cast itself in the role of a mediator or a partisan, and has come to be widely and rightly distrusted as a consequence.

I repeat what I said at the beginning: the objective of Al Qaeda is not the emancipation of the Palestinians but the establishment of tyranny in the Muslim world by means of indiscriminate violence in the non-Muslim world, and those who confuse the two issues are idiots who don't always have the excuse of stupidity.

However, this does not absolve us as citizens from the responsibility of demanding that our leaders be on the side of justice and of international law, for our own sake as well as everybody else's. And we may often have to uphold this view in spite of the unfavorable conditions—of "fallout shelter" paranoia and obsessive secrecy—that are created by our "own" governments.

There is no argument about the foe, in other words, and no real argument with it: only a settled determination to outlive and defeat this latest barbarism. Discovering friends and allies, discarding false ones and making new ones, will test our cultural and political intelligence to a hitherto-unknown degree. But the very complexity and subtlety of the task is one of the things that makes this war worth fighting.

The Age, September 5, 2002

⊀(8)⊁

It's a Good Time for War

In several of his demented sermons, in the days before he achieved global notoriety, Osama bin Laden made his followers a sort of promise. Defeating the Red Army in Afghanistan and bringing down the Soviet Union, he said, had been the hard part. The easy part—the destruction of the United States of America—was still to come. That task would be easy because America was corrupt and cowardly and rotten. It would not fight (as the debacle in Somalia had shown); it was a slave of the Jewish conspiracy; it cared only for comfort and materialism.

It involves no exaggeration to say that everything depends, and has depended, on proving bin Laden wrong. And not merely in proving him wrong, but in demonstrating exactly *how* wrong he is.

Of course, this weekend is partly, and rightly, being given over to remembrance. Everyone has his own indelible image of September 11. Mine is in part imaginary: It involves picturing the wolfish smiles on the faces of the second crew of hijackers as United Airlines Flight 175 screamed toward Manhattan and saw the flames and smoke already billowing from the first World Trade Center tower. With what delight they must have ramped up the speed of their plane, crammed with human cargo, and smashed into the second civilian target. But I also like to visualize the panic and dismay on the faces of those who stole United Airlines Flight 93 as they saw a posse of determined passengers ready to do or die over Pennsylvania rather than have the White House or the Capitol immolated by the scum of the earth. (I live in Washington, D.C., and can never pass either building without picturing how the scene might have looked if it were not for those exemplary volunteers. I also try hard to stay aware of my indebtedness to them.)

In order to get my own emotions out of the way, I should say briefly that on that day I shared the general register of feeling, from disgust to rage, but was also aware of something that would not quite disclose itself. It only became fully evident quite late that evening. And to my surprise (and pleasure), it was exhilaration. I am not particularly a war lover, and on the occasions when I have seen warfare as a traveling writer, I have tended to shudder. But here was a direct, unmistakable confrontation between everything I loved and everything I hated. On one side, the ethics of the multicultural, the secular, the skeptical, and the cosmopolitan. (Those are the ones I love, by the way.) On the other, the arid monochrome of dull and vicious theocratic fascism. I am prepared for this war to go on for a very long time. I will never become tired of waging it, because it is a fight over essentials. And because it is so *interesting*.

I had felt this way once before, on Valentine's Day 1989, when the Ayatollah Khomeini offered a bounty in his own name for the murder of a fiction writer then living in Western Europe. On that occasion, the response had not been so unanimous. The first President George Bush, when asked for a comment on the Khomeini *fatwa* against Salman Rushdie, had replied that as far as he could see, no American interests were involved.

In September 2001, there wasn't much evasive babble of that kind. It had become plain to any thinking person that Islamic absolutism was a deadly and immediate menace. Look at what it had done to its own societies: the Stone Age misery imposed upon Afghanistan or the traumas visited by fundamentalist gangs on Algeria or the state-enforced stultification in Saudi Arabia. If they would treat their "own" people like that, what might they have in store for us?

There's no time to waste on the stupid argument that such a deadly movement represents a sort of "cry for help" or is a thwarted expression of poverty and powerlessness. Osama bin Laden and his fellow dogmatists say openly that they want to restore the lost caliphate; in other words, the Muslim empire once centered at Constantinople. They are not anti-imperialists so much as nostalgists for imperialism. The gang that kidnapped and murdered *Wall Street Journal* reporter Daniel Pearl—and proudly made a video showing the ritual slaughter of a Jew—issued a list of demands on that same obscene video. One of those demands was for the resumption of US sales of advanced F-16 fighter jets to Pakistan. Only a complete moral idiot can believe for an instant that we are fighting against the wretched of the earth. We are fighting, as I said before, against the scum of the earth.

It is important to realize at the outset that a victory for those forces, of which bin Ladenism is only the most extreme, is in two senses of the word impossible. Impossible, obviously, from a moral point of view and from the viewpoint of survival. It has taken us a long time to evolve a society that, however imperfectly, respects political pluralism and religious diversity and the emancipation of the sexual life. A society that attempts to employ the objective standards of scientific inquiry and that has brought us the Hubble telescope and the unraveling of the chain of DNA. Clearly, there can be no compromise between this and the ravings of those who study dreams and are deluded by wild prophecies and who regard women as chattel and unbelievers as sacrificial animals. For them, the achievements of science are nothing, while the theft of WMDs counts as a holy task. Their degradation is bottomless.

This also entails the second sense in which their triumph is impossible. Even if it wished to go there, the Muslim world cannot be returned to the desert and to the precepts of the seventh century. Every such attempt has been a terrifying failure, just as every jihad has ended either in ignominious defeat or in fratricide among its partisans. In a broadcast just after September 11, bin Laden deputy Suleiman Abu Gheith warned Muslims living in the West not to reside in tall buildings or fly on airplanes, because the rain of death was not going to stop. There are many, many Muslims, and not just in the West, who do not care to be spoken to in that tone of voice.

I think that that broadcast should have been mandatory viewing and should have been followed by a robust reply delivered by a serious scholar or a duly elected politician. Instead, the Bush administration asked the American networks not to carry it, and national security adviser Condoleezza Rice even hinted suggestively that such transmissions might contain hidden codes. Well, I think we can take it as certain that Al Qaeda does not rely for its communications on the broadcast schedules of our treasured TV system. (It seems to have been able to arrange everything from flight training to bank accounts without even bothering to conceal its identity.)

But more to the point, why are we so timorous in the face of such a contemptible foe? Why did our vice president go into hiding? Why are we so bent on the useless collective punishment of law-abiding air travelers, none of whom are any better protected from a determined suicide-murderer than they were this time last year? What is the point of all these ominous "warnings" issued by the authorities, which resemble airport or subway announcements in being very loud but highly incomprehensible? Where is the spirit of Flight 93?

Of the gamut of emotions that made the scoreboard a year ago, many people reported a sense of powerlessness or helplessness. This is defeat in the mind. It is certainly true that the national security elite underestimated Al Qaeda before September 11, to an extent that verges upon criminal negligence. But that would be the worst justification for overestimating it now.

And people do not make the best decisions when they are afraid. It was a mistake to pass any law in the immediate aftermath of the assault. Congress should have insisted on a full accounting of the failures of the executive branch before submitting to that same branch's panicky demand for measures that infringe on the letter as well as the spirit of our Constitution. Imagine the grin on the faces of the enemy when they read that Canadians can no longer, with mere student visas, cross the border to take classes at US colleges. *That* should settle the terrorists' hash. No: When we remember that victory is certain we can at the same time stop scaring ourselves to death.

My most enduring memory of last fall, apart from the hauntingly beautiful weather that seemed to mock the prevailing anxiety, was of the maturity displayed by American society. Thousands of citizens are burned alive in an instant—some of them consumed by flames on camera—and there is no panic, no lynching, no looting to speak of. A few sick morons take out their ire on random Tibetans or Sikhs: The general disapproval is felt at once.

And for almost a month—a month—not a shot is fired in response, and there is no public demand for any theatrical or precipitate reprisal. Then, in a very well-calibrated international action, Afghanistan's Taliban regime is taken down and the Al Qaeda network is dispersed. Let the boasters of jihad remember this and be always reminded of it: Mullah Omar and his gang left "their" capital city of Kabul at dead of night and did not even bid farewell to the people they had so long exploited and tortured. Their guest bin Laden may or may not have met his end under the rubble in some obscure cave, as now seems likeliest. But whether or not he did, his last known action was to run away. As with every big-mouth cleric who ululates to an imaginary heaven about the bliss of suicide-murder, he preferred (and nominated) others to do the dying. In contrast to this cowardly hysteria, innumerable American civilians and soldiers acted with calm and humanity and courage.

I was in Pakistan, in Islamabad and Peshawar, and also in Kashmir during the war, and I am as scrupulous, I hope, about civilian casualties as the next person. I was highly impressed by the evolution of military strategy and tactics since the bombs-away inglorious days of the Vietnam era. Many of the points made by the antiwar movement have been consciously assimilated by the Pentagon and its lawyers and advisers. Precision weaponry is good in itself, but its ability to discriminate is improving and will continue to improve. Cluster bombs are perhaps not good in themselves, but when they are dropped on identifiable concentrations of Taliban troops, they do have a heartening effect.

The highest figure for "collateral damage" in the war in Afghanistan that I have seen is the untrustworthy figure of 3,000, which is compiled by suspect pacifist sources and takes no account of the refusal of the other side to identify itself. Such a figure, even if true, would hardly count as a "war" total at all, let alone a war that changed the entire future of a country. (To make a comparison that some idiots deliberately overlook, it is hardly more than the number of *intentional* civilian deaths in the trade center attacks in New York, where the total could easily have been much higher and where civilian aircraft were used to kill civilians.)

If you remember, there were also those who warned hysterically of a humanitarian disaster as a result of the bombing: a "silent genocide," as one Boston-area academic termed it. But to the contrary, the people of Afghanistan did not have to endure a winter with only the food and medicine that the primeval Taliban would have furnished them. They survived, and now the population has *grown* by almost 1.2 million, as refugees from the old, atrocious tyranny make their way home. Here is the first country in history to be bombed *out* of the Stone Age.

It's not over yet, as we must indeed keep telling ourselves, but thus far it is one of the most creditable military operations in history. And it was achieved with a minute fraction of the forces and resources that are at our disposal. There is not a government in the world that will ever again volunteer to play host to Al Qaeda or its surrogates and imitators.

For just this very reason—lest I sound too triumphalist—there is every cause for circumspection and care. We have time and force on our side, and we also have a culture that rightly claims superiority because of its attachment to objectivity and pluralism. This attachment is not emotional, it is intellectual. And the targets of our indiscriminate, fanatical foe are civilians, not generals or politicians. (Our foes wouldn't mind killing generals or politicians, of course, but their ideology counts all infidels as enemies, and civilians are easier to kill, and their level of soldiering is, well, a bit crude.)

So, as civilians in this war, and therefore as primary front-line targets, we do not need to submit to any culture of trust or loyalty or deference. We have a right to know who is in charge and what policies are being debated and what measures taken. We do not have to agree with the choice of any old ally in this struggle, and we dare not assume that any step taken in the name of the "national security" mantra is automatically OK.

Let me give some illustrations of what I mean: First, I'll take the international front. The most annoying thing, in arguing with peaceniks last fall, was confronting their refusal to see that a wholly new situation had arisen. They would insist on translating the fresh, challenging information back into the familiar language they already knew, of Vietnam or Nicaragua or the West Bank. Well, the same was true of the president's "axis of evil" speech, which attempted to fit the new reality into the reassuring old list of "rogue states" or official enemies. In particular, it seemed insane to include Iran in the "most-wanted" category.

The Iranian people, with no interference from outside, have in the past few years developed their own civil-society riposte to the archaic and bankrupt rule of the mullahs. With its dress and its music and its thirst for contact with the outside world, a generation has begun to repudiate theocracy and to insist that election results be respected. A free press is exploding from under the carapace, and electronic communications are eroding superstition. Iranian forces were extremely helpful in combating the Taliban, which had among other things been butchering their Shia co-religionists (as have bin Laden's allies in Pakistan).

There should by now have been a chorus from the American Congress and press and civil society demanding that the administration make good relations with Iran into a high priority. (By the way, the Iranians detest Saddam Hussein as well, and for excellent reasons.) Instead, we lump together potential friends with lethal enemies, and our elite cringes before Saudi Arabia, which would belong in any "axis." And why should our elite, which has got everything wrong in Iran from the shah to Oliver North's hostage-trading, be trusted just because this is an emergency? The most one can say here is that the "axis" rhetoric has been quietly dropped, but that's not good enough.

In case I should be accused of avoiding the question of Palestine, I should simply say that George W. Bush was right in making it plain to the Palestinians that suicide bombing, at this time or any other, would be suicidal only for them. But that does not dissolve America's long-standing promise to sponsor mutual recognition between equal populations—a promise that has been unkept for far too long and is now made more urgent rather than less.

Turning to the domestic side, I am still reeling from two telephone calls that I received at home last December. They were from people "in the loop," and they urged me to get myself and my family right out of town, right now. Intelligence had been received: A loose nuke was on the move, and Washington was the known target. "We're going. We're just telling some friends." I didn't go. Nor, after some hesitation, did I pass on the warning. (To whom? Anyway, I didn't believe that my sources could have such precise time-and-place information.)

Then I started to get angry. I'd already read about Washington's postal workers being felled by anthrax, while life-saving Cipro prescriptions were being distributed on Capitol Hill. And I've since read of the lucky few who are to receive immunization against smallpox. To repeat: The whole point of this war is that it pits us against those who deal in death *without discrimination*. Even so, we try to fight back in a discriminating manner. But why on earth discriminate among ourselves? If there was ever a time when the demand for comprehensive national health care should and could have been raised . . . Need I complete the sentence?

There is a tiny half-truth lurking in the gloating remarks made by some Europeans and others, to the effect that now "Americans will know what it's like." Fair enough. The lazy version of the pursuit of happiness was indeed interrupted by September 11, as other equally lazy versions have been ruptured since. But war, which was once cynically and cleverly defined as "the health of the state," need not be a one-way street. Previous conflicts, in the 1860s and 1940s, also deepened the attachment to democracy, law, and human rights. Within its own borders, the United States is already a potential microcosm of a secular, multinational democracy. We are the ones who have to decide whether such a system can long endure, at home or abroad. Rather than become nerve endings for nameless fear, we can each resolve to become more internationalist and to take a more forward role as citizens.

Last September is commonly said to have "changed everything," but it hasn't done so yet. As it does, we will move closer to a cause, and a country, that is already well worth fighting for.

Boston Globe (Online), September 8, 2002

⫷ 9 ⫸

Inside the Islamic Mafia

I remember laughing out loud, in what was admittedly a mirthless fashion, when Khalid Sheikh Muhammad, one of Osama bin Laden's most heavy-duty deputies, was arrested in Rawalpindi, Pakistan. Straining to think of an apt comparison, I fail badly. But what if, say, the Unabomber had been found hiding out in the environs of West Point or Fort Bragg? Rawalpindi is to the Pakistani military elite what Sandhurst is to the British, or St Cyr used to be to the French. It's not some boiling slum: It's the manicured and well-patrolled suburb of the officer class, very handy for the capital city of Islamabad if you want to mount a coup, and the site of Flashman's Hotel if you are one of those who enjoys the incomparable imperial adventure-stories of George MacDonald Fraser. Who, seeking to evade capture, would find a safe house in such a citadel?

Yet, in the general relief at the arrest of this outstanding thug, that aspect of the matter drew insufficient attention. Many words of praise were uttered, in official American circles, for the exemplary cooperation displayed by our gallant Pakistani allies. But what else do these allies have to trade, except Al Qaeda and Taliban suspects, in return for the enormous stipend they receive from the US treasury? Could it be that, every now and then, a small trade is made in order to keep the larger trade going?

One hesitates to utter thoughts like these, but they recur continually as one reads Bernard-Henri Lévy's latest book: *Who Killed Daniel Pearl?* (London: Duckworth, 2003). Everybody remembers—don't they?—the ghastly video put out on the Web by Pearl's kidnappers and torturers. It's the only live-action footage we possess of the ritual slaughter of a Jew, preceded for effect by his coerced confession of his Jewishness. Pearl was lured into a trap by the promise of a meeting with a senior religious demagogue, who might or might not have shed light on the life of the notorious "shoe-bomber," because of whom millions of us must take off our footwear at American airports every day, as if performing the pieties required for entering a mosque.

What a sick joke all this is, if you study Lévy's book with care. If you ever suspected that the Pakistani ISI (or Inter-services Intelligence) was in a shady relationship with the Taliban and Al Qaeda forces, this book materializes the suspicion and makes the very strong suggestion that Pearl was murdered because he was doing his job too well, not because he was a naive idealist who got into the wrong car at the wrong time. His inquiries had at least the potential for exposing the Pakistani collusion and double-dealing with jihad forces, in much the same pattern the Saudi Arabian authorities have been shown to follow—by keeping two sets of books, in other words, and by exhibiting only one set to Americans.

Like a number of those who take a moral stand on this, Bernard-Henri Lévy was a strong defender of Bosnia's right to exist, at a time when that right was being menaced directly by Serbian and Croatian fascists. It was a simplification to say that Bosnia was "Muslim," but it would also have been a simplification to say that the Bosnians were not Muslims. The best resolution of this paradox was to assert that Bosnia-Herzegovina stood for ethnic and cultural pluralism, and to say that one could defend Islam from persecution while upholding some other important values at the same time. I agree with M. Lévy that it was a disgrace at the time, and a tragedy in retrospect, that so few Western governments took this opportunity.

But now we hear, from those who were indifferent to that massacre of Muslims, or who still protest the measures that were taken to stop the massacre, that it is above all necessary for the West to be aware of Islamic susceptibilities. This plea is not made on behalf of the pluralistic citizens of Sarajevo, but in mitigation of Hamas and Hezbollah and Saddam Hussein. One of the many pleasures of Lévy's book is the care he takes to show the utter cynicism of the godfathers of all this. He quotes by name a Saudi lawyer who specializes in financial transactions:

> "Islamism is a business," he explains to me with a big smile. "I don't say that because it's my job, or because I see proof of it in my office ten times a day, but because it's a fact. People hide behind Islamism. They use it like a screen saying 'Allah Akbar! Allah Akbar!' But we know that here. We see the deals and the movements

behind the curtain. In one way or another, it all passes through our hands. We do the paperwork. We write the contracts. And I can tell you that most of them couldn't care less about Allah. They enter Islamism because it's nothing other than a source of power and wealth, especially in Pakistan. . . . Take the young ones in the madrassas. They see the high rollers in their SUVs having five wives and sending their children to good schools, much better than the madrassas. They have your Pearl's killer, Omar Sheikh, right in front of their eyes. When he gets out of the Indian prisons and returns to Lahore, what do the neighbors see? He's very well-dressed. He has a Land Cruiser. He gets married and the city's big-shots come to his wedding."

Everything we know about Al Qaeda's operations, as of those of Saddam Hussein, suggests that they combine the culture of a crime family or cartel with the worst habits of a bent multinational corporation. Yet the purist critics of "globalization" tend to assume that the spiritual or nationalistic claims of such forces still deserve to be taken at their own valuation, lest Western "insensitivity" be allowed to triumph.

And this in turn suggests another latent connection, which Lévy does not stress at all though he does dwell upon one of its obvious symptoms. The most toxic and devotional rhetoric of these Islamic gangsters is anti-Semitism. And what does anti-Semitism traditionally emphasize? Why, the moving of secret money between covert elites in order to achieve world domination! The crazed maps of future Muslim conquest that are pictured by the propaganda of jihad and that show the whole world falling to future Muslim conquest are drawn in shady finance-houses and hideaways of stolen gold and portable currency, in the capital cities of paranoid states, and are if anything emulations of the *Protocols of the Elders of Zion* rather than negations of them. Lévy's reformulation of an old term—"neo-anti-Judaism" instead of the worn-out phrase "anti-Semitism"—is harder on the tongue but more accurate as regards the corrupt and vicious foe with which we are actually dealing. His book was finished before it became clear that the "resistance" in Iraq was also being financed by an extensive mafia, which offers different bonuses for different kamikaze tactics, as it was already doing in Palestine and Kashmir.

In a recent conversation, M. Lévy said to me carefully that he doubts the conventional wisdom of the Western liberal, who believes that a settlement in Palestine will remove the inflammation that produces jihad. A settlement in Palestine would be a good thing in itself, to be sure. But those who believe in its generally healing power, he said, have not been following events in Kashmir. Indeed, it is from the Pakistani-Saudi periphery that the core challenge comes. I don't think that anyone who follows Lévy's inquiry into corruption and fanaticism, and the intimate bond between them, will ever listen patiently to any facile argument again.

Slate, September 25, 2003

◄(10)►

Al Qaeda's Latest Target

When I am at home, I never go near the synagogue unless, say, there is a bar or bat mitzvah involving the children of friends. But when I am traveling, in a country where Jewish life is scarce or endangered, I often make a visit to the shul. I always feel vaguely foolish doing this (the sensation of being a slight impostor is best conveyed in "Christian" terms by Philip Larkin's marvelous poem "Churchgoing") but as a result I have seen some fascinating evidences of survival in Damascus, in Havana, in Dubrovnik, in Sarajevo, and in Budapest, among other places. And more than a decade ago, I did go to the Neve Shalom synagogue in Istanbul.

This was slightly more than a side-trip of curiosity. Not long before my visit, a group of killers had thrown gasoline through the doors in mid-service, ignited it with a grenade or two, and then followed up with gunfire. This was more energetic than anything attempted on Kristallnacht. The people "claiming credit" for the "operation" (as the sayings now go) were the Abu Nidal group. I had met them, too, along with their leader, in their villa in Baghdad a few years previously. Of course, one must always be careful to insist that there is no "smoking gun" connecting Saddam Hussein to the activities pursued by his hon-ored guests. . . .

Last Saturday, the Neve Shalom community in Istanbul was hit again, this time along with another Jewish temple, by a truck bomb. There was a bar mitzvah in progress at the time, so the attackers could be assured of a fair generational cross-section of targets. It seems that the suicide-murderers who perpetrated the deed also killed a fair number of non-Jewish Turkish passersby. It also seems, according to the most plausible "claims," that the perpetrators were members of the Al Qaeda underworld. There appears little doubt that their action is related, however distantly, to Turkey's fairly neutral position in respect of the current battles in Iraq.

I have not yet read any article explaining how the frustrations of the oppressed Muslims of the world are alleviated by this deed, or how the wickedness of American foreign policy has brought these chickens home to roost, or how such slaughters are symptoms of "despair." Per-haps somebody is at work on such an article and hasn't quite finished it yet. (I have noticed, though, a slight tendency on the part of this school to shut up, at least for the time being.)

There is a vulgar reason for this reticence. In recent attacks from those gangs who have been busily fusing Saddamism with bin Lad-enism—and who didn't start this synthesis yesterday—it has been noticeable that Saudi citizens (the week before last), or Iraqi citizens (every day, but most conspicuously in the blasting of the Red Cross compound in Baghdad), or Indonesian citizens (in the bombing of the Marriott in Jakarta in August), or Moroccan citizens have been the chief or most numerous casualties. To this, one could add the Chris-tian Arabs whose famous restaurant in Haifa was blown up, along with its owners, on Yom Kippur. I sometimes detect a strained note in the coverage of this. Why would the jihadists be so careless, so to speak? Have they no discrimination, no tact?

Those who think this even semi-consciously have already forgot-ten what jihadists were doing in Algeria, Egypt, Afghanistan, and else-where, long before the assault on the World Trade Center (which also killed a substantial number of Muslims). It's pretty safe to say that the large majority of those murdered by Islamic holy warriors have not been Europeans or Americans as the term is usually understood. This is why I disagreed with the president when he described Sept. 11 as an attack "on America." It was true, but it was not the truth. The current jihad is still waged chiefly against Muslim states and societies and, as Istanbul proves, not just against dictatorial ones. (That last distinction is unsafe in itself, by the way, since the Afghanistan of the Taliban was more dictatorial and oppressive than Saudi Arabia or Algeria, and since bin Laden never conducted any operations against Saddam Hussein or his embassies or outposts.)

Whatever its faults, Turkey is a society with many elements of pluralism and democracy. (Just last week, in accordance with its expressed desire to conform with EU rules, it abolished capital punishment.) It also has a tradition of hospitality, offered in traditional Islamic terms, to the Jewish people. When expelled and dispossessed by Christian Europe, the Sephardim found refuge under the protection of the Caliph, in dominions of Islam as far apart as Bosnia and Baghdad. From this latest outrage, then, we can see how false the bin Ladenists are, even to their own expressed reverence for a lost Muslim empire. The worshippers at the Neve Shalom were not killed for building a settlement in the West Bank: They were members of a very old and honorable community who were murdered for being Jews. Their Turkish neighbors were casually murdered as "collateral damage."

This is in the nature and essence of the foe that we face. Try and bear it in mind, even as the networks speak so lazily of the same foe for "targeting Americans." Understanding why this is lazy is the whole justification of the war, just as it is the real reason why this war will be won.

Addendum: I wrote yesterday that, concerning the murders at the synagogues in Istanbul, I had "not yet read any article explaining how the frustrations of the oppressed Muslims of the world are alleviated by this deed, or how the wickedness of American policy has brought these chickens home to roost, or how such slaughters are symptoms of 'despair.' Perhaps somebody is at work on such an article and hasn't quite finished it yet. (I have noticed, though, a slight tendency on the part of this school to shut up, at least for the time being.)"

Goes to show how soft I am getting. Even as I was writing these words, the presses of the London *Guardian* were churning out the following paragraph, from someone named Fiachra Gibbons:

> So when six die, as they did on Saturday morning when their blood mingled with that of their Muslim neighbors blown to bits by a suicide bomber outside the Neve Shalom synagogue, the heart should miss a beat and the world weep. For we are mourning the loss of souls who had learned to span a supposedly unbridgeable gulf that is being daily widened by George Bush and our own dear, deluded leader.

In a way, this effort doesn't quite meet the standard of moral cretinism that I had suggested. It actually fails to make any link *at all* between the actions of the murderers and the policy of Bush and Blair. Rather, it simply *assumes* that the victims are to have their deaths attributed in this fashion. The prevalence of this assumption, along with its facile appearance in the pages of a great liberal newspaper, is something worth noting.

As the author undoubtedly knows—she elsewhere demonstrates some knowledge of Turkish Jewry—and as I reminded readers yesterday, the Neve Shalom synagogue has been lethally attacked before. The last occasion was in the late 1980s. At that time, the Reagan-Bush-Thatcher governments had for some years taken a pro–Saddam Hussein "tilt" in the Iran-Iraq war. I can't remember what the excuse of the Jew-killers was on that previous occasion, but it most certainly wasn't their hatred for regime change. Maybe they didn't come up with an excuse, imagining that the action spoke for itself. Anyway, why bother with a justification when there are so many peace-loving and progressive types willing to volunteer to make the excuses for you?

Slate, November 18, 2003

ᵛ⎰ 11 ⎱ᵛ

To Die in Madrid

I can remember when I was a bit of an ETA fan myself. It was in 1973, when a group of Basque militants assassinated Adm. Carrero Blanco. The admiral was a stone-faced secret police chief, personally groomed to be the successor to the decrepit Francisco Franco. His car blew up, killing only him and his chauffeur with a carefully planted charge, and not only was the world well rid of another fascist, but, more important, the whole scheme of extending Franco's rule was vaporized in the same instant. The dictator had to turn instead to Crown Prince Juan Carlos, who turned out to be the best Bourbon in history and who swiftly dismantled Franco's entire system. If this action was "terrorism," it had something to be said for it. Everyone I knew in Spain made a little holiday in their hearts when the gruesome admiral went sky-high.

The Basque country, with its historic capital in Guernica, had been one of the main battlegrounds against Hitler and Mussolini in their first joint aggression in Spain, and many European families adopted Basque orphans and raised money for the resistance. It is tedious to relate the story of ETA's degeneration into a gangster organization that itself proclaims a fascist ideology of Basque racial uniqueness, and anyway one doesn't need to bother, since nobody any longer argues that there is a "root cause" of ETA's atrocities. In the face of this kind of subhuman nihilism, people know without having to be told that the only response is a quiet, steady hatred and contempt, and a cold determination to outlast the perpetrators while remorselessly tracking them down.

However, it seems that some Spaniards, and some non-Spanish commentators, would change on a dime if last week's mass murder in Madrid could be attributed to the bin Ladenists. In that case not only would there be a root cause—the deployment of 1,300 Spanish soldiers in the reconstruction of Iraq—but there would also be a culpable person, namely Spain's retiring prime minister. By this logic, terrorism would also have a cure—the withdrawal of those Spanish soldiers from a country where Al Qaeda emphatically does not desire them to be.

Try not to laugh or cry, but some spokesmen of the Spanish Left have publicly proposed exactly this syllogism. I wonder if I am insulting the readers of *Slate* if I point out its logical and moral deficiencies:

Many Spaniards were among those killed recently in Morocco, where a jihadist bomb attack on an ancient Moorish synagogue took place in broad daylight. The attack was on Morocco itself, which was neutral in the recent Iraq war. It seems a bit late to demand that the Moroccan government change sides and support Saddam Hussein in that conflict, and I suspect that the Spanish Communist and socialist leadership would feel a little sheepish in making this suggestion. Nor is it obvious to me that the local Moroccan jihadists would stop bombing if this concession were made. Still, such a concession would be consistent with the above syllogism, as presumably would be a demand that Morocco cease to tempt fate by allowing synagogues on its soil in the first place.

The Turkish government, too, should be condemned for allowing its Prime Minister Tayyip Erdogan to visit the shattered synagogue in Istanbul after the latest mass murder (thus becoming, incidentally, the first Turkish prime minister ever to do so). Erdogan is also the first prime minister ever to be elected on an Islamist ticket. Clearly, he was asking for trouble and has not yet understood Al Qaeda's conditions for being allowed to lead a quiet life. Not that he hadn't tried—he prevented the US Army from approaching Baghdad through what is now known as the Sunni Triangle. He just hasn't tried hard enough.

It cannot be very long now before some slaughter occurs on the streets of London or Rome or Warsaw, as punishment for British and Italian and Polish membership of the anti-Saddam coalition. But perhaps there is still time to avoid the wrath to come. If British and Italian and Polish troops make haste to leave the Iraqis to their own "devices" (of the sort that exploded outside the mosques of Karbala and Najaf last month), their civilian cousins may still hope to escape the stern disapproval of the holy warriors. Don't ask why the holy warriors blow up mosques by the way—it's none of your goddam crusader-Jew business.

The other countries of NATO, which has now collectively adopted the responsibility for Afghanistan, should reconsider. As long as their forces remain on the soil of that country, they are liable to attract the sacred rage of the Muslim fighters. It will not be enough for Germany and France to have stayed out of Iraq. They cannot expect to escape judgment by such hypocritical means.

French schools should make all haste to permit not just the veil but the burqa, as well as to segregate swimming pools and playgrounds. Do they suppose that they deceive anybody when they temporize about God's evident will? Bombings will follow this blasphemy, as the night succeeds the day. It is written.

I find I can't quite decide what to recommend in the American case. I thought it was a good idea to remove troops from Saudi Arabia in any event (after all, we had removed the chief regional invader). But, even with the troops mainly departed, bombs continue to detonate in Saudi streets. We are, it seems, so far gone in sin and decadence that no repentance or penitence can be adequate. Perhaps, for the moment, it's enough punishment, and enough shame, just to know that what occurred in Madrid last week is all our fault. Now, let that sink in.

Slate, March 15, 2004

⫷ 12 ⫸

Murder by Any Other Name

Not to exaggerate or generalize or anything, but in the past week or so it seems to have become very slightly less OK to speak of jihad as an understandable reaction to underlying Muslim grievances. The murder of innocents in a Russian school may have been secondarily the result of a panic or a bungle by Vladimir Putin's "special forces," but nobody is claiming that the real responsibility lies anywhere but on the shoulders of the Muslim fanatics. And the French state's policy of defending secularism in its schools may have been clumsily and even "insensitively" applied, but nobody says that the kidnapping and threatened murder of two French reporters is thereby justified. As for the slaughter of the Nepalese workers in Iraq . . . you simply have to see the video and hear the Quranic incantations in the voice-over. (I use the words "murder" and "slaughter" by the way, and shall continue to do so, as I hope you will, too. How the *New York Times* can employ the term "execution" for these atrocities is beyond me.)

Even Abdul Rahman Al-Rashed, the general manager of Al-Arabiya television, was less euphemistic than that. In a column published under the unambiguous headline, "The Painful Truth: All the World Terrorists are Muslims!" he wrote, in the pan-Arab paper *Al-Sharq al-Awsat*: "Our terrorist sons are an end-product of our corrupted culture." According to a very interesting AP report from Maggie Michael, this was part of a wider refusal and denunciation across Arab and Muslim media. It wasn't *all* unambiguous—some critics said that the Chechen outrage was *so* bad that the Israelis must have been behind it—but it had a different tone from the usual trash about holy war and martyrdom. By the same token, nobody coerced the majority of French Muslim schoolchildren into turning up quiet and on time, almost all unveiled, on the day of the murder "deadline" set by the kidnappers in Iraq.

Often unspoken in commentary on attacks on America and Americans—and even worse, half-spoken—has been the veiled assumption that such things have a rough justice to them. The United States, with its globalizing blah-blah and its cowboy blah-blah, supposedly invites such wake-up calls. And the sorry fact is that French and Russian commentators and politicians have been noticeable for their promiscuity in this respect. It's also true that the French and Russian record could, if you looked at it in one way, be a real cause of sacred rage. (The French authorities have backed Saddam Hussein and many other regional despots, and the conduct of Russian soldiers in Chechnya makes Abu Ghraib look like a blip on the charts.) But no serious person would ever let these considerations obscure a full-out denunciation of those who deliberately make war on civilians. So let us ponder this serious moment, of solidarity with French and Russian victims, and hope to build upon it.

Any jeering can be saved for the strictly political, in which category I would include the recent speech of the new French foreign minister, Michel Barnier. In an address to the annual conference of French ambassadors on August 26, Barnier pointedly warned the assembled envoys that "France is not great when it is arrogant. France is not strong when it is alone." He very noticeably did not mention America, or American policy, even once. All that was lacking from his address was a self-criticism for French "unilateralism" and a promise that in future he would seek to "build alliances." Intelligent French people understand that the Bonapartist policy of the Chirac–de Villepin regime has been deeply damaging: You can see this in any French newspaper. In pledging to shape his own policy to conciliate the Elysée Palace, in other words, John Kerry seems to have once again chosen to change ships on a falling tide.

Another small but interesting development has occurred among my former comrades at the *Nation* magazine. In its "GOP Convention Issue" dated September 13, the editors decided to run a piece by Naomi Klein titled "Bring Najaf to New York." If you think this sounds suspiciously like an endorsement of Muqtada Sadr and his black-masked clerical bandits, you are not mistaken. The article, indeed, went somewhat further, and lower, than the headline did. Ms. Klein is known as a salient figure in the so-called anti-globalization movement, and for a book proclaiming her hostility to logos and other forms of oppression: She's not marginal to what remains of the Left. Her nasty, stupid article has evoked two excellent blog responses from two pillars of the *Nation* family: Marc Cooper in Los Angeles and Doug Ireland in New York. What gives, they want to know, with a supposed socialist-feminist offering swooning support to theocratic fascists? It's a good question, and I understand that it's ignited quite a debate among the magazine's staff and periphery.

When I quit writing my column for the *Nation* a couple of years ago, I wrote semi-sarcastically that it had become an echo chamber for those who were more afraid of John Ashcroft than Osama bin Laden. I honestly did not then expect to find it publishing actual endorsements of jihad. But, as Marxism taught me, the logic of history and politics is a pitiless one. The antiwar isolationist "Left" started by being merely "status quo": opposing regime change and hinting at moral equivalence between Bush's "terrorism" and the other sort. This conservative position didn't take very long to metastasize into a flat-out reactionary one, with Michael Moore saying that the Iraqi "resistance" was the equivalent of the Revolutionary Minutemen, Tariq Ali calling for solidarity with the "insurgents," and now Ms. Klein, among many others, wanting to bring the war home because any kind of anti-Americanism is better than none at all. These fellow-travelers with fascism are also changing ships on a falling tide: Their applause for the holy warriors comes at a time when wide swathes of the Arab and Muslim world are sickening of the mindless blasphemy and the sectarian bigotry. It took an effort for American pseudo-radicals to be outflanked on the Left by Ayatollah Sistani, but they managed it somehow.

Slate, September 7, 2004

⊰(13)⊱

Bush's Secularist Triumph

Many are the cheap and easy laughs in which one could indulge at the extraordinary, pitiful hysteria of the defeated Democrats. "Kerry won," according to one e-mail I received from Greg Palast, to whom the Florida vote in 2000 is, and always will be, a combination of Gettysburg and Waterloo. According to Nikki Finke of the *LA Weekly*, the Fox News channel "called" Ohio for Bush for reasons too sinister to enumerate. Gregory Maniatis, whose last communication to me had predicted an annihilating Democratic landslide, kept quiet for only a day or so before forwarding the details on how to emigrate to Canada. Thus do the liberals build their bridge to the 20th century.

Who can care about this pathos? Not I. But I do take strong exception to one strain in the general moaning. It seems that anyone fool enough to favor the re-election of the president is by definition a God-bothering, pulpit-pounding Armageddon-artist, enslaved by ancient texts and prophecies and committed to theocratic rule. I was instructed in last week's *New York Times* that this was the case, and that the Enlightenment had come to an end, by no less an expert than Garry Wills, who makes at least one of his many livings by being an Augustinian Roman Catholic.

I step lightly over the ancient history of Wills' church (which was the originator of the counter-Enlightenment and then the patron of fascism in Europe) as well as over its more recent and local history (as the patron, protector, and financier of child-rape in the United States, and the sponsor of the cruel "annulment" of Joe Kennedy's and John Kerry's first marriages). As far as I know, all religions and all churches are equally demented in their belief in divine intervention, divine intercession, or even the existence of the divine in the first place.

But all faiths are not always equally demented in the same way, or at the same time. Islam, which was once a civilizing and creative force in many societies, is now undergoing a civil war. One faction in this civil war is explicitly totalitarian and wedded to a cult of death. We have seen it at work on the streets of our own cities, and most recently on the streets of Amsterdam. We know that the obscene butchery of filmmaker Theo van Gogh was only a warning of what is coming in Madrid, London, Rome, and Paris, let alone Baghdad and Basra.

So here is what I want to say on the absolutely crucial matter of secularism. Only one faction in American politics has found itself able to make excuses for the kind of religious fanaticism that immediately menaces us in the here and now. And that faction, I am sorry and furious to say, is the Left. From the first day of the immolation of the World Trade Center, right down to the present moment, a gallery of pseudo-intellectuals has been willing to represent the worst face of Islam as the voice of the oppressed. How can these people bear to reread their own propaganda? Suicide murderers in Palestine—disowned and denounced by the new leader of the PLO—described as the victims of "despair." The forces of Al Qaeda and the Taliban represented as misguided spokespeople for anti-globalization. The blood-maddened thugs in Iraq, who would rather bring down the roof on a suffering people than allow them to vote, pictured prettily as "insurgents" or even, by Michael Moore, as the moral equivalent of our Founding Fathers. If this is liberal secularism, I'll take a modest, God-fearing, deer-hunting Baptist from Kentucky every time, as long as he didn't want to impose his principles on me (which our Constitution forbids him to do).

One probably should not rest too much on the similarity between bin Laden's last video and the newly available DVD of *Fahrenheit 9/11*. I would only say that, if bin Laden had issued a tape that with equal fealty followed the playbook of Karl Rove (and do please by all means cross yourself at the mention of this unholy name), it might have garnered some more attention. The Bearded One moved pedantically through Moore's bill of indictment, checking off the Florida vote-count in 2000, the "Pet Goat" episode on the day of hell, the violent intrusion into hitherto peaceful and Muslim Iraq, and the division between Bush and the much nicer Europeans. (For some reason, unknown to me at any rate, he did not attack the President for allowing the bin Laden family to fly out of American airspace.)

George Bush may subjectively be a Christian, but he—and the US armed forces—have objectively done more for secularism than the whole of the American agnostic community combined and doubled. The demolition of the Taliban, the huge damage inflicted on the Al Qaeda network, and the confrontation with theocratic saboteurs in Iraq represent huge advances for the non-fundamentalist forces in many countries. The "antiwar" faction even recognizes this achievement, if only indirectly, by complaining about the way in which it has infuriated the Islamic religious extremists around the world. But does it accept the apparent corollary—that we should have been pursuing a policy to which the fanatics had no objection?

Secularism is not just a smug attitude. It is a possible way of democratic and pluralistic life that only became thinkable after several wars and revolutions had ruthlessly smashed the hold of the clergy on the state. We are now in the middle of another such war and revolution, and the liberals have gone AWOL. I dare say that there will be a few domestic confrontations down the road, over everything from the Pledge of Allegiance to the display of Mosaic tablets in courtrooms and schools. I have spent all my life on the atheist side of this argument, and will brace for more of the same, but I somehow can't hear Robert Ingersoll or Clarence Darrow being soft and cowardly and evasive if it came to a vicious theocratic challenge that daily threatens us from within and without.

Slate, November 9, 2004

⊰ 14 ⊱

Jihad in the Netherlands

In 2003, at a conference held in Sweden, I was introduced to a member of the Netherlands parliament. She was a woman of hypnotizing beauty named Ayaan Hirsi Ali, who had become a star of the Dutch Liberal Party. Originally from Somalia, she had fled her country of origin in order to escape from genital mutilation and the real possibility that her family might sell her to a strange man twice her age. Becoming fluent in English and Dutch and radiating charisma, she had soon attracted attention by criticizing the refusal of the Muslim establishment in her adopted country to adapt itself to secular democracy. (Who knows how many brilliant women like herself are entombed for life within the confines of enslaving and stultifying theocracies?)

Today, she is living under police protection. In early November 2004, her friend and colleague Theo van Gogh was stabbed to death and then mutilated on a public street, evidently by a Muslim fanatic. Mr. Van Gogh, a descendant of the celebrated painter, was a filmmaker who had made a documentary about the maltreatment by Muslim authorities of Muslim women in Holland. The film had featured Ayaan Hirsi Ali, and a letter "addressed" to her was pinned, by a heavy knife, to the chest of the ritually slaughtered Van Gogh. The man arrested for the crime, identified as Mohammed Bouyeri, was further found to be carrying a "farewell note." (Apparently, he had hoped to die the death of a "martyr" at the scene of the crime, but the humane Dutch police only wounded him in the leg before subduing him.)

Both the open letter and the note are of extreme interest. The note speaks of *Tawheed*, which is the current Islamic extremist abuse of the Quranic word for "unity" or oneness against all heretics from Shia to Christian. This Salafist/bin Ladenist tendency also employs the term *takfir*, an approximate synonym for *excommunication* (and therefore slaughter) of infidels and heretics. The faction grouped behind this Quranic concept is the most noxious and cynical of the lot: its members allow themselves to consume pork and alcohol and consort with prostitutes if they are on a mission to deceive and destroy the infidel. (This explains the apparent "paradox" of the 9/11 hijackers who were seen cavorting in a nightclub in Florida shortly before mounting their assault on our civil society. It also means that the most outwardly "secular" Muslim might be just the one to fear. My friend Andrew Sullivan may be a hopeless Christian, but in discussing this special permission, awarded so generously to themselves by the godly, he made a truly secular observation. "How conveeenient," was the way he phrased it.)

The open letter is full of lurid and gloating accounts, lifted from the Quran, of the tortures that await apostates like Ayaan Hirsi Ali in hell. It refers to her throughout as "Miss Hirshi Ali," a mistake that has baffled some observers but which I think is obviously intended to make her sound more Jewish. The letter is obsessed with the Dutch Jews who are among the leadership of the Liberal Party and makes repeated references to anti-Gentile and racist remarks in Jewish scripture. Let's admit by all means that there are such references, but the ones cited by Bouyeri seem all to be lifted from a fundamentalist anti-Semitic Web site that has falsified the texts it pretends to be scrutinizing. Other evidence strongly suggests that his manifesto was written for him by a group that sent him out to kill.

When the bin Ladenist forces in Spain committed mass murder in the center of Madrid earlier in the year, they did so amid a huge controversy over the war in Iraq and on the eve of a general election. So badly did the Spanish government handle the affair—seeking to blame it all on a Basque nihilist faction—that many Spaniards were able implicitly to indict George W. Bush for the whole mess. This social and psychic suicide was not possible in the Dutch case. Holland gave up all concept of "empire" a generation ago. Moreover, it has since been the most generous and multicultural society in Europe, welcoming not only its former subjects from Indonesia but becoming a haven in general. And its reward has been to be targeted by *Tawheed*. One cannot emphasize enough that the victims here are not just secular artists like Theo van Gogh but people of Muslim origin who do not accept homicidal fundamentalism. This is the warning that many liberals have been overlooking or denying ever since the *fatwa* against Salman Rushdie in 1989.

And it is spreading: even as I write this, a Belgian legislator of Moroccan extraction, Mimount Bousakla, has been threatened with "ritual slaughter" for denouncing van Gogh's murder. Any thinking person can see that we will soon be facing *jihad* on the streets of Germany and France and England as well. A secret army has also been formed within our borders in the United States, though its triumphant first operation did not alert as many Europeans as it might have.

The Dutch are friendly and tolerant, but they do not like having this mistaken for weakness. A strong and hard reaction of decided outrage has set in. At first, the authorities misunderstood this. They sandblasted a mural that had been painted near the scene of the crime, which featured only the words "Thou shalt not kill." (The imam of a local mosque had of course complained that such a display was "racist incitement.") But people are now rightly fed up with having their own pluralism used against them, and the protest at this capitulation was almost as strong. I myself think it was the wrong mural to begin with. You cannot fight Islamic terror with Christianity, whether of the insipid or the crusader kind. The original commandment actually says "Thou shalt do no murder," thus making it almost the only one of the ten that makes any sense. But we do not prepare for murder when we resolve to defend ourselves and when we take the side of people like Ms. Hirsi Ali and Ms. Bousakla in the Islamic civil war that seeks to poison our society and enslave theirs.

Free Inquiry (February/March 2005)

⁗(15)⁗

We Cannot Surrender

Somewhere around London at about a quarter to nine yesterday morning, there must have been people turning on their TV and radio sets with a look of wolfish expectation.

I hope and believe that they were disappointed in what they got. There just wasn't quite enough giggle-value for the psychopath.

It must have been infernal underneath King's Cross, but above ground no panic, no screaming, no wailing and beating the air, no yells for vengeance.

I'm writing this in the early aftermath, but I would be willing to bet there will have been little or no bloody foolishness, either: no random attacks on mosques or shops or individuals. After all, devices on our buses and tubes are an open proclamation that the perpetrators don't care if they kill Muslims. Which, of course, is part of the point. When we use the weak and vague word "terrorism" we imply indiscriminate cruelty directed at civilians.

"Sadism" or "fascism" or "nihilism" would do just as nicely: all the venom that lurks just on the sub-human level of the human species.

In a tightly interwoven society, all that this poison has to do is ally itself with a certain low cunning.

People are afraid of plane crashes and of heights: in that sense 9/11 was the perfect strike on the collective unconscious. People are likewise afraid of fire and of crowded or subterranean conditions: the mind of the fascist is naturally attuned to exploit such dreads. I am guessing the planners of this coordinated atrocity hoped for more mayhem than they got, but the casualty figures are in a sense beside the point.

We all knew this was coming, and that one day a homely and familiar name like Tavistock Square would become a synonym for barbarism. The good old red London bus, a worldwide symbol of our capital, ripped to shards in an instant.

Random and "senseless" though such violence may appear, we also all know it expresses a deadly ideology; indeed that in some ways it is that ideology.

The preachers of this faith have taken care to warn us that they love death more than we love life. Their wager is that this makes them unstoppable. Well, we shall have to see. They certainly cannot prove their point unless we assist them in doing so.

My American friends have been impressed by the composure of the Londoners they have seen on the screen: I bet London Transport runs again rather sooner than US airlines resumed flying after 9/11.

I remember living in London through the Provisional IRA bombing in the 70s. I saw the very first car-bomb explode against the Old Bailey in 1972. There was no warning that time, but after a while a certain etiquette developed.

And, even as I detested the people who might have just as soon have blown me up as anyone else, I was aware there were ancient disputes involved, and that there was a potential political solution.

Nothing of the sort applies in this case. We know very well what the "grievances" of the jihadists are.

The grievance of seeing unveiled women. The grievance of the existence, not of the State of Israel, but of the Jewish people. The grievance of the heresy of democracy, which impedes the imposition of Sharia law. The grievance of a work of fiction written by an Indian living in London. The grievance of the existence of black African Muslim farmers, who won't abandon lands in Darfur. The grievance of the existence of homosexuals. The grievance of music, and of most representational art. The grievance of the existence of Hinduism. The grievance of East Timor's liberation from Indonesian rule. All of these have been proclaimed as a license to kill infidels or apostates, or anyone who just gets in the way.

For a few moments yesterday, Londoners received a taste of what life is like for the people of Iraq and Afghanistan, whose Muslim faith does not protect them from slaughter at the hands of those who think they are not Muslim enough, or are the wrong Muslim.

It is a big mistake to believe this is an assault on "our" values or "our" way of life. It is, rather, an assault on all civilization. I know perfectly well there are people thinking, and even saying, that Tony Blair brought this upon us by his alliance with George Bush.

A word of advice to them: try and keep it down, will you? Or wait at least until the funerals are over. And beware of the non-sequitur: you can be as opposed to the Iraq operation as much as you like, but you can't get from that "grievance" to the detonating of explosives at rush hour on London buses and tubes.

Don't even try to connect the two. By George Galloway's logic, British squaddies in Iraq are the root cause of dead bodies at home. How can anyone bear to be so wicked and stupid? How can anyone bear to act as a megaphone for psychotic killers?

The grievances I listed above are unappeasable, one of many reasons why the jihadists will lose.

They demand the impossible—the cessation of all life in favor of prostration before a totalitarian vision. Plainly, we cannot surrender. There is no one with whom to negotiate, let alone capitulate.

We shall track down those responsible. States that shelter them will know no peace. Communities that shelter them do not take forever to discover their mistake. And their sordid love of death is as nothing compared to our love of London, which we will defend as always, and which will survive this with ease.

Mirror, July 8, 2005

⑽ 16 ⑾

Yes, London Can Take It

If one must have cliché and stereotype (and evidently one must) then I would nominate the sturdy phlegmatic Londoner as the stock character who deserves to survive for at least another generation. Woken in the dark on the early morning of 7 July, and given the news that I and all British people had been expecting for some time, I made haste to turn on the television and was confronted at once by a man in his 30s with a shirt-front coated in blood. He was bleeding from his scalp, but was quite evenly telling his excited interviewer that "the gentleman next to me"—who was slightly off-screen—might be a superior witness since he had seen more of the actual flash and bang.

Further *vox populi* encounters disclosed an identical, almost camera-ready, ability to emulate the stoic forebears. I was cynically thinking, yes, that's all very well, but I can imagine panic and nightmare in the "tube" underneath King's Cross station, when I received an email from a teacher at King's College who had been caught up in the most hideous of the underground train bombs. He recounted the almost pedantic willingness of citizens to make way and say "after you" as the doors finally opened and as emergency staff made an appearance on the platforms. As anyone who regularly uses Edgware Road station, or anyone who goes to soccer matches, can attest, Londoners don't normally behave this politely, so again I assume that there is a subliminal script that so to speak "kicks in" when things get nasty.

Much of this elusive script is based on Noel Coward's sentimental ditty "London Pride," which was dusted off and given a fair old revival in the press on the following morning. Nobody who has read any serious account of life under the Nazi blitz can believe a word of it. Between 1940 and 1945, Londoners ran away, panicked, sent their children off to the country with labels around their necks, trampled each other in the rush to make tube stations into air-raid shelters (which the government at first refused to allow) and blamed Jews for jumping queues and hoarding goods. The rich moved complainingly into well-fortified hotels, and the police and firemen helped themselves to the contents of bombed or abandoned homes. Toward the end of the war, as guided missiles began to rain down from Germany, morale became very bad indeed. Read, if you like, Stephen Spender's account of being a fireman, or any selection of George Orwell's wartime "London Letters" to *Partisan Review.*

For all that, both men did develop an admiration for the essential toughness and humor of the Londoner. And at least it could be said that one note was almost never struck in those days. There were no serious demands for capitulation. But last Thursday the blood wasn't dry on the wall of the British Medical Association in Bloomsbury, with the lower stairway covered in body parts, before the call for surrender was being raised.

First out of the trap was George Galloway, the renegade Member of Parliament who has been Saddam Hussein's chief propagandist in Britain. Within hours of the atrocities, he had diagnosed their cause, or causes. These included the presence of British troops in Afghanistan and Iraq, the photographs from Abu Ghraib, and the state of affairs at Guantanamo. This can only mean that Galloway knows what was in the minds of the bombers, and knows that it was these subjects (and not, say, the Wahhabi hatred of unveiled women, or their fury at the liberation of East Timor) that had actually motivated the attacks. If he really knows that much about the killers, he should be asked to make a full disclosure of his sources to Scotland Yard. If he doesn't know, he should at least have waited until the blood was dry before opening his ugly mouth. Scant chance of the latter.

Galloway is an open supporter of the other side in this war, and at least doesn't try very hard to conceal the fact. Far more depressing are the insincere and inauthentic statements made by more "mainstream" types. The mayor of London, Ken Livingstone—another Blair-hater and another flirter with any local Imam who can bring him a few quick votes—managed to say that the murders were directed at "the working class," not the "powerful." That's true enough, but it doesn't avoid the implication that a jihadist bomb in, say, the Stock Exchange would have been less reprehensible. Another dismal statement, issued by the Muslim Council of Britain in concert with something called "Churches Together in Britain and Ireland," got as far as proclaiming that "no good purpose can be achieved by such an indiscriminate and cruel use of terror." This is to say too much and too little. It still hints that the purpose might be ill-served by the means. Further, it fails as an ecumenical statement in that it was evidently not submitted to Britain's large Jewish community for ratification. Why do I think that there were some in both the Muslim and Christian leaderships who thought that, in their proud "inclusiveness," they didn't need to go quite that far?

On the other hand, I must say that the leadership of "Imaan," a "social support group for Lesbian, Gay, Bisexual and Transgender Muslims," managed to issue a condemnation that was not shaded or angled in any way, and consisted of a simple, unequivocal denunciation and a statement of solidarity with the victims. That's the stuff. At last, the Churchill touch!

"London can take it!" That's what the patriotic proles are supposed to have yelled from the bomb-sites when Churchill toured the battered East End. London can indeed take it. It is a huge and resilient city, and if there were ten thousand jihadist guerrillas operating full time within its precincts, they could scarcely make a dent before they were utterly defeated. Once I had guiltily assured myself of the safety of my own daughter, I allowed myself to think that the long-awaited attack had not been as bad as many of us had expected. It was planned to be worse, and the next assault may be worse still. The tube stations selected for the mayhem show beyond doubt that the perpetrators must have expected to kill quite a number of Muslims, just as their co-thinkers have been doing in Kabul and Baghdad.

But another reflection now deposes the preceding one. In 2001 there was an enemy to hit back at, and some business to conclude with the Taliban. Since then, there has been unfinished business with Saddam Hussein and his notorious *fedayeen*. But from now on, we must increasingly confront the fact that the war within Islam is also a war within Europe. It's highly probable that the assassins of 7 July are British born, as were several Taliban fighters in the first round in Afghanistan. And the mirror image also exists. Many Muslims take the side of civilization and many European fascists and Communists are sympathetic to jihad.

These are not the bright, clear lines that many people fondly imagine to be heritable from a heroic past. But the nature of the enemy is somewhat similar. Like the fascists that they are, the murderers boast that they love death more than we love life. They imagine that this yell of unreason is intimidating and impressive. We shall undoubtedly go forward and put these grave matters to the proof but, meanwhile: Death to them and Long Live London!

Weekly Standard, July 18, 2005

◅(17)▻

Why Ask Why?

The return of murderous nihilism to Bali is highly instructive. It shows, first, that the fanatics of Islamism don't know how to stop. And it also shows that they never learn. How can Jemaah Islamiyah (JI), which almost ruined Indonesia's economy by its filthy attack three years ago, possibly have tried to repeat the same crime in the same place? If we look for answers to this question, we shall find answers that completely discredit the current half-baked apologies for terrorism.

I remember going to Bali from Jakarta in the summer of 2003. I had already toured the wreckage of the Marriott Hotel in the capital city, which was blown up by a suicide team just as I arrived, slaying several Muslim cab drivers who were waiting in line outside. The rage of the local population was something to be seen: The widows of the dead men were calling for the perpetrators to be tortured before they were executed. In Bali, which is a more mild and temperate place, a huge candlelit march had followed the bombings that had devastated the tourist hangouts in Kuta. I made a point of going to Legian Street, which had been the "ground zero" of this fiery atrocity, and of attending the opening of Paddy's Bar Reloaded, where so many genial Australians had been foully incinerated. The prevailing view was that JI had isolated itself and that the trial of the perpetrators would expose them to popular contempt—which indeed it did.

But if JI were rational, it wouldn't have attacked the bars and clubs and beaches of Kuta and Jimbaran in the first place. Indonesia is a mainly Muslim society, whose government takes a stern line against the war in Iraq and even Afghanistan. Its people, who are astonishingly hospitable to all foreigners, depend in millions of cases on tourism to make the difference between indigence and the minimum wage. Its elections feature Muslim political parties, many of them quite austere in their propaganda. Why on earth, then, would a fundamentalist group wish to bring discredit upon itself and ruin upon its neighbors by resorting to random slaughter?

Never make the mistake of asking for rationality here. And never underestimate the power of theocratic propaganda. The fanatics look at the population of Bali and its foreign visitors and they see a load of Hindus selling drinks—often involving the presence of unchaperoned girls—to a load of Christians. That in itself is excuse enough for mayhem. They also see local Muslims following syncretic and tolerant forms of Islam, and they yearn to redeem them from this heresy and persuade them of the pure, desert-based truths of Salafism and Wahhabism. (One of the men on trial in Bali had been in trouble before, in his home village, for desecrating local Muslim shrines that he regarded as idolatrous.) And then, of course, Australians must die. Why would that be? Well, is it not the case that Australia sent troops to help safeguard the independence of East Timor and the elections that followed it? A neighboring country that assists the self-determination of an Indonesian Christian minority must expect to have the lives of its holidaymakers taken.

Do not forget that on August 19, 2003, a gigantic explosion leveled the Canal Hotel in Baghdad, which then served as the Iraq headquarters of the United Nations. The materials used to do this were of a high military grade not available to any random "insurgent" and certainly came from the arsenals of the fallen regime. The main target—and principal victim—was Sergio Vieira de Mello, the dashing Brazilian who had been sent by Kofi Annan to reanimate the UN presence in Iraq. De Mello had been the most devoted and humane of the world body's civil servants and had won himself golden opinions in Cambodia, Lebanon, Sudan, and the Balkans. But it was his role as UN supervisor of the transition in East Timor that marked him for death. A communiqué from Al Qaeda gloated over the end of "the personal representative of America's criminal slave, Kofi Annan, the diseased Sergio de Mello, criminal Bush's friend." It went on to ask, "Why cry over a heretic? Sergio Vieira de Mello is the one who tried to embellish the image of America, the crusaders and the Jews in Lebanon and Kosovo, and now in Iraq. He is America's first man where he was nominated by Bush to be in charge of the UN after Kofi Annan, the criminal and slave of America, and he is the crusader that extracted a part of the Islamic land [East Timor]."

Consider this, look again at the awful carnage in Bali, and shudder if you ever said, or thought, that the bombs in London in July, or the bombs in Baghdad every day, or the bombs in Bali last Friday, are caused by any "policy" but that of the bombers themselves. Note the following:

1. East Timor was for many years, and quite rightly, a signature cause of the Noam Chomsky "Left." The near-genocide of its people is an eternal stain on Indonesia and on the Western states that were complicit or silent. Yet bin Ladenism wants not *less* of this killing and repression but *more*. Its demand to re-establish the caliphate is a pro-imperialist demand, not an anti-imperialist one.
2. Random bombings are not a protest against poverty and unemployment. They are a *cause* of poverty and unemployment and of wider economic dislocation.
3. Hinduism is considered by bin Ladenists to be a worse heresy even than Christianity or Judaism or Shiism, and its adherents, whether in Bali or Kashmir, are fit only for the edge of the sword. So, it is absurd to think of jihadism—which murders the poor and the

brown without compunction—as a movement against the rich and the "white."

So, what did Indonesia do to deserve this, or bring it on itself? How will the slaughter in Bali improve the lot of the Palestinians? Those who look for the connection will be doomed to ask increasingly stupid questions and to be content with increasingly wicked answers.

Slate, October 3, 2005

PART II

Hitchens on Iraq

◀ 18 ▶

Appointment in Samarra?

How would people be discussing the issue of "regime change" in Iraq if the question were not being forced upon them by the Administration? In other words, is the American and European and international audience for this debate no more than just that—an audience, complete with theater critics and smart-ass reviewers? Or to put the matter in still another way, would the topic of "regime change" be dropped if the Bush White House were not telegraphing all its military intentions toward Iraq while continuing to make an eerie secret of its political ones?

I approach this question as one who has been in favor of "regime change" in Iraq for quite a long time, and who considers himself a friend of those Iraqis and Iraqi Kurds who have risked so much to bring it about. I don't feel that I require official permission or exhortation to adopt the argument, but I do feel that it's a relinquishment of responsibility to abandon it. Unlike the chronically enfeebled and cowardly Democratic leadership in Congress, I don't beg like a serf for the President to "make his case" about WMDs. Nor do I feel comfortable waiting like a mendicant for him to speak out about the Kurds, or demanding that he pronounce in a less or more scary way about Saddam Hussein's underhanded friendship with the dark world of the international gangsters. I can make inquiries of my own, thanks all the same, and even form some conclusions.

The other day I was on some show with Senator Alan Simpson of Wyoming, a leading member of Washington's black-comedy troupe, who said that unless—like him—you had actually met Saddam Hussein you could have no conception of the reality of stone-cold evil. I reminded the Senator that on the occasion of his meeting with the Iraqi leadership, he had actually emerged to say that Saddam was getting an unfairly bad press, and recommended that he invite more reporters to record the achievements of the Baath Party. That was before the invasion of Kuwait, to which George Herbert Walker Bush and James Baker demonstrated an initially indulgent attitude. During the subsequent bombing of Baghdad, Senator Simpson was to the fore in denouncing Peter Arnett of CNN for being in Iraq at all, and later in circulating the allegation that Arnett had once had a brother-in-law who might have been a sympathizer of the Vietcong.

One can play this simple game, of hypocrisy and "double standards," indefinitely. I have played it myself and with better-seeded contestants than Senator Simpson. But a few nights ago I had a long conversation with my friend Dr. Barham Salih, the prime minister of the autonomous Kurdish region of Iraq, and thus one of the very few politicians in the area who have to face an election. He recently survived an assassination attempt by a gang that he is convinced is ideologically and organizationally linked to Al Qaeda. Salih is for a single standard: a democratic Iraq with a devolved Kurdistan (he doesn't like it when the Administration talks about Saddam Hussein gassing "his own people," because the Kurds are by no means Saddam's property). Salih speaks of a war "for Iraq" and not "on Iraq." He doesn't believe that the population can remove the dictator without outside help, but he also thinks the Turks are being given too much official consideration—partly because of their military alliance with Israel—in determining the outcome.

This is a serious dilemma for a serious person, who is being asked to stake his own life and the relative freedom of his people on the outcome. It's also a dilemma for us. Is the Bush Administration's "regime change" the same one the Iraqi and Kurdish democrats hope for? Rather than use the conservative language—of the risks of "destabilizing" the Middle East—liberals and radicals ought to be demanding that the Administration and Congress come clean about this. Meanwhile, one sees constant photo-ops of the President making nice with the Saudis, who have reasons of their own to worry about destabilization, while Kurdish leaders are met with in secret and at a much lower level.

"I am very disappointed with the Left," Salih told me. In the past the Kurdish cause was a major concern of the internationalist, human rights and socialist movements, but now a slight shuffling and evasiveness seems to have descended. Some of this obviously arises from a general reluctance to be identified with President Bush, but that, one hopes, is too paltry to explain much.

The other concern is more immediate. Since it is estimated by the Pentagon hawks that a war with Saddam Hussein (not, please, "with

Iraq") might well bring about the fall of the Hashemite monarchy in Jordan, and since we also know that there are those around General Sharon who are looking for a pretext to cleanse the Palestinians from the West Bank and expel them onto Jordanian soil, there exists the possibility that a serious moral and political disaster is in the making. Here, then, is a proposal that ought to command broad and deep support, including from the European "allies":

The government of Israel should be required to say, in public and without reservation, that it has no such plans and would never implement such a scheme. It should be informed in public by the President that this undertaking is required on penalty of regime change in case of default. This, after all, is no more than is regularly required from the Palestinians. And it is not just a matter of moral equivalence but of self-interest.

Sooner or later the Saddam Hussein regime *will* fall, either of its own weight or from the physical and mental collapse of its leader or from endogenous or exogenous pressure. On that day one will want to be able to look the Iraqi and Kurdish peoples in the eye and say that we thought seriously about their interests and appreciated that, because of previous interventions that were actually in Saddam's favor, we owed them a debt. It's this dimension that seems to me lacking in the current antiwar critique.

Nation, September 30, 2002

⫸ 19 ⫷

Taking Sides

I suppose I can just about bear to watch the "inspections" pantomime a second time. But what I cannot bear is the sight of French and Russian diplomats posing and smirking with Naji Sabry, Iraq's foreign minister, or with Tariq Aziz. I used to know Naji and I know that two of his brothers, Mohammed and Shukri, were imprisoned and tortured by Saddam Hussein—in Mohammed's case, tortured to death. The son of

Deputy Prime Minister Tariq Aziz was sentenced to twenty-two years of imprisonment last year; he has since been released and rearrested and released again, partly no doubt to show who is in charge. Another former friend of mine, Mazen Zahawi, was Saddam Hussein's interpreter until shortly after the Gulf War, when he was foully murdered and then denounced as a homosexual. I have known many regimes where stories of murder and disappearance are the common talk among the opposition; the Iraqi despotism is salient in that such horrors are also routine among its functionaries. Saddam Hussein likes to use as envoys the men he has morally destroyed; men who are sick with fear and humiliation, and whose families are hostages.

I don't particularly care, even in a small way, to be a hostage of Saddam Hussein myself. There is not the least doubt that he has acquired some of the means of genocide and hopes to collect some more; there is also not the least doubt that he is a sadistic megalomaniac. Some believe that he is a rational and self-interested actor who understands "containment," but I think that is distinctly debatable: Given a green light by Washington on two occasions—once for the assault on Iran and once for the annexation of Kuwait—he went crazy both times and, knowing that it meant disaster for Iraq and for its neighbors, tried to steal much more than he had been offered.

On the matter of his support for international nihilism, I have already written my memoir of Abu Nidal, the murderous saboteur of the Palestinian cause.[1] I have also interviewed the senior Czech official who investigated the case of Mohamed Atta's visit to Prague. This same official had served a deportation order on Ahmed Al-Ani, the Iraqi secret policeman who, working under diplomatic cover, was caught red-handed in a plan to blow up Radio Free Iraq, which transmits from Czech soil. It was, I was told (and this by someone very skeptical of Plan Bush), "70 percent likely" that Atta came to Prague to meet Al-Ani. Seventy percent is not conclusive, but nor is it really tolerable. Meanwhile, the Patriotic Union of Kurdistan holds several prisoners from the Ansar al-Islam gang, who for some reason have been trying to destroy the autonomous Kurdish regime in northern Iraq. These people have suggestive links both to Osama bin Laden and Saddam Hussein. It will perhaps surprise nobody that despite Kurdish offers of cooperation, our intrepid CIA has shown no interest in questioning these prisoners. (Incidentally, when is anyone at the CIA or the FBI going to be *fired*?) People keep bleating that Saddam Hussein is not a fundamentalist. But he did rejoice in the attacks on New York and Washington and Pennsylvania, and he does believe that every little bit helps.

I am much more decided in my mind about two further points. I am on the side of the Iraqi and Kurdish opponents of this filthy menace. And they are on the side of civil society in a wider conflict, which is the civil war now burning across the Muslim world from Indonesia to Nigeria. The theocratic and absolutist side in this war hopes to win it by exporting it here, which in turn means that we have no expectation of staying out of the war, and no right to be neutral in it. But there are honorable allies to be made as well, and from now on all of our cultural and political intelligence will be required in order to earn their friendship and help isolate and destroy their enemies, who are now ours—or perhaps I should say mine.

Only a fool would trust the Bush Administration to see all of this. I am appalled that by this late date no proclamation has been issued to the people of Iraq, announcing the aims and principles of the coming intervention. Nor has any indictment of Saddam Hussein for crimes against humanity been readied. Nothing has been done to conciliate Iran, where the mullahs are in decline. The Palestinian plight is being allowed to worsen (though the Palestinians do seem to be pressing ahead hearteningly with a "regime change" of their own). These misgivings are obviously not peripheral. But please don't try to tell me that if Florida had gone the other way we would be in better hands, or would be taking the huge and honorable risk of "destabilizing" our former Saudi puppets.

Moreover, it's obvious to me that the "antiwar" side would not be convinced even if all the allegations made against Saddam Hussein were proven, and even if the true views of the Iraqi people could be expressed. All evidence pointed overwhelmingly to the Taliban and Al Qaeda last fall, and now all the proof is in; but I am sent petitions on Iraq by the same people (some of them not so naïve) who still organize protests against the simultaneous cleanup and rescue of Afghanistan, and continue to circulate falsifications about it. The Senate adopted the Iraq Liberation Act without dissent under Clinton; the relevant

UN resolutions are old and numerous. I don't find the saner, Richard Falk—ish view of yet more consultation to be very persuasive, either.

This is something more than a disagreement of emphasis or tactics. When I began work for the *Nation* over two decades ago, Victor Navasky described the magazine as a debating ground between liberals and radicals, which was, I thought, well judged. In the past few weeks, though, I have come to realize that the magazine itself takes a side in this argument, and is becoming the voice and the echo chamber of those who truly believe that John Ashcroft is a greater menace than Osama bin Laden. (I too am resolutely opposed to secret imprisonment and terror-hysteria, but not in the same way as I am opposed to those who initiated the aggression, and who are planning future ones.) In these circumstances it seems to me false to continue the association, which is why I have decided to make this "Minority Report" my last one.

Nation, October 14, 2002

NOTE

1. Christopher Hitchens, "Hijackers I Have Known," *Nation*, September 16, 2002.

⪥ 20 ⪤

So Long, Fellow Travelers

George Bush made a mistake when he referred to the Saddam Hussein regime as "evil." Every liberal and leftist knows how to titter at such black-and-white moral absolutism. What the president should have done, in the unlikely event that he wanted the support of America's peace-mongers, was to describe a confrontation with Saddam as the "lesser evil."

This is a term the Left can appreciate. Indeed, "lesser evil" is part of the essential tactical rhetoric of today's Left, and has been deployed to excuse or overlook the sins of liberal Democrats, from President Clinton's bombing of Sudan to Madeleine Albright's veto of an international rescue for Rwanda when she was US ambassador to the United Nations. Among those longing for nuance, moral relativism— the willingness to use the term evil, when combined with a willingness to make accommodations with it—is the smart thing: so much more sophisticated than "cowboy" language.

Actually, the best case for a regime change in Iraq is that it *is* the lesser evil: better on balance than the alternatives, which are to confront Saddam later and at a time of his choosing, trust him to make a full disclosure to inspectors or essentially leave him alone.

You might think that the Left could have a regime-change perspective of its own, based on solidarity with its comrades abroad. After all, Saddam's ruling Baath Party consolidated its power by first destroying the Iraqi communist and labor movements, and then turning on the Kurds (whose cause, historically, has been one of the main priorities of the Left in the Middle East). When I first became a socialist, the imperative of international solidarity was the essential if not the defining thing, whether the cause was popular or risky or not. I haven't seen an anti-war meeting all this year at which you could even guess at the existence of the Iraqi and Kurdish opposition to Saddam, an opposition that was fighting for "regime change" when both Republicans and Democrats were fawning over Baghdad as a profitable client and geopolitical ally. Not only does the "peace" movement ignore the anti-Saddam civilian opposition, it sends missions to console the Baathists in their isolation, and speaks of the invader of Kuwait and Iran and the butcher of Kurdistan as if he were the victim and George W. Bush the aggressor.

Some peaceniks clear their throats by saying that, of course, they oppose Saddam Hussein as much as anybody, though not enough to support doing anything about him.

But some don't even bother to make this disavowal. In the United States, the main organizer of anti-war propaganda is Ramsey Clark, who perhaps understandably can't forgive himself for having been Lyndon Johnson's attorney general. However, he fails to live down this early disgrace by acting as a front man for a sinister sect—the International Action Center, cover name for the Workers World Party— which refuses to make any criticism of the Saddam regime. It is this quasi-Stalinist group, co-organized by a man with the wondrous name of Clark Kissinger, which has recruited such figures as Ed Asner and

Marisa Tomei to sign the "Not In Our Name" petition. Funny as this may be in some ways (I don't think the administration is going to war in the name of Ed Asner or Marisa Tomei, let alone Gore Vidal), it is based on a surreptitious political agenda. In Britain, the chief spokesman of the "anti-war" faction is a Labour MP named George Galloway, who is never happier than when writing moist profiles of Saddam and who says that the collapse of the Soviet Union was the worst moment of his life.

For the democratic and libertarian Left, that same moment was a high point and not a low one. But there were three ruling parties in the world that greeted the liberation of Eastern Europe with unreserved gloom. These were the Socialist Party of Serbia, the Baath Party of Iraq and the Workers' Party of North Korea, guided by their lugubrious yet megalomaniacal leaders. Since then, these three party-states and self-ish dictators have done their considerable best to ruin the promise of the post–Cold War years and to impose themselves even more ruthlessly on their own peoples and neighbors. It took a long time for the world to wake up to Slobodan Milosevic and even longer to get him where he belongs, which is in the dock. It will probably be even more arduous ridding ourselves of the menace of Saddam Hussein.

The most depressing thing, for me at any rate, has been to see so much of the Left so determined to hamper this process, which is why, after 20 years, I have given up my column in the *Nation* magazine. The Left has employed arguments as contemptible as those on whose behalf they have been trotted out. It maintained that any resistance to ethnic cleansing in Bosnia and Kosovo would lead to a wider war, chaos and/or the rallying of the Serbs to Milosevic. It forecast massive quagmires and intolerable civilian casualties. If this sounds familiar, it may be because you are hearing it again now and heard it last year from those who thought the Taliban–Al Qaeda base in Afghanistan was not worth fighting about.

But the element of bad faith in the argument is far worse than the feeble-minded hysteria of its logic. In the Balkans, those on the Left and Right who favored intervention could not live with the idea that Europe would permit the extermination of its oldest Muslim minority. At that point, the sensibilities of Islam did not seem to matter to the Ramsey Clarks and Noam Chomskys, who thought and wrote of national-socialist and Orthodox Serbia as if it were mounting a gallant resistance to globalization. (Saddam, of course, took Milosevic's side even though the Serb leader was destroying mosques and murdering Muslims.)

Now, however, the same people are all frenzied about an American-led "attack on the Muslim world." Are the Kurds not Muslims? Is the new Afghan government not Muslim? Will not the next Iraqi government be Muslim also? This meaningless demagogy among the peaceniks can only be explained by a masochistic refusal to admit that our own civil society has any merit, or by a nostalgia for Stalinism that I can sometimes actually taste as well as smell.

There is, of course, a soggier periphery of more generally pacifist types, whose preferred method of argument about regime change is subject change. The same people, in other words, who don't think that Saddam has any WMDs will argue the next moment that, if attacked, he will unleash them with devastating effect. Or they say that a Palestinian solution should come first, which would offer Saddam a very long lease, given the prospects of a final settlement with Israel (which, meantime, he would have the power and incentive to disrupt). Or they say we should try deterrence or containment—the two terms most ridiculed by the Left during the Cold War. And what about the fact that "we" used to be Saddam's backers? And, finally, aren't there other bad guys in the region, and isn't this a double standard?

The last two questions actually have weight, even if they are lightly tossed around. The serious response to the first one would be that, to the extent that the United States underwrote Saddam in the past, this redoubles our responsibility to cancel the moral debt by removing him. The serious response to the second one would involve noticing that the Saudi Arabian and Turkish oligarchies are, interestingly enough, also opposed to "regime change" in the region. And since when is the Left supposed to argue for preservation of the status quo? Even a halfway emancipated Iraq would hold out at least the promise of a better life for the Kurds (which annoys the Turks). Its oil resources, once freed up, could help undercut the current Saudi monopoly. Excellent. This is presumably unintelligible to those content to chant, "No war for oil," as if it were a matter of indifference who controlled the reserves of the region, or who might threaten to ignite or even irradiate these reserves if given the chance.

As someone who has done a good deal of marching and public speaking about Vietnam, Chile, South Africa, Palestine and East Timor in his time (and would do it all again), I can only hint at how much I despise a Left that thinks of Osama bin Laden as a slightly misguided anti-imperialist. (He actually says he wants to restore the old imperial caliphate and has condemned the Australian-led international rescue of East Timor as a Christian plot against Muslim Indonesia). Or a Left that can think of Milosevic and Saddam as victims.

Instead of internationalism, we find among the Left now a sort of affectless, neutralist, smirking isolationism. In this moral universe, the views of the corrupt and conservative Jacques Chirac—who built Saddam Hussein a nuclear reactor, knowing what he wanted it for— carry more weight than those of persecuted Iraqi democrats. In this moral universe, the figure of Jimmy Carter—who incited Saddam to attack Iran in 1980, without any UN or congressional consultation that I can remember—is considered axiomatically more statesman-like than Bush.

Sooner or later, one way or another, the Iraqi and Kurdish peoples will be free of Saddam Hussein. When that day comes, I am booked to have a reunion in Baghdad with several old comrades who have been through hell. We shall not be inviting anyone who spent this precious time urging democratic countries to give Saddam another chance.

Washington Post, October 20, 2002

⊸(21)⊷

I Wanted It to Rain on Their Parade

I had hoped that it would pour with rain during last Saturday's march for "peace."

Why? Exactly a week earlier in northern Iraq, a brave minister of the autonomous Kurdish government was foully done to death by a bunch of bin Laden clones calling themselves Ansar al-Islam.

Shawkat Mushir was lured under a flag of truce into a dirty ambush, in which he and several innocent bystanders—including an eight-year-old girl—were murdered.

There is already war in this part of Iraq, and on one side stands an elected Kurdish government with a multi-party system, 21 newspapers, four female judges, and a secular constitution.

In this area of an otherwise wretched and terrified country, oil revenues are spent on schools and roads and hospitals instead of for the upkeep of a parasitic and cruel military oligarchy.

The survivors of ethnic cleansing and torture and poison gas and chemical weapons—genocidal tactics which have cost the lives of at least 200,000 civilians—are rebuilding.

And they are fighting both the Al Qaeda forces and the tyranny of Saddam Hussein, which operate in an unspoken but increasingly obvious alliance. It's a sort of Hitler-Stalin pact.

In my opinion, these brave Kurds and their friends in the Iraqi opposition are fighting and dying on our behalf—and tackling our enemies for us.

It should be a cause for great pride that pilots of the Royal Air Force take a leading share in patrolling the skies over northern Iraq, protecting a decade-long experiment in successful regime change.

During the many years I spent on the Left, the cause of self-determination for Kurdistan was high on the list of principles and priorities—there are many more Kurds than there are Palestinians and they have been staunch fighters for democracy in the region.

It would have been a wonderful thing if hundreds of thousands of people had flooded into London's Hyde Park and stood in solidarity with this, one of the most important struggles for liberty in the world today.

Instead, the assortment of forces who assembled demanded, in effect, that Saddam be allowed to keep the other five-sixths of Iraq as his own personal torture chamber.

There are not enough words in any idiom to describe the shame and the disgrace of this.

I went to the last such "peace" demonstration in Hyde Park last autumn and found it was pretty easy to distinguish between the two main tendencies.

These were:

1. Those who knew what they were doing and
2. Those who did not.

Among the first tendency—the animating and organizing force—were an easily-recognizable bunch of clapped-out pseudo-Marxists who, deep in their hearts, have a nostalgia for the days of the one-party State and who secretly regard Saddam as an anti-imperialist.

They were assisted by an impressive number of fundamentalist Muslims, who mouth the gibberish slogans of holy war but who don't give a damn for the suffering inflicted by Saddam on their co-religionists.

A more gruesome political alliance I have never seen.

Then came the sincere, fuddled stage-army of the good—people who think that a remark such as "peace is better than war" is an argument in itself. Their latest cry is that "inspections" should be given "more time." I am always impressed by sweet people who are evidence-proof.

The surveillance tapes recently played to the United Nations show conclusively, among other things, that the ranks of the "inspectors" have been heavily penetrated by Iraqi secret police agents, who now know where and when "inspections" will be.

So let's have "more time" for a lot more of that, shall we? And don't let's ask what Saddam wants the extra time for.

Just in the past few weeks, every stop-gap straw-man argument of the peaceniks has been shot down in flames.

Yes, dear, I am afraid that there are bin Laden agents taking shelter in Baghdad.

Yes, Mr bin Laden seems to think that Saddam's cause is, with reservations, one that a Muslim fascist ought to support. Yes, there are weapons and systems, found even by the bumbling inspectors, that Saddam had sworn he did not have.

Yes, sorry to break it to you but the Iraqi regime does have a special police department that inspects the inspectors.

And—are you sitting down?—the French are owed several billion dollars by Saddam for their past help in supplying the sinews of aggression against Iran, Kuwait and Kurdistan.

The Russian government, too, is seeking lucrative contracts in the Iraqi market and is being rewarded with such contracts for its slithery behavior at the UN.

Excuse me, comrades, but that is "blood for oil."

Meanwhile, 14 or so European governments, including most of those recently emancipated from Stalinism and also the only Muslim state in Europe (Albania), have signed a statement supporting the case for the removal of Saddam's wicked, conspiring, menacing regime.

I think I would prefer to have Vaclav Havel in my corner than the grotesque, corrupt, cynical dandy Jacques Chirac.

Now, I cheerfully admit that the experience of finding itself on the right side in this region is new to Washington (and to London, for that matter).

And one must be vigilant in ensuring that the "regime change" argument is not just picked up and then discarded by the coalition forces.

But one has to distinguish sharply between those who have learned from past crimes and blunders involving Saddam, and those who have not.

And this test does not apply only to governments or States. The last time that the "peace" marchers assembled, they would have spared the government of the Taliban.

The time before that, they would have spared the regime of Slobodan Milosevic.

Thank goodness that such opinions no longer count, however many people may be persuaded to hold them.

Soon, the Iraqi people will have a chance to express their own opinion, which will be more interesting and more complex than the facile banners and placards that we have already grown bored with.

I desperately wanted it to absolutely pour with rain on Saturday's demonstration—heavy rain on the just and the unjust, and a touch of hard rain and hail on the silly who are being led by the sinister.

Mirror, February 18, 2003

⟪ 22 ⟫

Weapons and Terror

It's fascinating to be this far into the post-Saddam period and still to be arguing about weapons, about terror, and about Saddam. According to one school, the total effect of the whole thing has been to expose WMD claims as a sham, ratchet up the terror network, and give Saddam a chance at a populist comeback.

I don't think that this can be quite right. I still want to reserve my position on whether anything will be found, but I did write before the war, and do state again (in my upcoming book *A Long Short War*) that obviously there couldn't have been very many weapons in Saddam's hands, nor can the coalition have believed there to be. You can't station tens of thousands of men and women in uniform on the immediate borders of Iraq for several months if you think that a mad dictator might be able to annihilate them with a pre-emptive strike.

The Iraqis also tended to admit things in reverse. In other words, it was only at the height of the Blix moment in 2003 that they conceded how near they had been to a nuclear weapon in 1990, when almost nobody believed they had such a capacity. And we know how many chemical and biological weapons they possessed at one time because they reluctantly handed over long lists stating what they were.

Thus if nothing has been found so far, and if literally nothing (except the mobile units predicted and described by one defector) is found from now on, it will mean that the operation was a success. The stuff must have been destroyed, or neutralized, or work on it must have been abandoned during the long grace period that was provided by the UN debates. One senior UN inspector adds a caveat to that, which is worth stressing. The intention of the regime to acquire weapons at some point, or to reacquire them, should not be doubted. There are many blueprints and many brains and many computer discs full of know-how. These would be nearly if not actually impossible to discover, and they will now not be reassembled by a Baathist government. Thus if you take my line of the "long short war," and a timeline of 1990 to 2003, Saddam Hussein went from being a threshold nuclear potentate with the capacity to invade Kuwait to an ex-potentate unable even to deploy his Republican Guard. This was the outcome of a series of measures, from sanctions to bombing, designed to create the conditions for regime change or to make regime change (desirable for numberless other reasons) possible. The anti-war movement opposed even the sanctions at first and the military part of the operation at all times. But Iraq is now disarmed, and who will argue that it was not the believable threat of intervention that brought this about?

Perhaps half-aware that this is true, anti-war Democrats and some others are now saying that the world has nonetheless been made more dangerous because of the threat of additional terrorism. Some stuff may have gone missing, and the fanatics may have been encouraged. Well, they can't have this both ways, either. If there was stuff to go missing, then it was there all along, wasn't it? And it wasn't being kept for recreational use. The incompetence of the US protective and investigative teams, in this and in some other areas (like the elementary delivery of supplies and repairs) doesn't alter that fact. As to the terrorists who (remember?) had "no connection" to Saddam Hussein, they seem moved nonetheless to take revenge for his fall. Can that possibly mean they feel they have lost a friend?

Let us skip over this obvious point and inquire about what they managed. In Saudi Arabia, which is a fertile place for anti-Western feeling of all sorts, they managed to kill a number of Saudi officials and bystanders while inflicting fairly superficial damage on Western interests. Widespread and quite sincere denunciation of this has been evident across Saudi society. While in Morocco, where the evidence for an Al Qaeda connection is not so plain, whatever organization did set off the suicide attacks in Casablanca has isolated itself politically. Please try to remember that Al Qaeda and its surrogates are engaged in a war with Muslims as well: They boast of attacking the West in order to impress or intimidate those Muslims who are wavering. But they are steadily creating antibodies to themselves in the countries where they operate. The jihadists who murdered tourists in Egypt were widely execrated and not just because they threatened to ruin the tourist industry. The Bali bombers in Indonesia caused something of the same effect. The recent suicide atrocities in Jerusalem and Tel

Aviv were clearly directed, by their timing, against elements in the Palestinian Authority who want to make a deal.

This is where all our political and cultural intelligence will be required. In a civil war within the Islamic world, secularists and liberals have the chance to make many allies against theocracy and its gruesome tactics. It is not just Christian Nigerians who oppose the imposition of *Sharia* law in that country and the stoning of Amina Lawal. As the jihadists begin to explode themselves and their devices on Arab streets, they will not fulfill the usual prediction of bringing ever more recruits to bin Laden. Quite the contrary. Instead, and as in Afghanistan and Iran, there will be more people willing to oppose theocratic absolutism. Of course this political project can be called a "war" because it does also necessitate the use of remorseless force. But when the murderers strike next on American or European soil, it won't prove that it was wrong to fight them, and it certainly won't demonstrate that we brought it on ourselves by making them cross (i.e., by fighting back). It will remind us that it is indeed a war. So, it's depressing to see that, just as many Arabs and Muslims are turning against bin Ladenism, some Western liberals are calling for a capitulation in the mind and hinting that this war is either avoidable or, even worse, not worth fighting, lest it offend the enemy.

Slate, May 20, 2003

⤙ 23 ⤚

Restating the Case for War

The following is a dense paragraph of apparent prescience that was first published in 1998:

> Trying to eliminate Saddam, extending the ground war into an occupation of Iraq, would have violated our guideline about not changing objectives in midstream, engaging in "mission creep," and incurred incalculable human and political costs. Apprehending

him was probably impossible. We had been unable to find Noriega in Panama, which we knew intimately. We would have been forced to occupy Baghdad and, in effect, rule Iraq. The coalition would instantly have collapsed, the Arabs deserting it in anger and other allies pulling out as well. Under these circumstances, there was no viable "exit strategy" we could see, violating another of our principles. Furthermore, we had been self-consciously trying to set a pattern for handling aggression in the post–Cold War world. Going in and occupying Iraq, thus unilaterally exceeding the United Nations's mandate, would have destroyed the precedent of international response to aggression that we hoped to establish. Had we gone the invasion route, the United States could conceivably still be an occupying power in a bitterly hostile land.

This is taken from Chapter 19 of *A World Transformed*, by President Bush senior and Gen. Brent Scowcroft. With allowance made for a few differences of emphasis (and of confusion, possibly willful, about the historical record—Manuel Noriega was in fact fairly easily apprehended), it is now the pattern for an emerging conventional wisdom. Like its more recent emulators, extending from many Democratic candidates to an increasing number of commentators, it represents the anti-Saddam war, or the "regime change" campaign, as something elective and voluntary rather than as something inescapable. (It is also, you may notice, the same logic that was used by Bush, Scowcroft, and others to justify staying out of Bosnia.)

I have noticed lately a distressing tendency on the part of those who support the intervention in Iraq to rest their case largely on under-reported good news. Now, it is certainly true, as I have said myself, that there is much to celebrate in the new Iraq. The restoration of the ecology of the southern marshes, the freedom to follow the majority Shiite religion, the explosion of new print and electronic media, the emancipation of the schools and universities, and the consolidation of Kurdish autonomy are all magnificent things. But those who want to take credit for them must also axiomatically accept the blame for the failure to anticipate huge lacunae in the provision of power, water, and security.

More to the point, one has to be prepared to support a campaign—or a cause—that is going badly. The president has been widely lampooned by many a glib columnist for saying that increased violence is not necessarily a cause for despair and may even be evidence of traction. He is, in fact, quite right to take this view, which was first expressed, to my knowledge, by Gen. John Abizaid. Those who murder the officials of the United Nations and the Red Cross, set fire to oil pipelines and blow up water mains, and shoot down respected clerics outside places of worship are indeed making our point for us. There is no justifiable way that a country as populous and important as Iraq can be left at the mercy of such people. And—here is my crux—there never was.

The counsel of prudence offered above by Bush and Scowcroft was all very well as far as it went. But it did leave Saddam Hussein in power, and it did (as its authors elsewhere concede) involve the United States in watching from the sidelines as Iraqis were massacred for rebelling on its side and in its name. It left the Baathist regime free to continue work on WMDs, which we know for certain it was doing on a grand scale until at the very least 1995. And it left Saddam free to continue to threaten his neighbors and to give support and encouragement to jihad forces around the world. (The man most wanted in the 1993 bombing of the World Trade Center, Abdul Rahman Yasin, fled straight from New Jersey to Baghdad, though there are still those in our "intelligence" services who prefer to grant Saddam the presumption of innocence in this and many other matters.) It also left Saddam Hussein free to try and assassinate former President Bush on his postwar visit to Kuwait—an act of such transparent lunacy that it far transcends any sneers about George W. wanting to avenge his daddy. (It also demonstrates, by the way, Saddam Hussein's urgent personal need for a revenge for 1991—a consideration that deserves more attention than it has received.)

This already lousy status quo was volatile and unstable. Saddam Hussein's speeches and policies were becoming ever more demented and extreme and ever more Islamist in tone. The flag of Iraq was amended to include a verse from the Quran, and gigantic mosques began to be built in Saddam's own name. Even if, as seems remotely possible, he was largely bluffing about WMDs, this conclusion would destroy the view maintained by many liberals that, for all his crimes, Saddam understood the basic logic of deterrence and self-preservation. (That he was "in his box," as the saying went.) Not only was he able to defy the United Nations, but with French and Russian collusion, he was also increasingly able to circumvent sanctions. The "box" was falling apart, and its supposed captive was becoming more toxic. As he became older and madder, there emerged the real prospect of a succession passing to either Uday or Qusay Hussein, or to both of them. Who could view that prospect with equanimity? (Qusay Hussein was at the heart of the concealment program, for centrifuges and other devices, that has recently been partly exposed by David Kay's report.)

Meanwhile, the no-fly zones managed to protect the Kurds and Shiites from a repeat performance of the mass murders of 1991 and earlier but did not prevent, for example, the planned destruction of the largest wetlands in the Middle East, home to the 5,000-year-old civilization of the Marsh Arabs. The smoke from this drain-and-burn atrocity was visible from the space shuttle. I shall leave open the question of whether "we" had any responsibility to prevent this and other mutilations and tortures of Iraqi society, except to say that the meltdown and trauma of that society, now so visible to all, were always inescapably in our future and would in any case have had consequences beyond themselves for the wider region. The continuation of this regime was indeed an imminent threat, at least in the sense that it was a permanent threat.

The question then, becomes this: Should the date or timing of this unpostponable confrontation have been left to Saddam Hussein to pick? The two chief justifications offered by the Bush administration (which did mention human rights and genocide at its first presentation to the United Nations, an appeal that fell on cold as well as deaf ears) were WMDs and terrorism. Here, it is simply astonishing how many people remain willing to give Saddam Hussein the benefit of the doubt. The late Dr. David Kelley, whose suicide has so embarrassed the Blair government, put it very plainly in an article he wrote just before the war. Seriousness about "inspections" required a regime change in Iraq—no credible inspection could be conducted on any other terms. This point has since been amply vindicated by the Kay inquiry, still in its early stages, which has already unearthed compelling evidence of a complex concealment program, of the designing of missiles well beyond the permitted legal range, of the intimidation of scientists and witnesses, and of the incubation (in some cases hidden in scientists' homes) of deadly biological toxins. Some of the other leads have turned out to be false, or at any rate not proved, and no major stockpiles have yet been found. Nonetheless, the Baathists declared a very impressive stockpile as late as 1999 and never cared to inform the UN inspectorate what they had done with it. (*If* they destroyed it themselves, it deserves to be pointed out, they were in gross and open breach of the relevant resolutions, which anticipated this tactic and specified that all weapons were to be turned over, listed, classified, and only then neutralized in the presence of certified witnesses.)

Before the war, it was a staple of anti-interventionist argument that Saddam was too well-armed to be attacked and would unleash WMDs in a horrific manner. (Chancellor Gerhard Schröder of Germany opposed the war despite being—possibly wrongly—informed by his intelligence services that Saddam was no more than three years away from acquiring a nuclear bomb.) Any failures of prediction on this point can thus be shared equally, but there is no moral equivalence between them. Thanks to the intervention, Saddam Hussein has been verifiably disarmed, and a full accounting of his concealment and acquisition programs is being conducted. Where is the objection to that? Why so much surliness and resentment?

I am pleased to notice the disappearance from the peacenik argument of one line of attack—namely that Saddam Hussein was "too secular" to have anything to do with jihad forces. The alliance between his murderous fedayeen and the jihadists is now visible to all—perhaps there are some who are still ready to believe that this connection only began this year. Meanwhile, an increasing weight of disclosure shows that the Iraqi Mukhabarat both sought and achieved contact with the bin Laden forces in the 1990s and subsequently. Again, was one to watch this happening and hope that it remained relatively low-level?

The literal-minded insistence that all government rhetoric be entirely scrupulous strikes me, in view of the above, as weird. It can only come from those who were not willing to form, or to defend, positions of their own: in other words, those for whom Saddam would not have been a problem unless Bush tried to make him into one. An example:

In trying to justify the earlier eviction of Saddam from Kuwait, Secretary of State James Baker put forward the case that "jobs" were the main justification. I thought that to be both stupid and ignoble at the time (and was generally antiwar at that date) but did not think that it automatically, or even partially, invalidated the case for restoring Kuwaiti sovereignty by force of arms.

Arguments about democracy and reform cannot be phrased in terms of UN resolutions—especially when two of the relevant regime's clients are among the permanent membership of the Security Council—but there is every reason to believe that the United States has chosen the right side in the region, in principle as well as in practice. To take the salient case of Iran, does anybody believe that the mullahs' regime would have agreed to searches and inspections, or that Messrs Straw, de Villepin, and Fischer would have been able to seize the initiative on behalf of the European Union, except in the case that a) the main rival of Iran had been itself disarmed and b) a certain pedagogic lesson had been instilled? And that is to leave to one side the coming "people power" revolution in Iran itself, which seems to have been substantially encouraged by the "regime change" policy next door.

We are fighting for very large principles, in other words, and for extremely high stakes. And yes, part of the proof of this is the horror and terror and misery involved. Only a few months ago, the first elected president of Serbia, Zoran Djindjic, was shot down in the street by the alliance of mafiosi and ethnic fascists who constitute the legacy of Slobodan Milosevic. That gruesome reverse took place years after Milosevic himself had been put under arrest (and only a short while after the corpse of his murdered predecessor, Ivan Stambolic, had been finally unearthed). But do you want to try and imagine what former Yugoslavia would look like now if there had not been an international intervention (postponed and hobbled by the United Nations) to arrest the process of aggression and ethnocide? Both Bush and Scowcroft—and Baker—did make the irresponsible decision to let the Balkans bleed, which is why I mistrust the counsel of prudence that I opened by quoting and find even more suspect the tendency of today's Left to take refuge in neutralist and conservative isolationism.

Slate, November 5, 2003

⚛(24)⚛

The Literal Left

The truly annoying thing that I find when I am arguing with opponents of the regime-change policy in Iraq is their dogged literal-mindedness. "Your side said that coalition troops would be greeted with 'sweets and flowers!'" Well, I have seen them with my own eyes being ecstatically welcomed in several places. "But were there actual *sweets and flowers*?" Then again, "You said there was an alliance between bin Laden and Saddam, and now people think that Saddam was behind 9/11." Well, the administration hasn't said there was a 9/11 connection, but there are reams of verifiable contact between Al Qaeda and Baghdad. Bin Laden supported Saddam, and his supporters still do, and where do you think this lovely friendship was going? "But there's no *direct link* between Saddam and 9/11." Finally, "You said that weapons of mass destruction would be found, and they haven't been." Well, what I said in my book *A Long Short War* was that the programs were latent—which is why we wouldn't face WMD in case of an invasion, as the peace movement kept saying we would—but that I had been believably told of stuff hidden in a mosque and that I had every reason to think that Saddam Hussein was trying to make up for what he'd lost or illegally destroyed by buying it off the shelf from North Korea. Incidentally, if the Iraqis destroyed the stocks they had once declared, they were in serious breach of the UN resolutions, which stipulated that they be handed over and accounted for. "But they said they'd find *actual stuff.*"

This is not just tiresome in itself. It convinces me that, if the Bush and Blair administrations had not raised the overdue subject of Saddam's hellish regime, nobody else was going to. Aided by occasional political ineptitude in Washington and London, the opponents of the policy have done no better than act as if Iraq had nothing to do with them and maintain that things were all right as they were, or at any rate could only be made worse by an intervention. The idea that Iraq's state and society were headed for confrontation and implosion anyway just doesn't occur to such minds.

I think that this is why the David Kay report has received such a grudging audience for its important findings. I pause to note, just for my own sake, that the report contains a photograph of laboratory equipment stacked in a mosque. Much more salient is the story of Saddam's dealings with Kim Jong-Il, which was written up at length by David Sanger and Thom Shanker in the *New York Times* on December 1.

You may remember the secret and disguised shipload of North Korean Scuds, intercepted on its way to Yemen by the Spanish navy just before war began last March. Now downloaded hard drives from Iraqi government computers, plus interviews with Iraq officials and scientists, have established that Saddam Hussein was trying to buy Rodong missiles from Pyongyang and was hoping to purchase the rights to the North Korean production line. The significance of this is obvious enough: The Rodong missile has a range much greater than that prohibited to Iraq by the UN resolutions. It also makes sense: North Korea is bankrupt and starving and exports only weapons and drugs while Saddam's Iraq had plenty of spare off-the-record cash in American dollars. The intended transshipment point and the site of the negotiations, Syria in both instances, also indicates that Syria has long been at least a passive profiteer from the sanctions imposed on its neighbor.

Even more interesting is the fashion in which the deal broke down. Having paid some $10 million dollars to North Korea, the Iraqi side found that foot-dragging was going on—this is the discussion revealed on one of the hard drives—and sought a meeting about where the money might be refunded. North Korea's explanation for its slipped deadline was that things were getting a little ticklish. In the month before the coalition intervened in Iraq, Saddam's envoys came back empty-handed from a meeting in Damascus. It doesn't take a rocket scientist (just for once I can use this expression without toppling into cliché) to deduce that the presence of a large force all along Iraq's borders might have had something to do with North Korea's cold feet.

So the "drumbeat" scared off the deal-makers, and Saddam Hussein never did get Rodong missiles, which might have been able to hit targets far away from Iraq. Elsewhere in the Kay report, there is convincing evidence that Iraqi scientists were working on missiles, and missile fuels, with ranges longer than those permitted by the United Nations. So there is an explanation for why the completed and readied material was never "found" by inspectors before or after the invasion: It hadn't been acquired quite yet. Which meant that Saddam could not confront the international community in the way that North Korea has lately been doing, by brandishing weapons that do in fact have deterrent power. As in previous cases—the parts of a nuclear centrifuge found in the yard of Iraqi scientist Mahdi Obeidi, for example— the man in charge of these covert weapons programs was Saddam's son Qusay. I find I can live with the idea that Qusay never got to succeed his father as Kim Jong-Il did. Imagine a North Korea, with attitude, on the sea lanes of the Persian Gulf—and with "deniable" but undeniable ties to Al Qaeda. That was in our future if action had not been taken.

There were predictions made by the peaceniks, too, that haven't come literally true, or true at all. There has been no refugee exodus, for example, of the kind they promised. No humanitarian meltdown, either. No mass civilian casualties. All of these things would of course come to pass, and right away, if the Iraqi "resistance" succeeded in sabotaging the coalition presence. But I refuse to believe that any anti-war person is so keen on vindication as to wish for anything like that.

Slate, December 4, 2003

⚜(25)⚜

Guerrillas in the Mist

Having been screened by the special operations department of the Pentagon last August, *The Battle of Algiers* is now scheduled for a run at the New York Film Forum. Unless I am wrong, this event will lead to a torrent of pseudo-knowing piffle from the armchair guerrillas (well, there ought to be a word for this group). I myself cherished the dream of being something more than an armchair revolutionary when I first saw this electrifying movie. It was at a volunteer work-camp for internationalists, in Cuba in the summer of 1968. Che Guevara had only been dead for a few months, the Tet rising in Vietnam was still a fresh and vivid memory, and in Portuguese Africa the revolution was on the upswing. I went to the screening not knowing what to expect and was so mesmerized that when it was over I sat there until they showed it again. I was astounded to discover, sometime later on, that Gillo Pontecorvo had employed no documentary footage in the shooting of the film: It looked and felt like revolutionary reality projected straight onto the screen.

When I next saw it, in Bleecker Street in the Village in the early 1970s, it didn't have quite the same shattering effect. Moreover, in the audience (as in that Cuban camp, as I later found out) there were some idiots who fancied the idea of trying "urban guerrilla" warfare inside the West itself. The film had a potently toxic effect on Black Panthers, Weathermen, Baader-Meinhof, and Red Brigade types. All that needs to be said about that "moment" of the Left is that its practitioners ended up dead or in prison, having advanced the cause of humanity by not one millimeter.

Those making a facile comparison between the Algerian revolution depicted in the film and today's Iraq draw an equally flawed analogy. Let me mention just the most salient differences.

1. Algeria in 1956—the "real time" date of the film—was not just a colony of France. It was a department of metropolitan France. The slogan of the French Right was *Algérie Française*. A huge population of French settlers lived in the country, mainly concentrated in the coastal towns. The French had exploited and misgoverned this province for more than a century and were seeking to retain it as an exclusive possession.

2. In 1956, the era of French and British rule in the Middle East had already in effect come to an end. With the refusal by President Eisenhower to countenance the Anglo-French-Israeli attack on Egypt at Suez in November of that year, the death-knell of European colonialism had struck. There was no military tactic that could have exempted a near-bankrupt France from this verdict. General Massu in Algiers could have won any military victory he liked and it would have changed nothing. Frenchmen as conservative as Charles de Gaulle and Raymond Aron were swift to recognize this state of affairs.

Today, it is Arab nationalism that is in crisis, while the political and economic and military power of the United States is virtually unchallengeable. But the comparison of historical context, while decisive, is not the only way in which the Iraq analogy collapses. The French could not claim to have removed a tyrannical and detested leader. They could not accuse the Algerian nationalists of sponsoring international terrorism (indeed, they blamed Gamal Abdel Nasser in Egypt for fomenting the FLN in Algiers itself). They could not make any case that Algerian nationalism would violate the Non-Proliferation Treaty or even threaten to do so. Thus, French conscripts—not volunteers— and Algerian rebels were sacrificed for no cause except the lost and futile one of French reaction. The right-wing generals of the Algeria campaign, and some of the extreme settlers, actually did conduct an urban guerrilla rearguard action of their own, in Paris as well as Algeria, and did try to bring off a military coup against de Gaulle, but they had been defeated and isolated by 1968.

I would challenge anybody to find a single intelligent point of comparison between any of these events and the present state of affairs in Iraq. The only similarity that strikes the eye, in point of guerrilla warfare, is that the toughest and most authentic guerrilla army in Iraq— the Kurdish *peshmerga*—is fighting very effectively on the coalition side. Not even the wildest propaganda claims of the Baathist and jihadist sympathizers allege that the tactics of General Massu are being employed by General Abizaid or General Sanchez: Newspaper and political party offices are being opened not closed, and just last month the Saddam ban on Iraqi pilgrims making the hajj to Mecca was rescinded.

If one wants to make a serious Algerian analogy, however, there are far more recent events on which to base a comparison. During the 1990s a very bitter war was fought, in the casbah of Algiers and Oran as well as in the countryside, between the FLN (now an extremely shabby ruling party) and the forces of Islamic jihad. A very great number of people were slaughtered in this war, which featured torture and assassination and terror of every description. I have seen estimates of deaths that exceed 150,000. The FLN eventually won the war with the backing of three forces: the Algerian army, the secularized urban middle class, and the Berbers or Kabyles who make up one of the Arab world's largest non-Arab minorities. It wasn't very pretty, and it involved the use of some repulsive measures, but if Algeria had fallen to the fundamentalists the bloodbath would have been infinitely worse and the society would have been retarded almost to the level of Afghanistan. Millions of people would have left or tried to leave, creating a refugee crisis in France and perhaps giving M. Jean-Marie Le Pen (a brutish and boastful veteran of the first Algerian war) an even better shot at the presidency than he managed in his upset first-round triumph in 2002. Fascism would have been the all-round winner.

That "Battle of Algiers," not Pontecorvo's outdated masterpiece, is replete with examples and parallels that ought to be of great interest and relevance to ourselves. Can an Arab and Muslim state with a large non-Arab minority and many confessional differences defeat the challenge of a totalitarian and medieval ideology? In this outcome, we and our Arab and Kurdish friends have a stake, whereas in the battles of the past (as of the present) one can only applaud the humiliation of French unilateralism and neocolonialism, whether it occurs on-screen or off.

Slate, January 2, 2004

◄(26)►

Fallujah

There must be a temptation, when confronted with the Dantesque scenes from Fallujah, to surrender to something like existential despair. The mob could have cooked and eaten its victims without making things very much worse. One especially appreciated the detail of the heroes who menaced the nurses, when they came to try and remove the charred trophies.

But this "Heart of Darkness" element is part of the case for regime-change to begin with. A few more years of Saddam Hussein, or perhaps the succession of his charming sons Uday and Qusay, and whole swathes of Iraq would have looked like Fallujah. The Baathists, by playing off tribe against tribe, Arab against Kurd and Sunni against Shiite, were preparing the conditions for a Hobbesian state of affairs. Their looting and beggaring of the state and the society—something about which we now possess even more painfully exact information—was having the same effect. A broken and maimed and traumatized Iraq was in our future no matter what.

Obviously, this prospect could never have been faced with equanimity. Iraq is a regional keystone state with vast resources and many common borders. Its implosion would have created a black hole, sucking in rival and neighboring powers, tempting them with opportunist interventions and encouraging them to find ethnic and confessional proxies. And who knows what the death-throes of the regime would have been like? We are entitled, on past experience, to guess. There could have been deliberate conflagrations started in the oilfields. There might have been suicidal lunges into adjacent countries. The place would certainly have become a playground for every kind of nihilist and fundamentalist. The intellectual and professional classes, already gravely attenuated, would have been liquidated entirely.

All of this was, only just, averted. And it would be a Pangloss who said that the dangers have receded even now. But at least the international intervention came before the whole evil script of Saddam's crime family had been allowed to play out. A subsequent international intervention would have been too little and too late, and we would now being holding an inquest into who let this happen—who in other words permitted in Iraq what Bill Clinton and Madeleine Albright and Kofi Annan permitted in Rwanda, encouraged by the Elysée.

Prescience, though, has now become almost punishable. Thanks in part to Richard Clarke's showmanship (and to the crass ineptitude of the spokesmen for the Bush administration) it is widely considered laughable to have even thought about an Iraqi threat. Given Saddam's record in both using and concealing WMDs, and given his complicity—at least according to Mr. Clarke—with those who bombed the World Trade Center in 1993 and with those running Osama bin Laden's alleged poison factory in Sudan, any president who did *not* ask about a potential Baathist link to terrorism would be impeachably failing in his duty.

It's becoming more and more plain that the moral high ground is held by those who concluded, from the events of 1991, that it was a mistake to leave Saddam Hussein in power after his eviction from Kuwait. However tough that regime-change might have been, it would have spared the lives of countless Iraqis and begun the process of nation-rebuilding with 12 years' advantage, and before most of the awful damage wrought by the sanctions-plus-Saddam "solution." People like Paul Wolfowitz are even more sinister than their mocking foes believe. They were against Saddam Hussein not just in September 2001 but as far back as the 1980s. (James Mann's excellent book *Rise of the Vulcans*, greatly superior to Richard Clarke's, will I hope not be eclipsed by it. It contains an account that every serious person should ponder.)

I debate with the opponents of the Iraq intervention almost every day. I always have the same questions for them, which never seem to get answered. Do you believe that a confrontation with Saddam Hussein's regime was inevitable or not? Do you believe that a confrontation with an Uday/Qusay regime would have been better? Do you know that Saddam's envoys were trying to buy a weapons production line off the shelf from North Korea (*vide* the Kay report) as late as last March? Why do you think Saddam offered "succor" (Mr. Clarke's word) to the man most wanted in the 1993 bombings in New York? Would you have been in favor of lifting the "no fly zones" over northern and southern Iraq; a 10-year prolongation of the original "Gulf War"? Were you content to have Kurdish and Shiite resistance fighters do all the fighting for us? Do you think that the timing of a confrontation should have been left, as it was in the past, for Baghdad to choose?

I hope I do not misrepresent my opponents, but their general view seems to be that Iraq was an elective target; a country that would not otherwise have been troubling our sleep. This ahistorical opinion makes it appear that Saddam Hussein was a new enemy, somehow chosen by shady elements within the Bush administration, instead of one of the longest-standing foes with which the United States, and indeed the international community, was faced. So, what about the "bad news" from Iraq? There was always going to be bad news from there. Credit belongs to those who accepted—can we really decently say pre-empted?—this long-term responsibility. Fallujah is a reminder, not just of what Saddamism looks like, or of what the future might look like if we fail, but of what the future held before the Coalition took a hand.

Wall Street Journal, April 2, 2004

◃(27)▹

Vietnam?

Here is how the imperialist plot in Iraq was proceeding until recently. The Shiite Muslim pilgrimages to Najaf and Karbala and the Sunni pilgrimages to Mecca and Medina had been recommenced after a state ban that had lasted for years and been enforced in blood. A new dinar had been minted, without the face of the dictator, and was on its way to becoming convertible. (Indeed, recent heists at the Beirut and Baghdad airports suggested that the Iraqi currency was at last worth stealing.) The deliberately parched and scorched wetlands of the south were being re-flooded. At the end of June, the American headquarters was to be converted into an embassy. At that point, almost $100 billion was to become available for the reconstitution of the Iraqi state and society. By the end of the year, campaigning would be under way for the first open election in Iraqi memory, and the only such election in the region (unless you count Israel).

There are those—not conspicuous for their bravery under a less indulgent regime—who would prefer not to give this process a chance to breathe. For them, it is nobler to take hostages and dismember prisoners and to conceal explosives in the bodies of dead dogs. When confronted with those who were brave under the previous regime, they tend to back away. (I don't see Muqtada Sadr taking on the Kurdish *peshmerga* any time soon, and I'd be fascinated to see what happened if he did. He has said that "Kurdistan is the enemy of God.")

Of what does this confrontation remind you? Why, of Vietnam, says Sen. Edward Kennedy. No, more like Lebanon in 1982, says the *New York Times*. The usually admirable Colbert King, in the *Washington Post*, asking how we got ourselves into this, compares pro-American Iraqis to the Uncle Toms on whom liberal opinion used to rely for advice about the black ghetto. And Thomas Friedman, never more than an inch away from a liberal panic of his own, has decided that it is Kurdish arrogance—in asking to keep what they already have—that has provoked theocratic incendiarism.

If the United States were the nation that its enemies think it is, it could quite well afford to Balkanize Iraq, let the various factions take a chunk each, and make a divide-and-rule bargain with the rump. The effort continues, though, to try and create something that is simultaneously federal and democratic. Short of that, if one absolutely has to fall short, the effort must continue to deny Iraq to demagogues and murderers and charlatans. I can't see how this compares to the attempt to partition and subjugate Vietnam, bomb its cities, drench its forests in Agent Orange, and hand over its southern region to a succession of brutal military proxies. For one thing, Vietnam even at its most Stalinist never invaded and occupied neighboring countries (or not until it took on the Khmer Rouge), never employed weapons of genocide inside or outside its own borders, and never sponsored gangs of roving nihilist terrorists. If not all its best nationalists were Communists, all its best Communists were nationalists, and their combination of regular and irregular forces had beaten the Japanese and French empires long before the United States even set foot in the country, let alone before the other Kennedy brothers started assassinating the very puppets they had installed there.

As for Lebanon: Gen. Sharon in 1982 set out to "solve" the Palestinian problem by installing a fascist-minded Phalange Party, itself a minority of the Christian minority, in Beirut. (To watch American policy in Iraq, you would never even know that there was a 6 percent Christian minority there.) And Sharon invaded a country that already had a large population of Palestinian refugees, a country that had committed no offense against international law except to shelter those Palestinians—against their will and that of Lebanon—to begin with.

Colbert King is actually nearer the mark than he knows. Those Arab Iraqis who take a pro-American line do have a tendency to be secular, educated, and multicultural. They also, often, have had to spend time in exile (as 4 million Iraqis have been compelled to do), and many of them have barely had time to come home and start over. Then there is a potential majority, according even to the most depressing opinion polls, who want to be given time to think. The above qualifications don't apply so much to Iraqi Kurdistan, which did its own fighting and doesn't suffer so much from that elusive feeling of "humiliation," and where the "street" is pro-American. This does force us to face the fact that there is no pro-Western militia, with ready-made slogans of religion and nationalism and "martyrdom" and Kalashnikovs to spare. And facing that fact means asking whether we will abandon the nascent Iraqi civil society to those who do have those things.

The scenes in Fallujah and Kut and elsewhere are pre-figurations of what a transfer of power would have looked like, unedited, in the absence of coalition forces. This is the Iraq that had been prepared for us by more than a decade of sanctions-plus-Saddam, with a new lumpen class of impoverished, disenfranchised, and paranoid people, with bullying, Khomeini-style, Wahhabi-style and Baath-style forces to compete for their loyalty. Such was the future we faced anyway. This is implicitly admitted by those antiwar forces who asked, "Why not Zimbabwe?" or, "Why not Rwanda?"

I could give a list of mistakes that I think the Bremer administration has made, but none that would have justified theocratic barbarism. I don't feel I should give free advice to officers in the field, but if the locations seized by Sadr or his Sunni counterparts had been left to their own devices for a few days, there is some reason to think that the local population would have gotten a glimpse of that future and rejected it. A few days rule by the inflamed Party of God . . . Or what about a quarter-century of it, as the Iranian people have just had to endure?

Here is the reason that it is idle to make half-baked comparisons to Vietnam. The Vietnamese were not our enemy, let alone the enemy of the whole civilized world, whereas the forces of jihad are our enemy and the enemy of civilization. There were some Vietnamese, even after the whole ghastly business, who were sorry to see the Americans leave. There were no Lebanese who were sad to see the Israelis leave. There would be many, many Iraqis who would be devastated in more than one way if there was another Somalian scuttle in their country. In any case, there never was any question of allowing a nation of this importance to become the property of *Clockwork Orange* holy warriors.

Slate, April 12, 2004

⟨ 28 ⟩

Second Thinking

At least there's no question about the flavor of the week. It's a scoop of regime-change second-thoughts, with a dash of "who lost Iraq by gaining it?" Colin Powell, who has never been wise before any event (he was for letting Bosnia slide and didn't want even to move an aircraft carrier on the warning—which he didn't believe—that Saddam was about to invade Kuwait), always has Bob Woodward at his elbow when he wants to be wise afterwards. Richard Clarke has never been asked any questions about his insistence that the United States stay away from Rwanda. Many of those who were opposed to any military intervention now tell us that they always thought it should have been at least twice as big.

To give an example of the latter school: E.J. Dionne in the *Washington Post* has just instructed his readers that Fallujah and the Sunni triangle would more likely have been under control the first time around, except that we refused the offer of help from the Turks. Dionne, whose politics are an etiolated version of the Dorothy Day/Michael Harrington Catholic-pacifist school, is the soft-left's William Safire in this thirst for Turkish power. At the time, I thought it was impressive that the United States refused Turkey's arrogant pre-condition, which was a demand that Turkish troops be allowed into Iraqi Kurdistan. Apart from the fact that there was and is no threat from that quarter, such a concession would have negated our "regime change" claims.

Now we hear on all sides, including Lakhdar Brahimi of the United Nations, that de-Baathification was also a mistake. Can you imagine what the antiwar critics, and many Iraqis, would now be saying if the Baathists had been kept on? This point extends to Paul Bremer's decision to dissolve the Baathist armed forces. That could perhaps have been carried out with more tact, and in easier stages. But it was surely right to say that a) Iraq was the victim of a huge and parasitic military, which invaded externally and repressed internally; and b) that young Iraqi men need no longer waste years of their lives on nasty and stultifying conscription. Moreover, by making it impossible for any big-mouth brigadier or general to declare himself the savior of Iraq in a military coup, the United States also signaled that it would not wish to rule through military proxies (incidentally, this is yet another gross failure of any analogy to Vietnam, El Salvador, Chile, and all the rest of it).

In parallel with this kind of retrospective brilliance, we continue to hear from those whose heroic job it is to keep on exposing the open secret. Fresh bulletins continue to appear from the faction that knows the awful truth: Saddam's Iraq was considered a threat by some people even before Osama bin Laden became famous. I still recommend Kenneth Pollack's book *The Threatening Storm* as the best general volume here. Published well before the war and by a member of the Clinton NSC whose pre-Kuwait warnings had been overruled by the first Bush administration, it openly said that continuing coexistence with Saddam Hussein had become impossible and that the aftermath of September 11, 2001, made it thinkable at last to persuade public opinion that this was so. More than any other presentation, this prepared the ground for the intervention. I remember it being rather openly on sale and being considered the argument that you had to beat.

Pollack rested more of his case than he now finds comfortable[1] on the threat from Iraqi WMD. That these used to be a threat is no more to be denied than the cheerful fact that we can now be sure that they no longer are. (And being sure is worth something, by the way, unless you would have preferred to take Saddam's word for it.) So, should it now be my own turn? What did I most get wrong? Hell, I'm not feeling masochistic today. But come on, Hitchens, the right-thinking now insist that you concede at least *something*.

The thing that I most underestimated is the thing that least undermines the case. And it's not something that I overlooked, either. But the extent of lumpen Islamization in Iraq, on both the Khomeinist and Wahhabi ends (call them Shiite and Sunni if you want a euphemism that insults the majority), was worse than I had guessed.

And this is also why I partly think that Colin Powell, as reported by Woodward, was right. He apparently asked the president if he was willing to assume, or to accept, responsibility for the Iraqi state and society. The only possible answer, morally and politically, would have been "yes." The United States had already made itself co-responsible for Iraqi life, first by imposing the sanctions, second by imposing the no-fly zones, and third by co-existing with the regime. (Three more factors, by the way, that make the Vietnam comparison utterly meaningless.) This half-slave/half-free compromise could not long have endured.

The antiwar Left used to demand the lifting of sanctions without conditions, which would only have gratified Saddam Hussein and his sons and allowed them to rearm. The supposed neutrals, such as Russia and France and the United Nations, were acting as knowing profiteers in a disgusting oil-for-bribes program that has now been widely exposed. The regime-change forces said, in effect: Lift the sanctions and remove the regime. But in the wasted decade of sanctions-plus-Saddam, a whole paranoid and wretched fundamentalist underclass was created and exploited by the increasingly Islamist propaganda of the Baath Party. This also helps explain the many overlooked convergences between the supposedly "secular" Baathists and the forces of jihad.

When fools say that the occupation has "united" Sunni and Shiite, they flatter the alliance between the proxies of the Iranian mullahs and the Saudi princes. And they ignore the many pleas from disputed and distraught towns, from Iraqis who beg not to be abandoned to these sadistic and corrupt riffraff. One might have seen this coming with greater prescience. But it would have made it even more important not to leave Iraq to the post-Saddam plans of such factions. There was no way around our adoption of Iraq, as there still is not. It's only a pity that the decision to intervene was left until so many years had been consumed by the locust.

Slate, April 19, 2004

NOTE

1. See Pollack's contribution to "Liberal Hawks Reconsider the Iraq War," *Slate*, January 12, 2004.

⊰(29)⊱

Abu Ghraib Isn't Guernica

Ian McEwan observed recently that there were, in effect, two kinds of people: those who could have used or recognized the words "Abu Ghraib" a few years ago, and those to whom it became a new term only last year. And what a resonant name it has indeed become. Now the Colombian painter Fernando Botero has produced a sequence of lurid and haunting pictures, based on the photographs taken by American war criminals, with which he hopes to draw attention to the horrors inflicted there. But his true ambition, he says, is to do for Abu Ghraib what Picasso did for Guernica.

The first of these ambitions is probably otiose: Where in the world are the images of Abu Ghraib not already notorious? (One of the cleansers of Darfur, only recently, employed them as a *tu quoque* to pre-empt any American condemnation of his activities.)

The second ambition is a bit dubious. It's also a bit stale: An article by Jonathan Steele in Britain's *Guardian* has already employed the Guernica comparison—this time to compare it to the US Marine Corps' re-taking of Fallujah.

Guernica did have a certain reputation, as a town, before it was immortalized by Pablo Picasso. It was the historic capital of the Basques of Spain, and its famous oak tree was the spot where Spanish monarchs took an oath to protect Basque liberties. Its destruction from the air by German aircraft allied with Gen. Franco was considered not just an atrocity in itself, but a warning of a future Nazi blitzkrieg against Europe, and this is the potency that the painting still possesses, even if you agree with the Marxist and Third-Worldist art critic John Berger, in his *The Success and Failure of Picasso*, that it was one of the master's crudest works.

Abu Ghraib was by no means celebrated as an ancestral civic and cultural center before the year 2004. To the Iraqis, it was a name to be mentioned in whispers, if at all, as "the house of the end." It was a Dachau. Numberless people were consigned there and were never heard of again. Its execution shed worked overtime, as did its torturers, and we are still trying to discover how many Iraqis and Kurds died in its precincts. At one point, when it suffered even more than usual from chronic overcrowding, Saddam and his sons decided to execute a proportion of the inmates at random, just to cull the population. The warders then fanned out at night to visit the families of the prisoners, asking how much it would be worth to keep their son or brother or father off the list. The hands of prisoners were cut off, and the proceedings recorded on video for the delight of others. I myself became certain that Saddam had reached his *fin de régime*, or his Ceaușescu moment, when he celebrated his 100-percent win in the "referendum" of 2003 by releasing all the nonpolitical prisoners (the rapists and thieves and murderers who were his natural constituency) from Abu Ghraib. This sudden flood of ex-cons was a large factor in the horrific looting and mayhem that accompanied the fall of Baghdad.

I visited the jail a few months later, and I can tell you about everything but the stench, which you would have to smell for yourself. Layers of excrement and filth were being shoveled out; cells obviously designed for the vilest treatment of human beings made one recoil. In the huge, dank, cement gallery where the executions took place, a series of hooks and rings hung over a gruesome pit. Efforts were being made to repaint and disinfect the joint, and many of the new inmates were being held in encampments in the yard while this was being done, but I distinctly remember thinking that there was really no salvaging such a place and that it should either be torn down and ploughed over or turned into a museum.

Instead, it became an improvised center for anyone caught in the dragnet of the "insurgency" and was filled up with suspects as well as armed supporters of Baathism and bin Ladenism. There's no need to restate what everyone now knows about what happened as a consequence. But I am not an apologist if I point out that there are no more hangings, random or systematic. The outrages committed by Pvt. England and her delightful boyfriend were first uncovered by their superiors. And seven of Saddam's amputees—those whose mutilations were filmed and distributed as a warning—have been flown to Houston, Texas—Texas, capital of redneck barbarism!—to be fitted with new prosthetic hands. A film about this latter episode, titled *A Show of Hands*, has been made by Don North and was, I believe, shown on the

Al Hurra network. But I don't think that 1-in-100,000,000 people has seen it; certainly nobody in comparison with the universal dissemination of photographs of recreational sadism. Sr. Botero, who usually works with flab, has done some leaner and meaner paintings in this case. But they resemble less the metaphors of Picasso than the starkly literal efforts of Goya to represent the crumpled and twisted bodies of the second of May. And that is somehow appropriate, since Goya was divided in his own mind between Spanish patriotism and a covert sympathy for the Napoleonic forces, which, even at second hand, were bringing the principles of 1789 to his own benighted state.

The superficially clever thing to say today is that Lynndie England represents all of us, or at any rate all her superiors, and that the liberation of Iraq is thereby discredited. One odd effect of this smug view is to find her and her scummy friends—the actual inflictors of pain and humiliation—somehow innocent, while those senior officers who arrested them and put them on trial are somehow guilty. There is something faintly masochistic and indecent about that conclusion.

There's also something indecent about any comparison of this with the struggle of the Spanish Republic. If Fallujah is "Guernica," then the US Marines are Herman Goering's Condor Legion. If Abu Ghraib is "Guernica," then the US Army is a part of the original "Axis" between Hitler, Mussolini, and Franco. I wonder if any sympathizer of this view would accept its apparent corollary: that the executions and tortures inflicted by the Spanish Communists—crimes now denied by nobody, though Picasso excused them at the time—axiomatically discredit the anti-fascist cause? And this distortion of the record is all the more extraordinary, since a much more natural analogy is close at hand. Gen. Franco's assault on the Spanish Republic—an assault that claimed to be, and was, a rebel "insurgency" against the elected government—consisted of an alliance of fascist parties, religious extremists, and Muslim fighters. It was led by the frightened former oligarchy, and its cause was preached from the pulpit, and its foot-soldiers were Moorish levies from North Africa and "volunteers" from Germany and Italy. How shady it is that our modern leftists and peaceniks can detect fascism absolutely everywhere except when it is actually staring them in the face. The next thing, of course, if we complete the historic analogy, would be for them to sign a pact with it. And this, some of them have already done.

Slate, May 9, 2005

⊲(30)⊳

History and Mystery

When the *New York Times* scratches its head, get ready for total baldness as you tear out your hair. A doozy classic led the "Week in Review" section on Sunday. Portentously headed "The Mystery of the Insurgency," the article rubbed its eyes at the sheer lunacy and sadism of the Iraqi car bombers and random murderers. At a time when new mass graves are being filled, and old ones are still being dug up, writer James Bennet practically pleaded with the authors of both to come up with an intelligible (or defensible?) reason for his paper to go on calling them "insurgents."

I don't think the *New York Times* ever referred to those who devastated its hometown's downtown as "insurgents." But it does employ this title every day for the gang headed by Abu Musab al-Zarqawi. With pedantic exactitude, and unless anyone should miss the point, this man has named his organization "Al Qaeda in Mesopotamia" and sought (and apparently received) Osama bin Laden's permission for the franchise. Did Al Qaeda show "interest in winning hearts and minds . . . in building international legitimacy . . . in articulating a governing program or even a unified ideology," or any of the other things plaintively mentioned as lacking by Mr. Bennet?

The answer, if we remember our ABC, is yes and no, with yes at least to the third part of the question. The bin Ladenists did have a sort of "governing program," expressed in part by their Taliban allies and patrons. This in turn reflected a "unified ideology." It can be quite easily summarized: the return of the Ottoman Empire under a caliphate and a return to the desert religious purity of the seventh century (not quite the same things, but that's not our fault). In the meantime, anyway, war to the end against Jews, Hindus, Christians, unbelievers, and Shiites. None of the "experts" quoted in the article appeared to have remembered these essentials of the Al Qaeda program, but had they done so, they might not be so astounded at the promiscuous way in which the Iraqi gangsters pump out toxic anti-Semitism, slaughter Nepalese and other Asian guest-workers on video and gloat over the death of Hindus, burn out and blow up the Iraqi Christian minority, kidnap any Westerner who catches their eye, and regularly inflict massacres and bombings on Shiite mosques, funerals, and assemblies.

A letter from Zarqawi to bin Laden more than a year ago, intercepted by Kurdish intelligence and since then well-authenticated, spoke of Shiism as a repulsive heresy and the ignition of a Sunni-Shiite civil war as the best and easiest way to thwart the Crusader-Zionist coalition. The actions since then have precisely followed the design, but the design has been forgotten by the journal of record. The bin Laden and Zarqawi organizations, and their co-thinkers in other countries, have gone to great pains to announce, on several occasions, that they will win because they love death, while their enemies are so soft and degenerate that they prefer life. Are we supposed to think that they were just boasting when they said this? Their actions demonstrate it every day, and there are burned-out school buses and clinics and hospitals to prove it, as well as mosques (the incineration of which one might think to be a better subject for Islamic protest than a possibly desecrated Quran, in a prison where every inmate is automatically issued with one).

Then we might find a little space for the small question of democracy. The Baath Party's opinion of this can be easily gauged, not just from its record in power but from the rancid prose of its founding fascist fathers. As for the bin Ladenists, they have taken extraordinary pains to say, through the direct statements of Osama and of Zarqawi, that democracy is a vile heresy, a Greek fabrication, and a source of profanity. For the last several weeks, however, the *Times* has been opining every day that the latest hysterical murder campaign is a result of the time it has taken the newly elected Iraqi Assembly to come up with a representative government. The corollary of this mush-headed coverage must be that, if a more representative government were available in these terrible conditions (conditions supplied by the gangsters themselves), the homicide and sabotage would thereby decline. Is there a serious person in the known world who can be brought to believe such self-evident rubbish?

On many occasions, the jihadists in Iraq have been very specific as well as very general. When they murdered Sergio Vieira de Mello, the brilliant and brave UN representative assigned to Baghdad by Kofi Annan, the terrorists' communiqué hailed the death of the man who had so criminally helped Christian East Timor to become independent of Muslim Indonesia. (This was also among the "reasons" given for the bombing of the bar in Bali.) I think I begin to sense the "frustration" of the "insurgents." They keep telling us what they are like and what they want. But do we ever listen? *Nah*. For them, it must be like talking to the wall. Bennet even complains that it's difficult for reporters to get close to the "insurgents": He forgets that his own paper has published a conversation with one of them, in which the man praises the invasion of Kuwait, supports the cleansing of the Kurds, and says that "we cannot accept to live with infidels."

Ah, but why would the "secular" former Baathists join in such theocratic mayhem? Let me see if I can guess. Leaving aside the formation of another well-named group—the Fedayeen Saddam—to perform state-sponsored jihad before the intervention, how did the Baath Party actually rule? Yes, it's coming back to me. By putting every Iraqi citizen in daily fear of his or her life, by random and capricious torture and murder, and by cynical divide-and-rule among Sunnis, Shiites, and Kurds. Does this remind you of anything?

That's not to say that the paper doesn't have a long memory. Having once read in high school that violence is produced by underlying social conditions, the author of this appalling article refers in lenient terms to "the goal of ridding Iraq of an American presence, a goal that may find sympathy among Iraqis angry about poor electricity and water service and high unemployment." Bet you hadn't thought of that: The water and power are intermittent, so let's go and blow up the generating stations and the oil pipelines. No job? Shoot up the people waiting to register for employment. To the insult of flattering the psychopaths, Bennet adds his condescension to the suffering of ordinary Iraqis, who are murdered every day while trying to keep essential services running.

(Baathism, by the way, comes in very handy in crippling these, because the secret police of the old regime know how things operate, as well as where everybody lives. Or perhaps you think that the attacks are so "deadly" because the bombers get lucky seven days a week?)

This campaign of horror began before Baghdad fell, with the execution and mutilation of those who dared to greet American and British troops. It continued with the looting of the Baghdad museum and other sites, long before there could have been any complaint about the failure to restore power or security. It is an attempt to put Iraqi Arabs and Kurds, many of them still traumatized by decades of well-founded fear, back under the heel of the Baath Party or under a home-grown Taliban, or the combination of both that would also have been the Uday/Qusay final solution. Half-conceding the usefulness of chaos and misery in bringing this about, Bennet in his closing paragraph compares jihadism to 19th-century anarchism, which shows that he hasn't read Proudhon, Bakunin or Kropotkin either.

In my ears, "insurgent" is a bit like "rebel" or even "revolutionary." There's nothing axiomatically pejorative about it, and some passages of history have made it a term of honor. At a minimum, though, it must mean "rising up." These fascists and hirelings are not rising up, they are stamping back down. It's time for respectable outlets to drop the word, to call things by their right names (Baathist or bin Ladenist or jihadist would all do in this case), and to stop inventing mysteries where none exist.

Slate, May 16, 2005

⟨ 31 ⟩

Unmitigated Galloway

Every journalist has a list of regrets: of stories that might have been. Somewhere on my personal list is an invitation I received several years ago, from a then-Labour Member of Parliament named George Galloway. Would I care, he inquired, to join him on a chartered plane to

Baghdad? He was hoping to call attention to the sufferings of the Iraqi people under sanctions, and had long been an admirer of my staunch and muscular prose and my commitment to universal justice (I paraphrase only slightly). Indeed, in an article in a Communist party newspaper in 2001 he referred to me as "that great British man of letters" and "the greatest polemicist of our age."

No thanks, was my reply. I had my own worries about the sanctions, but I had also already been on an officially guided visit to Saddam's Iraq and had decided that the next time I went to that terrorized slum it would be with either the Kurdish guerrillas or the US Marines. (I've since fulfilled both ambitions.) Moreover, I knew a bit about Galloway. He had had to resign as the head of a charity called "War on Want," after repaying some disputed expenses for living the high life in dirt-poor countries. Indeed, he was a type well known in the Labour movement. Prolier than thou, and ostentatiously radical, but a bit too fond of the cigars and limos and always looking a bit odd in a suit that was slightly too expensive. By turns aggressive and unctuous, either at your feet or at your throat; a bit of a backslapper, nothing's too good for the working class: what the English call a "wide boy."

This was exactly his demeanor when I ran into him last Tuesday on the sidewalk of Constitution Avenue, outside the Dirksen Senate Office Building, where he was due to testify before the subcommittee that has been uncovering the looting of the UN Oil-for-Food program. His short, cocky frame was enveloped in a thicket of recording equipment, and he was holding forth almost uninterrupted until I asked him about his endorsement of Saddam Hussein's payment for suicide-murderers in Israel and the occupied territories. He had evidently been admirably consistent in his attention to my humble work, because he changed tone and said that this was just what he'd expect from a "drink-sodden ex-Trotskyist popinjay." It takes a little more than this to wound your correspondent—I could still hold a martini without spilling it when I was "the greatest polemicist of our age" in 2001—but please note that the real thrust is contained in the word "Trotskyist." Galloway says that the worst day of his entire life was the day the Soviet Union fell. His existence since that dreadful event has involved the pathetic search for an alternative fatherland. He has recently written that, "just as Stalin industrialized the Soviet Union, so on a different scale Saddam plotted Iraq's own Great Leap Forward." I love the word "scale" in that sentence. I also admire the use of the word "plotted."

As it happens, I adore the street-fight and soap-box side of political life, so that when the cluster had moved inside, and when Galloway had taken his seat flanked by his aides and guards, I decided to deny him the 10 minutes of unmolested time that otherwise awaited him before the session began. Denouncing the hearings as a show-trial the previous week, he had claimed that he had written several times to the subcommittee (whose members he has publicly called "lickspittles") asking to be allowed to clear his name, and been ignored. The subcommittee staff denies possessing any record of such an overture. Taking a position near where he was sitting, I asked him loudly if he had brought a copy of his letter, or letters. A fresh hose of abuse was turned upon me, but I persisted in asking, and after awhile others joined in—receiving no answer—so at least he didn't get to sit gravely like a volunteer martyr.

Senators Norm Coleman and Carl Levin then began the proceedings, and staff members went through a meticulous presentation, with documents and boards, showing the paperwork of the Iraqi State Oil Marketing Organization and the Iraqi Oil Ministry. These were augmented by testimony from an (unnamed) "senior Saddam regime official," who had vouched for the authenticity of the provenance and the signatures. The exhibits clearly showed that pro-Saddam political figures in France and Russia, and at least one American oil company, had earned the right to profit from illegal oil-trades, and had sweetened the pot by kicking back a percentage to Saddam's personal palace-building and mass grave-digging fund.

In several cases, the documents suggested that a man named Fawaz Zureikat, a Jordanian tycoon, had been intimately involved in these transactions. Galloway's name also appears in parentheses on the Zureikat papers—perhaps as an *aide-memoire* to those processing them—but you must keep in mind that the material does not show transfers directly to Galloway himself; only to Zureikat, his patron and partner and friend. In an analogous way, one cannot accuse Scott Ritter, who made a ferocious documentary attacking the Iraq war, of being in Iraqi pay. One may be aware, though, that the Iraqi-American businessman who financed that film, Shakir al-Khafaji, has since shown up in the captured Oil-for-Food correspondence.

After about 90 minutes of this cumulative testimony, Galloway was seated and sworn, and the humiliation began. The humiliation of the deliberative body, I mean. I once sat in the hearing room while a uniformed Oliver North hectored a Senate committee and instructed the legislative branch in its duties, and not since that day have I felt such alarm and frustration and disgust. Galloway has learned to master the word "neocon" and the acronym "AIPAC," and he insulted the subcommittee for its deference to both of these. He took up much of his time in a demagogic attack on the lie-generated war in Iraq. He announced that he had never traded in a single barrel of oil, and he declared that he had never been a public supporter of the Saddam Hussein regime. As I had guessed he would, he made the most of the anonymity of the "senior Saddam regime official," and protested at not knowing the identity of his accuser. He improved on this by suggesting that the person concerned might now be in a cell in Abu Ghraib.

In a small way—an exceedingly small way—this had the paradoxical effect of making me proud to be British. Parliament trains its sons in a hard school of debate and unscripted exchange, and so does the British Labour movement. You get your retaliation in first, you rise to a point of order, you heckle and you watch out for hecklers. The torpid majesty of a Senate proceeding does nothing to prepare you for a Galloway, who is in addition a man without embarrassment who has stayed just on the right side of many inquiries into his character and his accounting methods. He has, for example, temporarily won a libel case against the *Daily Telegraph* in London, which printed similar documents about him that were found in the Oil Ministry just after the fall of Baghdad. The newspaper claimed a public-interest defense, and did not explicitly state that the documents were genuine. Galloway, for his part, carefully did not state that they were false, either. The case has now gone to appeal.

When estimating the propensity of anyone to take money or gifts, one must also balance the propensity of a regime to offer them. I once had an Iraqi diplomat contact in London, who later became one of Saddam's ministers. After inviting him to dinner one night, I noticed that he had wordlessly left a handsome bag, which contained a small but nice rug, several boxes of Cuban cigars (which I don't smoke), and several bottles of single malt Scotch. I was at the time a fairly junior editor at a socialist weekly. More recently, I have interviewed a very senior and reliable UN arms inspector in Iraq, who was directly offered an enormous bribe by Tariq Aziz himself, and who duly reported the fact to the US government. If the Baathists would risk approaching this particular man, it seems to me, they must have tried it with practically everybody. Quite possibly, though, the Saddam regime decided that Galloway was entirely incorruptible, and would consider such an inducement beneath him.

Such speculation to one side, the subcommittee and its staff had a tranche of information on Galloway, and on his record for truthfulness. It would have been a simple matter for them to call him out on a number of things. First of all, and easiest, he had dared to state under oath that he had not been a defender of the Saddam regime. This, from the man who visited Baghdad after the first Gulf war and, addressing Saddam, said: "Sir, I salute your courage, your strength, your indefatigability." How's that for lickspittling? And even if you make allowances for emotional public moments, you can't argue with Galloway's own autobiography, blush-makingly entitled *I'm Not the Only One*, which was published last spring and from which I offer the following extracts:

The state of Kuwait is "clearly a part of the greater Iraqi whole, stolen from the motherland by perfidious Albion." (Kuwait existed long before Iraq had even been named.) "In my experience none of the Baath leaders have displayed any hostility to Jews." The post–Gulf war massacres of Kurds and Shia in 1991 were part of "a civil war that involved massive violence on both sides." Asked about Saddam's palaces after one of his many fraternal visits, he remarked, "Our own head of state has a fair bit of real estate herself." Her Majesty the Queen and her awful brood may take up a lot of room, but it's hardly comparable to one palace per province, built during a time of famine. Discussing Saddam's direct payments to the families of suicide-murderers—the very question he had refused to answer when I asked him—he once again lapsed into accidental accuracy, as with the Stalin comparison, and said that "as the martyred know, he put Iraq's money where his mouth was." That's true enough: It was indeed Iraq's money, if a bit more than Saddam's mouth.

At the hearing, also, Galloway was half-correct in yelling at the subcommittee that he had been a critic of Saddam Hussein when Donald Rumsfeld was still making friendly visits to Baghdad. Here, a brief excursion into the aridities of Left history may elucidate more than the Galloway phenomenon.

There came a time, in the late 1970s, when the Iraqi Communist party realized the horrific mistake it had made in joining the Baath party's Revolutionary Command Council. The Communists in Baghdad, as I can testify from personal experience and interviews at the time, began to protest—too late—at the unbelievable cruelty of Saddam's purge of the army and the state: a prelude to his seizure of total power in a full-blown fascist coup. The consequence of this, in Britain, was the setting-up of a group named CARDRI: the Campaign Against Repression and for Democratic Rights in Iraq. Many democratic socialists and liberals supported this organization, but there was no doubting that its letterhead and its active staff were Communist volunteers. And Galloway joined it. At the time, it is at least half true to say, the United States distinctly preferred Saddam's Iraq to Khomeini's Iran, and acted accordingly. Thus a leftist could attack Saddam for being, among other things, an American client. We ought not to forget the shame of American policy at that time, because the preference for Saddam outlived the war with Iran, and continued into the postwar Anfal campaign to exterminate the Kurds. In today's "antiwar" movement, you may still hear the echoes of that filthy compromise, in the pseudo-ironic jibe that "we" used to be Saddam's ally.

But mark the sequel. It must have been in full knowledge, then, of that repression, and that genocide, and of the invasion of Kuwait and all that ensued from it, that George Galloway shifted his position and became an outright partisan of the Iraqi Baath. There can be only two explanations for this, and they do not by any means exclude one another. The first explanation, which would apply to many leftists of different stripes, is that anti-Americanism simply trumps everything, and that once Saddam Hussein became an official enemy of Washington the whole case was altered. Given what Galloway has said at other times, in defense of Slobodan Milosevic for example, it is fair to assume that he would have taken such a position for nothing: without, in other words, the hope of remuneration.

There was another faction, however, that was, relatively speaking, nonpolitical. During the imposition of international UN sanctions on Iraq, and the creation of the Oil-for-Food system, it swiftly became known to a class of middlemen that lavish pickings were to be had by anyone who could boast an insider contact in Baghdad. This much is well known and has been solidly established, by the Volcker report and by the Senate subcommittee. During the material time, George Galloway received hard-to-get visas for Iraq on multiple occasions, and admits to at least two personal meetings with Saddam Hussein and more than ten with his "dear friend" Tariq Aziz. But as far as is known by me, he confined his activity on these occasions to pro-regime propaganda, with Iraqi crowds often turned out by the authorities to applaud him, and provide a useful platform in both parliament and the press back home.

However, his friend and business partner, Fawaz Zureikat, didn't concern himself so much with ideological questions (though he did try to set up a broadcasting service for Saddam). He was, as Galloway happily testified, involved in a vast range of deals in Baghdad. But Galloway's admitted knowledge of this somehow does not extend to Zureikat's involvement in any Oil-for-Food transactions, which are now *prima facie* established in black and white by the subcommittee's report. Galloway, indeed, has arranged to be adequately uninformed about this for some time now: It is two years since he promised the BBC that he would establish and make known the facts about his Zureikat connection.

Here then are these facts, as we know them without his help. In 1998, Galloway founded something, easily confused with a charity, known as the Mariam Appeal. The ostensible aim of the appeal was to provide treatment in Britain for a 4-year-old Iraqi girl named Mariam Hamza, who suffered from leukemia. An announced secondary aim was to campaign against the sanctions then in force, and still a third, somewhat occluded, aim was to state that Mariam Hamza and many others like her had contracted cancer from the use of depleted-uranium shells by American forces in the first Gulf war. A letter exists, on

House of Commons writing paper, signed by Galloway and appointing Fawaz Zureikat as his personal representative in Iraq, on any and all matters connected to the Mariam Appeal.

Although it was briefly claimed by one of its officers that the Appeal raised most of its money from ordinary citizens, Galloway has since testified that the bulk of the revenue came from the ruler of the United Arab Emirates and from a Saudi prince. He has also conceded that Zureikat was a very generous donor. The remainder of the funding is somewhat opaque, since the British Charity Commissioners, who monitor such things, began an investigation in 2003. This investigation was inconclusive. The commissioners were able to determine that the Mariam Appeal, which had used much of its revenue for political campaigning, had not but ought to have been legally registered as a charity. They were not able to determine much beyond this, because it was then announced that the account books of the Appeal had been removed, first to Amman, Jordan, and then to Baghdad. This is the first charity or proto-charity in history to have disposed of its records in that way.

To this day, George Galloway defiantly insists, as he did before the senators, that he has "never seen a barrel of oil, owned one, bought one, sold one, and neither has anybody on my behalf." As a Clintonian defense this has its admirable points: I myself have never seen a kilowatt, but I know that a barrel is also a unit and not an entity. For the rest, his defense would be more impressive if it answered any charge that has actually been made. Galloway is not supposed by anyone to have been an oil trader. He is asked, simply, to say what he knows about his chief fundraiser, nominee, and crony. And when asked this, he flatly declines to answer. We are therefore invited by him to assume that, having earlier acquired a justified reputation for loose bookkeeping in respect of "charities," he switched sides in Iraq, attached himself to a regime known for giving and receiving bribes, appointed a notorious middleman as his envoy, kept company with the corrupt inner circle of the Baath party, helped organize a vigorous campaign to retain that party in power, and was not a penny piece the better off for it. I think I believe this as readily as any other reasonable and objective person would. If you wish to pursue the matter with Galloway himself, you will have to find the unlisted number for his villa in Portugal.

Even if the matter of subornation and bribery had never arisen, there would remain the crucial question of Iraq itself. It was said during the time of sanctions on that long-suffering country that the embargo was killing, or had killed, as many as a million people, many of them infants. Give credit to the accusers here. Some of the gravamen of the charge must be true. Add the parasitic regime to the sanctions, over 12 years, and it is clear that the suffering of average Iraqis must have been inordinate.

There are only two ways this suffering could have been relieved. Either the sanctions could have been lifted, as Galloway and others demanded, or the regime could have been removed. The first policy, if followed without conditions, would have untied the hands of Saddam. The second policy would have had the dual effect of ending sanctions and terminating a hideous and lawless one-man rule. But when the second policy was proposed, the streets filled with people who absolutely opposed it. Saying farewell to the regime was, evidently, too high a price to pay for relief from sanctions.

Let me phrase this another way: Those who had alleged that a million civilians were dying from sanctions were willing, nay eager, to keep those same murderous sanctions if it meant preserving Saddam! This is repellent enough in itself. If the Saddam regime was cheating its terrified people of food and medicine in order to finance its own propaganda, that would perhaps be in character. But if it were to be discovered that any third parties had profited from the persistence of "sanctions plus regime," prolonging the agony and misery thanks to personal connections, then one would have to become quite judgmental.

The bad faith of a majority of the Left is instanced by four things (apart, that is, from mass demonstrations in favor of prolonging the life of a fascist government). First, the antiwar forces never asked the Iraqi Left what it wanted, because they would have heard very clearly that their comrades wanted the overthrow of Saddam. (President Jalal Talabani's party, for example, is a member in good standing of the Socialist International.) This is a betrayal of what used to be called internationalism. Second, the Left decided to scab and blackleg on the Kurds, whose struggle is the oldest cause of the Left in the Middle East. Third, many leftists and liberals stressed the cost of the Iraq intervention as against the cost of domestic expenditure, when if they had been looking for zero-sum comparisons they might have been expected to cite waste in certain military programs, or perhaps the cost of the "war on drugs." This, then, was mere cynicism. Fourth, and as mentioned, their humanitarian talk about the sanctions turned out to be the most inexpensive hypocrisy.

George Galloway—having been rightly expelled by the British Labour party for calling for "jihad" against British troops, and having since then hailed the nihilism and sadism and sectarianism that goes by the lazy name of the Iraqi "insurgency" or, in his circles, "resistance"—ran for election in a new seat in East London and was successful in unseating the Labour incumbent. His party calls itself RESPECT, which stands for "Respect, Equality, Socialism, Peace, Environment, Community, Trade Unionism." (So that really ought to be RESPECTU, except that it would then sound less like an Aretha Franklin song and more like an organ of the Romanian state under Ceaușescu.)

The defeated incumbent, Oona King, is of mixed African and Jewish heritage, and had to endure an appalling whispering campaign, based on her sex and her combined ethnicities. Who knows who started this torrent of abuse? Galloway certainly has, once again, remained adequately uninformed about it. His chief appeal was to the militant Islamist element among Asian immigrants who live in large numbers in his district, and his main organizational muscle was provided by a depraved sub-Leninist sect called the Socialist Workers party. The servants of the one god finally meet the votaries of the one-party state. Perfect. To this most opportunist of alliances, add some Tory and Liberal Democrat "actical voters" whose hatred of Tony Blair eclipses everything else.

Perhaps I may be allowed a closing moment of sentiment here? To the Left, the old East End of London was once near-sacred ground. It was here in 1936 that a massive demonstration of longshoremen, artisans, and Jewish refugees and migrants made a human wall and drove back a determined attempt by Sir Oswald Mosley's Blackshirts to mount a march of intimidation. The event is still remembered locally as "The Battle of Cable Street." That part of London, in fact, was one of the few places in Europe where the attempt to raise the emblems of fascism was defeated by force.

And now, on the same turf, there struts a little popinjay who defends dictatorship abroad and who trades on religious sectarianism at home. Within a month of his triumph in a British election, he has flown to Washington and spat full in the face of the Senate. A megaphone media in London, and a hysterical fan-club of fundamentalists and political thugs, saw to it that he returned as a conquering hero and all-round celeb. If only the supporters of regime change, and the friends of the Afghan and Iraqi and Kurdish peoples, could manifest anything like the same resolve and determination.

Weekly Standard, May 30, 2005

⊰(32)⊱

Losing the Iraq War

Another request in my in-box, asking if I'll be interviewed about Iraq for a piece "dealing with how writers and intellectuals are dealing with the state of the war, whether it's causing depression of any sort, if people are rethinking their positions or if they simply aren't talking about it." I suppose that I'll keep on being asked this until I give the right answer, which I suspect is "Uncle."

There is a sort of unspoken feeling, underlying the entire debate on the war, that if you favored it or favor it, you stress the good news, and if you opposed or oppose it you stress the bad. I do not find myself on either side of this false dichotomy. I think that those who supported regime change should confront the idea of defeat, and what it would mean for Iraq and America and the world, every day. It is a combat defined very much by the nature of the enemy, which one might think was so obviously and palpably evil that the very thought of its victory would make any decent person shudder. It is, moreover, a critical front in a much wider struggle against a vicious and totalitarian ideology.

It never seemed to me that there was any alternative to confronting the reality of Iraq, which was already on the verge of implosion and might, if left to rot and crash, have become to the region what the

Congo is to Central Africa: a vortex of chaos and misery that would draw in opportunistic interventions from Turkey, Iran, and Saudi Arabia. Bad as Iraq may look now, it is nothing to what it would have become without the steadying influence of coalition forces. None of the many blunders in postwar planning make any essential difference to that conclusion. Indeed, by drawing attention to the ruined condition of the Iraqi society and its infrastructure, they serve to reinforce the point.

How can so many people watch this as if they were spectators, handicapping and rating the successes and failures from some imagined position of neutrality? Do they suppose that a defeat in Iraq would be a defeat only for the Bush administration? The United States is awash in human rights groups, feminist organizations, ecological foundations, and committees for the rights of minorities. How come there is not a huge voluntary effort to help and to publicize the efforts to find the hundreds of thousands of "missing" Iraqis, to support Iraqi women's battle against fundamentalists, to assist in the recuperation of the marsh Arab wetlands, and to underwrite the struggle of the Kurds, the largest stateless people in the Middle East? Is Abu Ghraib really the only subject that interests our humanitarians?

The *New York Times* ran a fascinating report, under the byline of James Glanz, on July 8. It was a profile of Dr. Alaa Tamimi, the mayor of Baghdad, whose position it would be a gross understatement to describe as "embattled." Dr. Tamimi is a civil engineer and convinced secularist who gave up a prosperous exile in Canada to come home and help rebuild his country. He is one among millions who could emerge if it were not for the endless, pitiless torture to which the city is subjected by violent religious fascists. He is quoted as being full of ideas, of a somewhat Giuliani-like character, about zoning enforcement, garbage recycling, and zero tolerance for broken windows. If this doesn't seem quixotic enough in today's gruesome circumstances, he also has to confront religious parties on the city council and an inept central government that won't give him a serious budget.

Question: Why have several large American cities not already announced that they are going to become sister cities with Baghdad and help raise money and awareness to aid Dr. Tamimi? When I put this question to a number of serious anti-war friends, their answer was to the effect that it's the job of the administration to allocate the money, so that there's little room or need for civic action. I find this difficult to credit: For day after day last month I could not escape the news of the gigantic "Live 8" enterprise, which urged governments to do more along existing lines by way of debt relief and aid for Africa. Isn't there a single drop of solidarity and compassion left over for the people of Iraq, after three decades of tyranny, war, and sanctions and now an assault from the vilest movement on the face of the planet? Unless someone gives me a persuasive reason to think otherwise, my provisional conclusion is that the human rights and charitable "communities" have taken a pass on Iraq for political reasons that are not very creditable. And so we watch with detached curiosity, from dry land, to see whether the Iraqis will sink or swim. For shame.

Slate, August 8, 2005

⁖(33)⁖

A War to Be Proud Of

Let me begin with a simple sentence that, even as I write it, appears less than Swiftian in the modesty of its proposal: "Prison conditions at Abu Ghraib have improved markedly and dramatically since the arrival of Coalition troops in Baghdad."

I could undertake to defend that statement against any member of Human Rights Watch or Amnesty International, and I know in advance that none of them could challenge it, let alone negate it. Before March 2003, Abu Ghraib was an abattoir, a torture chamber, and a concentration camp. Now, and not without reason, it is an international byword for Yankee imperialism and sadism. Yet the improvement is still, unarguably, the difference between night and day. How is it possible that the advocates of a post-Saddam Iraq have been placed on the defensive in this manner? And where should one begin?

I once tried to calculate how long the post–Cold War liberal Utopia had actually lasted. Whether you chose to date its inception from the fall of the Berlin Wall in November 1989, or the death of Nicolae Ceaușescu in late December of the same year, or the release of Nelson Mandela from prison, or the referendum defeat suffered by Augusto Pinochet (or indeed from the publication of Francis Fukuyama's book about the "end of history" and the unarguable triumph of market liberal pluralism), it was an epoch that in retrospect was over before it began. By the middle of 1990, Saddam Hussein had abolished Kuwait and Slobodan Milosevic was attempting to erase the identity and the existence of Bosnia. It turned out that we had not by any means escaped the reach of atavistic, aggressive, expansionist, and totalitarian ideology. Proving the same point in another way, and within approximately the same period, the theocratic dictator of Iran had publicly claimed the right to offer money in his own name for the suborning of the murder of a novelist living in London, and the *génocidaire* faction in Rwanda had decided that it could probably get away with putting its long-fantasized plan of mass murder into operation.

One is not mentioning these apparently discrepant crimes and nightmares as a random or unsorted list. Khomeini, for example, was attempting to compensate for the humiliation of the peace agreement he had been compelled to sign with Saddam Hussein. And Saddam Hussein needed to make up the loss, of prestige and income, that he had himself suffered in the very same war. Milosevic (anticipating Putin, as it now seems to me, and perhaps Beijing also) was riding a mutation of socialist nationalism into national socialism. It was to be noticed in all cases that the aggressors, whether they were killing Muslims, or exalting Islam, or just killing their neighbors, shared a deep and abiding hatred of the United States.

The balance sheet of the Iraq war, if it is to be seriously drawn up, must also involve a confrontation with at least this much of recent history. Was the Bush administration right to leave—actually to confirm—Saddam Hussein in power after his eviction from Kuwait in 1991? Was James Baker correct to say, in his delightfully folksy manner, that the United States did not "have a dog in the fight" that involved ethnic cleansing for the mad dream of a Greater Serbia? Was the Clinton administration prudent in its retreat from Somalia, or wise in its opposition to the UN resolution that called for a preemptive strengthening of the UN forces in Rwanda?

I know hardly anybody who comes out of this examination with complete credit. There were neoconservatives who jeered at Rushdie in 1989 and who couldn't see the point when Sarajevo faced obliteration in 1992. There were leftist humanitarians and radicals who rallied to Rushdie and called for solidarity with Bosnia, but who—perhaps because of a bad conscience about Palestine—couldn't face a confrontation with Saddam Hussein even when he annexed a neighbor state that was a full member of the Arab League and of the UN (I suppose I have to admit that I was for a time a member of that second group). But there were consistencies, too. French statecraft, for example, was uniformly hostile to any resistance to any aggression, and Paris even sent troops to rescue its filthy clientele in Rwanda. And some on the hard Left and the brute Right were also opposed to any exercise, for any reason, of American military force.

The only speech by any statesman that can bear reprinting from that low, dishonest decade came from Tony Blair when he spoke in Chicago in 1999. Welcoming the defeat and overthrow of Milosevic after the Kosovo intervention, he warned against any self-satisfaction and drew attention to an inescapable confrontation that was coming with Saddam Hussein. So far from being an American "poodle," as his taunting and ignorant foes like to sneer, Blair had in fact leaned on Clinton over Kosovo and was insisting on the importance of Iraq while George Bush was still an isolationist governor of Texas.

Notwithstanding this prescience and principle on his part, one still cannot read the journals of the 2000/2001 millennium without the feeling that one is revisiting a hopelessly somnambulist relative in a neglected home. I am one of those who believe, uncynically, that Osama bin Laden did us all a service (and holy war a great disservice) by his mad decision to assault the American homeland four years ago. Had he not made this world-historical mistake, we would have been able to add a Talibanized and nuclear-armed Pakistan to our list of the threats we failed to recognize in time. (This threat still exists, but it is no longer so casually overlooked.)

The subsequent liberation of Pakistan's theocratic colony in Afghanistan, and the so-far decisive eviction and defeat of its bin Ladenist guests, was only a reprisal. It took care of the last attack. But what about the next one? For anyone with eyes to see, there was only one other state that combined the latent and the blatant definitions of both "rogue" and "failed." This state—Saddam's ruined and tortured and collapsing Iraq—had also met all the conditions under which a country may be deemed to have sacrificed its own legal sovereignty. To recapitulate: It had invaded its neighbors, committed genocide on its own soil, harbored and nurtured international thugs and killers, and flouted every provision of the Non-Proliferation Treaty. The United Nations, in this crisis, faced with regular insult to its own resolutions and its own character, had managed to set up a system of sanctions-based mutual corruption. In May 2003, had things gone on as they had been going, Saddam Hussein would have been due to fill Iraq's slot as chair of the UN Conference on Disarmament. Meanwhile, every species of gangster from the hero of the *Achille Lauro* hijacking to Abu Musab al Zarqawi was finding hospitality under Saddam's crumbling roof.

One might have thought, therefore, that Bush and Blair's decision to put an end at last to this intolerable state of affairs would be hailed, not just as a belated vindication of long-ignored UN resolutions but as some corrective to the decade of shame and inaction that had just passed in Bosnia and Rwanda. But such is not the case. An apparent consensus exists, among millions of people in Europe and America, that the whole operation for the demilitarization of Iraq, and the salvage of its traumatized society, was at best a false pretense and at worst an unprovoked aggression. How can this possibly be?

There is, first, the problem of humorless and pseudo-legalistic literalism. In Saki's short story *The Lumber Room*, the naughty but clever child Nicholas, who has actually placed a frog in his morning bread-and-milk, rejoices in his triumph over the adults who don't credit this excuse for not eating his healthful dish: "'You said there couldn't possibly be a frog in my bread-and-milk; there was a frog in my bread-and-milk,' he repeated, with the insistence of a skilled tactician who does not intend to shift from favorable ground." Childishness is one thing—those of us who grew up on this wonderful Edwardian author were always happy to see the grown-ups and governesses discomfited. But puerility in adults is quite another thing, and considerably less charming. "You said there were WMDs in Iraq and that Saddam had friends in Al Qaeda ... Blah, blah, pants on fire." I have had many opportunities to tire of this mantra. It takes ten seconds to intone the said mantra. It would take me, on my most eloquent C-SPAN day, at the very least five minutes to say that Abdul Rahman Yasin, who mixed the chemicals for the World Trade Center attack in 1993, subsequently sought and found refuge in Baghdad; that Dr. Mahdi Obeidi, Saddam's senior physicist, was able to lead American soldiers to nuclear centrifuge parts and a blueprint for a complete centrifuge (the crown jewel of nuclear physics) buried on the orders of Qusay Hussein; that Saddam's agents were in Damascus as late as February 2003, negotiating to purchase missiles off the shelf from North Korea; or that Rolf Ekeus, the great Swedish socialist who founded the inspection process in Iraq after 1991, has told me for the record that he was offered a $2 million bribe in a face-to-face meeting with Tariq Aziz. And these eye-catching examples would by no means exhaust my repertoire, or empty my quiver. Yes, it must be admitted that Bush and Blair made a hash of a good case, largely because they preferred to scare people rather than enlighten them or reason with them. Still, the only real strategy of deception has come from those who believe, or pretend, that Saddam Hussein was no problem.

I have a ready answer to those who accuse me of being an agent and tool of the Bush-Cheney administration (which is the nicest thing that my enemies can find to say). Attempting a little levity, I respond that I could stay at home if the authorities could bother to make their own case, but that I meanwhile am a prisoner of what I actually do know about the permanent hell, and the permanent threat, of the Saddam regime. However, having debated almost all of the spokespeople for the antiwar faction, both the sane and the deranged, I was recently asked a question that I was temporarily unable to answer. "If what you claim is true," the honest citizen at this meeting politely asked me, "how come the White House hasn't told us?"

I do in fact know the answer to this question. So deep and bitter is the split within official Washington, most especially between the Defense Department and the CIA, that any claim made by the former has been undermined by leaks from the latter. (The latter being those who maintained, with a combination of dogmatism and cowardice not seen since Lincoln had to fire General McClellan, that Saddam Hussein was both a "secular" actor and—this is the really rich bit—a rational and calculating one.)

There's no cure for that illusion, but the resulting bureaucratic chaos and unease has cornered the president into his current fall-back upon platitude and hollowness. It has also induced him to give hostages to fortune. The claim that if we fight fundamentalism "over there" we won't have to confront it "over here" is not just a standing invitation for disproof by the next suicide-maniac in London or Chicago, but a coded appeal to provincial and isolationist opinion in the United States. Surely the elementary lesson of the grim anniversary that will shortly be upon us is that American civilians are as near to the front line as American soldiers.

It is exactly this point that makes nonsense of the sob-sister tripe pumped out by the Cindy Sheehan circus and its surrogates. But in reply, why bother to call a struggle "global" if you then try to localize it? Just say plainly that we shall fight them everywhere they show themselves, and fight them on principle as well as in practice, and get ready to warn people that Nigeria is very probably the next target of the jihadists. The peaceniks love to ask: When and where will it all end? The answer is easy: It will end with the surrender or defeat of one of the contending parties. Should I add that I am certain which party that ought to be? Defeat is just about imaginable, though the mathematics and the algebra tell heavily against the holy warriors. Surrender to such a foe, after only four years of combat, is not even worthy of consideration.

Antaeus was able to draw strength from the earth every time an antagonist wrestled him to the ground. A reverse mythology has been permitted to take hold in the present case, where bad news is deemed to be bad news only for regime-change. Anyone with the smallest knowledge of Iraq knows that its society and infrastructure and institutions have been appallingly maimed and beggared by three decades of war and fascism (and the "divide-and-rule" tactics by which Saddam maintained his own tribal minority of the Sunni minority in power). In logic and morality, one must therefore compare the current state of the country with the likely or probable state of it had Saddam and his sons been allowed to go on ruling.

At once, one sees that all the alternatives would have been infinitely worse, and would most likely have led to an implosion—as well as opportunistic invasions from Iran and Turkey and Saudi Arabia, on behalf of their respective interests or confessional clienteles. This would in turn have necessitated a more costly and bloody intervention by some kind of coalition, much too late and on even worse terms and conditions. This is the lesson of Bosnia and Rwanda yesterday, and of Darfur today. When I have made this point in public, I have never had anyone offer an answer to it. A broken Iraq was in our future no matter what, and was a responsibility (somewhat conditioned by our past blunders) that no decent person could shirk. The only unthinkable policy was one of abstention.

Two pieces of good fortune still attend those of us who go out on the road for this urgent and worthy cause. The first is contingent: There are an astounding number of plain frauds and charlatans (to phrase it at its highest) in charge of the propaganda of the other side. Just to tell off the names is to frighten children more than Saki ever could: Michael Moore, George Galloway, Jacques Chirac, Tim Robbins, Richard Clarke, Joseph Wilson . . . a roster of gargoyles that would send Ripley himself into early retirement. Some of these characters are flippant, and make heavy jokes about Halliburton, and some disdain to conceal their sympathy for the opposite side. So that's easy enough.

The second bit of luck is a certain fiber displayed by a huge number of anonymous Americans. Faced with a constant drizzle of bad news and purposely demoralizing commentary, millions of people stick out their jaws and hang tight. I am no fan of populism, but I surmise that these citizens are clear on the main point: It is out of the question—plainly and absolutely out of the question—that we should surrender the keystone state of the Middle East to a rotten, murderous alliance between Baathists and bin Ladenists. When they hear the fatuous insinuation that this alliance has only been created by the resistance to it, voters know in their intestines that those who say so are soft on crime and soft on fascism. The more temperate anti-warriors, such as Mark Danner and Harold Meyerson, like to employ the term "a war of choice." One should have no problem in accepting this concept. As they cannot and do not deny, there was going to be another round with Saddam Hussein no matter what. To whom, then, should the "choice" of time and place have fallen? The clear implication of the anti-choice faction—if I may so dub them—is that this decision should have been left up to Saddam Hussein. As so often before . . .

Does the president deserve the benefit of the reserve of fortitude that I just mentioned? Only just, if at all. We need not argue about the failures and the mistakes and even the crimes, because these in some ways argue themselves. But a positive accounting could be offered without braggartry, and would include:

1. The overthrow of Talibanism and Baathism, and the exposure of many highly suggestive links between the two elements of this Hitler-Stalin pact. Abu Musab al Zarqawi, who moved from Afghanistan to Iraq before the coalition intervention, has even gone to the trouble of naming his organization Al Qaeda in Mesopotamia.
2. The subsequent capitulation of Gaddafi's Libya in point of WMDs—a capitulation that was offered not to Kofi Annan or the EU but to Blair and Bush.
3. The consequent unmasking of the A.Q. Khan network for the illicit transfer of nuclear technology to Libya, Iran, and North Korea.
4. The agreement by the United Nations that its own reform is necessary and overdue, and the unmasking of a quasi-criminal network within its elite.
5. The craven admission by President Chirac and Chancellor Schröder, when confronted with irrefutable evidence of cheating and concealment, respecting solemn treaties, on the part of Iran, that not even this will alter their commitment to neutralism. (One had already suspected as much in the Iraqi case.)
6. The ability to certify Iraq as actually disarmed, rather than accept the word of a psychopathic autocrat.
7. The immense gains made by the largest stateless minority in the region—the Kurds—and the spread of this example to other states.
8. The related encouragement of democratic and civil society movements in Egypt, Syria, and most notably Lebanon, which has regained a version of its autonomy.

9. The violent and ignominious death of thousands of bin Ladenist infiltrators into Iraq and Afghanistan, and the real prospect of greatly enlarging this number.

10. The training and hardening of many thousands of American servicemen and women in a battle against the forces of nihilism and absolutism, which training and hardening will surely be of great use in future combat.

It would be admirable if the president could manage to make such a presentation. It would also be welcome if he and his deputies adopted a clear attitude toward the war within the war: in other words, stated plainly, that the secular and pluralist forces within Afghan and Iraqi society, while they are not our clients, can in no circumstance be allowed to wonder which outcome we favor.

The great point about Blair's 1999 speech was that it asserted the obvious. Coexistence with aggressive regimes or expansionist, theocratic, and totalitarian ideologies is not in fact possible. One should welcome this conclusion for the additional reason that such coexistence is not desirable, either. If the great effort to remake Iraq as a demilitarized federal and secular democracy should fail or be defeated, I shall lose sleep for the rest of my life in reproaching myself for doing too little. But at least I shall have the comfort of not having offered, so far as I can recall, any word or deed that contributed to a defeat.

Weekly Standard, September 5, 2005

◄ 34 ►

Anti-War, My Foot

Saturday's demonstration in Washington, in favor of immediate withdrawal of coalition forces from Iraq, was the product of an opportunistic alliance between two other very disparate "coalitions." Here is how the *New York Times* (after a front-page and an inside headline, one of them reading "Speaking Up Against War" and one of them reading "Antiwar Rallies Staged in Washington and Other Cities") described the two constituencies of the event: "The protests were largely sponsored by two groups, the Answer Coalition, which embodies a wide range of progressive political objectives, and United for Peace and Justice, which has a more narrow, antiwar focus." The name of the reporter on this story was Michael Janofsky. I suppose that it is possible that he has never before come across "International ANSWER," the group run by the "Worker's World" party and fronted by Ramsey Clark, which openly supports Kim Jong-Il, Fidel Castro, Slobodan Milosevic, and the "resistance" in Afghanistan and Iraq, with Clark himself finding extra time to volunteer as attorney for the *génocidaires* in Rwanda. Quite a "wide range of progressive political objectives" indeed, if that's the sort of thing you like. However, a dip into any database could have furnished Janofsky with well-researched and well-written articles by David Corn and Marc Cooper—to mention only two radical Left journalists—who have exposed "International ANSWER" as a front for (depending on the day of the week) fascism, Stalinism, and jihadism.

The group self-lovingly calling itself "United for Peace and Justice" is by no means "narrow" in its "antiwar focus" but rather represents a very extended alliance between the Old and the New Left, some of it honorable and some of it redolent of the World Youth Congresses that used to bring credulous priests and fellow-traveling hacks together to discuss "peace" in East Berlin or Bucharest. Just to give you an example, from one who knows the sectarian makeup of the Left very well, I can tell you that the Worker's World Party—Ramsey Clark's core outfit—is the product of a split within the Trotskyist movement. These were the ones who felt that the Trotskyist majority, in 1956, was wrong to denounce the Russian invasion of Hungary. The WWP is the direct, lineal product of that depraved rump. If the "United for Peace and Justice" lot want to sink their differences with such riffraff and mount a joint demonstration, then they invite some principled political criticism on their own account. And those who just tag along . . . well, they just tag along.

To be against war and militarism, in the tradition of Rosa Luxemburg and Karl Liebknecht, is one thing. But to have a record of consistent *support* for war and militarism, from the Red Army in Eastern

Europe to the Serbian ethnic cleansers and the Taliban, is quite another. It is really a disgrace that the liberal press refers to such enemies of liberalism as "antiwar" when in reality they are straight-out pro-war, but on the other side. Was there a single placard saying, "No to Jihad"? Of course not. Or a single placard saying, "Yes to Kurdish self-determination" or "We support Afghan women's struggle"? Don't make me laugh. And this in a week when Afghans went back to the polls, and when Iraqis were preparing to do so, under a hail of fire from those who blow up mosques and UN buildings, behead aid workers and journalists, proclaim *fatwas* against the wrong kind of Muslim, and utter hysterical diatribes against Jews and Hindus.

Some of the leading figures in this "movement," such as George Galloway and Michael Moore, are obnoxious enough to come right out and say that they support the Baathist-jihadist alliance. Others prefer to declare their sympathy in more surreptitious fashion. The easy way to tell what's going on is this: Just listen until they start to criticize such gangsters even a little, and then wait a few seconds before the speaker says that, bad as these people are, they were invented or created by the United States. That bad, huh? (You might think that such an accusation—these thugs were cloned by the American empire for God's sake—would lead to instant condemnation. But if you thought that, gentle reader, you would be wrong.)

The two preferred metaphors are, depending on the speaker, that the bin Ladenists are the fish that swim in the water of Muslim discontent or the mosquitoes that rise from the swamp of Muslim discontent. (Quite often, the same images are used in the same harangue.) The "fish in the water" is an old trope, borrowed from Mao's hoary theory of guerrilla warfare and possessing a certain appeal to comrades who used to pore over the Little Red Book. The mosquitoes are somehow new and hover above the water rather than slip through it. No matter. The toxic nature of the "water" or "swamp" is always the same: American support for Israel. Thus, the existence of the Taliban regime cannot be swamplike, presumably because mosquitoes are born and not made. The huge swamp that was Saddam's Iraq has only become a swamp since 2003. The organized murder of Muslims by Muslims in Pakistan, Iraq, and Afghanistan is only a logical reaction to the summit of globalizers at Davos. The stoning and veiling of women must be a reaction to Zionism. While the attack on the World Trade Center—well, who needs reminding that chickens, or is it mosquitoes, come home to roost?

There are only two serious attempts at swamp-draining currently under way. In Afghanistan and Iraq, agonizingly difficult efforts are in train to build roads, repair hospitals, hand out ballot papers, frame constitutions, encourage newspapers and satellite dishes, and generally evolve some healthy water in which civil-society fish may swim. But in each case, from within the swamp and across the borders, the most poisonous snakes and roaches are being recruited and paid to wreck the process and plunge people back into the ooze. How nice to have a "peace" movement that is either openly on the side of the vermin, or neutral as between them and the cleanup crew, and how delightful to have a press that refers to this partisanship, or this neutrality, as "progressive."

Slate, September 26, 2005

PART III

Hitchens on the Left

⊰ 35 ⊱

An Interview with Christopher Hitchens, Part I

Radicalism, Liberty, and the Post-Socialist World[1]

RHYS SOUTHAN: How does your younger contrarian self differ from your older one?

CHRISTOPHER HITCHENS: The book [*Letters to a Young Contrarian*] forces me to ask that question, and yet I don't quite. I must say that I've always found the generational emphasis on the way that my youth was covered to be very annoying. There were a lot of other people born in April 1949, and I just don't feel like I have anything in common with most of them. I forget who it was who said that generation—age group, in other words—is the most debased form of solidarity. The idea of anyone who was born around that time having an automatic ticket to being called "a 60s person" is annoying to me. Especially membership in the specific group that I could claim to have been a part of: not just of "the 60s," but of *1968*. There's even a French term for it: *soixante-huitard*. You can now guess roughly what the political parameters were for me at the time. And you can also guess at least one of the sources of my irritation, which is that by generational analysis, Bill Clinton and I are of the same kidney and same DNA. I repudiate that with every fiber.

But I'm postponing an answer to your question. In those days, I was very much in rebellion against the state. The state had presented itself to [my fellow protestors and me], particularly through the Vietnam War, in the character of a liar and a murderer. If, at a young age, you are able to see your own government in that character, it powerfully conditions the rest of your life. I was taught very early on that the state can be, and is, a liar and a murderer. Yet I have to concede that I didn't think there was a problem *necessarily* with the state, or government, or collective power.

I had been interested in libertarian ideas when I was younger. I set aside this interest in the 60s simply because all the overwhelming political questions seemed to sideline issues of individual liberty in favor of what seemed then to be grander questions. I suppose what would make me different now is that I am much more inclined to stress those issues of individual liberty than I would have been then. And to see that they do possess, with a capital H and a capital I, Historical Importance, the very things that one thought one was looking for.

RS: When did your focus change? In *Letters*, you write that you've "learned a good deal from the libertarian critique" of the idea that the individual belongs to the state and you praise a friend who taught you that "the crucial distinction between systems . . . was no longer ideological. The main political difference was between those who did, and those who did not, believe that the citizen could—or should—be the property of the state."

CH: It's hard to assign a date. I threw in my lot with the Left because on all manner of pressing topics—the Vietnam atrocity, nuclear weapons, racism, oligarchy—there didn't seem to be any distinctive libertarian view. I must say that this still seems to me to be the case, at least where issues of internationalism are concerned. What is the libertarian take, for example, on Bosnia or Palestine?

There's also something faintly ahistorical about the libertarian worldview. When I became a socialist it was largely the outcome of a study of history, taking sides, so to speak, in the battles over industrialism and war and empire. I can't—and this may be a limit on my own imagination or education—picture a libertarian analysis of 1848 or 1914. I look forward to further discussions on this, but for the moment I guess I'd say that libertarianism often feels like an optional philosophy for citizens in societies or cultures that are already developed or prosperous or stable. I find libertarians more worried about the over-mighty state than the unaccountable corporation. The great thing about the present state of affairs is the way it combines the worst of bureaucracy with the worst of the insurance companies.

What I did was to keep two sets of books in my mind. I was certainly interested in issues that have always interested libertarians—defining what the limits to state power are. The first political issue on which I'd ever decided to take a stand was when I was in my teens and before I'd become a socialist. It was the question of capital punishment. A large part of my outrage toward capital punishment was exactly the feeling that it was arrogating too much power to the government. It was giving life-and-death power to the state, which I didn't think it deserved, even if it could use it wisely. I was convinced it could not and did not.

In the mid-1970s, I first met someone whom I've gotten to know better since, Adam Michnik, one of the more brilliant of the Polish dissidents of the time. Michnik made the luminous remark you quoted about the citizen and his relation to the state. I remember thinking, "Well, that's a remark that's impossible to forget."

RS: So, do you still consider yourself a socialist?

CH: Brian Lamb of C-SPAN has been interviewing me on and off for about 20 years, since I'd first gone to Washington, which is roughly when his own *Washington Journal* program began. As the years went by, he formed the habit of starting every time by saying: "You haven't been on the show for a bit. Tell me, are you still a socialist?" And I would always say, "Yes, I am." I knew that he hoped that one day I would say, "No, you know what, Brian, I've seen the light, I've seen the error of my ways." And I knew that I didn't want to give him this satisfaction, even if I'd had a complete conversion experience.

The funny thing is that, recently, he stopped asking me. I don't know why. And just about at that point, I had decided that however I would have phrased the answer—I didn't want to phrase it as someone repudiating his old friends or denouncing his old associations—I no longer would have positively replied, "I am a socialist."

I don't like to deny it. But it simply ceased to come up, as a matter of fact. And in my own life there's a reason for that.

There is no longer a general socialist critique of capitalism—certainly not the sort of critique that proposes an alternative or a replacement. There just is not and one has to face the fact. Though I don't think that the contradictions, as we used to say, of the system are by any means all resolved.

RS: Many socialists have a radically anti-authoritarian disposition, even though the policies they would enact end up being authoritarian. What causes this divide?

CH: Karl Marx was possibly the consummate anti-statist in his original writings and believed that the state was not the solution to social problems, but the outcome of them, the forcible resolution in favor of one ruling group. He thought that if you could give a name to utopia, it was the withering away of the state. Certainly those words had a big effect on me.

The reason why people tend to forget them, or the Left has a tendency to forget them in practice, has something to do with the realm of necessity. If you make your priority—let's call it the 1930s—the end of massive unemployment, which was then defined as one of the leading problems, there seemed no way to do it except by a program of public works. And, indeed, the fascist governments in Europe drew exactly the same conclusion at exactly the same time as Roosevelt did, and as, actually, the British Tories did not. But not because the Tories had a better idea of what to do about it. They actually favored unemployment as a means of disciplining the labor market.

You see what I mean: Right away, one's in an argument, and there's really nothing to do with utopia at all. And then temporary expedients become dogma very quickly—especially if they seem to work.

Then there's the question of whether or not people can be made by government to behave better. They can certainly be made to behave worse; fascism is the proof of that, and so is Stalinism. But a big experience, and this gets us a bit nearer the core of it, a very big influence on a number of people my age was the American civil rights movement, and the moral grandeur of that and also the astonishing speed and exclusiveness of its success. A lot of that did involve asking the government to condition people's behavior, at least in the sense of saying there are certain kinds of private behavior that are now not lawful. And there seemed to be every moral justification for this, and I'm not sure I wouldn't still say that there was.

But it's become too easily extended as an analogy and as a metaphor—and too unthinkingly applied. In my memory, the demand of the student radical was for the university to stop behaving as if it was my parent, *in loco parentis*. They pretend they're your family, which is exactly what we've come here to get away from. We don't want the dean telling us what we can smoke or who we can sleep with or what we can wear, or anything of this sort. That was a very important part of the 60s.

Now you go to campus and student activists are continuously demanding more supervision, of themselves and of others, in order to assure proper behavior and in order to ensure that nobody gets upset. I think that's the measure of what I mean.

RS: Does that explain Ralph Nader's popularity among students during last year's election? He came across as a contrarian in his campaign, and became a hero to a lot of college students. You supported him, too. But he's essentially a curmudgeon with a conservative disposition who advocated lots of regulation.

CH: If I separate in my mind what it is that people like about Ralph, I'm certain the first thing is this: There are people who support him who don't agree with him politically at all, or have no idea of what his politics are. I would be hard-put to say that I knew what his politics were, but the quality that people admired of him was certainly his probity, his integrity. It's just impossible to imagine Ralph Nader taking an under-the-table campaign donation or a kickback. Or arranging to have someone assassinated, or any of these kinds of things. That's not a small thing to say about somebody.

You're right that his approach to life is in many ways a very conservative one. He leads a very austere, rather traditional mode of life. I met him first about 20 years ago. He contacted me, in fact, as he'd admired something I'd written. We met, and the main outcome of this was a 20-year campaign on his part to get me to stop smoking. In fact, he even offered me a large-ish sum of money once if I would quit. Almost as if he were my father or my uncle. Yes, generally speaking, he is a believer in the idea that government can better people, as well as condition them. But he's not an authoritarian, somehow. The word would be *paternalist*, with the state looking after you, rather than trying to control you. But there are some of us who don't find the state, in its paternal guise, very much more attractive. In fact, it can be at its most sinister when it decides that what it's doing is for your own good.

I certainly wish I wasn't a smoker and wish I could give it up. But I'm damned if I'll be treated how smokers are now being treated by not just the government, but the government ventriloquizing the majority. The majoritarian aspect makes it to me more repellent. And I must say it both startles and depresses me that an authoritarian majoritarianism of that kind can have made such great strides in America, almost unopposed. There's something essentially un-American in the idea that I could not now open a bar in San Francisco that says, "Smokers Welcome."

RS: The Right and the Left have joined together in a war against pleasure. What caused this?

CH: The most politically encouraging event on the horizon—which is a very bleak one politically—is the possibility of fusion or synthesis of some of the positions of what is to be called Left and some of what is to be called libertarian. The critical junction could be, and in some ways already is, the "War on Drugs."

The War on Drugs is an attempt by force, by the state, at mass behavior modification. Among other things, it is a denial of medical rights, and certainly a denial of all civil and political rights. It involves a collusion with the most gruesome possible allies in the Third World. It's very hard for me to say that there's an issue more important than that at the moment. It may sound like a hysterical thing to say, but I really think it's much more important than welfare policy, for example. It's self-evidently a very, very important matter. Important enough, perhaps, to create this synthesis I've been looking for, or help to do that.

RS: What are the signs that political fusion between some libertarians and some leftists is happening?

CH: One reason the War on Drugs goes on in defiance of all reason is that it has created an enormous clientele of people who in one way or another depend upon it for their careers or for their jobs. That's true of congressmen who can't really get funding for their district unless it's in some way related to anti-drug activity. There's all kinds of funding that can be smuggled through customs as anti-drug money—all the way to the vast squads of people who are paid to try to put the traffic down, and so forth. So what's impressive is how many people whose job it has been to enforce this war are coming out now and saying that it's obviously, at best, a waste of time.

The other encouraging sign is that those in the political-intellectual class who've gone public about it have tended to be on what would conventionally have been called the Right. Some of them are fairly mainstream Republicans, like the governor of New Mexico. *National Review*, under the ownership of William Buckley, published a special issue devoted to exposing the fallacies and appalling consequences of the War on Drugs. I thought that should have been the *Nation* that did that. I now wouldn't care so much about the precedence in that. It wouldn't matter to me who was first any longer. I don't have any allegiances like that anymore. I don't ask what people's politics are. I ask what their principles are.

RS: Has your own shift in principles changed your relationship with the *Nation*?

CH: For a while it did. I thought at one point that I might have to resign from the magazine. That was over, in general, its defense of Bill Clinton in office, which I still think was a historic mistake made by left-liberals in this country. It completely squandered the claim of a magazine like the *Nation* to be a journal of opposition. By supporting Clinton, the *Nation* became a journal more or less of the consensus. And of the rightward moving consensus at that, because I don't think there's any way of describing Bill Clinton as an enemy of conservatism.

I'd been made aware by someone in the Clinton administration of what I thought was criminal activity. At any rate, the administration engaged in extraordinarily reprehensible activity by way of intimidating female witnesses in an important case. I decided that I would be obstructing justice if I'd kept the evidence to myself. That led to me being denounced in the *Nation* as the equivalent of a McCarthyite state invigilator, which I thought was absurd. Where I live, the White House is the government. So if one attacks it, one isn't reporting one's friends to the government, so to speak, by definition.

The controversy shows the amazing persistence of antediluvian categories and habits of thought on the Left, and these were applied to me in a very mendacious and I thought rather thuggish way. I had to make an issue of it with the magazine, and I was prepared to quit. But we were able to come to an agreement. They stopped saying this about me, in other words.

But there is no such thing as a radical Left anymore. *Ça n'existe pas.* The world of Gloria Steinem and Jesse Jackson, let's say, has all been, though it doesn't realize it, hopelessly compromised by selling out to Clintonism. It became, under no pressure at all, and with no excuse, and in no danger, a voluntary apologist for abuse of power.

It couldn't wait to sell out. It didn't even read the small print or ask how much or act as if it were forced under pressure to do so. I don't think they've realized how that's changed everything for them. They're not a Left. They're just another self-interested faction with an attitude toward government and a hope that it can get some of its people in there. That makes it the same as everyone else—only slightly more hypocritical and slightly more self-righteous.

RS: In *Letters to a Young Contrarian*, you talk about how it was libertarians—specifically Milton Friedman and Alan Greenspan—who did the most to end the draft by persuading President Nixon's special commission on the matter that mandatory military service represented a form of slavery. Is it the contrarians from unexpected ranks that enact real change?

CH: Absolutely. Mr. Greenspan and Mr. Friedman used my mantra correctly by saying the draft would make the citizen the property of the state. To argue against them, however, I'll quote someone whom neither of them particularly likes, but whom I think they both respect. John Maynard Keynes said somewhere—I think in *Essays in Persuasion*—that many revolutions are begun by conservatives because these are people who tried to make the existing system work and they know why it does not. Which is quite a profound insight. It used to be known in Marx's terms as revolution from above.

It would indeed come from enlightened and often self-interested members of the old regime who perfectly well knew that the assurances being given to the ruler were false. That the system didn't know what was going on or how to provide for itself, but couldn't bear to acknowledge that fact and had no means for self-correction. That is indeed how revolutions often begin.

RS: What do you think about the anti-globalization movement? Is it contrarian or radical in your sense?

CH: There was a long lapse where it seemed that nobody took to the streets at all, and where the idea of taking to the streets had begun to seem like something really from a bygone era. It came back very suddenly, initially in Seattle. In some kind of promethean way, the idea was passed on and contained, perhaps like fire in a reed, only to break out again.

In a way I should have been pleased to see that, and I suppose in some small way I was, but a lot of this did seem to me to be a protest against modernity, and to have a very conservative twinge, in the sense of being reactionary. It's often forgotten that the Port Huron Statement, the famous Students for a Democratic Society [SDS] document, was in part a protest against mechanization, against bigness, against scale, against industrialization, against the hugeness and impersonality of, as it thought of it, capitalism. There were elements of that that I agreed with at the time, particularly the interface between the military and the industrial [segments of society].

I do remember thinking that it had a sort of archaic character to it, exactly the kind of thing that Marx attacked, in fact, in the early critiques of capitalism. What SDS seemed to want was a sort of organic, more rural-based, traditional society, which probably wouldn't be a good thing if you could have it. But you can't, so it's foolish to demand such a thing. This tendency has come out as the leading one in what I can see of the anti-globalization protesters. I hear the word *globalization* and it sounds to me like a very good idea. I like the sound of it. It sounds innovative and internationalist.

To many people it's a word of almost diabolic significance—as if there could be a non-global response to something.

RS: This anti-global approach seems especially surprising coming from the Left.

CH: The Seattle protesters, I suppose you could say, in some ways came from the Left. You couldn't say they came from the Right, although a hysterical aversion to world government and internationalism is a very, very American nativist right-wing mentality. It's the sort that is out of fashion now but believe me, if you go on radio stations to talk about Henry Kissinger, as I have recently, you can find it. There are people who don't care about Kissinger massacring people in East Timor, or overthrowing democracy in Chile, or anything of that sort. But they do believe he's a tool of David Rockefeller, and the Trilateral Commission, and the secret world government. That used to be a big deal in California in the 50s and 60s with the John Birch Society.

There are elements of that kind of thing to be found in the anti-globalization protests, but the sad thing is that practically everything

I've just said wouldn't even be understood by most of the people who attend the current protests, because they wouldn't get the references.

RS: You've called yourself a socialist living in a time when capitalism is more revolutionary.

CH: I said this quite recently. I'm glad you noticed it. Most of the readers of the *Nation* seemed not to have noticed it. That was the first time I'd decided it was time I shared my hand. I forget whether I said I was an ex-socialist, or recovering Marxist, or whatever, but that would have been provisional or stylistic. The thing I've often tried to point out to people from the early days of the Thatcher revolution in Britain was that the political consensus had been broken, and from the Right. The revolutionary, radical forces in British life were being led by the conservatives. That was something that almost nobody, with the very slight exception of myself, had foreseen.

I'd realized in 1979, the year she won, that though I was a member of the Labour Party, I wasn't going to vote for it. I couldn't bring myself to vote conservative. That's purely visceral. It was nothing to do with my mind, really. I just couldn't physically do it. I'll never get over that, but that's my private problem.

But I did realize that by subtracting my vote from the Labour Party, I was effectively voting for Thatcher to win. That's how I discovered that that's what I secretly hoped would happen. And I'm very glad I did. I wouldn't have been able to say the same about Reagan, I must say. But I don't think he had her intellectual or moral courage. This would be a very long discussion. You wouldn't conceivably be able to get it into a *Reason* interview.

Marx's original insight about capitalism was that it was the most revolutionary and creative force ever to appear in human history. And though it brought with it enormous attendant dangers, [the revolutionary nature] was the first thing to recognize about it. That is actually what the *Manifesto* is all about. As far as I know, no better summary of the beauty of capital has ever been written. You sort of know it's true, and yet it can't be, because it doesn't compute in the way we're taught to think. Any more than it computes, for example, that Marx and Engels thought that America was the great country of freedom and revolution and Russia was the great country of tyranny and backwardness.

But that's exactly what they did think, and you can still astonish people at dinner parties by saying that. To me it's as true as knowing my own middle name. Imagine what it is to live in a culture where people's first instinct when you say it is to laugh. Or to look bewildered. But that's the nearest I've come to stating not just what I believe, but everything I ever have believed, all in one girth.

Reason Online (November 2001)

NOTE

1. Although this interview, originally entitled "Free Radical," appeared in *Reason Online* in November 2001, it was conducted before the September 11 attacks.

◄(36)►

Don't. Be. Silly. An Open Letter to Martin Amis

Dearest Martin,

You know how it is with kind friends. If a disobliging word is published about one, in, let's say, the letters column of the *Sheep-Shearer's Gazette* in the south island of New Zealand, they will take infinite pains to get word of it to you by fax or email. So I have lately been reading bushels of stuff about myself, generated by reviews of your book on Stalinism. I wince on my own behalf a good deal as I wade through, but I don't forget to wince for you as well. Hardened as I am to hostile or philistine reviews, I can still imagine that you must be at least disappointed by the treatment you have been getting. And in a way it must be worse than all that journo-sludge concerning your teeth or your divorce, because the subject that's being slighted here is the grave and momentous one of the victims of "Koba."

My sympathy is tinged with annoyance, all the same. What did you imagine would happen if you elected to write on such a Himalayan topic, and then pygmified it by addressing so much of it to me?[1] If you remember, I did try to warn you about this over a year ago. I find myself embarrassed almost every day at the thought of an actual gulag survivor reading this, or even reading about it, and finding his or her experience reduced to a sub-Leavisite boys' tiff, gleefully interpreted as literary fratricide by hacks who couldn't care a hoot for the real subject.

As it happens, I think that there are passages of really magnificent endeavor in your book, but anyone who wants to know where and how I differ on the history and the analysis can direct their jolly search engines to my mega-review in the *Atlantic Monthly* ["Lightness at Midnight," September 2002].

I also thought it would be churlish to pass up the "open letter" invitation that you extend in your sarcastically headed "Comrade Hitchens" chapter. Aside from the distressing matter of proportion that I just mentioned, and the question of your sources and interpretations, there also remains our political disagreement. In what you claim to recall of my views, and of the views of James Fenton, there is an unpardonable assumption that the Left of 68 was not only morally null about Stalin, but also frivolous and selfish. I am not going to let this pass. I've lived to see the brave and serious and self-sacrificing war-resisters of the Vietnam era written off as draft-dodgers and privileged sissies, which is to say that I've seen a huge lie become widely accepted. You help circulate part of this lie yourself, when you echo the fantastic assertion, originally fabricated by paranoid reactionaries, that American soldiers returned from Vietnam to face "execration." And here is how you perform your duty to memory, about events with which you did have a nodding acquaintance:

> In my first year at Oxford (autumn 1968) I attended a demonstration against the resuppression of Czechoslovakia. Some 60 or 70 souls were present. We heard speeches. The mood was sorrowful, decent. Compare this to the wildly peergroup-competitive but definitely unfakable emotings and self-lacerations of the crowds outside the American embassy in Grosvenor Square, where they gathered in their tens of thousands.

I wince again at the sly way you contrast your own sorrowful decency to the unseemly saturnalia of the time, but as you perfectly well know

I was one of the organizers of that event in Oxford, and James Fenton was there too (in a crowd, incidentally, that contained many more "souls" than you say). The group of which I was then a member, the International Socialists, organized pro-Czech events around the country and even managed to fling leaflets in Russian onto the decks of Soviet merchant vessels in British ports. I was actually in Cuba on the day of the invasion, and managed to distribute some "anti-Soviet" materials on the streets of Havana. I'm reasonably proud of that, though if you had asked me at the time, I'd have been proudest of having hosted Dr Eduardo Mondlane, the founder of Frelimo, at a reception in my tiny college room. He was murdered shortly afterwards by the Portuguese secret police, but he's still remembered as the gentle and highly civilized father of Mozambican independence and the impetus given to revolution in southern Africa that year has now resulted, at some remove, in the triumph of Nelson Mandela.

How you know about Grosvenor Square I can't imagine: I'm willing to testify that there was some "emoting" all right, and that there could well have been more—the My Lai massacre had occurred only the day before, though we didn't quite realize it. The "lacerations," though, were supplied—as in Chicago and Paris and elsewhere—by the forces of law and order.

You say sneeringly that the "New Left" of the 60s represented "revolution as play" and that its "death throes" took the form of "vanguard terrorism." The atom of truth in this—or the grain of received wisdom—doesn't excuse you. That year, the unstoppable fusion of the American civil rights movement with the largest-ever citizen movement against a war—a war of atrocity and aggression about which we now know that everything we even suspected was true—brought about the legal emancipation of black America, and compelled the warmakers to begin their retreat. Not bad. Not bad at all—even if there were a few hippies and druggies and freaks involved here and there (though I can't resist adding that there wasn't much hedonism on the battlefields of Mozambique). If I am embarrassed to recall anything about my politics at that time—and I'll admit to the odd wince—it is chiefly because I wish I had done very much more than I did.

What else was happening that year? Well, the West German comrades—led by a young Rudi Dutschke who had escaped from East Berlin—launched a critical movement that broke the shady silence of the post–Third Reich consensus. In France, the 10-year period of one-man rule was abruptly and, yes, if you insist, joyously terminated. Much of southern and NATO Europe was under military dictatorship at the time: I still see old friends from Spain and Portugal and Greece whose activities in those days meant the breaking-open of prison states only a short while later.

Most interesting of all, in my memory, was the direct confrontation this involved with Stalin's heirs. Our faction at any rate was in close touch with student and worker groups in Poland and Czechoslovakia, where open rebellion against the sclerotic Warsaw pact regimes was breaking out. The regimes themselves seemed to get the point. Moscow directly ordered the French Communist party to help put down the rebellion against De Gaulle, and Brezhnev both sought and received Lyndon Johnson's advance assurance that a Red Army invasion of Prague would be considered an "internal affair."

For a short, exhilarating while, it seemed that the permafrost could be melted from below. And this idea did not experience any "death throes." It became subterranean, and re-emerged in 1989. Of the dissident heroes of that later revolution, I can think of several who I first met on or around the barricades of 1968. And many of them also did tremendous work in helping to save the people of Bosnia a few years further on.

Not long ago, I took part in quite a serious discussion, initiated by the man who had served the longest term of imprisonment in communist Yugoslavia, about naming a street in the Kosovo capital of Pristina after Leon Trotsky. (You make rather a boast of not having read the Old Man, but his book of reportage on the 1912 Balkan wars is one of the finest polemics ever composed, not to say one of the most prescient.)

Some exemplary people and causes, in other words, could not be said to be quite decided on the lethal question of bolshevism: the only revolution that had ever defeated its enemies. That there was an element of power-worship here I'm quite prepared to concede, and those involved, including myself, are obliged to subject themselves to self-criticism. But your attempted syllogism invites a direct comparison with Hitlerism, and levels the suggestion of moral equivalence to the Nazis at, say, the many "hard Left" types who worked for Dr Martin Luther King. My provisional critique of this ahistorical reasoning would fit into three short italicized sentences. *Don't. Be. Silly.*

I see from some of the more vulgar and stupid responses to your book that the specter of Trotskyism once again stalks the land and I think I am in a strong position to promise you that all such talk is idle. It's over. But how would you know that? You report on how you took the pedantic trouble to ask me—should it be Trotskyist or Trotsky-ite? And you add that I told you several times that only Stalinists or ignorant people say the latter. And then you go and call the POUM—George Orwell's party—"Trotskyite."

By the way, that's a factual error as well as an aesthetic one, and I wish it was the only such. A poor return for my labors, I must say. I am glad I didn't try to tell you any more about Rosa Luxemburg, who was probably more of a historical heroine to us, not least because her warnings about Leninism had been the earliest, not to say the most lucid and courageous. But then one had to face the argument that if she and her comrades had been more ruthless and more Leninist, the militarist German Right might have been crushed in 1919 instead of, with infinitely more suffering and woe, in 1945. This is and was a deeply serious and troubling question (though I must say that its least serious consequence is that you have pissed me off by making light of it).

You demand that people—you prefer the term "intellectuals"—give an account of their attitude to the Stalin terror. Irritatingly phrased though your demand may be, I say without any reservation that you are absolutely right to make it. A huge number of liberals and conservatives and social democrats, as well as communists, made a shabby pact with "Koba," or succumbed to the fascinations of his power. Winston Churchill told Stalin's ambassador to London, before the war, that he had quite warmed to the old bastard after the Moscow Trials, which had at least put down the cosmopolitan revolutionaries who Churchill most hated. T. S. Eliot returned the manuscript of *Animal Farm* to George Orwell, well knowing that his refusal might condemn it to non-publication, because he objected to its "Trotskyite" tone. (You can read all about this illuminating episode in my little book on Orwell [*Orwell's Victory*].) I think we can say fairly that the names of Churchill and Eliot are still highly regarded in conservative political and cultural circles. You have a certain reputation for handling irony and paradox. How could you miss an opportunity like this, and sound off like a *Telegraph* editorialist instead, hugging the shore and staying with the script?

However, while all of those and many other dirty compromises were being made, the Bulletin of the Left Opposition was publishing exactly the details, of famine and murder and deportation and misery, that now shock you so much. I evidently wasted my breath in telling you this, but there exists a historical tradition of Marxist writers—Victor Serge, C. L. R. James, Boris Souvarine and others—who exposed and opposed Stalin while never ceasing to fight against empire and fascism and exploitation. If the moral and historical audit is to be properly drawn up, then I would unhesitatingly propose the members of this derided, defeated diaspora, whose closest British analogue and ally was Orwell, as the ones who come best out of the several hells of the last century. A pity that you felt them beneath your notice.

Your letter to me is addressed from what sounds like a pretty cushy spot in Uruguay, where you sometimes repair. You make it appear idyllic—"a place of thousand-mile beaches." As you have probably heard, it has been calculated that during the 1970s, one tenth of the Uruguayan population was forced into exile, while one in every 50 of the remainder was processed through the military and police prison system and that in those prisons new heights of innovation—especially but by no means exclusively in psychological torture—were attained. (Behaviorism was involved; detainees were forced to watch Charlie Chaplin movies and punished if they laughed. You can look it up in Lawrence Weschler's harrowing book, *A Miracle, a Universe: Settling Accounts with Torturers*.) Quite an impressive number of Uruguayans are still looking for members of their families.

The Uruguayan oligarchy was probably smart in making few claims for itself while it was doing this. It certainly didn't announce that it was trying to bring about a workers' paradise. The mere boast that it was doing it in order to ward off communism was enough to keep the weapons and "advisers" coming from my home town of Washington DC, and to procure an uncritical silence from most western "intellectuals."

You scorn the sinister illusion of human perfectibility, as well you may. But—though I don't criticize you for idealizing Uruguay as a counter revolutionary tourist—I do earnestly hint to you that there may yet be more scope for radical human improvement. And by the way, and since you linger too long on the subject of mirth, you say that nobody laughed at Hitler. Well, the fellow traveler Charlie Chaplin seems to have contrived it.

This whole exchange between us comes at an unsettling time for me, because I think that a huge section of the "Left" has fatally condemned itself by flirting with, or actually succumbing to, a creepy concept of "moral equivalence" between the United States and its (actually our) enemies—whether Christian Orthodox thugs in the Balkans or Islamic fascists in Afghanistan or national socialists in Mesopotamia. Talk about wincing—I can scarcely bear to read the drivel and bad faith that is now emitted by some of my former comrades. However, and though I am now without allegiances, I still choose to regard the term "comrade" as a title of honor, and one which betrays itself rather than fulfils itself in such negations. It was always a sorrow to me—I can tell you this now—that my dearest friend showed no real interest in such apparent metaphysics, and I'm sorry all over again that you have written on the subject in such a way as to give pleasure to those who don't love you, as I do.

Fraternally, then, Christopher

Guardian, September 4, 2002

NOTE

1. Hitchens is referring to Amis's 2002 book *Koba the Dread: Laughter and the Twenty Million*, the concluding section of which reproaches Hitchens for what Amis sees as his indulgent embrace of the socialist project.

⤳(37)⤶

Europe's Status Quo Left

A Review of *Language, Politics, and Writing: Stolentelling in Western Europe* by Patrick McCarthy

At a time when "European" cultural opinion is so much sought after and discussed by Americans of liberal temper, and considered suspect by so many Americans of the conservative school, one might do much worse than to consult the work of a man of Irish descent, reared in South Wales, who teaches in Bologna (at the Paul H. Nitze School of the Johns Hopkins University campus there) and whose expertise is the modern history and politics of France. I have derived great pleasure and instruction from both reading and conversing with Patrick McCarthy in the past, and so I opened his collection of essays on the interweaving of 20th-century Europe's political and literary history with some impatience.

This impatience, I regret to report, still persists. Elegant and allusive as *Language, Politics, and Writing* often is, it has something inescapably blasé and laconic about. Let me simply cite what McCarthy says about European culture and Islam, on an early page of his introduction:

> Culture—hopefully defined more precisely—gets a long chapter of its own because it is probably the greatest problem that young Europeans will have to face. European culture is becoming one of many and has to confront "others." In particular, it must confront "the other," namely, Islam. Europe's record is not encouraging (nor is Islam's), but we have the resources in our culture to create a dialogue rather than a war. Whatever President Bush may say, September 11 was not just an act of terrorism; it was the fruit of a breakdown of communications that has deep historical roots. Catching Osama bin Laden may be an excellent undertaking, but the real goal is to learn to live with and talk to, not about, Islam.

When this passage departs from cliché and tautology, it is only to fall into error. The word "hopefully" is employed in just the way one teaches students to avoid. "Nor" should be "neither." Nothing is added, in American or European campus lingo, by putting a simple concept such as "the other" (or "others") in pseudo-significant apostrophes. Culture, however precisely defined it is "hopefully" going to be, either is, or probably is, the greatest "problem" that all humans will "have to face." (There doesn't seem to be, in other words, any chance of something so obvious not being the case.) By the way, when exactly was "European culture" not "one of many," including many European ones? But are we therefore to view the many Islams as identical or as a homogenous "Islam"? Then one would hate to see, if only from the standpoint of metaphor mixture, the fruit of a breakdown. But no doubt this unlikely collision would have—as everything surely does—"deep historical roots."

The political references are sloppy in the same way. The US president did not refer to the events of September 11, 2001, as "just an act of terrorism." Among other things, he defined those events as an act of war and meant what he said. Moreover, and whatever one may think of his choice of terms, the president made and continues to make a strenuous effort to enforce a distinction between discrepant interpretations of Islam. McCarthy's final sentence here is merely complacent: He allows that a hunt for Al Qaeda might be all very well—as if it did not concern him all that much—while taking second place to his own reflections on cultural coexistence. How searching might these reflections be? Not all that profound, if they depend upon a false distinction between talking "to" someone and talking "about" something.

I am again only taking McCarthy at his word when he makes a core announcement on the very same page:

> If I were asked to sum up the book's theme in a sentence, I would refer to Primo Levi's statement that a man who gives up trying to be understood by those around him is headed only for the gas-chamber. (And what of Auschwitz? Is it not good that the last half-century has not produced another set of death-camps in Western Europe? Yes of course, even if that is a low target to set oneself.

Moreover, the ex-Yugoslavia has witnessed forms of cruelty almost equal the crimes of the Nazis.)

This passage hovers on the verge of gibberish. In what sense did Levi say such a thing? Are we to conclude that those who despair of being understood are themselves headed for the gas chamber or instead that they are pushing others in that direction? If the first, then was Diogenes the Cynic bound for Treblinka? If the second, then are the postmodern theorists bent on genocide? Meanwhile, please bear in mind that Western Europe must have been very mutually intelligible in the last half century, since it produced no death camps. Except that there were, apparently, death camps (though they were located just across the Adriatic from Western Europe). The "stolentelling" in the subtitle of this book comes from James Joyce and implies that all language has been annexed from other languages. I knew that. I also knew that Joyce worked in Paris and Trieste as well as Dublin. But this cultural conceit is no excuse for such obfuscation.

McCarthy announces the limitations of his own concept of "Europe." He means it to comprise the British Isles and the mainland, excluding Spain and Eastern Europe and (he might have added) Scandinavia. That's good, because many people have come to employ the terms "Europe" and "the Europeans" in a manner that is either too embracing or too finite. Within this severely circumscribed compass (I should have thought that Milan Kundera was a "Western" force by now), McCarthy's main unintended limitation is his tendency to swing between very learned and expert micro-observations and much more questionable macro ones. Sometimes, the micro-learning has to be elucidated by the reader, which is no bad thing. McCarthy makes enough glancing references to Celtic and Gaelic nationalism, whether Welsh, Irish, or Breton, to allow the inference that there was a consistent overlap between this form of Romanticism and modern forms of fascism.

The bulk of the collection consists of exegeses, either of other books or other authors. In discussing authorship, McCarthy rather tentatively proposes Roland Barthes's distinction—which he at first terms a sharp one—between *écrivain* and *écrivant*. The first practitioner, we are informed, considers language an end in itself: a process of musing upon how rather than why. The second confronts the why or the whys. This distinction is only introduced to be dropped, since the only times McCarthy employs it are to say that two great authors—Antonio Gramsci and George Orwell—decisively combined both roles in one. (Toward the end of the book, McCarthy also says in passing that Margaret Drabble's novels show her sometimes as *écrivain* and at other times as *écrivant,* but since he doesn't stipulate which works are which we are no further enlightened.)

Let me give another example of the lazy transition between a specific and a general reference. McCarthy doesn't venture far from conventional wisdom when he nominates the Dreyfus case as a defining moment in the evolution of modern France: pitting cosmopolitanism against anti-Semitism, civil society against the army, "intellectuals" against the Roman Catholic Church, and objective standards of justice against mystical ones. Later, while discussing the divorce scandal that ruined the career of Charles Stuart Parnell, so stirred James Joyce, and so greatly retarded the cause of Irish nationalism, he calls it "arguably Ireland's Dreyfus case." This assertion is plainly ridiculous, as well as anachronistic. Parnell was dead before the Dreyfus case occurred and was never tried for anything himself. The only possible analogy is the lamentable fact that in both "cases" (in my opinion as well as that of McCarthy), the Roman Catholic hierarchy committed itself on the wrong side. The defensive word "arguably" must have been inserted in a moment of unease.

There should have been more such moments. As any student of Joyce ought to know, the "ordinary" speech of everyday discourse lies in wait for the critical writer, with its numbing clichés ready to hand. Thus, it is just as true to say, of the Northern Ireland "Good Friday" agreement, that the Irish Republican Army was brought by force "to the conference table" as it is to say the British government was. It is equally true to say the global economy increases the number of the included as it is to say the number of the excluded has risen (McCarthy's preferred formulation).

Carelessness stalks the book in a way that might have been less irritating at a less urgent time. How can the novelist Alan Sillitoe have "supported" the "Suez fiasco" of 1956? You can be pro-invasion but not pro-fiasco, as anyone fluent in Italian may confirm. Orwell was never "invalided out" of Spain and wouldn't have been able to write *Homage to Catalonia* if he had been. I would not say, reviewing Jean-Paul Sartre's *La Nausée,* that "Like Orwell's Winston, Roquentin cannot keep a diary because he has nothing to put in it." Again, the opposite is the case. Finally, it's not undue nitpicking to notice the repeated misspelling of important names—Salman Rushdie, Jesse Owens, and Brian Friel—even though some of these must be blamed on cretinous copyediting. (Harold Macmillan, who receives more than a dozen misspelled mentions, was part owner of the family-named firm that actually published this book.)

I have a fondness for many of the same writers as McCarthy does: Levi, Oscar Wilde, Gramsci, Giuseppe Tomasi di Lampedusa, Albert Camus, Seamus Heaney, and the English "realist" writers of the 1950s and later (Sillitoe being the one most deserving of the revival he receives in these pages). The essay comparing Levi and Céline and their impossibly different attitudes to the German "New Order" in Europe is highly audacious and can lead to sleep deprivation. A rare fair-mindedness is displayed in considering the many-sidedness of Sartre. But I kept noticing opportunities missed: Of course it's true, as Heaney says, that Catholics and Protestants use different idioms, and of course the Irish would not have turned the tables on England if it had tried to preserve the Gaelic language in the United States. But didn't Wilde long ago point out the essentially liberating nature of the United States for the Irish? I can't agree with McCarthy that Lampedusa's *The Leopard* is a "right-wing novel" (it always struck me as a masterly formulation of the conflict between the forces and relations of production), but suppose that I consent for the sake of argument. Wouldn't now—with Umberto Bossi in political alignment with Silvio Berlusconi—be the ideal moment to revisit Gramsci's concept of Italy as two nations, southern and northern? McCarthy repeatedly passes up such cross-references, and one can't but suspect that this is because they might interfere with a settled attitude.

Patrick McCarthy is honest enough to give us an account of his own political affiliations, which have oscillated between the Aneurin Bevan wing of British Labour, the Gaulliste and Mitterandiste interpretations of radical Francophilia, and the Enrico Berlinguer period of Italian Euro-communism. Some in the United States might think of McCarthy's pedigree as fairly "hard" Left; I think I can detect the symptoms also of the soft. But what his collection of essays illustrates is something insufficiently remarked upon: the evolution of the European Left into a status-quo force, somewhat inclined to sit out the storm and to content itself with essentially voyeuristic comments on the brashness of the United States. (The great exception, if it is indeed to be counted as a "Left" one, is Tony Blair, who receives only the most superficial mention here.) I was once as happy as anyone to sit with McCarthy and to discuss Gramsci's *Prison Notebooks* or the ambiguities of Sartre's *Les Tempes Modernes.* I still enjoy these pursuits, though they occasionally strike me now as comparable to well-conducted tours of Atlantis. Perhaps that's why the cultivated guides have such a marked tendency to gurgle, as they make their appointed rounds.

Foreign Policy (July/August 2003)

⤜(38)⤛

Left-Leaving, Left-Leaning

A Review of *Left Illusions* by David Horowitz and *Not Without Love* by Constance Webb

Not long ago, having expressed some disagreements in print with an old comrade of long standing,[1] I was sent a response that he had published in an obscure newspaper [*Counter Punch*, August 20, 2003]. This riposte referred to my opinions as "racist." I would obviously scorn to deny such an allegation on my own behalf. I would, rather, prefer to repudiate it on behalf of my former friend. He had known me for many years and cooperated with me on numerous projects, and I am quite confident that he would never have as a collaborator anyone he suspected of racial prejudice. But it does remind me, and not for the first time, that quarrels on the Left have a tendency to become miniature treason trials, replete with all kinds of denunciation. There's a general tendency—not by any means confined to radicals but in some way specially associated with them—to believe that once the lowest motive for a dissenting position has been found, it must in some way be the real one.

This is a vulgar error, with its roots in the intellectual atmosphere of the Stalin period, and it is the central preoccupation of David Horowitz's latest collection of apostasy. I should say at the outset that I have known or at least met Horowitz at almost every stage of his political evolution (and I confess that one of these collected essays defends me against some piece of calumny from a few years back. That article begins—quite correctly in a way—by saying that he knows full well that by taking my side he is throwing me a lifebelt made out of the heaviest possible cement).

To have met Horowitz in Berkeley at the end of the 60s, when he was running the now-legendary *Ramparts* magazine, was to have encountered a rather cocky and prickly guy, aware of his status as a celebrity of the New Left. Our meeting wasn't a huge success. Rather daringly, he reprints some of his essays from this period, which hold up fairly well and, in the case of the article on Israel and the Left, show a prose superior to some of his post-defection pieces. Next time we ran into each other it was 1982. Horowitz was defending then-Israeli Defense Minister Ariel Sharon's war in Lebanon and had already published an essay about his growing disillusionment with the anti-Americanism of the Left. He was half in and half out at that stage: When I inquired where he was politically, he replied that he'd ceased to be a Deutscher-ite and become a Kolakowski-ist. I include this reminiscence because it will please those readers on the Left who get the reference and because it shows how intent and minute was Horowitz's self-scrutiny. In the 1984 presidential election, he came out enthusiastically for Ronald Reagan, which made me think that he had kissed farewell to fine distinctions. In 1988 he convened a famous conference of former radicals who had developed "Second Thoughts." It occurred, perhaps unfortunately, at the crescendo of the Iran-contra scandal—which didn't make Reagan look all that good—and just as Mikhail S. Gorbachev was beginning the dismantling of the Soviet Empire. If that latter momentous process vindicated anyone, it was perhaps Isaac Deutscher (who had believed in a version of "reform Communism") almost as much as it was Leszek Kolakowski, who had maintained that the USSR was quite beyond reform. With the Cold War so to speak behind us, I suspected that Horowitz would find life without the old enemy a little dull. How much of an audience would there be for his twice-told tale about growing up in a doggedly loyal Communist Party family and his agonizing over the series of wrenches and shocks that had detached him from Marxism altogether? But then, I didn't anticipate that in the fall of 2001 I would be reading solemn polemics by leading intellectualoids, proposing a strict moral equivalence—moral equivalence at best, in some cases—between America and the Taliban. Nor did I expect to see street theater antiwar demonstrations, organized by open admirers of Fidel Castro and Slobodan Milosevic and Kim Jong Il, united in the sinister line of, in effect, "hands off Saddam Hussein." So I admit that I now find the sardonic, experienced pessimism in Horowitz's book a bit more serviceable than I once did. No matter what the shortcomings of US policy may have been in the post-2001 crisis, it is clear at least to me that much of the Left has disgraced itself either by soft-headed neutralism or, in the case of a very noticeable minority, by something rather like open sympathy for the enemies of civilization. The May-June issue of *New Left Review*, for example, contained an editorial calling not just for solidarity with the "resistance" in Iraq but with Kim Jong Il in his stand against imperialism!

Horowitz must be correct in proposing that this calamity has its roots in a more general failure of historical self-criticism—as we used to call it—and on this matter he can sometimes be right even when he is wrong. (For example, he was essentially neutral when it came to the confrontation with Milosevic.) There really is a cultural layer, in academia as well as outside it, that considers Joseph McCarthy to have been far more opprobrious than Josef Stalin. This doesn't mean that there's any excuse for McCarthyism, and Horowitz doesn't offer one, but nor does it pardon those who make cultural icons, even today, out of uncritical Stalinists such as writer Dalton Trumbo (now being celebrated off Broadway), Alger Hiss (defended by *The New Yorker* under Tina Brown) or Angela Davis (welcomed by faculties on campuses where Horowitz's pamphlets are effectively ruled to be non-kosher). The Davis example is essential, because at the heart of the Horowitz critique is a deep scar, inflicted by the protracted and bitter argument about race in America.

Horowitz's parents devoted themselves to the early civil rights struggle, and he grew up on Communist adulation of Paul Robeson.

When the Black Panther Party emerged in Oakland, he and his fellow Berkeleyites were in a good position to offer them help, and Horowitz found them a bookkeeper, an African American friend named Betty Van Patter. Bookkeeping was a rather exiguous skill in a party that swiftly turned to shakedowns and mob tactics, and Van Patter was killed and dumped into San Francisco Bay. There is no doubt now, and there was precious little then, of the Panther leadership's complicity in this revolting crime. But there was then, and there still is, a certain amount of shuffling in the ranks when mention of that responsibility comes up. For Horowitz at any rate, her killing was his equivalent of Kronstadt or the Hitler-Stalin pact: a political as well as emotional breaking point. Those who complain of his often harsh and bitter tone may suspect him of sublimating his own feeling of guilt: He doesn't deny that. His main preoccupation has become the countering of race-based politics on the cultural Left, including a high-profile campus campaign against the "reparations for slavery" initiative. I am appalled at the refusal of some student newspapers to take Horowitz's paid ads on this topic: I do sometimes wince, though, at the tone of "And after all we've done for you . . ." that he takes when replying to what he thinks of as exorbitant black demands. Nonetheless, it's not for those on the Left who so often reach for the *ad hominem* attack to suddenly take a high tone when Horowitz calls it as he sees it.

Race and the Left also form the core of Constance Webb's memoir, *Not Without Love*. Here we read of how a bewitching young woman, fired with every sort of idealism, became a Trotskyist militant in the Fresno area in the hot period of the 1930s and later the lover of that movement's most brilliant and charismatic member, the late C. L. R. James. Originally from Trinidad but thoroughly Anglicized, at least to the extent that he had mastered English literature, James wrote the classic *Black Jacobins*, a luminous study of Toussaint L'Ouverture's slave rebellion in Haiti, combining a staunch eminence as the mind of the anti-colonial revolution with an intransigent opposition to Stalinism. This portrait of a man, gentlemanly to a high degree but practically irresistible to women, is beautifully drawn by a woman who seems to have been entirely irresistible to men. Indeed, much of the charm of the memoir is supplied by Webb's frank admission that, as a model and actress, she knew she was to some extent living by her cover-girl looks. (She describes a moment of sexual horror with Salvador Dali that confirms and redoubles everything one had ever suspected about him.) She socialized, as a white person, on the other side of "the color line," but she earned her living on the white side, and her recollection of the days when racism was legal and institutional is as shocking and dispiriting as such memories always are.

Webb has already published a fascinating biography of Richard Wright, and in these pages she gives a firsthand account of her acquaintance, through James, with black America's literary aristocracy, from Ralph Ellison and Chester Himes to James Baldwin. The parallel account of the tiny but dramatic world of the Trotskyist and post-Trotskyist groupuscule doesn't need a specialized knowledge to be understood and is a tribute to some heroic and under-appreciated activity. One is reminded that some people stay on the Left for the same reason that some people leave it: because of matters of principle.

Los Angeles Times, November 16, 2003

NOTE

1. Hitchens is referring to Edward Said.

⫸ 39 ⫷

Polymath with a Cause

A Review of *From Oslo to Iraq and the Road Map* by Edward W. Said

Edward Said, who died last September after an astonishingly tenacious duel with leukemia, had at least three interlocking careers and perhaps four. He was a most accomplished literary critic, who combined a reverence for canonical English with an awareness of postmodern methods. He was what I like to call a civilizational critic as well, interpreting Eastern and Western societies to each other and mapping, in his best known work, *Orientalism*, an attack on scholarly presumption that altered the perspective of a generation. He was a full-time volunteer on behalf of the cause of the dispossessed Palestinian people. And he was a musician of concert-playing standard.

Each of these commitments contained its own fold or irony or duality. Said became shocked by the anti-literary and philistine tone of much postmodern academic fashion. He was as ready to attack insularity and tribalism in the Arab world as he was to excoriate the condescension of the Anglo-American professoriat. As a member of the Anglican minority from Palestinian Jerusalem, and as a man temperamentally opposed to cruelty and violence, he was not an apologist for jihadism or for the tactics that have so much degraded the Palestinian cause. And, as a promoter of the theory and practice of music, he found his warmest collaborator in the Israeli conductor Daniel Barenboim, with whom he founded a program to bring Jewish and Arab orchestral prodigies closer together.

His unofficial fifth career, as a regular columnist in Arab-world newspapers such as *Al-Hayat* in London and *Al-Ahram* in Egypt, was the scene where many of these complexities played themselves out, and it forms the material collected in these pages. (And here is the point where I should declare that we were friends, as well as one-time collaborators on an anthology about Palestinian rights.) As someone who is Said's distinct inferior as a litterateur, and who knows nothing of music, and could not share in his experience of being an exiled internationalist, I try not to suspect myself of envy when I say that he was at his very weakest when he embarked on the polemical.

This weakness arose from two causes. First, Said was extremely emotional and very acutely conscious of unfairness and injustice. No shame in that, I hardly need add. But he felt himself obliged to be the unappointed spokesman and interpreter for the unheard and the misunderstood, and this could sometimes tempt him to be propagandistic. We ended up having a bitter personal quarrel over the "regime change" policy of the United States in Afghanistan and Iraq, but the disagreement actually began almost a quarter of a century before that, with the publication of easily his worst book: *Covering Islam*. In that volume, published just after the Khomeini revolution in Iran, he undertook to explain something—Western ignorance of Muslim views—that certainly needed explication. But he ended up inviting us to take some of those Muslim grievances at their own face value. I remember asking him then how he—a secular Anglican with a love of political pluralism and of literary diversity—could hope to find any home, for himself or his principles, in an Islamic republic. He looked at me as if I had mentioned the wrong problem or tried to change the subject.

Then again, during the Algiers summit of the PLO in 1986, he was prominent among those who called for the Palestinians to revise their "charter" and to accept a two-state solution. There was an important element of nobility in this: Those who had lost their homes in Palestine in 1947–48 had decided that they would not demand "the right of return" for themselves, but would sacrifice this goal for the sake of the occupied inhabitants of the West Bank and Gaza. In those days, Edward was very much an admirer of Yasser Arafat and published a flattering profile of him—in *Interview* magazine—that I don't believe he ever anthologized. But by 1993, with Arafat on the White House lawn and mutual recognition occurring between Israel and the PLO, he had announced that the old man was too corrupt and too undemocratic to be taken seriously. (The Clinton administration really wanted Said on that lawn: I can remember George Stephanopoulos asking me to try to persuade him, which I was made to regret doing as soon as I attempted it.)

One could hand this volume to anybody who doubted, or who had managed not to know about, the daily suffering of Palestinians under Israeli occupation. With great moral energy, Said details the reality of confiscated land, demolished homes and brutal restrictions. He registers, with especial strength, the sheer humiliation of all this. A Palestinian born in the town of his great-grandparents has to accept arbitrary rule by people who have just arrived from Russia or the United States, many of whom do not speak (as many Palestinians do) either Hebrew or Arabic. How can this possibly be justified? Some answer the question nonsensically, by claiming that God awarded this entire territory to the Jews. Others say that the imperative of a Jewish homeland constitutes a sort of meta-historical override. To the latter, Said gave a very dignified response, saying that his people's case was also unique in that they were and are "the victims of the victims."

But, since the case is unequal to begin with, and confronts largely unarmed Arab farmers with a military superpower that has nuclear weapons, it seems beside the point to complain that any negotiations are therefore unfair also. This is the line taken by Said, and also by Tony Judt, the former kibbutznik and now a distinguished academic at New York University, who contributes a highly eloquent introduction. Just as peace does not need to be made between friends, so redress is not demanded between equals. It may well be, as both Judt and Said imply, that the whole Zionist enterprise was a mistake to begin with and that Palestine should be a political entity that awards citizenship without distinction of ethnicity and religion. (For what it's worth, I think so, too.) But in the meanwhile, it is no more probable that Jews and Christians will want to mingle freely with Hamas and Islamic Jihad than it is that Muslim olive-growers will welcome gun-toting settlers from Brooklyn. And—to get specific—if Edward Said believes that Arafat is the Palestinian version of "Papa Doc" Duvalier, as he once told me and as he reaffirms here, why should the Israelis accept an interlocutor that he himself would reject? As he points out with rage, Arafat has since announced that he now wishes he had stayed with the Oslo negotiations. But at whose expense, really, is this awful irony?

The book is disfigured by some vulgarities that are not worthy of their author. To say that George Mitchell and Warren Rudman, former senators who worked on a very imperfect peace plan, are "among the highest-paid members of the Israeli lobby" is cheap, to put it no higher. To say that Arab Americans were beaten in the streets after September 11 because of the inciting speeches of Paul Wolfowitz, as Said actually did write in the exalted pages of the *London Review of Books*, is to resort to the silliest kind of demagogy. Worst of all is an entire article slandering the distinguished Iraqi dissident author Kanan Makiya. This is an essay written in tones of almost sub-literate violence and containing allegations—of a direct subsidy from Saddam Hussein to Makiya, for example—that Said knew to be false and defamatory. It should never have been written, and it most decidedly should not have been reprinted.

There is a contradiction at the center of this collection. Edward Said, to his credit and honor, repeatedly confronted his Arab readership with stern criticism of their own shortcomings, and of the abject failures and horrible crimes of their regimes and their leaders. But never once did he allow that American or British policy, directed at changing those regimes, could be justified. He cites the dreadful case

of the Egyptian social scientist Saadedin Ibrahim, unjustly accused
and imprisoned by a state security court in Cairo for pursuing his objective and detached research. Well, who sent observers to Ibrahim's
trial and protested his sentence? The US State Department, that's who.
(In New York not long ago, the now-released Ibrahim told me that he
had personally celebrated the downfall of Saddam Hussein.) In similar
fashion, Said would steadily denounce the Taliban and the Iraqi Baath
Party, while reserving even more vitriol for what he calls "the devasta-
tion of Afghanistan" by the Western intervention. At his lowest point,
he even claimed that the looting and destruction of the Iraqi national
museum was a deliberate act of American imperial vandalism, designed to intimidate Iraqis by a show of force. The uplifting thing about
contradictions is that they can illuminate, by debate and contrast, and
may point the way toward a synthesis. The sad thing about this book is
the deliberate way in which it forecloses that possibility.

Washington Post, August 15, 2004

◄(40)►

Susan Sontag: An Obituary

Between the word "public" and the word "intellectual" there falls, or
ought to fall, a shadow. The life of the cultivated mind should be private, reticent, discreet: Most of its celebrations will occur with no audience, because there can be no applause for that moment when the
solitary reader gets up and paces round the room, having just noticed
the hidden image in the sonnet, or the profane joke in the devotional
text, or the secret message in the prison diaries. Individual pleasure of
this kind is only rivaled when the same reader turns into a writer, and
after a long wrestle until daybreak hits on his or her own version of the
mot juste, or the unmasking of pretension, or the apt, latent literary
connection, or the satire upon tyranny.

The 20th century was perhaps unusual in the ways in which it
forced such people to quit their desks and their bookshelves and to

enter the agora. Looking over our shoulders, we do not find that we have much respect or admiration for those who simply survived, or who kept the private life alive. We may owe such people more than we know, but it is difficult to view them as exemplary. Our heroes and heroines are those who managed, from Orwell through Camus and Solzhenitsyn, to be both intellectual and engaged. (This combination of qualities would also be true of a good number of our fools and villains, from Céline to Shaw, with Sartre perhaps occupying the middle position.)

Susan Sontag passed an extraordinary amount of her life in the pursuit of private happiness through reading and through the attempt to share this delight with others. For her, the act of literary consumption was the generous parent of the act of literary production. She was so much impressed by the marvelous people she had read—beginning with Jack London and Thomas Mann in her girlhood, and eventually comprising the almost Borgesian library that was her one prized possession—that she was almost shy about offering her own prose to the reader. Look at her output and you will see that she was not at all prolific.

If it doesn't seem like that—if it seems as if she was always somewhere in print—it is because she timed her interventions very deftly. By the middle 1960s, someone was surely going to say something worth noticing about the energy and vitality of American popular culture. And it probably wasn't going to be any of the graying manes of the old *Partisan Review* gang. Sontag's sprightly, sympathetic essays on the diminishing returns of "high culture" were written by someone who nonetheless had a sense of tradition and who took that high culture seriously (and who was smart enough to be published in *Partisan Review*). Her acute appreciation of the importance of photography is something that now seems uncontroversial (the sure sign of the authentic pioneer), and her "Notes on 'Camp'" were dedicated to the memory of Oscar Wilde, whose fusion of the serious and the subversive was always an inspiration to her, as it is, I can't resist adding, to too few female writers.

In a somewhat parochial time, furthermore, she was an internationalist. I once heard her rather sourly described as American culture's "official greeter," for her role in presenting and introducing the writers of other scenes and societies. There was no shame in *that* charge: She—and Philip Roth—did a very great deal to familiarize Americans with the work of Czeslaw Milosz and Danilo Kiš, Milan Kundera and György Konrád. In *Against Interpretation*, published in 1966, she saw more clearly than most that the future defeat of official Communism was inscribed in its negation of literature. When Arpad Goncz, the novelist who eventually became a post-Communist president of Hungary, was invited to the White House, he requested that Susan be placed on his guest list. It's hard to think of any other American author or intellectual who would be as sincerely mourned as Susan will be this week, from Berlin to Prague to Sarajevo.

Mention of that last place name impels me to say another thing: this time about moral and physical courage. It took a certain amount of nerve for her to stand up on stage, in early 1982 in New York, and to denounce martial law in Poland as "fascism with a human face." Intended as ironic, this remark empurpled the anti-anti-Communists who predominated on the intellectual Left. But when Slobodan Milosevic adopted full-out national socialism after 1989, it took real guts to go and live under the bombardment in Sarajevo and to help organize the Bosnian civic resistance. She did not do this as a "tourist," as sneering conservative bystanders like Hilton Kramer claimed. She spent real time there and endured genuine danger. I know, because I saw her in Bosnia and had felt faint-hearted long before she did.

Her fortitude was demonstrated to all who knew her, and it was often the cause of fortitude in others. She had a long running battle with successive tumors and sarcomas and was always in the front line for any daring new treatment. Her books on illness and fatalism, and her stout refusal to accept defeat, were an inspiration. So were the many anonymous hours and days she spent in encouraging and advising fellow sufferers. But best of all, I felt, was the moment when, as president of American PEN, she had to confront the Rushdie affair in 1989.

It's easy enough to see, now, that the offer of murder for cash, made by a depraved theocratic despot and directed at a novelist, was a warning of the Islamist intoxication that was to come. But at the time, many of the usual "signers" of petitions were distinctly shaky and nervous, as were the publishers and booksellers who felt themselves under threat and sought to back away. Susan Sontag mobilized a tremendous campaign of solidarity that dispelled all this masochism and capitulation. I remember her saying hotly of our persecuted and hidden friend: "You know, I think about Salman *every second*. It's as if he was a *lover*." I would have done anything for her at that moment, not that she asked or noticed.

With that signature black-on-white swoosh in her hair, and her charismatic and hard-traveling style, she achieved something else worthy of note—the status of celebrity without any of the attendant tedium and squalor. She resolutely declined to say anything about her private life or to indulge those who wanted to speculate. The nearest to an indiscretion she ever came was an allusion to *Middlemarch* in the opening of her 1999 novel *In America*, where she seems to say that her one and only marriage was a mistake because she swiftly realized "not only that I was Dorothea but that, a few months earlier, I had married Mr. Casaubon.")

A man is not on his oath, said Samuel Johnson, when he gives a funeral oration. One ought to try and contest the underlying assumption here, which condescendingly excuses those who write *nil nisi bonum* of the dead. Could Susan Sontag be irritating, or hectoring, or righteous? She most certainly could. She said and did her own share of foolish things during the 1960s, later retracting her notorious remark about the white "race" being a "cancer" by saying that it slandered cancer patients. In what I thought was an astonishing lapse, she attempted to diagnose the assault of September 11, 2001, as the one thing it most obviously was not: "a consequence of *specific* [sic] American alliances and actions." Even the word "general" would have been worse in that sentence, but she had to know better. She said that she didn't read reviews of her work, when she obviously did. It could sometimes be very difficult to tell her anything or to have her admit that there was something she didn't know or hadn't read.

But even this insecurity had its affirmative side. If she was sometimes a little permissive, launching a trial balloon only to deflate it later (as with her change of heart on the filmic aesthetic of Leni Riefenstahl) this promiscuity was founded in curiosity and liveliness. About 20 years ago, I watched her having an on-stage discussion with Umberto Eco in downtown New York. Eco was a bit galumphing—he declared that his favorite novel was *Lolita* because he could picture himself in the part of Umberto Umberto. Susan, pressed to define the word "polymath," was both sweet and solemn. "To be a polymath," she declared, "is to be interested in everything—and in nothing else." She was always trying to do too much and square the circle: to stay up late debating and discussing and have the last word, then get a really early night, then stay up reading, and then make an early start. She adored trying new restaurants and new dishes. She couldn't stand affectless or bored or cynical people, of any age. She only ventured into full-length fiction when she was almost 60, and then discovered that she had a whole new life. And she resisted the last malady with terrific force and resource, so that to describe her as life-affirming now seems to me suddenly weak. Anyway—death be not proud.

Slate, December 29, 2004

⁜(41)⁜

An Interview with Christopher Hitchens, Part II

Anti-Fascism, Reactionary Conservatism, and the Post–September 11 World

JAMIE GLAZOV: I'd like to begin with your intellectual journey. You were, at one time, a man of the Left and, if I am correct, a Trotskyist. What led you to this political disposition? It is often said that a lot of our personal psychology and character lead us to our political outlooks. When you look back, does this apply to you in any way? Tell us a bit about your attraction to the Left, Trotskyism, Isaac Deutscher, etc.

CHRISTOPHER HITCHENS: At the time and place when I came to political awareness, which was in the early mid-1960s in England, the governing Establishment was that of the Labour Party in its most corrupt and opportunist form and in Washington (which we all understood as the real capital), it was that of the Democratic machine of LBJ. The charm and appeal of the "social democratic" project was thus very slight. And, coming from a generation which had read *Darkness* *at Noon* and *Nineteen Eighty Four* before being exposed to any Marxist influence, the option of illusions in orthodox Communism did not seriously exist. I think it is this formative background that meant that, in Western Europe at least, the radical and insurgent spirit was attracted to one form or another of "Trotskyism."

In 1968—I of course like to think of myself as having been a "Sixty Eighter" or even *soixante-huitard* rather than merely a "Sixties person"—there seemed the chance not only of contesting the atrocious imperial war in Vietnam but of ending the dictatorial regimes of De Gaulle, Franco, Salazar and Papadopoulos, and of extending this movement across the Berlin Wall. And we have some successes to boast of: the battering that the old order received in that year was to prove terminal in the short run, both East and West.

One is in danger of sounding like an old-fart veteran if one goes on too long about this, but to have been involved in street-arguments in Havana while Chicago was erupting and Prague being subjugated was to feel oneself part of a revolutionary moment. What I didn't understand then was that this was the very end of something—the revolutionary Marxist tradition—rather than a new beginning of it. But it had its aspect of honor and of glory. Its greatest culmination turned out to be in 1989, when the delayed or postponed effects of 1968 helped bring down the Berlin Wall altogether. It's not very well understood by the mainstream, but many Czechs and Poles and East Germans of my acquaintance, with more or less "Trotskyist" politics, played a seminal part in those events. And I did my best to stay on their side through those years.

The figure of Trotsky himself, as leader of the "Left Opposition" to Stalin, has many deformities. But I still think he comes out of the 20th century as a great figure of courageous and engaged dissent, and of the fusion of intellect and action. In my writing, I try to pay respect to the literary and intellectual figures associated with this tradition, from C. L. R. James to Victor Serge. The best-known of this group is of course George Orwell, though he is often not celebrated for that reason.

I am anticipating your next question, but there is in fact a "red thread" that still connects my past to my present views. In discussing things with my Iraqi and Kurdish comrades over the past decade or so, for example, I was quite struck by how many of them came to the struggle against Saddam Hussein by means of some of the same memories, books and traditions that I did. The best of the Iraqi dissident authors, Kanan Makiya, whose books everyone simply has to read if they want to be part of the argument, is the foremost example.

JG: After 9/11, you publicly broke with the Left. You resigned from the *Nation* magazine and came out forcefully supporting Bush's efforts in Afghanistan and Iraq. Tell us a bit about this turning point in your life. What was the final straw? Was it an excruciating decision? Surely it took a lot of courage to make it. After all, it entailed facing the fact that you yourself may have been wrong on some things and that, well, perhaps that you were also in the company of people that maybe it was a mistake to be in the company of. Tell us a little bit about the intellectual journey here, the decisions you had to make, and perhaps some of the pain—and bravery—that came along with making them.

CH: Well, there's no bravery involved (as there has been, for example, in Kanan's case). And my "turning points" are not quite the ones you suppose. The realization that we were in a cultural and political war with Islamic theocracy came to me with force and certainty not on 11 September 2001 but on 14 February 1989, when the Ayatollah Khomeini offered money in his own name to suborn the murder of my friend Salman Rushdie. On that occasion, as you may forget, the conservative and neo-conservative movement was often rather stupid and neutral, in the case of the Bush establishment because of its then-recent exposure as a sordid client of Khomeini's in the Iran-contra scandal, and in the case of many neo-cons because they thought Salman was an ally of Third World rebellions, especially the Palestinian one.

The realization that American power could and should be used for the defense of pluralism and as a punishment for fascism came to me in Sarajevo a year or two later. Here, the coalition of forces that eventually saved former Yugoslavia from aggression and ethnocide was made up of some leftists, many Jews and Muslims in America and Europe, many if not most of the neo-conservatives, and Tony Blair's Labour Government. The mass of mainstream conservatives in America and Britain were indifferent if not openly hostile, and of course many peaceniks kept to their usual line that intervention only leads to quagmires. That was an early quarrel between me and many of my *Nation* colleagues, and it was also the first time I found myself in the same trench as people like Paul Wolfowitz and Jeanne Kirkpatrick: a shock I had to learn to get over.

On 11 September I was actually in Whitman College, in Washington State, giving the "Scoop" Jackson memorial lecture at his *alma mater*. Slightly to my surprise, the college and the Jackson family had invited me to speak about my indictment of Henry Kissinger. But on reflection I understood that I needn't have been so startled: Henry Jackson had always disliked Kissinger for his willingness to sell out the Soviet Jews to Brezhnev, for example, and I point out in my book that it was Kissinger who told Gerald Ford to refuse Solzhenitsyn an invitation to the White House, and who later groveled to the Chinese Stalinists right after Tiananmen Square. He was soft on Communism, as well as on fascism and military dictatorship. (He also opposed any move to stop, let alone to depose, Slobodan Milosevic.)

Watching the towers fall in New York, with civilians incinerated on the planes and in the buildings, I felt something that I couldn't analyze at first and didn't fully grasp (partly because I was far from my family in Washington, who had a very grueling day) until the day itself was nearly over. I am only slightly embarrassed to tell you that this was a feeling of exhilaration. Here we are then, I was thinking, in a war to the finish between everything I love and everything I hate. Fine. We will win and they will lose. A pity that we let them pick the time and place of the challenge, but we can and we will make up for that.

As to the "Left" I'll say briefly why this was the finish for me. Here is American society, attacked under open skies in broad daylight by the most reactionary and vicious force in the contemporary world, a force which treats Afghans and Algerians and Egyptians far worse than it has yet been able to treat us. The vaunted CIA and FBI are asleep, at best. The working-class heroes move, without orders and at risk to their lives, to fill the moral and political vacuum. The moral idiots, meanwhile, like Falwell and Robertson and Rabbi Lapin, announce that this clerical aggression is a punishment for our secularism. And the governments of Pakistan and Saudi Arabia, hitherto considered allies on our "national security" calculus, prove to be the most friendly to the Taliban and Al Qaeda.

Here was a time for the Left to demand a top-to-bottom house-cleaning of the state and of our covert alliances, a full inquiry into the origins of the defeat, and a resolute declaration in favor of a fight to the end for secular and humanist values: a fight which would make friends of the democratic and secular forces in the Muslim world. And instead, the near-majority of "Left" intellectuals started sounding like Falwell, and bleating that the main problem was Bush's legitimacy. So I don't even muster a hollow laugh when this pathetic faction says that I, and not they, are in bed with the forces of reaction.

JG: When a leftist leaves the ranks, he often loses many, if not all, of his friends. In my own experience with leftists, I have learned that when they "like" people, they do not like them for who the people are as actual human beings, but for how their structure of political ideals conforms to their own. If you are a leftist in a leftist crowd and you all of a sudden like George W. Bush and love capitalism, chances are you will soon be made into a non-person.

You were once close friends with individuals such as Alexander Cockburn, Sidney Blumenthal, etc. But it appears not any more. Did your leftist friends abandon you? Or the other way around? Was this dislocation hurtful to you? Did it surprise you?

CH: In fairness to Mr Blumenthal, it must be said that it was I who attacked him first. As for Mr Cockburn, if I admire him as a somewhat *ad hominem* polemicist (which I still do, though I think he long ago reached the point of diminishing returns) then I can't very well complain when his fire is turned in my direction. Some lurid things have been said about me—that I am a racist, a hopeless alcoholic, a closet homosexual and so forth—that I leave to others to decide the truth of. I'd only point out, though, that if true these accusations must also have been true when I was still on the correct side, and that such shocking deformities didn't seem to count for so much then. Arguing with the Stalinist mentality for more than three decades now, and doing a bit of soap-boxing and street-corner speaking on and off, has meant that it takes quite a lot to hurt my tender feelings, or bruise my milk-white skin.

There are also a number of my old comrades, I must say, who have been very solid and eloquent in defending civil society against totalitarianism and theocracy, in America and Europe and the Middle East, and I recognize the *esprit* of 1968 in many of them, even as this has come to mean less to me personally.

JG: What do you consider yourself to be now? Are you still a leftist? Are you a conservative? Do you want to be embraced by neo-conservatives? Or are these labels—and questions—meaningless/inaccurate to you?

CH: The last time that I consciously wrote anything to "save the honor of the Left," as I rather pompously put it, was my little book on the crookedness and cowardice and corruption (to put it no higher) of Clinton. I used leftist categories to measure him, in other words, and to show how idiotic was the belief that he was a liberal's champion. Again, more leftists than you might think were on my side or in my corner, and the book was published by Verso, which is the publishing arm of the *New Left Review*. However, if a near-majority of leftists and liberals choose to think that Clinton was the target of a witch-hunt and the victim of "sexual McCarthyism," an Arkansan Alger Hiss in other words, you become weary of debating on their terms and leave them to make the best of it. Which I now see I was beginning to do anyway.

I have been taunted on various platforms recently for becoming a neo-conservative, and have been the object of some fascinating website and blog stuff, from the isolationist Right as well as from the peaceniks, who both argue in a semi-literate way that neo-conservativism is Trotskyism and "permanent revolution" reborn.

Sometimes, you have to comb an overt anti-Semitism out of this propaganda before you can even read it straight. And I can guarantee you that none of these characters has any idea at all of what the theory of "permanent revolution" originally meant.

However, there is a sort of buried compliment here that I find I am willing to accept. The neo-cons, or some of them, decided that they would back Clinton when he belatedly decided for Bosnia and Kosovo against Milosevic, and this even though they loathed Clinton, because the battle against religious and ethnic dictatorship in the Balkans took precedence. This, by the way, was partly a battle to save Muslims from Catholic and Christian Orthodox killers. That impressed me. The neo-cons also took the view, quite early on, that coexistence with Saddam Hussein was impossible as well as undesirable. They were dead right about that. They had furthermore been thinking about the menace of jihadism when most people were half-asleep.

And then I have to say that I was rather struck by the way that the *Weekly Standard* and its associated voices took the decision to get rid of Trent Lott earlier this year, thus removing an embarrassment as well as a disgrace from the political scene. And their arguments were on points of principle, not "perception." I liked their ruthlessness here, and their seriousness, at a time when much of the liberal Left is not even seriously wrong, but frivolously wrong, and babbles without any sense of responsibility. (I mean, have you *read* their sub-Brechtian stuff on Halliburton . . . ?) And revolution from above, in some states and cases, is—as I wrote in my book *A Long Short War*—often preferable to the status quo, or to no revolution at all.

The matter on which I judge people is their willingness, or ability, to handle contradiction. Thus Paine was better than Burke when it came to the principle of the French revolution, but Burke did and said magnificent things when it came to Ireland, India and America. One of them was in some ways a revolutionary conservative and the other was a conservative revolutionary. It's important to try and contain multitudes. One of my influences was Dr Israel Shahak, a tremendously brave Israeli humanist who had no faith in collectivist change but took a Spinozist line on the importance of individuals. Gore Vidal's admirers, of whom I used to be one and to some extent remain one, hardly notice that his essential critique of America is based on Lindbergh and "America First"—the most conservative position available. The only real radicalism in our time will come as it always has—from people who insist on thinking for themselves and who reject party-mindedness.

JG: You took many anti-American positions during the Cold War. Do you regret any of them? Now that you look back, were you wrong in any way? And if you do not think you were wrong, how is that reconcilable with your pro-American positions today in the War on Terror, Iraq, etc? Why is it right to defend freedom in the face of Saddam and Osama, but not in the face of Soviet totalitarianism?

CH: Again, I don't quite share the grammar of your question, and I dispute the right of conservatives to be automatically complacent on these points. My own Marxist group took a consistently anti-Moscow

line throughout the "Cold War," and was firm in its belief that the Soviet Union and its European empire could not last. Very few people
believed that this was the case: the best known anti-Communist to advance the proposition was the great Robert Conquest, but he himself
insists that part of the credit for such prescience goes to Orwell. More
recently, a very exact pre-figuration of the collapse of the USSR was
offered by two German Marxists, one of them from the West (Hans
Magnus Enzensberger) and one from the East (Rudolf Bahro, the accuracy of whose prediction was almost uncanny). I have never met an
American conservative who has even heard of, let alone read, either of
these authors.

Reasonably certain in the view that the official enemy was being
over-estimated (as it famously was by the CIA, for example, until at
least 1990) and that it would be eclipsed, I also believed that the conflict was never worth even the risk of a nuclear war. I was right about
that. And I detested the way that "Cold War" rhetoric was used to justify things, like the salvage of French colonialism in Indochina or the
prolonging of white rule in Southern Africa, which were deservedly
doomed in the first place and which in their origins predated the Bolshevik Revolution. I was right about that, too. I did believe that an
alternative version of democratic socialism was available to outweigh
and replace both global empires, though I find that this conviction has
fallen away from me and may never have been a real option—though I
am not ashamed of having upheld it.

JG: You refer to the "alternative version of democratic socialism" that
you wished "was available to outweigh and replace both global empires." In reference to both of the sides of the Cold War, you appear
to be implying some kind of moral equivalency between a system that
liquidated 100 million human beings in the 20th century and another
system, within which you lived, that allowed you to gain many material
and cultural rewards for criticizing it. Can it be denied that America
represented freedom, democracy and the forces of "good" in the face
of Soviet communism?

CH: Yes it can be denied in very many cases. Just to give you one example in which I was very much involved myself, there is no doubt
that the United States imposed a dictatorship, with a fascist ideology,
on Greece (a NATO member and member of the Council of Europe)

in 1967. This was done simply in order that the wrong party not win the upcoming elections. The result was a disastrous war in the Eastern Mediterranean as well as the stifling of liberty in Greece. One could go on—I have never seen anyone argue that the mass murder in East Timor, for example, helped to bring down the Berlin Wall. You might want to look at my little book on Henry Kissinger, which shows what much more conservative historians have elsewhere established—that during the Nixon years the USA was a rogue state. Alas those were not the only such years.

My self-criticism here would be a different one from the one you solicit. I was more pessimistic than I should have been about the likelihood of the United States reforming itself. In the long run, the Constitutional and democratic impulses reasserted themselves. To put it shortly, I much prefer an America that removes Saddam Hussein to the America that helped install and nurture him—and unlike you I am not willing to overlook these important pre-existing facts.

JG: I am not sure what is so complicated about the fact that in a world of good and evil, the forces of good must sometimes temporarily ally themselves with certain unlikable forces against the most terrible and dangerous evils of the time. But we'll have to return to this theme perhaps in another exchange.

I'd like to get back to the Left and the War on Terror. As a person who is familiar with the leftist mindset, why do you think the Left has taken the position it does on the War on Terror? Despots and terrorists like Saddam and Osama are the greatest persecutors of all leftist ideals and values. How can the Left not be violently opposed to such figures and the systems they lead? Where are radical western feminists, for instance, screaming for the rights of women under militant Islam?

CH: Concerning Iraq, I have to remind you that those of us who took the regime-change position (I invited the readers of my *Nation* column to support the Iraqi National Congress and the Patriotic Union of Kurdistan several years ago) were confronted first by the arguments of Bush Senior—who wrote openly that it was better and safer to leave Saddam in power in 1991—and of Bush Junior, who ran against Gore on the question of "nation building." We also had to fight against the CIA, as we indeed still do, and against the Buchanan-type forces grouped around the magazine *The American Conservative*. Finally, we faced the conservative Arabists of the State Department and at least half of the staff of Kissinger Associates. So don't be so goddam cocky about who was, or was not "pro-American." Having changed my own mind after the end of the first "Gulf War," I had at least as many arguments to conduct with Washington's right wing as I did with the soft or the dogmatic Left, and would not wish this any other way.

JG: I would like to focus in on *the Left's* mindset. What is it deep down in the heart of a leftist anti-war activist that spawns his opposition to Bush in the face of an evil such as Saddam and Osama?

CH: There is a noticeable element of the pathological in some current leftist critiques, which I tend to attribute to feelings of guilt allied to feelings of impotence. Not an attractive combination, because it results in self-hatred.

JG: What, in your view, should the US do in Iraq? In the War on Terror in general? Must we pursue the policy of pre-emptive strikes?

CH: The Bush administration was right on the main issue of removing Saddam as the pre-condition, but I whimper when I think of the opportunities that have since been missed. The crucial thing was obviously the empowerment of the Iraqis: I don't like this being adopted as a grudging final resort. And it seems nobody will be fired for failing to think about things—like generators for heaven's sake—that are simply an aspect of American "can do" culture. The humiliating attempt to involve the Turkish army in Iraq—which is one of the things I flatly disagree with Wolfowitz about—should never have been permitted in the first place.

The anti-war and neutralist forces share the blame here, because there was nothing to stop them saying, very well Mr. President, let us commonly design a plan for a new Iraq and think about what will be needed. Instead, all energy had to be spent on convincing people that Iraq should no longer be run by a psychotic crime family—which if the other side had had its way, it still would be. And we could be looking forward to the Uday/Qusay succession!

The "pre-emption" versus "prevention" debate may be a distinction without much difference. The important thing is to have it understood that the United States is absolutely serious. The jihadists have in the past bragged that America is too feeble and corrupt to fight. A lot is involved in disproving that delusion on their part.

JG: Are you hopeful that we will win the War on Terror against militant Islam and rogue regimes?

CH: Since I do still find that I use the method of historical materialism (not yet surpassed by any rival) I think it's worth stating some unarguable propositions. First—all *jihads* have always failed. The last serious one, which was the declaration of a holy war by the Ottoman Empire in 1914, ended by the loss of that empire as well as the loss of the war, and was a defeat and erasure so complete that many people who hear Osama bin Laden's call for the restoration of the Caliphate don't even know what he's screeching about. Lesser *jihads* tend to consume themselves in quarrels over spoils or doctrines: an irrational view of the world will tell against you in the end, as is shown by the crazy and self-destructive tactics now being pursued by Islamists in Saudi Arabia, Indonesia, Turkey and elsewhere. They wish to be martyrs—we should be willing to help.

Second—dictatorship is a very unstable and uncertain (and highly vulnerable) method of rule. Third, no combination of dictatorship and clericalism can possibly stand against the determined power of the United States. In other words, the eventual result is certain victory, military and political, however long the task may take. It can be useful to bear this in mind. The job of citizens is to make sure that this American power really is self-determined, and not left either to professionals or to amateurs. We are not watching for the outcome of this war: we are participants in it and had better comport ourselves as such.

JG: Last question: in terms of your own position on Iraq and the War on Terror, are you making any headway or inroads in leftist ranks? Are any segments of the Left receptive to your message? How have you been received by the Left in general with your stance?

CH: Most of the leftists I know are hoping openly or secretly to leverage difficulty in Iraq in order to defeat George Bush. For innumerable reasons, including the one I cited earlier, I think that this is a tactic and a mentality utterly damned by any standard of history or morality. What I mainly do is try to rub that in.

As I've told you before, there are some former comrades who take a decent position but they all half-understand that it's now an anomalous one in terms of the "Left" as a whole. Some pessimistic liberals who don't wish to sabotage the effort still describe the war against jihadism and dictatorship as "unwinnable."

My short reply is that it is un-loseable. We still haven't captured Radovan Karadzic or Ratko Mladic, who are hiding somewhere in Europe ten years after murdering over 10,000 Muslims in one day. But their protector regime is gone and one day they will be caught or killed. Osama bin Laden is dead in my opinion, and probably has been dead for more than a year. Saddam Hussein is alive, but not where he planned to be.

The Taliban and the Baath and the Serbian Socialist Party will not regain power, however much violence they muster. These are facts. The combat as a whole will never be "over," because it is part of a permanent struggle between reason and unreason, among other things. But to assert that rather minimal point is also to assert that the enemy cannot win. Given the proven nature of that enemy, I hope I need not say any more about what I think of its subconscious sympathizers, let alone its overt ones.

JG: What is your general disposition towards the Israel-Palestine conflict?

CH: One of the advantages of a Marxist and internationalist training is that it exposes one to the early writings of those Jewish cosmopolitans who warned from the first day that Zionism would be a false Messiah for the Jews and an injustice to the Arabs. Nothing suggests to me that they were wrong on these crucial points. If I could re-wind the tape I would stop Herzl from telling the initial demagogic lie (actually two lies) that a land without a people needs a people without a land. And, if Palestine actually had been uninhabited, I would still have said that Jews have no business seeking Messianic or Biblical ghettoes. That's the way I think, and I am simply disgusted by the lunatic propaganda which even now argues that to make Jews "safer" there should be settlements built on stolen land in the middle of the Gaza strip, for example.

Those who propose this are deluding the Jews and oppressing and robbing the Arabs, and while they may well bring on Armageddon (as some of them openly desire to do) they will of course fail to bring on the coming of the Messiah, let alone the "second" such coming in which their even more moronic Christian fundamentalist friends affect to believe. I think it an urgent task of the United States to dissociate entirely from this enterprise, and for the Supreme Court to rule that no American funds be used for the illegal establishment of religion in the occupied territories.

Mistaken as it is as an ethno-nationalist quasi-religious ideology, Zionism may have entirely failed to prove itself justifiable or sustainable, but nonetheless has founded a sort of democratic state which isn't any worse in its practice than many others with equally dubious origins. And we are of course now faced with Islamic nihilists who oppose any Jewish presence in Palestine at all, and who act accordingly. (Unless you believe, as some pacifists seem to do, that suicide-murderers slay themselves and others, including Christian Arabs, either out of "despair" or in order to bring about a two-state solution. I have no time to waste on that delusion, either.)

The United States is free to say at any time that it can and will guarantee the 1947/8 frontiers of Israel, and will make this defense perimeter part of the western alliance, but that it will not provide one cent for annexation and colonization, let alone for fanatical religious proselytisation. General Sharon would have to reject this offer of perpetual "security," because of the thuggish ideology of his own party. But the evidence is that a majority of Israeli Jews and Jewish Americans would support it, on principle. Why does this not happen, and why do we gamble the whole future of regime-change in the region on the wishes of a handful of demented zealots? At least partly because of the influence of the Christian lobby, which completes my point about the poisonous effect of the three monotheisms. The war upon which we are engaged is a war for Enlightenment values, in which all religious fundamentalists are actual or potential traitors. It's well beyond time that we recognized this elementary fact, and began to act upon it.

JG: You refer to settlements being built on "stolen land." But the Jews never "stole" anyone's land. The Palestine Mandate was never a nation, let alone even a political entity of any kind. It was a "mandate" that was created by the British from the remnants of the Turkish Empire after World War I. 10% of it was given to the Jews and 90% to the Palestinian Arabs.

Israel "occupied" the territories in a defensive war in which Arabs sought to wipe Israel out of existence. How do the Israelis give this land back if the neighbors who tried to exterminate them still refuse to recognize Israel's right to exist? Even international law legitimizes Israel for occupying the land after defeating its aggressors.

Question: why do you focus on Israeli "occupation" when you know that if Arabs desist from their desire and effort to obliterate Israel, that all kinds of land can be given to all kinds of Palestinians and Arabs?

CH: The Balfour Declaration and the Sykes-Picot agreement preceded the Palestine Mandate, and planned for a disastrous partition of the region which we are still (or those of us who know about it) compelled to regret. If you give the most cursory attention to the writings of Herzl and Nordau and other founders of the Zionist movement, or if you read the memoirs of Yitzhak Rabin closer to our own day, you will notice at once that they knew that a confrontation with the Arab inhabitants of Palestine was unavoidable. This was because they wanted their land, and wanted it without its inhabitants. The historic mistake—even if we agree that there was no ethical error involved— was the assumption that in time the Arabs would simply get used to this expropriation. To describe this is a mistake is of course a colossal understatement as well as a punishable euphemism.

The theft of land continues to this moment in the specific as well as the general sense: a farmer whose great-grandfather worked the same olive grove can be evicted without notice to make room for a settlement or a road or a wall, and told that such a flagrant confiscation is justifiable because he is not a Jew. This is a scandal, and its roots are inscribed in Israeli law, and I have never seen it justified. The only actual justification offered is that god awarded the land to one tribe a good many years ago, and of course this appalling racist and messianic delusion—employed by Israel's Prime Minister without apology—only makes a terrible situation even worse.

I might add that this program of colonization was well under way before there were any suicide bombers, and was ruthlessly continued during the unarmed *intifada* of the 1980s, as it was during every single day of the Oslo negotiations. You are quite mistaken about international law, which explicitly forbids interference with the demography and ownership of territories occupied in wartime. Meanwhile, leading Israeli conservatives speak openly about a "transfer" or mass deportation of the remaining Arab population, and boast that this is no more than what they began doing in 1947/1948.

Let me add a word for your Republican readers. I would be opposed to this maltreatment of the Palestinians if it took place on a remote island with no geopolitical implications. It is a matter of principle. However, the exorbitance of Sharon and his cronies is now such that it has attracted the criticism of the last four heads of the Shin Beth. What strikes me in this is the sheer wanton selfishness of the thing: for the sake of a doomed racist colonization the Israeli zealots are prepared to destroy the entire possibility of regime-change in the region (an enterprise that leaves them cold in any case because it doesn't involve the fulfillment of insane biblical prophecies).

Mr Bush, to his credit, has become the first President to use the term "Palestinian state." And he has criticized the building of the wall that both locks in and extends the occupation. Every one of the potential Democratic nominees takes an opportunistic pro-Israeli view that consists of irresponsible pandering. One of my reasons for favoring the re-election of the President is that only given a second term is he likely to speak up properly. He shouldn't wait, of course. He should say immediately: "General Sharon, tear down this wall!" Dream on, you may say. I'm not an optimist here, as you will see from my earlier reply about Armageddon without the Messiah. But I know from experience that none of Bush's liberal and Democratic rivals will even come close to this, and so I am a "lesser evil" person on this rather crucial point.

In the last sentence of your question, by the way, you appear to negate what you say in your first one.

JG: No contradiction. The basic point is that Israel has always been ready to provide land for peace. It is ready to do the same now. But the intent of the Arabs and Palestinians to wipe out the Jewish homeland, rather than to build a Palestinian homeland, is what constitutes the tragedy.

So I guess we reach this question then: do you think there is any realistic solution to this problem? If you were able to have some influence in the "peace process," would there be any kind of idea or agenda that you would push for?

CH: Well, the problem of Palestine is not, I hope, so anguishing and cataclysmic that it needs my personal solution. I do think, much of the time, that the moment for a decent solution may be in our past not in our future, and that a horrific outcome awaits. One of the haunting phrases of the *Manifesto* is the least noted: Marx and Engels speak soberly not of the victory of one side or another but of "the common ruin of the contending classes," and this is a better description of 1871 and 1905, to say nothing of 1914 and 1917, than they are usually given credit for.

Still, the solution of a local land-dispute between competing petty tribes ought not to be beyond the wit of man. The argument is contained within a quadrilateral. Either one side can defeat and expel or exterminate the other. Or there can be a sharing of the territory. Or the conflict may exhaust and destroy both parties. Or the status quo—a kind of armed and unstable apartheid truce—can be assumed to continue indefinitely.

There are no other options. So, to take the above in order, it can easily be seen that the fourth one is impossible. Neither Jews nor Arabs can go on as they are, and the demographic facts are ruthlessly telling. This in turn makes more fearful and more toxic the other two "solutions," each of which would involve ethnic cleansing and war and each of which would therefore involve—since ethnic cleansing would not be forgiven or forgotten—even worse wars in the future, not excluding ethnocidal attempts.

The second solution was adopted by Yitzhak Rabin because he had looked the alternatives in the face and had even thought of trying them. His murder by a Jewish fascist was a calamity, and I remember thinking at the time that it might make the nightmare options more thinkable.

In my opinion, Israel doesn't "give up" anything by abandoning religious expansionism in the West Bank and Gaza. It does itself a favor, because it confronts the internal clerical and chauvinist forces which want to instate a theocracy for Jews, and because it abandons a scheme which is doomed to fail in the worst possible way. The so-called "security" question operates in reverse, because as I may have said already, only a moral and political idiot would place Jews in a settlement in Gaza in the wild belief that this would make them safer.

Of course this hard-headed and self-interested solution of withdrawal would not satisfy the jihadists. But one isn't seeking to placate them. One is seeking to destroy and discredit them. At the present moment, they operate among an occupied and dispossessed and humiliated people, who are forced by Sharon's logic to live in a close yet ghettoized relationship to the Jewish centers of population. Try and design a more lethal and rotten solution than that, and see what you come up with.

The principal reason why this trivial squabble has become so dangerous to all of us is the "faith based" element. Even for the so-called secular Jewish nationalists, it always had to be Jerusalem and Hebron. (Never mind the silly idea of turning Jewish watchmakers from Hungary into farmers: now it turns Jewish bullies from Brooklyn into vigilantes.) What did they imagine would be the response of the followers of the Prophet? I think myself that not even the most secular and internationalist Palestinian could be expected to bear the indignity of being first chucked out of his land and then told that oranges didn't grow in the "desert" of Haifa until 1948. One must not insult or degrade or humiliate people, let alone deport or dispossess them. Nor is one permitted to lie about history.

The United States now has—as elsewhere—to split the difference between principle and pragmatism, and it can if it wishes to do so. I feel sad that this is the best that can be done, and I shudder when I think of the missed chances, but a peace must now be imposed and the moment for performing this action is long overdue.

Frontpage, December 10, 2003

PART IV

Critical Responses and Exchanges

◄(42)►

Letter to the *Nation*, October 1, 2001

NOAM CHOMSKY

Editors' Note: The following is a summary of Chomsky's letter to the Na-tion magazine. Readers are encouraged to access the full transcript of the letter, which, as of the publication of this book, is available at www. thenation.com/doc/20011015/chomsky20011001.

Chomsky was asked by the *Nation* to respond to two articles by Chris-topher Hitchens: "Against Rationalization" and "Of Sin, the Left, and Islamic Fascism" (see chapters 3 and 4, respectively, in this volume). "After refusing several times," he "reluctantly" agreed to do so.

Chomsky begins by questioning Hitchens's refusal to credit a com-parison between the September 11 attacks and President Clinton's rocketing of the Al Shifa pharmaceutical plant in Khartoum in August 1998. Referring to the latter, Chomsky observes that it inflicted a vast human toll, resulting in the deaths of hundreds of thousands of peo-ple. "To regard the comparison to September 11 as outrageous," he as-serts, is to "express extraordinary racist contempt for African victims of a shocking crime."

Chomsky then proceeds to challenge the accusation, mounted by Hitchens, that he is an apologist for terror. On the contrary, he insists, by addressing the "grievances expressed by people of the Middle East region, rich to poor, secular to Islamist," I am simply following the "the course that would be followed by anyone who hopes to reduce the likelihood of further atrocities rather than simply to escalate the cycle of violence, in the familiar dynamics, leading to even greater catastro-phes here and elsewhere."

Chomsky concludes by suggesting that "the fair and sensible reac-tion" to Hitchens's comments is to treat them as evidence of "some ab-erration, and to await the return of the author to the important work that he has often done in the past."

HITCHENS RESPONDS

The two related questions before the house are these. Can the attacks of September 11 be compared to an earlier outrage committed by Americans? And should they be so compared?

Noam Chomsky does not rise much above the level of half-truth in his comparison of the September 11 atrocities to Clinton's rocketing of Sudan. Since his remarks are directed at me, I'll instance a less-than-half-truth as he applies it to myself. I "must be unaware," he writes, that I "express such racist contempt for African victims of a terrorist crime." With his pitying tone of condescension, and his insertion of a deniable but particularly objectionable innuendo, I regret to say that Chomsky displays what have lately become his hallmarks.

I have a very clear memory of the destruction of the Al Shifa chemical plant in Khartoum on August 20, 1998, and of the false claim made by the Administration that it had sought out and destroyed a nerve gas facility that was linked to Osama bin Laden's shady business empire. I wrote a series of columns in the *Nation*, dated October 5, October 19 and November 16, 1998. The first one of these was re-circulated on the web by *Salon* magazine. I then wrote an expanded essay for the January 1999 issue of *Vanity Fair*. And the chapter in my book *No One Left to Lie To*, titled "Clinton's War Crimes," is a summary and digest of all the above. I quoted Tom Carnaffin, the British engineer who had helped construct the plant. I quoted the German ambassador, Werner Daum, who had recently toured it. I interviewed one of the world's leading authorities on inorganic chemistry, Professor R.J.P. Williams. I interviewed Milton Bearden, a retired CIA station chief. My conclusions, which were stated earlier and at greater length than by any of the journalists cited by Chomsky, were that the factory was a medical and pharmaceutical facility, unrelated in any way to the holdings of bin Laden, and that this could and should have been known in advance. In any case, I argued, the United States had no right to hit Sudanese territory without at least first requesting an inspection of the plant. In short, as I put it, several times and in several different ways, "only one person was killed in the rocketing of Sudan. But many more have died, and will die, because an impoverished country has lost its chief source of medicines and pesticides." As I also phrased it, the President had "acted with caprice and brutality and with a complete disregard for international law, and perhaps counted on the indifference of the press and public to a negligible society like that of Sudan."

Thus I think I am indeed "unaware," with or without Chomsky's lofty permission, of my propensity for racist contempt. Since Chomsky reads the *Nation* and seems to have a clip-file on Al Shifa, he is in a position to know my views if he cares to. I think I can say without immodesty that I wrote more, and earlier, about this scandal than any other person. I also helped the late John Scanlon in preparing the basis for a lawsuit by the owner of the factory, Saleh Idris, seeking compensation from the US government. That suit is still active.

I have to say that I didn't get an unambiguous response from the Left at the time, because there were those who were uneasy at the allegation that Clinton had "wagged the dog." (The bombing took place as Miss Lewinsky was returning to the grand jury, and secured him a nauseating "bounce" in the opinion polls.) It was felt in some "progressive" quarters that to make too much of the atrocity was to "give ammunition" to the Republicans. I may be mistaken, but I don't remember Noam Chomsky circulating the news of the war crime when it would have made any difference. Certainly not with the energy he does now—by way of a comparison with the massacres in New York and Washington and Pennsylvania.

How exact is this comparison? Chomsky is obviously right when he says that one must count "collateral" casualties, though it isn't possible to compute the Sudanese ones with any certainty. (And he makes a small mistake: The Sudanese regime demanded at the UN only that there be an on-site inspection of the destroyed factory—a demand that the United States resisted, to its shame.) But must one not also measure intention and motive? The clear intention of the September 11 death squads was to maximize civilian deaths in an area renowned for its cosmopolitan and multi-ethnic character. (The New York Yemeni community alone is "missing" some 200 members, mainly push-cart vendors in the nearby streets.) The malicious premeditation is very evident and manifest: The toll was intended to be very much higher than it was. And I believe I have already pointed out that the cruise missiles fired at Sudan were not crammed with terrified civilian kidnap victims. I do not therefore think it can be argued that the hasty, politicized and wicked decision to hit the Al Shifa plant can be characterized as directly homicidal in quite the same way. And I don't think anyone will be able to accuse me of euphemizing the matter.

(Incidentally, the *New York Times* for October 2 carried a report on page B4. The World Bank now estimates that the shock suffered by the international economy as a result of September 11 will have the following effects on poorer societies. "It is estimated that 40,000 children worldwide will likely die from disease and malnutrition and 10 million people will fall below the bank's extreme poverty line of $1 dollar a day or less as a result of slower economic growth." No doubt Chomsky will wish to factor this in. Or will he prefer to say that the World Bank is the problem in the first place? His casuistry appears to be limitless.)

In a brilliant article in *The New Yorker* ("The Missiles of August"), Seymour Hersh reconstructed the decision-making that led to the Al Shifa raid. He found that four of the five Joint Chiefs had been kept in the dark about it, as had Louis Freeh of the FBI, who was then in Africa investigating the ghastly bombings of two neighboring US Embassies. I was myself able to find several senior people at the State Department and the CIA who had urged against the strike at the time and who could prove it, and would let their own names be used for quotation. It was as near to a purely presidential decision, replete with Strangelovian opportunism, as could be. Never mind for now whether this strengthens my case for trying Clinton—a case that Chomsky makes without realizing it. How fair is it to say that "the United States" decided in advance on all those Sudanese deaths? It might be fairer than one might like, but it still wouldn't come up to the Al Qaeda standard.

As one who spent several weeks rebutting it, and rebutting it in real time, I can state that the case for considering Al Shifa as a military target was not an absolutely hollow one. (One of the main Sudanese opposition groups, for example, had identified it as a bin Laden facility engaged in the manufacture of nerve gas.) In one way this makes little difference, because Clinton never demanded an inspection and because a nerve gas plant can't be folded like a tent and moved overnight. So that what was committed was certainly an aggression. However, at least a makeshift claim of military targeting could be advanced: President Clinton and his contemptible Defense Secretary Cohen did not boast of having taught Sudanese civilians a lesson. Furthermore, the Sudanese regime had been sheltering and nurturing Osama bin Laden, had been imposing its own form of Islamic dictatorship and has in other respects a filthy record. And two embassies had just been blown up in Kenya and Dar es Salaam, with the infliction of very many hundreds of African civilian casualties, by men in bin Laden's network. (It's not specially pointful to this argument, but Chomsky's touching belief in the then-imminence of regional peace strikes me as naïve.) I thus hold to my view that there is no facile "moral equivalence" between the two crimes.

But this by no means exhausts my disagreement with Chomsky. Suppose that we agree that the two atrocities can or may be mentioned in the same breath. Why should we do so? I wrote at the time (the *Nation*, October 5, 1998) that Osama bin Laden "hopes to bring a 'judgmental' monotheism of his own to bear on these United States." Chomsky's recent version of this is "considering the grievances expressed by people of the Middle East region." In my version, then as now, one confronts an enemy who wishes ill to our society, and also to his own (if impermeable religious despotism is considered an "ill"). In Chomsky's reading, one must learn to sift through the inevitable propaganda and emotion resulting from the September 11 attacks, and lend an ear to the suppressed and distorted cry for help that comes, not from the victims, but from the perpetrators. I have already said how distasteful I find this attitude. I wonder if even Chomsky would now like to have some of his own words back? Why else should he take such care to quote himself deploring the atrocity? Nobody accused him of not doing so. It's often a bad sign when people defend themselves against charges which haven't been made.

To be against rationalization is not the same as to be opposed to reasoning. By all means we must meet the challenge to our understanding. I think that the forces represented by Al Qaeda and the Taliban are fairly easy to comprehend, but not very easy to coexist with. I also believe that we would do well to take them at their word. I even believe that it is true that September 11 was a hinge event. Chomsky gives me the impression of regarding it as an inconvenience. With some irritation and impatience, he manages to assimilate it to his pre-existing worldview, and then goes on as if nothing much had happened. I think it would be flattering to describe this as an exercise in clarification.

And I think it also contains a serious danger of euphemism, in that it purportedly connects the mass murder of our fellows to causes (such as the emancipation of the Palestinians from occupation) which are much better considered in their own right. To propose the connection is inevitably to flatter Al Qaeda, even if only indirectly. If I seem to exaggerate, then pray consider this passage from page 39 of Chomsky's most recent book: *A New Generation Draws the Line: Kosovo, East Timor and the Standards of the West* (London: Verso, 2000):

> The huge slaughter in East Timor is (at least) comparable to the terrible atrocities that can plausibly be attributed to Milosevic in the earlier wars in Yugoslavia, and responsibility is far easier to assign, with no complicating factors. If proponents of the "repetition of Bosnia" thesis intend it seriously, they should certainly have been calling for the bombing of Jakarta—indeed Washington and London—in early 1998 so as not to allow in East Timor a repetition of the crimes that Indonesia, the US, and the UK had perpetrated there for a quarter-century. And when the new generation of leaders refused to pursue this honorable course, they should have been leading citizens to do so themselves, perhaps joining the bin Laden network. These conclusions follow straightforwardly, if we assume that the thesis is intended as something more than apologetics for state violence.

Here, the pretense of remorseless logic degenerates into flat-out irrationality. "These conclusions follow straightforwardly"? The accusations against Milosevic are "plausible"? A year ago it would have been possible to notice the same thing that strikes the eye today: Chomsky's already train-wrecked syllogisms seem to entail the weird and sinister assumption that bin Laden is a ventriloquist for thwarted voices of international justice. (For more on this, see an excellent forthcoming essay on Chomsky's work in *The American Prospect*, authored by Professor Jeffrey Isaac of the University of Indiana, to whom I am indebted.)

If there is now an international intervention, whether intelligent and humane, or brutal and stupid, against the Taliban, some people will take to the streets, or at least mount some "Candle in the Wind" or "Strawberry Fields" peace vigils. They did not take to the streets, or even go moist and musical, when the Administration supported the Taliban. But that was, surely, just as much an intervention? An intervention, moreover, that could not even pretend to be humane or democratic? I had the same concern about those who did not object when the United States safeguarded Milosevic, but did protest when it finally turned against him. Am I supposed not to notice that these two groups of "anti-interventionists" are in fact the same people?

Concluding, then. I have begun to think that Noam Chomsky has lost or is losing the qualities that made him a great moral and political tutor in the years of the Indochina war, and that enabled him to write such monumental essays as his critique of the Kahan Commission on Sabra and Shatila or his analysis of the situation in East Timor. I don't say this out of any "more in sorrow than anger" affectation: I have written several defenses of him and he knows it. But the last time we corresponded, some months ago, I was appalled by the robotic element both of his prose and of his opinions. He sought earnestly to convince me that Vaclav Havel, by addressing a joint session of Congress in the fall of 1989, was complicit in the murder of the Jesuits in El Salvador that had occurred not very long before he landed in Washington. In vain did I point out that the timing of Havel's visit was determined by the November collapse of the Stalinist regime in Prague, and that on his first celebratory visit to the United States he need not necessarily take the opportunity to accuse his hosts of being war criminals. Nothing would do, for Chomsky, but a strict moral equivalence between Havel's conduct and the mentality of the most depraved Stalinist. (He's written this elsewhere, so I break no confidence.) I then took the chance of asking him whether he still considered Ed Herman a political co-thinker. Herman had moved from opposing the bombing of Serbia to representing the Milosevic regime as a victim and as a nationalist peoples' democracy. He has recently said, in a ludicrous attack on me, that the "methods and policies" of the Western forces in Kosovo were "very similar" to the tactics of Al Qaeda, an assertion that will not surprise those who are familiar with his style. Chomsky knew perfectly well what I was asking, and why, but chose to respond by saying that he did not regard anybody in particular as a co-thinker. I thought then that this was a shady answer; I now think that it may also have been an unintentionally prescient one. I don't believe that any of those who have so anxiously sought his opinions in the past three weeks have felt either inspired or educated by them, because these opinions are a recipe for nothingness. And only an old admiration should prevent me from adding, nothingness at the very best.

Nation (Online), October 4, 2001

⁴⁽ 43 ⁾ᵘ

Letter to the *Nation*, January 10, 2002

EDWARD S. HERMAN

Editors' Note: The following is a summary of Herman's letter to the Nation. *As of the publication of this book, the full transcript of the letter is available at www.thenation.com/doc/20020128/letter.*

Herman begins by questioning Hitchens's self-proclaimed radical credentials. Defining the essence of "liberalism" as, via L. T. Hobhouse, an aversion to force, Herman dismissively observes that Hitchens can't even be described as a liberal.

Herman then goes on to castigate Hitchens for his view that the war in Afghanistan was executed with an almost "pedantic policy" of avoiding civilian casualties, and did not cause a "serious loss of civilian life":

> Marc Herold has calculated, on the basis of news reports alone, that more than 3,500 Afghan civilians have been killed by US bombs, more than in the Trade Center bombings, which Hitchens considered an extremely serious loss of human life. Hitchens ignores the effect of the war—and deliberate Bush actions denying food supplies—on a starving population, which has frightened all those working in food relief. Erwin van't Land, of Doctors Without Borders, stated in late November that "the situation deteriorated during the past two months of bombing, as large parts of the Afghan population dependent on international aid for survival [some 3.5 million people] did not receive it."

"But," says Herman, "Hitchens knows better, just as he *knows* that the kind and gentle Bush Administration is 'pedantically' avoiding civilian casualties" (emphasis in original).

Herman concludes by dismissing Hitchens's claim that Bush's war can be defended from the Left. "At this point in his political journey," he reflects, "we may have a long wait to find an imperialist war that Christopher Hitchens will not find to be a left's and just war."

HITCHENS RESPONDS

I'm happy to let readers decide for themselves about my ideological character. But I don't mind having it said that I favor physical force against fascism, and even relish it. And I think Hobhouse is a dubious source for determining that liberalism equals pacifism. Whether Herman is a pacifist or not I neither know nor care: that he isn't an ally in battles against fascism is already notorious.

Shortly after September 11 he wrote that the attack on the World Trade Center was reminiscent of the methods employed by NATO to get Milosevic out of Kosovo. Now his dismal search for moral equivalence leads him to find serendipity in the apparent symmetry of casualty figures. Well it now looks as if—supposing his Afghan civilian numbers to be correct—there have been more people killed in Afghanistan than in New York, Washington and Pennsylvania combined. So perhaps his crass utilitarianism will lead him to announce that the coalition's counterstroke against the Taliban and Al Qaeda is not merely as bad as, but actually worse than, the September 11 aggression.

I, however, will continue to presume that it is obvious that those murdered in America on that day were not "collateral damage." Their murders were the direct object of the "operation." By contrast, we have had repeated and confirmed reports of frustration on the part of American targeters in Afghanistan, frequently denied permission to open fire because of legal constraints imposed by the Pentagon. This is actually a tribute to the work of the antiwar movement over the years; it seems paltry in more than one way to be sneering at it.

Since every member of Al Qaeda has to be counted as a potential suicide bomber, and since their Taliban protectors had created vast hunger and misery in Afghanistan, the true humanitarian cost of finding and killing them cannot be reckoned in Herman's simple arithmetic. Nor can his outdated and arcane citations alter the fact that aid of all kinds is now reaching those who most need it. The necessary condition for that was always a short and hard-fought war. Unless of course, for "humanitarian" reasons, one was prepared to leave the Taliban/Al Qaeda regime in place. I would not direct such a slur against Herman, even though I can't help noticing that General Galtieri, trainer of the *contras*, might still be in possession of both Argentina and the Malvinas if Herman's counsel had been heeded. The chances of that, however, have grown slimmer over the years and are now approaching the nonexistent.

Finally, when I spoke in Chicago I said that the war against Islamic fascism had been going on for some time before the Bush family joined in, that it involved and involves a confrontation with the oligarchies of Pakistan and Saudi Arabia, and that it was therefore more a question of whether he should be allowed to join our (not "my") war. Herman misses the point and the joke, and I would put this down to his customary sloppiness if it wasn't that, in his other misrepresentations of my published views on Ashcroftism, he seems to be actuated by malice as well.

Nation (Online), January 10, 2002

⫷ 44 ⫸

Christopher Hitchens: The Dishonorable Policeman of the Left

SCOTT LUCAS

It was a sudden, devastating attack. The perpetrator struck mercilessly, leaving no time for a considered response. When he had finished, the "Left" was in ruins.

"I have no hesitation in describing this mentality, carefully and without heat," the author wrote heatedly, "as soft on crime and soft on fascism. No political coalition is possible with such people and, I'm thankful to say, no political coalition with them is now necessary. It no longer matters what they think."

And, with that strike, we could rest assured that no dissent—no quibbling about military action against Afghanistan; no worries about the bypassing of the United Nations or the International Court of Justice; no concerns that the Israel-Palestine issue, the tensions in Saudi Arabia, Pakistan, Indonesia or the Philippines would remain even after Osama bin Laden and Mullah Omar had been hunted down; no mention of the long-term expansion of American power for motives perhaps less noble than the "war on terrorism"—would rise from the smoldering target of this invective. For the attacker was not Donald Rumsfeld but the self-proclaimed "contrarian," the "singularly insightful . . . critic of American policy and culture" (*Reason* magazine), the "honorable man of the left" (*Atlantic* magazine), that "authentic voice of dissent" (the *Observer*), Christopher Hitchens.

Hitchens's assault was masterful. He gave it non-partisan respectability by launching it across the Anglo-American political spectrum: The London *Evening Standard* on 19 September 2001; the *Nation*, almost the only semblance of a mainstream "Left" journal in the US, on 24 September; the *Guardian* and the *Spectator* in the following three days. His past record—as vilifier of Pinochet's Chile and scourge of Bill Clinton's "Monicagate," of air strikes against Iraq and the Sudan, and, above all, for tracking the "war criminal" Henry Kissinger—established his claim to being the honorable policeman of the Left, attacking it in order to save it.

Since then, Hitchens has worked his beat masterfully. In addition to his periodic walkabouts in the *Guardian*, the *Mirror* and the *Evening Standard*, there has been the unveiling of his tome *Letters to a Young Contrarian*, an appearance on Start the Week, the references to his latest book-length mission, *Orwell's Victory* (in which he binds history to the present by exalting the "decent Englishman" George and smiting evildoers such as Raymond Williams). There has even been time to inspire, with wit and wine, Lynn Barber's tribute in the *Observer*. Hitch has toned down the polemic and moved to other concerns—he's traveled through India and revisited his persistent target Kissinger—but still he lurks behind the forelock, ready to pounce if the bad lefties reassemble to suck up to Islam: "I'm not surprised at criticism from the 'Ramadanistas' . . . I don't care what they think . . . It's one long bleat from these guys and gals."

But it ain't the final reel for our hero yet. Sheriff Hitchens rode into London on 15 May, saddling up for a debate on "the war on terrorism," and found that all his carpet-bombing, daisy-cutting rhetoric hadn't wiped out the "Left."

On the podium, there was top schoolmarm Onora O'Neill, with her pragmatic approach to nation states and human rights, politely asking about the evidence to prove Hitchens's "Islamic fascist" conspiracy (in which he characterizes Islam as one homogenized entity, committed to imposing Sharia law across the globe). There was Jacqueline Rose, the Freudian with the heart of gold, linking Hitchens's rhetoric to that of Tony Blair, Ariel Sharon and Osama bin Laden: "At best, two boys in a playground fighting, at worst two dead men talking . . . very exciting, very ineffectual, and very dangerous." There was Anatole Lieven, too thoughtful by half. He reminded the Sheriff that he, Lieven, had supported a retaliatory strike against Al Qaeda, but then he became a pest with his depression because the US had not developed "a new commitment to humanitarian principles and a new sense of international law and international institutions," and warned that a "war on Islam" would never succeed.

And there, at the other end of the table, was Tariq Ali. He tried to hide his menace behind his smile, he checked his black hat at the door, but we still knew that he was a quick-draw barb-slinger. He quipped about the "thinker president" and labeled Hamid Karzai an "old US agent." And he warned that "the effects of this business are by no means over," inconveniently noting the tenuous situation in Pakistan and the collective blind eye to Saudi support for Al Qaeda.

The Sheriff was soon agitated, scribbling notes and scanning the audience, cheek in hand. He tested his learned one-liners against the villainous Ali—"I'll try to avoid casuistry as well as prolixity"; he tried his chastising one-liners—"I hope we've heard the last of the sneering [at President Bush]. We've certainly heard the first of it"; he fell back on his best 9/11 phrases—"civilian airliners turned into cruise missiles."

But, while it may have worked in Peoria, it wasn't going down well in London. Hitchens's opening shots met largely with a "been there, heard that" response. Defensive, then desperate, he moved from target to target: how about *fatwas* from Iran? Sharia law in Nigeria? Synagogues burned in Tunisia? Synagogues burned and trashed in London? Immigrants bringing the rise of Jean-Marie Le Pen in France? Everywhere the "destruction of society where only one book is allowed"? No joy. Only when the Sheriff mentioned the rightness of action in Kosovo were some of the citizenry moved.

By contrast, Jacqueline Rose's comments on the dangers of warrior language were warmly received, and she was loudly commended when she took on Hitchens's free association that "theocratic fascism" was even responsible for the Dreyfus affair: "It was the French, not Islamic theocracy, that put Dreyfus on trial." Hitchens snapped at the audience: "You'll clap anything?"

For the Sheriff, the evening had already turned into High Noon: he was taking on all of us. He lashed out: "I won't bore you with that moral mushy stuff [about airliners/cruise missiles/terrified passengers], even if many of you have already forgotten it"—and encountered booing and heckling. (To its credit, the audience, as well as the moderator, immediately silenced the hecklers.) When he was booed for turning aside a question derisively, he redoubled the challenge to the audience: "If you knew how you sound when you hissed, you wouldn't do it. You sound like such berks." And, always, there was his sneer and mocking handclap when those listening responded to a point that was not his: "Anyone can get more applause than me."

It had come to this. An elderly gentleman challenged the Sheriff over the dangers of US foreign policy. The Sheriff shot back wildly, "I assume you are from the subcontinent," and tried to finish off his assailant: "I wouldn't expect you to think otherwise with your ideology." The gentleman replied in agitation: "I am not from the subcontinent." Hitchens blustered, "We can all make mistakes." Off mike, he said: "well, he certainly looks like he's from the subcontinent."

It didn't have to be this way. In the first few days after 11 September, Hitchens was not attacking (except for George W. Bush, "a shadow framed by powerful advisers and handlers, a glove puppet with little volition of his own and a celebrated indifference to foreign affairs"): he was cautioning that "the question [Americans] are asking is how—not why."

But then something happened. Maybe it was the horror and agony of losing a friend, the CNN commentator Barbara Olson, in the attacks. Maybe it was the surge of anger and mourning for the loss of a "big, free, happy, carefree society." Maybe it was just the pressure of writing quickly for newspapers clamoring for answers. Probably it was all of these.

Hitchens had a little think for Americans, for all of us, and came up with an easy "why" in the *Evening Standard*: "The people who destroyed the World Trade Center, and used civilians as accessories, are not fighting to free Gaza. They are fighting for the right to throw acid in the faces of unveiled women in Kabul and Karachi." The petty-minded might have quibbled at the easy slippage from "the people who destroyed the World Trade Center" to the unnamed "they" who may have had nothing to do with the attack, who may even have condemned it, but who were undoubtedly scarring women and blowing up the Buddha. (He was not the only person to make this maneuvre: Bush also pulled it off the following day in his speech to Congress, the one that put the Taliban, rather than Osama bin Laden, in the US cross-hairs.)

But Hitchens was already beyond such objections, beyond the need for any understanding of the complexities of the region, of Islam, of "America." The enemy was not just over there, he was here. Suitably buoyed by this discovery, he crushed his foes with a bombardment of invective: "Liberal masochism is of no use to us at a time like this, and Muslim self-pity even less so. Self-preservation and self-respect make it necessary to recognize and name a lethal enemy when one sees one."

No link was too tenuous, no tone too shrill for our intrepid protector. Hitchens assured us that if "brave American civilians" had not been allowed "to mount a desperate resistance" on United Airlines Flight 93, which crashed in the Pennsylvania countryside, "I would be looking out at a gutted Capitol or charred White House, and reading Pinter or Pilger on how my neighborhood had been asking for it." The assertion of Sam Husseini, the director of the US-based Institute for Public Accuracy, that Al Qaeda "could not get volunteers to stuff envelopes if Israel had withdrawn from Jerusalem like it was supposed to—and the US stopped the sanctions and the bombing on Iraq," was not the "why" that Hitchens wanted. So it became "a simple refusal to admit that a painful event has occurred . . . a cheery rationalization of something ghastly . . . a crude shifting of blame."

This was "with us or against us" intellectual warfare, a "ha ha ha to the pacifists," a warning to the moaning "peaceniks" and any other bin Ladens: "There are more of us and we are both smarter and nicer, as well as surprisingly insistent that our culture demands respect, too."

This victory won, Hitchens's macho swagger has taken a knock recently. He was unsettled by his new bedfellows' "axis of evil," "the symbolic phrase for everything that has become risky and dubious and opportunistic about the new Bush foreign policy," even as he fell into confused hand-wringing about Iraq, where he could not wish away the problems of *realpolitik* with his moral wand—"in many ways, the United States quite likes the Saddam regime." (C'mon, Christopher, no liberal whining!) And the silence on the Israeli-Palestinian imbroglio of the "authentic voice of dissent," a prominent supporter of a Palestinian state and critic of Ariel Sharon, was finally broken on 15 April with a column for the new-look *Mirror*.

But, after seeing Hitchens at the debate, organized by the *London Review of Books*, I fear these thoughtful moments will be rare. "The Hitch" is no longer an activist, no longer a participant in the real debates about power and who wields it, no more a source for thought. No, he is an industry, posing in trench coat with a cigarette dangling from his top lip,[1] hailed as "one of the few remaining practitioners of the five-hour, two-bottle lunch." And, naturally, the most profitable industry is a monopoly. So he packages himself, surreally, not just as a policeman but the only policeman of "a radical Left that no longer exists."

Just as Orwell eventually saw himself as Charles Dickens, "a type hated with equal hatred by all the smelly little orthodoxies which are now contending for our souls," Hitchens now sees himself as Orwell (who, as the cover of *Orwell's Victory* reminds us, also dangled a cigarette from his top lip), the lone voice of decency among the ranks of a naive and/or nasty Left.

It's an effective tactic. Like Orwell, Hitchens has made himself the poster boy of "principled opposition," even as he sides with the dominant powers in the US, by wielding a scatter-gun, "common-sense" rhetoric that does not have to deal with troubling political or economic considerations. He need not worry about such details. Only he, in his words, has "elementary morals." All others, with their "oppositional stance" (like Orwell's pacifists who were the accomplices of fascism, like his "pansy" leftist writers), can cower with their Al Qaeda allies or whimper in the op-ed columns of the *Guardian*.

I don't care when the hapless Andrew Sullivan of the *Sunday Times*, through columns repetitively void, or his preening website, thrashes against the "Left." I read Mark Steyn's "loud bloke in a pub" opinions in Conrad Black's newspaper from the same safe distance that I would keep from any loud bloke in a pub. But Hitchens, because of his past affiliations, the quality and persistence of much of his writing, and especially his *cause celebre* against Kissinger, has street cred.

This is more than a semantic scrap, more than a sideshow to keep the intelligentsia gossiping. It is more than another contest between Christopher and Tariq for the soul of 68. We are well beyond 9/11, with the bodies piling up and human rights suspended in the West Bank; with detainees languishing uncharged not only in Camp X-Ray, but in American and British jails; with the United States desperate to unleash its bombers over Baghdad, to stare down Tehran, to crush insurgencies everywhere from Colombia to the Philippines, to topple governments that do not meet the "with us or against us" criterion. In a "war on terrorism" that is highly elastic, Hitchens's rhetoric of "Islamic fascism" stretches conveniently.

So, Sheriff, before you ride into the sunset, into Washington's sanctuary, I'm calling you out. Before you have another pop at the dissent of the "Left," do it fairly, where someone can respond with the political, economic, military and, yes, moral considerations that you might be shoving aside. If you are going to reduce your opposition to stick men and women, "voluntary apologists for abuse of power" standing in the way of "the model revolution [of] the American experiment," hang around for an answer before your five-hour lunch.

Name the time, the place and the medium. This time, bring some evidence along with your one-liners. I'll be there.

New Statesman, May 27, 2002

NOTE

1. This is a reference to the cover of *Letters to a Young Contrarian*, which shows Hitchens dressed in a trench coat and smoking a cigarette.

⟅ 45 ⟆

Letter to the *Nation*, January 6, 2003

STUDS TERKEL

I was fascinated by the letters between Christopher Hitchens and Katha Pollitt.[1] There was a throwaway reference in Hitchens's piece that caught my attention. It was a reference to Gore Vidal, at whom he threw a rabbit punch, among others. I was suddenly reminded of a moment in the late, late, late of the evening when Hitch and I got smashed. It was just a couple of years ago.

He was in Chicago in re his excellent Kissinger book. During those blurry moments at my house, and very delightful they were, he confided that in some quarters he was regarded as the successor to Gore Vidal as America's pre-eminent man of letters. I've a hunch that Vidal may have a comment on that, especially now.

My point is a simple one: vanity. It's probably the least of our seven deadly sins; all of us have a touch of it, more or less. In some cases, more than less. Saddam Hussein is not the subject of this note; nor the nature of our approach toward the mass murderer. Chris has his opinion; the *Nation*'s editors have theirs. It is the manner in which he has behaved toward those who differ with him: his *ad hominem* assaults on their intelligence and integrity. It is his vulgarity of language, so unlike the guy I knew, that knocked me for a loop.

I have always admired Hitchens's insights, elegance of style and sharpness of wit. I still do. But the turn he has taken—the sharp one— is more in the direction of Becky than of Orwell. I'm afraid that his psyche is now more possessed of vanity than of fairness.

I am somewhat embarrassed in revealing a conversation that took place under the influence of booze. It is something of a foul blow. Yet I am merely pointing out that below-the-belt punching is a game that two can play. It's a nasty game, kid.

PS: Chris, I miss your stuff in the *Nation* very much. It discombobulates me that your stalwart Orwellian self has become aligned with the wanton boy swatting flies. Remember the line from *King Lear*: "As flies to wanton boys, are we to the gods; / They kill us for their sport." That a wanton boy, at this moment in history, is the most powerful man in the world is an absurd fact. It's a scenario that can have been written only by that master of outrageous humor W. C. Fields. It grieves me that one as gifted as you has chosen to play second banana to the wanton boy in a burlesque skit that's not very funny. Come back, Chris; the martini is waiting. On second thought, I withdraw the invitation. Difficulties might ensue. We'd reflect, of course, on the wanton boy's appointment of Kissinger as truth-seeker. But as we mellowed with a drink or two, we'd probably reminisce about our dear old friend Jessica Mitford and what she'd make of things today; and of you. Five gets you ten she'd have said, "Christopher Hitchens, poor boy, since his conversion, has been transmogrified from a witty observer of the human comedy to a bloody bore, seated at the far-right end of the bar." As you may surmise, Kiddo, it would wind up as a somewhat less than pleasant visit. I'd find the memory of Mitford much better company than the presence of Hitchens. Thus, at this moment, I'm drinking alone, hoisting one to Jessica (Decca, as we called her) and her dreams; and mine; and young Christopher's.

Nation, January 6, 2003

NOTE

1. See "The Hitchens-Pollitt Papers," in *Nation*, December 16, 2002.

HITCHENS RESPONDS

I am hoping that an open letter to my readers won't seem unduly conceited or solipsistic. Every month for years, the letters editors at the *Nation* would send me the correspondence regarding me and ask me if I wanted to reply, and each time I would say no, don't bother, the letters column belongs to the readers, I have my own space in the magazine, I won't respond unless accused of fabrication, child-abuse, racism etc.

However, there have been so many attacks on me from *Nation* quarters in the recent past that I wonder from time to time if people think I am shy, or shifty, or have nothing to say in my own defense. . . . This thought occurred to me with especial force when I saw the ignoble letter from Studs Terkel given such huge play by the *Nation*'s editors. (On this occasion, I might add, I received no advance warning. But perhaps I'd surrendered that privilege by resigning my column.)

Consider this: In April of 2001 I was in Chicago on a book tour. Mutual friends conveyed an invitation from Terkel to call on him, and said that he needed some cheering-up after the death of his wife. So, round there I went. I'd be a hypocrite if I said I was keen on the idea, because I'd paid a similar call—again at his insistence—a couple of years before, and there is a limit to how many times you can hear the identical anecdotes from a man who is too full of himself, as well as too deaf, to listen even to your appreciation. Anyway, Terkel's mode (unvarying on the few occasions I've run into him) is one of affirmative over-praise. He won't let you defend yourself from the charge of being a great guy. Once again, he loudly hymned me as the heir to James Cameron—a good egg who was once a journalistic inspiration to us all. I can take praise as well as the next man but, when this became tiring, deflected it into false modesty. Gore Vidal had kindly mentioned me as his inheritor and I said, perhaps incautiously, that now that I had that on my dust-jacket blurb I needed no further promotion. Embarrassing? You bet. But I have two witnesses to this, and one of them was taping it for some possible profile of one or other of us. Again to repeat—this drop-by at Terkel's home was not my idea. Nor was my mention of Vidal his discovery. As for the idea that I have "rabbit-punched" Gore—what can I say? If I could rabbit-punch the author of *Julian* and *Lincoln*, I would need no endorsement. I merely said that Vidal made an allegation of complicity against the White House in the matter of September 11, and so he did. You can look it up in the London *Observer*. Time passes and I part company with the *Nation* family. Of course I don't and can't insist on their reading the only blurb on my last collection of essays, or indeed any of the reviews of it, several of which mentioned the over-generous Vidal encomium. But out of the blue comes a semi-coherent letter from Terkel, which is awarded the leading space on the *Nation*'s letters page, and goes on for almost a column and a half, and which "reveals" that I mentioned the blurb, which was on the stands in Chicago long before I arrived there.

Now perhaps you will wonder if I am not making an absurd fuss. But when I quit the magazine, it was only after a series of appeals not to do so, and a number of assurances from Victor [Navasky] and Katrina [Vanden Heuvel] that there would be no bad blood on their side. (I said that I, too, would keep things impersonal when or if asked.) They go back a long way with Terkel. He is one of the grand old men of their tradition. Thus, when he writes a long and foolish but—in his mind—revealing letter, they do wrong by him in publishing it. Do they ring and say—"Studs, it's your call but are you sure you want to do this?" Not a bit. Nor do they contact me to ask if the story is even half-true (which they would quite certainly have done if the positions were reversed). They let him make an idiot of himself, because they think it affords the chance to be unpleasant to me. Thus does the Left expend itself.

You can't fail to notice the main theme of Terkel's letter. Comb out the Chicago semi-tough big-shoulder affectations, from "kid" to "Kiddo," and the subject is booze. He can't stay off it (the subject I mean). As it chances, this is now the main line of attack upon your humble servant. It is said, from *Counter Punch* upwards, that I am an irredeemable drunk, and the despair of my few remaining friends. Terkel says that on this occasion it was martinis—which I haven't touched since my second daughter was born in 1993—and also says that he was "smashed" himself, which he may well have been. But no guest could be "smashed" in a house as ungenerous as his, and I was overdue for a date elsewhere and anxious to be on my way, and I have two witnesses and a video. So he's probably staying with what he understands to be a safe jest.

Nobody who knows me thinks that I drink too little, and I could probably stand to imbibe less. It's both an advantage and a disadvantage to have a tolerance for alcohol. But I sometimes wonder what those who don't know me must think. The reputation now approaches the legendary. Yet in the past year I turned out quite a few columns and essays, and produced a book or so, and mounted the podium several times a month, and appeared on TV or radio several times a week, and flew to many cities and many countries, and taught numerous classes and seminars. I was never late for anything, whether deadline or appointment, and have never taught on any campus that hasn't invited me back. I also managed to drive Route 66 from start to finish while somehow avoiding either arrest or collision. And I told a couple of radio stations that, yes, I would appear to debate either Alexander Cockburn or John Pilger, but the initial invitations were never followed up. In their shoes, I'd have taken on an incoherent alcoholic any time.

It's said, further, that I have been a slave to the bottle since heaven knows when. If true—which it is not—this would logically mean that the rot set in when I was still on the right side of the Left. But the question didn't come up then, if you follow me. Yet at a recent lunch at the offices of the *New Statesman*, no less a person than Professor Noam Chomsky tells his hosts that he hasn't bothered reading me since my attack on Mother Teresa (which was almost a decade ago) and that this is because of my hopelessly boozed-out state. As it happens, I know this to be untrue, both because I was in civil correspondence with Chomsky until mid-2001, and because he has barely seen me lift a glass. He is adhering to a party line. An odd line, too, since nobody will say that Gore Vidal is famous for abstention, or the late Jessica Mitford (shamefully enlisted as a potential posthumous critic of mine by Terkel). One of the nicest things about Alexander Cockburn is his demonstration of love and loyalty on the subject of his late father, who I had the pleasure of meeting more than once. In his own account, Alexander pays especial tribute to the old man's fondness for drink, which never seems to have incapacitated him.

I suppose therefore that I should be uplifted by all this, since an *ad hominem* attack is almost by definition an admission that my enemies would rather not engage with my arguments. I can't quite make that claim, however. They do engage with my arguments. They generally do so in the status-quo, safety-first mode that now distinguishes so much of the Left, insisting not that such and such a line on Iraq, say, is wrong on principle, but that it is too risky or too hazardous. I would have let the whole *ad hominem* business drop, or pass, if it wasn't that the Terkel stuff somehow crossed my line. It was lousy of the *Nation* to allow him to make an ass of himself, lousy of them to do so as a way of trying to embarrass me, and lousy of them to make it a lead letter even in a slow week. Of course, Terkel also takes the mindless view that Bush is more dangerous (and more capricious) than Saddam Hussein or Osama bin Laden. He misuses *Lear* to advance the line about flies and wanton boys. But how ill white hairs become a fool and jester, and how cynical of Navasky and Vanden Heuvel to exploit an actual friend against a (now decidedly) former one.

My faint suspicion is that this is a warm-up for the impending publication of Sidney Blumenthal's $600,000 book, which may well venture into *ad hominem* territory in an attempt to redeem for Farrar, Straus and Giroux an advance which I predict they'll have to eat. I have already told Blumenthal, through channels, that he's entirely welcome to try this but he'd better be ready to be repaid in his own coin. I'm even wondering, after spending more than three decades in the service of the *New Statesman* and the *Nation*, and keeping my ears and eyes open, how it would look if I repaid all my new foes in the currency of gossip and hearsay.

I'll close by saying that I called Terkel to ask if it was all right if I recounted my memory of the evening (he said yes). And I am writing at this length only for people who choose to see it.

> "Hitchens's Open Letter to Readers and Letter Exchange with Victor Navasky," Christopher Hitchens Web, 2003

⸬(46)⸬

Hitchens as Model Apostate

NORMAN FINKELSTEIN

I'm occasionally asked whether I still consider myself a Marxist. Even if my "faith" had lapsed, I wouldn't advertise it, not from shame at having been wrong (although admittedly this would be a factor) but rather from fear of arousing even a faint suspicion of opportunism. To borrow from the lingo of a former academic fad, if, in public life, the "signifier" is "I'm no longer a Marxist," then the "signified" usually is, "I'm selling out." No doubt one can, in light of further study and life experience, come to repudiate past convictions. One might also decide that youthful ideals, especially when the responsibilities of family kick in and the prospects for radical change dim while the certainty of one's finitude sharpens, are too heavy a burden to bear; although it might be hoped that this accommodation, however understandable (if disappointing), were accomplished with candor and an appropriate degree of humility rather than, what's usually the case, scorn for those who keep plugging away. It is when the phenomenon of political apostasy is accompanied by fanfare and fireworks that it becomes truly repellent.

Depending on where along the political spectrum power is situated, apostates almost always make their corrective leap in that direction, discovering the virtues of the status quo. "The last thing you can be accused of is having turned your coat," Thomas Mann wrote to a convert to National Socialism right after Hitler's seizure of power. "You always wore it the 'right' way around." If apostasy weren't conditioned by power considerations, one would anticipate roughly equal movements in both directions. But that's never been the case. The would-be apostate almost always pulls towards power's magnetic field, rarely away. However elaborate the testimonials on how one came to "see the light," the impetus behind political apostasy is—pardon my cynicism—a fairly straightforward, uncomplicated affair: to cash in, or keep cashing in, on earthly pleasures. Indeed, an apostate can even capitalize on the past to increase his or her current exchange value. Professional ex-radical Todd Gitlin never fails to mention, when denouncing those to his left, that he was a former head of Students for a Democratic Society (SDS). Never mind that this was four decades ago; although president of my sixth-grade class 40 years ago, I don't keep bringing it up. Shouldn't there be a statute of limitations on the exploitation of one's political past? In any event, it's hard to figure why an acknowledgment of former errors should enhance one's current credibility. If, by a person's own admission, he or she had got it all wrong, why should anyone pay heed to his or her new opinions? Doesn't it make more sense attending to those who got there sooner rather than later? A member of the Flat-Earth Society who suddenly discovers the world is round doesn't get to keynote an astronomers' convention. Indeed, the prudent inference would seem to be, once an idiot, always an idiot. It's child's play to assemble a lengthy list—Roger Garaudy, Boris Yeltsin, David Horowitz, Bernard Henri-Levy . . .—bearing out this commonsensical wisdom.

Yet, an apostate is usually astute enough to understand that, in order to catch the public eye and reap the attendant benefits, merely registering this or that doubt about one's prior convictions, or nuanced disagreements with former comrades (which, after all, is how a reasoned change of heart would normally evolve), won't suffice. For, incremental change, or fundamental change by accretion, doesn't get the buzz going: there must be a dramatic rupture with one's past. Conversion and zealotry, just like revelation and apostasy, are flip sides of the same coin, the currency of a political culture having more in common with religion than rational discourse. A rite of passage for apostates peculiar to US political culture is bashing Noam Chomsky. It's the political equivalent of a bar mitzvah, a ritual signaling that one has "grown up"—i.e., grown out of one's "childish" past. It's hard to pick up an article or book by ex-radicals—Gitlin's *Letters to a Young Activist*, Paul Berman's *Terror and Liberalism . . .*—that doesn't include a hysterical attack on him. Behind this venom there's also a transparent psychological factor at play. Chomsky mirrors their idealistic past as well as sordid present, an obstinate reminder that they once had principles but no longer do, that they sold out but he didn't. Hating to be reminded, they keep trying to shatter the glass. He's the demon from the past that, after recantation, no amount of incantation can exorcise.

Two altogether opposed political stances can each draw an audience's attention. One is to be politically consistent, but nonetheless original in one's insights; the other, an inchoate form of apostasy, is to bank on the shock value of an occasional, wildly inconsistent outburst. The former approach, which Chomsky exemplifies, requires hard work, whereas the latter is a lazy substitute for it. Thus Nat Hentoff, the hip (he *loves* jazz) left-liberal writer, would jazz up his interminably dull *Village Voice* columns by suddenly coming out against abortion or endorsing Clarence Thomas's Supreme Court nomination. The master at this pose of maverick unpredictability used to be Christopher Hitchens. Amidst a fairly typical leftist politics, he would suddenly ambush unsuspecting readers with his opposition to abortion, admiration of the misogynist and juvenile lyrics of 2 *Live Crew* ("I think that's very funny"), or support for Columbus's extermination of Native Americans ("deserving to be celebrated with great vim and gusto"). Immediately the talk of the town became, "Did you read Hitchens this week?"

Although a tacit assumption equates unpredictability with independence of mind, it might just as well signal lack of principle. As if to bear out this point, Hitchens has now repackaged himself as a full-fledged apostate. For maximum pyrotechnical effect, he knew that the "awakening" had to be as abrupt as it was extreme: if yesterday he counted himself a Trotskyist and Chomsky a comrade, better now to announce that he supports Bush and counts Paul Wolfowitz a comrade. Their fates crossed when Wolfowitz and Hitchens both immediately glimpsed in September 11 the long-awaited opportunity: for Wolfowitz, to get into Iraq, for Hitchens, to get out of the Left. While public display of angst doesn't itself prove authenticity of feeling (sometimes it might prove the reverse), a sharp political break must, for one living a political life, be a wrenching emotional experience. The rejection of one's core political beliefs can't but entail a rejection of the person holding them: if the beliefs were wrong, then one's *whole being* was wrong. Repudiating one's comrades must also be a sorrowful burden. It is not by chance that "fraternity" is a prized value of the Left: in the course of political struggle, one forges, if not always literally, then, at any rate, spiritually, blood bonds. Yet, the élan with which Hitchens has shed his past and, spewing venom, the brio with which he savages former comrades is a genuine wonder to behold. No doubt he imagines it is testament to the mettle of his conviction that past loyalties don't in the slightest constrain him; in fact, it's testament to the absence of any conviction at all.

Hitchens collects his essays during the months preceding the US attack on Iraq in *The Long Short War*. He sneers that former comrades organizing the global anti-war demonstrations "do *not* think that Saddam Hussein is a bad guy at all" (emphasis in original), and the many millions marching in them consist of the "blithering ex-flower child or ranting neo-Stalinist." Similarly, he ridicules activists pooling their meager resources for refreshments at a fundraiser—they are not among the chosen at a *Vanity Fair* soiree—as "potluck peaceniks" and "potluckistas." Yet, he is at pains to inform readers that all his newly acquired friends are "friends for life." As with the solicitude he keeps expressing for the rights of Arab women, it seems that Hitchens protests too much. The famous aphorism quoted by him that nations have no permanent allies, only permanent interests, might be said to apply, *mutatis mutandis*, to himself as well. Indeed, his description of a psychopath—"incapable of conceiving an interest other than his own and perhaps genuinely indifferent to the well-being of others"—comes perilously close to a self-portrait. To discover our true human nature, Freud once wrote, just reverse society's moral exhortations: if the Commandment says not to commit adultery, it's because we all want to. This simple game can be played with Hitchens as well: when he avows, "I attempt to write as if I did not care what reviewers said, what peers thought, or what prevailing opinion might be," one should read, "My every word is calculated for its public effect."

Hitchens has riotous fun heaping contempt on several of the volunteer "human shields" who left Iraq before the bombing began. They "obviously didn't have the guts," he jeers, hunkered down in his Washington foxhole. Bearing witness to his own bravery, Hitchens reports in March 2003 that, although even the wife of *New York Times* columnist Tom Friedman is having doubts about going to war, "I am fighting to keep my nerve"—truly a profile in courage, as he exiles himself in the political wilderness, alongside the Bush administration, Congress, a majority of US public opinion, and his employers in the major media. Outraged at the taunt that he who preaches war should perhaps consider fighting it, Hitchens impatiently recalls that, since September 11, "civilians at home are no safer than soldiers abroad," and that, in fact, he's not just a target but *the* main target: "The whole point of the present phase of conflict is that we are faced with tactics that are directed *primarily at civilians*. . . . It is amazing that this essential element of the crisis should have taken so long to sink into certain skulls" (emphasis in original). No doubt modesty and tact forbid Hitchens from drawing the obvious comparison: while cowardly American soldiers frantically covered themselves in protective gear and held their weapons at the ready, he patrolled *his* combat zone in Washington, DC unencumbered. Lest we forget, Hitchens recalls that ours is "an all-volunteer army" where soldiers willingly exchange "fairly good pay" for "obedience" to authority: "Who would have this any other way?" For sure, not those who will never have to "volunteer."

It's a standing question as to whether the power of words ultimately derives from their truth value or if a sufficiently nimble mind can endow words with comparable force regardless of whether they are bearers of truth or falsity. For those who want to believe that the truth content of words does matter, reading the new Hitchens comes as a signal relief. Although redoubtable as a left-wing polemicist, as a right-wing one he only produces doubt, not least about his own mental poise. Deriding Chomsky's "very vulgar" harnessing of facts, Hitchens wants to go beyond this "empiricism of the crudest kind." His own preferred epistemology is on full display, for all to judge, in *The Long Short War.* To prove that, after supporting dictatorial regimes in the Middle East for 70 years, the US has abruptly reversed itself and now wants to bring democracy there, he cites "conversations I have had on this subject in Washington." To demonstrate the "glaringly apparent" fact that Saddam "infiltrated, or suborned, or both" the UN inspection teams in Iraq, he adduces the "incontrovertible case" of an inspector offered a bribe by an Iraqi official: "The man in question refused the money, but perhaps not everybody did." Citing "the brilliant film called *Nada,*" Hitchens proposes this radical redefinition of terrorism: "the tactic of demanding the impossible, and demanding it at gunpoint." Al Qaeda is accordingly terrorist because it posits an impossible world of "clerical absolutism" but, judging by this definition, the Nazi party wasn't terrorist because it posited a possible world without Jews. Claiming that every country will resort to preemptive war, and that pre-emptive is indistinguishable from preventive war, Hitchens infers that all countries "will invariably decide that violence and first use are justified" and none can be faulted on this account—which makes you wonder why he's so hot under the collar about Saddam's invasion of Kuwait.

Hitchens maintains that that "there is a close . . . fit between the democratically minded and the pro-American" in the Middle East—like "President for Life" Hosni Mubarak, King Abdullah of Jordan . . . ; that Washington finally grasped that "there *were* 'root causes' behind the murder-attacks" (emphasis in original)—but didn't Hitchens ridicule any allusion to "root causes" as totalitarian apologetics?; that "racism" is "anti-American as nearly as possible by definition"; that "evil" can be defined as "the surplus value of the psychopath"—is there a *Bartlett's* for worst quotations?; that the US's rejoining of UNESCO during the Iraq debate proved its commitment to the UN; that "empirical proofs have been unearthed" showing that Iraq didn't comply with UN resolutions to disarm; that since the UN solicits US support for multilateral missions, it's "idle chatter" to accuse the US of acting unilaterally in Iraq; that the likely killing of innocent civilians in "hospitals, schools, mosques and private homes" shouldn't deter the US from attacking Iraq because it is proof of Saddam's iniquity that he put civilians in harm's way; that those questioning billions of dollars in postwar contracts going to Bush administration cronies must prefer them going to "some windmill-power concern run by Naomi Klein"— is this dry or desiccated wit?

On one page Hitchens states that the world fundamentally changed after September 11 because "civilians are in the front line as never before," but on another page he states that during the 1970s, "I was more than once within blast or shot range of the IRA and came to understand that the word 'indiscriminate' meant that I was as likely to be killed as any other bystander." On one page he states that, even if the US doesn't attack or threaten to attack, "Saddam Hussein *is not going to survive. His regime is on the verge of implosion*" (emphases in original), but on another page he states that "only the force of American arms, or the extremely credible threat of that force, can bring a fresh face to power." On one page he states that the US seems committed to completely overhauling Iraq's political system, but on another page he states that replacing Saddam with "another friendly general . . . might be ideal from Washington's point of view." On one page he states that "*Of course* it's about oil, stupid" (emphasis in original), but on another page he states that "it was not for the sake of oil" that the US went to war. In one paragraph he states that the US must attack Iraq even if it swells the ranks of Al Qaeda, but in the next paragraph he states that "the task of statecraft" is not to swell its ranks. In one sentence he claims to be persuaded by the "materialist conception of history," but in the next sentence he states that "a theory that seems to explain everything is just as good at explaining nothing." In the first half of one sentence he argues that, since "one cannot know the future," policy can't be based on likely consequences, but in the second half he concludes that policy should be based on "a reasoned judgment about the evident danger."

Writing before the invasion, Hitchens argued that the US must attack even if Saddam offers self-exile in order to capture and punish this heinous criminal. Shouldn't he urge an attack on the US to capture and punish Kissinger? And, it must attack because Saddam started colluding with Al Qaeda after the horrific crimes of September 11. Should the US have been attacked for colluding with Saddam's horrific crimes, not after but while they unfolded, before September 11? France is the one "truly 'unilateralist' government on the Security Council," according to Hitchens, a proof being that 20 years ago it sank a Greenpeace vessel—next to which the US wars in Central America apparently pale by comparison. He assails French President Jacques Chirac, in a masterful turn of phrase, as a "balding Joan of Arc in drag," and blasts France with the full arsenal of *Berlitz*'s "most commonly used French expressions." For bowing to popular anti-war sentiment in Germany, German Chancellor Gerhard Schroeder stands accused of "cheaply" playing "this card," while in the near-unanimous opposition of the Turkish people to war Hitchens detects evidence of "ugly egotism and selfishness." He says that Wolfowitz wants "democracy and emancipation"—which must be why Wolfowitz rebuked the Turkish military for not stepping in after the Turkish people vetoed participation in the war. A "principled policy cannot be measured," Hitchens sniffs, "by the number of people who endorse it." But for a principled democrat the number of people endorsing a policy does decide whether to implement it. Hitchens's notion of democracy is his "comrade," ex-Trotskyist but ever-opportunist Kanan Makiya, conjuring up a "complex and ambitious plan" to totally remake Iraq in Boston and presenting it for ratification at an émigré conference in London. The invective he hurls at French, German and Turkish leaders for heeding the popular will shows that Hitchens hasn't, at any rate, completely broken faith with his past: contemptuous of "transient polls of opinion," he's still a Trotskyist at heart, guiding the benighted masses to the Promised Land, if through endless wars and safely from the rear.

Most of *The Long Short War* is given over to parsing words. According to Hitchens, all the key terms of the debate on Iraq were meaningless. In his hands this is probably true. For many years Hitchens awed readers with his formidable control over the English language. Now his ego delights in testing whether, through sheer manipulation of words, he can pass off flatulent emissions as bouquets. It perhaps would be funny watching fatuous readers fawn over gibberish—were not human life at stake. Hitchens can't believe a word he's saying. In contrast to bursting windbags like Vaclav Havel, Hitchens is too smart to take his vaporizings seriously. It's almost an inside joke as he signals each ridiculous point with the assertion that it's "obvious." Hitchens resembles no one so much as the Polish émigré hoaxer, Jerzy Kosinski, who, shrewdly sizing up intellectual culture in America, used to give, before genuflecting Yale undergraduates, lectures on such topics as "The Art of the Self: the theory of 'Le Moi Poetique' (Binswanger)." Translation: for this wanger it's all about *moi*. Kosinski no doubt had a good time of it until, outed as a fraud, he had enough good grace, which Hitchens plainly lacks, to commit suicide. And for Hitchens it's also lucrative nonsense that he's peddling. It's not exactly a martyr's fate defecting from the *Nation*, a frills-free liberal magazine, to *Atlantic Monthly*, the well-heeled house organ of Zionist crazies. Although Kissinger affected to be a "solitary, gaunt hero," Hitchens says, in reality he was just a "corpulent opportunist." It sounds familiar.

Counter Punch, September 10, 2003

HITCHENS RESPONDS

In his delightful memoir of his father, Alexander Cockburn recalls Claud's method of dealing with unwelcome bills, and with the ominous red-tinted follow-up letters that often succeeded them. The old man composed a fantasy-response, informing his creditors that every six months he would throw all his unpaid bills into a basket, stir them with a stick, and then take out two or three and pay them at random. "One more nasty letter from you and you're out of the game."

I could spend a lot of my time replying to attacks on my person, but I now play a version of the Cockburn roulette. (I don't respond to assaults from the "Counterpunch" source at all: this is because I like Alexander and his family, and because I think there's something satisfying in having him much more fascinated by my writing than I can any longer be by any of his.) Every now and then, though, kind friends hasten to send me a collector's item of abuse and the recent one from the Norman Finkelstein website [subsequently posted at *Counter Punch*] is a keeper. Out of the basket it comes.

It is headed "Fraternally yours, Chris,"[1] which is supposedly the way that I "used to sign off" my correspondence. I very often still do end my letters with the old salutation of the British Labor movement, but it's usually without the "yours" and I have never signed a letter "Chris" in my life—chiefly because it isn't my name. I tried everything I knew to stop Norman calling me "Chris" but I couldn't get him to desist. This is a detail, but it does indicate a man who—even his friends would agree on this—was a slightly more ardent talker than listener.

The essay is a study in apostasy and will apparently form part of a new introduction to Finkelstein's book *The Rise and Fall of Palestine.* Since that's a serious subject, I'm hoping that its publisher sees this in time and avoids the embarrassment of conflating Finkelstein's ill-argued personal grudges with the fate of a struggling people.

My book *A Long Short War*, about the liberation of Iraq, is a fairly terse and modest pamphlet, made up of handy bite-sized polemics, each of them dated to see how well or badly it holds up in retrospect. It's not a work in which one can easily get bogged down. But Finkelstein manages to get himself entangled in the text to a wince-making degree. Thus he says that I describe the followers of the anti-war demonstrations as "ex-flower children" or "neo Stalinists," while that was my description only of the organizers. His appreciation of irony and contradiction, very keen in his own mind, is klutzy in the extreme when laboriously downloaded from that mind onto the page. Thus, he reminds me that I witnessed "indiscriminate" bombings by the Provisional IRA in the 1970s, which I certainly did. He then triumphantly counterposes this to a statement on another page, where I say that after 11 September 2001 "civilians are in the front line as never before." This dull attempt at a "gotcha" collapses instantly upon itself—unless you are ready to believe that the Al Qaeda movement hasn't promoted anti-civilian warfare to a newer and higher degree. (I don't actually know Finkelstein's answer to this question: in December 2001 he gave an exhaustive interview, reprinted in *Counter Punch,* in which he stated: "Frankly, part of me says—even though everything since September 11th has been a nightmare—'you know what, we deserve the problem on our hands because some things bin Laden says are true.'" Which part of you, Norman, was that? And which part am I arguing with? And wasn't September 11th also "a nightmare": not just "everything since"?)

Some of the things the Nazis said were "true," too (about Stalinism, say, before they made a pact with it, and about the Treaty of Versailles). This is a subject on which Finkelstein rightly claims some expertise, but he seems willing to make a fool of himself on his own turf in a crass attempt to insult me. I define terrorism as "the tactic of demanding the impossible, and demanding it at gunpoint." Judging by this, says Finkelstein, "the Nazi Party wasn't terrorist because it posited a world without Jews." He really must be more careful. First, we do not lack words of condemnation for the Third Reich, and "Nazi" is the least of these, because it is the most literal. Second, the other definitions we possess—of which "genocidal" would be one—are terms that don't exhibit the same ambiguity as "terrorist" does. "Terrorist," indeed, is almost a euphemistic word when compared to "totalitarian." Third, I am presuming that Norman Finkelstein will agree with me that Nazism did manifest a high degree of irrationality, not only in its attempt at Judaeocide but also in its declaration of war on three fronts against three great powers, aimed at the preposterous fantasy of Aryan world domination. I do think that Al Qaeda is doomed because of similar jihadist and millennial delusions. In my essay, I was attempting to distinguish it from, say, Hezbollah, which is a local politico-clerical-military faction with (relatively) limited and defined aims. I'm not sure, though, that this distinction would lead me to emulate Finkelstein, who called in public and in print for "solidarity with Hezbollah" on his notorious visit to Lebanon. The reason that he gave for this wild piece of promiscuity was that Hezbollah was being targeted for elimination by the United States and Israel. Tempting though it might be—and though his own logic might seem to necessitate it—I shall not accuse Norman Finkelstein of demanding solidarity with Al Qaeda on what would be the precisely identical grounds. But from someone who identifies with Hezbollah and half-sympathizes with Al Qaeda, I am not sure I am ready to hear that it is I who have capitulated to the forces of reaction.

In other words—and to return to my book for a moment—I was attempting to enforce distinctions rather than blur them. I think that any fair-minded reader, who had my little book to hand while reading Finkelstein's screed, would agree that he fails to bring off any of the rhetorical or logical coups on which he rushes to congratulate himself.

It's true that I am sometimes rude—always on purpose, I trust—but not as crude as Finkelstein's own use of references to flatulence, psychopathy or the "bursting windbag" Vaclav Havel. Anyway, do please purchase a copy of my reasonably-priced pamphlet and let me know if you disagree.

Much more absorbing than all this is the question of motive—which seems to fairly obsess Finkelstein—and also of authenticity. Throughout his essay, he seems to argue that nobody could criticize the Left except for the most mercenary and opportunist reason. There are and have been such defectors of course, but the idea of treason and pelf being at the root of it all is a flat negation of a long history of honorable and courageous re-thinking, from Kautsky to Koestler. I wouldn't claim to be on this chart at all, but it must at least be thinkable, to anyone except Finkelstein, that I could have succeeded as a mere journalist while writing nothing at all about Noam Chomsky. In fact I wrote a long and much-circulated defense of him in the 1980s, and have never repudiated it. (As Finkelstein knows, though he falsely states the contrary, I have never disowned, in the *auto da fe* sense, any of my past on the Left.) I had some kind words for Chomsky in a book of mine that was in proof when 11 September hit, and didn't remove them as I could have done. Unlike many on the Left, who circulate Stalinist defamations of Orwell, Chomsky for example has always taken an "Orwellian" position as regards objective and historical truth. I had begun to disagree with him very seriously over his lenience towards Milosevic and his opposition to the military rescue of Bosnia and Kosovo from attempted ethnocide, and if Finkelstein thinks that this position of mine was inspired by the lust for gold from major magazines he is welcome to the thought.

I looked up some earlier Chomsky a while ago, to see how it held up in retrospect, and I was pleased to find that some of the classic essays—on B.F. Skinner and behaviorism, on the press and East Timor, and on the Kahan Commission into Sabra and Shatila—are still imperishable. This will not be said, I think, of the 2001 talk in which Chomsky described the American intervention in Afghanistan as "a silent genocide." Finkelstein appears to think that any criticism of that stupidity would only indicate severe moral decrepitude in the person making it. He's thus put in the position of one to whom Chomsky is above all criticism: not exactly a compliment to the once-great skeptic and inquirer.

Finkelstein himself has not achieved guru status and may not desire it (though I insist that anyone reading this far should pay a visit to his website and scan the cartoon which he thinks makes him look good. It's a real eye-opener for students of repressed narcissism). I have profited very much from his work on Palestine, and on Germany. His demolitions of Joan Peters and Daniel Goldhagen will be in any future anthology of the best investigative scholarship, and Edward Said and I, when we put together the collection *Blaming the Victims*, essentially structured it around the Peters essay.

Obviously therefore I can't be the best judge when this great cold and clear eye is trained upon myself. But what is all this gunk about "armchairs"? He can't seem to stay off the subject. As it happens, I have been in Iraq three times, very cautiously and prudently, during time of war. This doesn't necessarily give me any edge in any argument. If the "armchair" point has any value, though, it must apply to those who argue against the war as well, and who can view the struggle against Saddam Hussein with a neutral spectator's eye. (I may be optimistic when I describe this stance as neutral: I do sometimes lapse into generosity.) I would perhaps do better in making this point if I made it on behalf of Kanan Makiya, who did not conduct his battle only in Boston and in London, as Finkelstein spitefully and sneeringly says, but who exposed himself to considerable danger in embattled Iraqi Kurdistan and has returned to his volatile country to live and to take part in the very arduous conflict over its future. Incidentally, I don't know by what grandly-assumed right Finkelstein refers to the Iraqi and Kurdish dedicatees of my book as my "newly acquired friends." I have known them all for quite some time, and my solidarity with them is indeed in part a solidarity with people who have taken more risks than I have.

As you will see if you look up my chapter on the "armchair," I point out that if soldiering were to be a qualification for comment in wartime, we would have to discount the views of most women, and of all men over military age, all well as all those whose disabilities prevented them from fighting. This would also obviously entail disqualifying all pacifists and anti-warriors, almost by definition. Such an outcome would I hope be detestable to Finkelstein, who has spent some useful time as a civilian observer on the West Bank. So why does he embrace an argument that would so clearly tell against him? Or is he willing to leave all the fighting to Hezbollah?

A sure sign of ineptitude and malice is manifested when one's attacker is willing to cover himself with mud in order to try and make some of it adhere to his target. Finkelstein's essay begins with a lugubrious self-interrogation about his own "Marxism," and his staunch unwillingness to repudiate it lest he be suspected, even by himself, of "selling out." But mark the sequel. In another attempted "gotcha" he trips over the rug by writing: "In one sentence [Hitchens] claims to be persuaded by the 'materialist conception of history,' but in the next sentence he states that 'a theory that seems to explain everything is just as good at explaining nothing.'" Now, anyone who knows anything at all about the materialist conception of history knows that it is *not* a theory that seems, or even claims, to explain everything. It is a method of examining the dynamics of the economy and society, now adopted because of its relative rigor by a number of non-Marxist historians. (For a good explication of the ABC, see Professor Gerry Cohen's *Karl Marx's Theory of History: A Defense*.) Only the philistine and the ignorant continue to maintain that it is a "determinist" or "predictive" procedure. But in order, or so he imagines, to score a point at my expense, Finkelstein happily joins with this reactionary crowd. Don't fret, Norman—nobody will notice if you cease proclaiming your adherence to an ideology you do not understand. Marx understood contradiction: you can't even rise to the level of paradox.

This cheap turn to anti-intellectualism does not, it seems to me, reach the standard of Finkelstein's previous work. So we both seem to be lamenting each other's degeneration. He says it's axiomatically reactionary to change: I would warn him that it can be very conservative to remain the same. I however don't know him well enough to make the *ad hominem* insinuation that his alteration of tone is due to some impulse of corruption or to secret and shameful worship of violence. And he certainly doesn't know me well enough (even to call me by my right name). Not all changes of mind, I would urge on him softly, are symptoms of decay. There is the equal and opposite danger of ossification, dogmatism, party-mindedness and sclerosis. And yes, it does and will show in the style.

. . .

PS I don't want to be accused of avoiding Finkelstein's unbelievably facile challenge about moral equivalence. Should the United States, he asks with the triumphant cackle of a hen laying an outsize egg, have been liable to invasion for sheltering Kissinger or cosseting Saddam? I'd actually like to know Finkelstein's answer to his own question. I imagine he would have to reluctantly say no, unless Messrs Putin and Chirac and the Arab League gave their permission for the strike, or unless Kofi Annan was in vindictive mood. However, the kernel of the question isn't necessarily diminished by the shallowness or hypocrisy of the person asking it.

Let me give an example of how this matter may nonetheless be taken seriously. In a recent debate with Turkish spokesmen on Capitol Hill, I found myself for the hundredth time involved with the issue of the Armenian genocide. (Finkelstein's willingness to take Turkish opinion at its face value is incidentally one of the many deformities of his piece: Turkey disliked regime change in Iraq because it feared the growing power of Iraqi Kurdish autonomy: a topic which Finkelstein continues to airbrush from the entire discussion.) As usual when the Armenian question comes up, Turkey's apologists at first deny that the massacres ever took place. But as the argument persists, they invariably say that the Armenians took the Russian side in the First World War and were thus asking for trouble. In other words, the Armenians deserved the massacre that never took place. At this point I ask the Turks to invert the argument and apply it to themselves. Turkey took the side of Germany; many Armenians the side of Russia. Had Armenians been stronger, would they have been justified in putting all the Turks to the sword? I've never heard a coherent reply to this challenge but, when speaking with Armenian comrades, I do not encourage them to apply Turkish logic in reverse.

Moral equivalence needs careful handling. In the two slipshod examples given by Finkelstein, I think that the answer would be no but that the US ought to be putting its own war-criminals on trial. Indeed, that would have been a far better cause for the American Left than its sterile campaign of neutralism in respect of men like Milosevic and Saddam. In the case of the rocket attack on Sudan in August 1998, conducted by Clinton without any demand for inspection, any recourse to the United Nations, any discussion with allies or any consultation with Congress, I can't see any reason in law or morality why the Sudanese government, repellent though it is, wouldn't have been entitled to conduct a retaliatory strike, provided that it was against a military target. I wrote about this war-crime extensively at the time, and received exactly zero support from the Finkelstein-Chomsky faction, who avoided all mention of the atrocity until it could be flung into the scales after September 11, in order to cancel or balance out the Al Qaeda aggression against civilians of all nationalities living and working in New York. One can only have contempt for casuistry on this scale, and for those who think it clever to ask serious questions in an unserious way, and who then run away from the answer.

PPS. Finkelstein's words about me have been freely available on this website for some time. I hope that my response will also be available on his. (And, when you surf into the Finkelstein world, don't forget to check out that cartoon.)

"A Few Words of Fraternal Admonition to 'Norm' Finkelstein,"
Christopher Hitchens Web, 2004

NOTE

1. The sub-heading of Finkelstein's article is "Hitchens as Model Apostate."

⁓(47)⤙

Obituary for a Former Contrarian

DENNIS PERRIN

Bright spring afternoon. Hitch and I spend it in his fave DC pub just down the street from his spacious apartment. At the long polished bar, he sips a martini, I swig Tanqueray on ice offset by pints of ale. The pub's TV is flashing golf highlights while the jukebox blasts classic rock. We're chatting about nothing in particular when the juke begins playing "Moonshadow" by Cat Stevens. Hitch stops talking.

His face tightens. Eyes narrow. I know this look—I saw it on *Crossfire* when he nearly slugged a Muslim supporter of the Ayatollah's *fatwa* against Salman Rushdie. I saw it during a Gulf War panel discussion at Georgetown when he responded to some pro-war hack with a precision barrage of invective, followed by the slamming down of the mike, causing a brief reverb in the speakers.

And here it was again.

"No," he said, shaking his head, exhaling Rothman smoke. "No—get rid of that!" Bartender asks, "Excuse me?" "Get rid"—gesturing to the music in the air—"of that." "Can't. Someone played that song." "Well, fuck it then."

Don't know if Hitch is serious. Yes, his anger about the *fatwa* is real and understandable. And the fact that the former Cat Stevens, Yusef Islam, endorsed the mullahs' death sentence clearly enraged him. But getting shitty over "Moonshadow"?

"You know," I say, "Yusef Islam renounced everything about his past. He hates Cat Stevens more than you do. He gave away or destroyed all his gold records. If you really want to show your disgust for him, embrace Cat Stevens. Play his stuff loud and often. Whistle 'Peace Train' or 'Oh Very Young' when you pass the local mosque." Hitch listens, head down, fresh Rothman lit. "No. Never. Fuck them both." "Moonshadow" ends. Pat Benatar—or was it Whitesnake?—takes over, and we resume drinking.

That was about 12 years ago. Another lifetime. Back then Christopher Hitchens was It to me—my mentor, more or less. Just a few years before, I'd left the misery-filled comedy improv scene to work as a media activist and critic. Learned to write political essays on the job for a ratty New York East Village weekly. Raw execution. Tortured metaphors. Sentences so rank they needed quicklime. Yet I muddled on, read Alexander Cockburn's "Beat the Devil" and Hitch's "Minority Report" in the *Nation* for inspiration. Got the nerve to send a few columns to each. Cockburn was pleasant and encouraging in his reply, but Hitch went further. He typed up a letter praising some of my takes, criticizing others, showing me where he thought I misstepped, and so on, then closed by inviting me out for a drink whenever he was in New York or I in DC.

That's when it started.

These days Christopher is vilified by many who once agreed with him, or at least respected his talent. We all know the story of The 9/11 Transformation: the former socialist and Beltway snitch who finally showed his true colors as a shill for W's gang. Some of his former friends, like Cockburn, have gone beyond political disagreement into personal insults, mostly aimed at Hitch's weight and drinking habits. (Dr. Alex also attempted some psychotherapy.) Some, like Sidney Blumenthal, affect an arch, dismissive posture, as if Hitch were little more than a distraction in the Grand Scheme. I've done my share of slagging too, mostly on a discussion list I belong to, but also to him, and I try to keep my criticisms politically and aesthetically based. Yet it's hard for me to erase the fond memories I have of Hitch.

See, Hitch engaged me. Whenever I was in DC for a talk or conference or simply visiting friends, I spent at least one night at Christopher's, and there, in the early hours at his large dining room table, Hitch held court. He talked about his early activist days in England, analyzed the current scene, riffed on political figures while steadily pounding red wine and chain-smoking his Rothmans. I tried to keep up on all fronts, but he was in another league. So I sat back, took in the spectacle. Far from blurring or dulling his mind, booze seemed to sharpen him. I was awed by his eloquence. I learned. (When his book *Letters to a Young Contrarian* was released, a friend asked if I'd read it. "Why?" I replied. "I lived it.")

Above all, Christopher was kind and generous. He listened. He could be self-deprecating and intensely funny. He also had (and still seems to have) a weakness for gossip. This was often entertaining, though once when Andrew Sullivan joined us for drinks, the gossip took a swift dive into the bowels of the *New Republic*, a loathsome mag personified by Sullivan, who remains one of the most arrogant, pretentious jerks I've ever met. I wondered then how Hitch could stomach his type, but overlooked it in favor of the access I enjoyed.

My most intense period with him came during the first Gulf War. It was Christopher's prime. His pieces in the *Nation* and *Harper's* then were tonic. Read pages 75–98 from his collection *For the Sake of Argument* and see for yourself, especially now. Here's the close of his January 1991 *Harper's* cover story, "Realpolitik in the Gulf: A Game Gone Tilt":

The call [to war] was an exercise in peace through strength. But the cause was yet another move in the policy of keeping a region divided and embittered, and therefore accessible to the franchisers of weaponry and the owners of black gold. An earlier regional player, Benjamin Disraeli, once sarcastically remarked that you could tell a weak government by its eagerness to resort to strong measures. The Bush administration uses strong measures to ensure weak government abroad, and has enfeebled democratic government at home. The reasoned objection must be that this is a dangerous and dishonorable pursuit, in which the wealthy gamblers have become much too accustomed to paying their bad debts with the blood of others.

This is the high point—the place where Hitch got it and fluently expressed it. Though hardly soft on Saddam, he still understood the imperial pecking order, the context in which vast power is wielded, the cynicism of it, the horror. He eviscerated the Bush gang with substance and style, and ripped through its apologists. Hitch was hitting all cylinders when he came across Bill Clinton in New Hampshire. Christopher had met his match: an Arkansas political pro with blood money behind him, a hustler and charmer impervious to journalistic assault, a con man so skilled at lying that even those wise to his game were impressed with his performance. Hitch, of course, went straight for Clinton's throat. But he never could get his hands on Clinton, and this fed a frustration that became an obsession.

By this time, Hitch and I saw each other intermittently, spoke by phone occasionally. I'd learned all I could from him and moved on. But I continued to read him and catch his TV appearances when possible. I was sympathetic to his anti-Clintonism, but there was something different about him. Hitch seemed harsher, meaner, sloppier in his attacks. His hatred of Bill and Hillary led him to link arms with the likes of Ann Coulter and the insane David Horowitz, a man who shouts "TREASON!" every 90 seconds. What the fuck? I thought. Why was Christopher going this twisted route? Whenever I asked him about it, he'd be polite but vague. He maintained that he wasn't bound by ideology, so appearing with Coulter at a Free Republic gathering meant little compared to the larger fight against Clinton. "I'll take what I can get," he said.

There was one thing Clinton did that Hitch approved of: bombing Serbia. Opposing it at first, Hitch soon banged the NATO drum in every available outlet. Milosevic wasn't a mere regional thug with blood on his hands—he was a genocidal monster who, if left alone, would wipe out every Muslim and Kosovar he could catch. Stopping him now would spare Europe another Hitleresque nightmare.

Well, maybe. As Hitch once told me, anybody is capable of anything: "Never be surprised by grim disclosure. Welcome it." But it appeared that Hitch's nuanced takes on global events and imperial designs were becoming grimmest black and white. Question his support for the bombing and you risked being called a pro-Slobo dupe. He was energized by the violence. Plugged into the Machine.

By the time of Clinton's impeachment, Christopher became better known for outrage than as a talented essayist. For every literary piece he'd pen for the educated set in the *London Review of Books*, there were outbursts on *Hardball* and in his once-fine *Nation* column. Even though Clinton had stopped Milosevic from gobbling all of Europe, Hitch still couldn't stand him. And his distaste for Clinton led him to testify in the impeachment process, which soon led to charges that he betrayed his friend, the Clinton loyalist Sidney Blumenthal.

I felt bad for Hitch—he was getting raked good in the press, and old allies like Alexander Cockburn penned truly nasty attacks on his character. I wrote a long defense of Christopher in answer to Cockburn's "Hitch the Snitch" tirade, but I wasn't fully behind him. Like many on the Left, I too wanted to see Clinton impeached, but for heavier crimes than lying about blowjobs. And I didn't want to help advance Tom DeLay's agenda. But Hitch could care less about this. Getting Clinton was all that mattered, and this mania drove him to shift his attacks to Al Gore during the 2000 campaign, supposedly on behalf of Ralph Nader, but also in the cynical service of George W. Bush.

And thus the table was set for the final course, which came on 9/11/01. Osama bin Laden provided Christopher the carnage-strewn opening he was waiting for, and soon after the Towers fell and the Pentagon's fires were put out, Hitch went off like he's never gone off before. Everybody to his left was a terrorist stooge. America was no longer an imperialist power. George W. Bush was a Noble Warrior for Enlightenment Values. From the wreckage of 9/11 came a new American Dawn, and Hitch soaked in its rays.

At first I was flabbergasted by the venom Hitch directed at people like Noam Chomsky and Howard Zinn (though, curiously enough, not at his old friend Edward Said, who didn't join Christopher's Liberation Squad). Then, after reading his arguments for smashing the Taliban and their Al Qaeda "guests" in Afghanistan, along with Ahmed Rashid's fine book *Taliban*, I eventually came out in favor of the US hitting those who backed the 9/11 attacks, if only to scatter them and knock them off balance.

When I explained my hesitant conversion to Hitch over the phone, he seemed delighted, and told a mutual friend that I was moving to "the right side."

Hmmm.

It's true I was pissed about the attacks on New York, my adopted hometown. And it's true that I took (and take) Al Qaeda seriously and support undermining if not destroying them through international cooperation and effort. But I'm not a supporter of Bush's regime by any stretch, and was adamantly against the US invasion of Iraq, knowing full well that plans for that attack predated 9/11 and had nothing to do with "liberation" or democracy, much less self-defense. Whatever goodwill the US garnered after Al Qaeda's hit was squandered by the administration's lust for expansionist war on its narrow terms. Can't support that.

The other difference is that, unlike Christopher, I do not revel in blasting apart strangers. There was a mean streak in me during the Afghan campaign where I did make light of Taliban and Al Qaeda dead. But inside I knew that plenty more noncombatants were getting butchered, which bothered me. Plus I wasn't as gung-ho or dismissive about torturing prisoners at Guantanamo as were many of the war's supporters. Hitch has written about weapons that "shame us" and shown some concern for those chopped up by the US. Yet, more often than not, he's celebrated Bush's military attacks, and is critical when he thinks Bush isn't ruthless enough.

DC has finally gotten to him. That must be the main explanation. Yes, there are other factors to consider, but the DC Beast frames and distorts the thinking. Few on the Beltway's A List fret about crushing other countries. They enjoy it. They like the view from atop the growing pile of bodies. Always have. You can't live among these types for 20-plus years without some of their madness infecting your brain. And I'm afraid this madness, and the verbiage that covers it, is becoming more evident in Christopher.

I can barely read him anymore. His pieces in the Brit tabloid the *Mirror* and in *Slate* are a mishmash of imperial justifications and plain bombast; the old elegant style is dead. His TV appearances show a smug, nasty scold with little tolerance for those who disagree with him. He looks more and more like a Ralph Steadman sketch. And in addition to all this, he's now revising what he said during the buildup to the Iraq war.

In several pieces, including an incredibly condescending blast against Nelson Mandela, Hitch went on and on about WMD, chided readers with "Just you wait!" and other taunts, fully confident that once the US took control of Iraq, tons of bio/chem weapons and labs would be all over the cable news nets—with him dancing a victory jig in the foreground. Now he says WMD were never a real concern, and that he'd always said so. It's amazing that he'd dare state this while his earlier pieces can be read at his website. But then, when you side with massive state power and the cynical fucks who serve it, you can say pretty much anything and the People Who Matter won't care.

Currently, Hitch is pushing the line, in language that echoes the reactionary Paul Johnson, that the US can be a "superpower for democracy," and that Toms Jefferson and Paine would approve. He's also slammed the "slut" Dixie Chicks as "fucking fat slags" for their rather mild critique of our Dear Leader. He favors Bush over Kerry, and doesn't like it that Kerry "exploits" his Vietnam combat experience (as opposed to, say, re-election campaign stunts on aircraft carriers).

Sweet Jesus. What next? I'm afraid my old mentor is not the truth-telling Orwell he fancies himself to be. He's becoming a coarser version of Norman Podhoretz.

Minneapolis City Pages, July 9, 2003

◄ 48 ►

Farewell Hitch

GEORGE SCIALABBA

If a hall of fame were established for contemporary book reviewers—
well, why not? There's one for ad executives, poker players, and probably porn stars—Christopher Hitchens would very likely be its second
inductee. (James Wood, of course, would be the first.) About an amazing range of literary and political figures—Proust, Joyce, Borges, Byron,
Bellow, Orhan Pamuk, Tom Paine, Trotsky, Churchill, Conor Cruise
O'Brien, Israel Shahak, and a hundred others—he has supplied the basic information, limned the relevant controversies, hazarded an original perception or two, and thrown out half a dozen fine phrases, causing
between fifteen and forty-five minutes of reading time to pass entirely
unnoticed. His very, very frequent political columns have occasionally
seemed tossed off, it's true; but his books about Cyprus, the Palestinians, the British monarchy, and the Elgin Marbles are seriously argued.
Though he lives in Washington, DC, and is said to be very fond of fancy
parties, he has famously insulted and called for the incarceration of a sitting President and a ubiquitously befriended diplomat and Nobel laure-
ate. And he appears on all those self-important TV talk shows without
wearing a tie. How can you not admire someone like that?

Actually, it's not so difficult, I've discovered. All the someone in
question has to do is begin thinking differently from me about a few
important matters, and in no time I find that his qualities have sub-
tly metamorphosed. His abundance of colorful anecdotes now looks
like incessant and ingenious self-promotion. His marvelous copious-
ness and fluency strike me as mere mellifluous facility and mechani-
cal prolixity. A prose style I thought deliciously suave and sinuous I
now find preening and over-elaborate. His fearless cheekiness has become truculent bravado; his namedropping has gone from endearing
foible to excruciating tic; his extraordinary dialectical agility seems
like resourceful and unscrupulous sophistry; his entertaining literary
asides like garrulousness and vulgar display; his bracing contrariness,
tiresome perversity. Strange, this alteration of perspective; and even

stranger, it sometimes occurs to me that if he changed his opinions again and agreed with me, all his qualities would once more reverse polarity and appear in their original splendor. A very instructive experience, epistemologically speaking.

Then again, it's not just his changing his mind that's got my goat. His and my hero Dwight Macdonald did that often enough. But one may do it gracefully or gracelessly. Even when all the provocations Hitchens has endured are acknowledged (especially the not-infrequent hint that booze has befogged his brain), they don't excuse his zeal not merely to correct his former comrades but to bait, ridicule, and occasionally slander them, caricaturing their arguments and questioning their good faith. Not having recognized a truth formerly ought to make you more patient, not less, with people who do not recognize it now; and less certain, not more, that whomever you currently disagree with is contemptibly benighted. Besides, if you must discharge such large quantities of remonstrance and sarcasm, shouldn't you consider saving a bit more of them for your disagreements—he must still have some, though they're less and less frequently voiced, these days—with those who control the three branches of government and own the media and other means of production?

Hitchens might want to insist, contrarily, that although he has changed his allies, he has not changed his opinions. Unlike, say, David Horowitz, he still believes that the Cold War was an inter-imperial rivalry, the Vietnam War was immoral, the overthrow of Allende was infamous, and American support for Mobutu, Suharto, the Greek colonels, the Guatemalan and Salvadoran generals, the Shah of Iran, and the Israeli dispossession of Palestinians was and is indefensible. He still believes in progressive taxation; the New Deal; vigilant environmental, occupational safety, and consumer protection regulation; unions (or some form of worker self-organization); and, in general, firm and constant opposition to the very frequent efforts of the rich and their agents to grind the faces of the poor. It's just that he now cordially despises most of the people who proclaim or advocate these things. Why?

It began with the Balkan wars. Hitchens supported NATO intervention, in particular the bombing of Serbia in March of 1999. Some of his opponents on the Left argued that NATO gave up too easily on (or indeed sabotaged) diplomacy, was wrong not to seek UN authorization to use force, and may have precipitated a humanitarian catastrophe (the flight and deportation of hundreds of thousands of Kosovar Albanians after the bombing began) that might not otherwise have occurred. Hitchens replied furiously—though not, by and large, to these arguments; rather, to other ones, either nonexistent or easier to refute: for example, opposition "in principle in any case to any intervention," and insistence that in view of its imperialist past the United States could never in any circumstances be a force for good. His most reflective comments did seem to take his opponents' point: "Skeptical though one ought to be about things like the reliance of NATO on air power and the domination of the UN by the nuclear states, the 'double standard' may still be made to operate against itself." But such moments were few. Since 9/11, reflectiveness and skepticism have gone on holiday from his political writing. Logic and good manners have also frequently called in sick. "Embattled" is too mild a description of his state of mind; it's been inflamed. Those who returned different answers than he did to the questions "Why did 9/11 happen?" and "What should we do about it?" were not to be taken seriously. They were Osama's useful idiots, "soft on crime and soft on fascism," their thinking "utterly rotten to its very core." What provoked that last epithet was a suggestion, by a pro-Arab-American commentator, that "bin Laden could not get volunteers to stuff envelopes if Israel had withdrawn from Jerusalem ... and the US stopped the sanctions and bombing of Iraq." Hitchens went ballistic. The hapless fool who wrote this, he thundered, either "knows what was in the minds of the murderers," in which case "it is his solemn responsibility to inform us of the source of his information, and also to share it with the authorities," or else he doesn't know, in which case it is "rash" and "indecent" to speculate.

Hitchens proceeded to speculate. Al Qaeda, like its allies the Taliban, aims first "to bring their own societies under the reign of the most pitiless and inflexible declension of Sharia law," and then, since it regards all unbelievers as "fit only for slaughter and contempt," it will seek to "spread the contagion and visit hell upon the unrighteous." Talk of "Muslim grievances" is rubbish; Al Qaeda's only grievance is that it has not yet enslaved the whole world. Jihad means, simply, the obligatory conquest or destruction of everything outside Islam.

Hitchens has asserted this insistently: for him, to talk about "grievances expressed by the people of the Middle East" in connection with 9/11 is obscene. Bin Laden and Al Qaeda are "medieval fanatics"; they "wish us ill"; no more need be said. To presume to "lend an ear to the suppressed and distorted cry for help that comes, not from the victims, but from the perpetrators" just amounts to "rationalizing" terror. Denouncing one's opponents as soft on terror has been the first or last resort of many scoundrels in the political debates of the past few decades in America. (Actually, it's such a dubious tactic that even the scoundrels don't usually get further than broad hints.) One is surprised to see Hitchens doing it. But even more important: Is he right about Al Qaeda? Does he know "what was in the minds of the murderers"?

In *Imperial Hubris* and its predecessor, *Through Our Enemies' Eyes*, veteran CIA analyst Michael Scheuer, former head of the Agency's Al Qaeda task force, writes:

Bin Laden and most militant Islamists [are] motivated by . . . their hatred for a few, specific US policies and actions they believe are damaging—and threatening to destroy—the things they love. Theirs is a war against a specific target and for specific, limited purposes. While they will use whatever weapon comes to hand—including WMDs—their goal is not to wipe out our secular democracy, but to deter us by military means from attacking the things they love. Bin Laden *et al.* are not eternal warriors; there is no evidence that they are fighting for fighting's sake, or that they would be lost for things to do without a war to wage. . . . To understand the perspective of the [tens or hundreds of millions of] supporters of bin Laden, we must accept that there are many Muslims in the world who believe that US foreign policy is irretrievably biased in favor of Israel, trigger happy in attacking the poor and ill-defended Muslim countries, Sudan, Iraq, Afghanistan, Somalia, and so forth; rapacious in controlling and consuming the Islamic world's energy resources; blasphemous in allowing Israel to occupy Jerusalem and US troops to be based in Saudi Arabia; and hypocritical and cruel in its denial of Palestinian rights, use of economic sanctions against the Muslim people of Iraq, and support for the Muslim world's absolutist kings and dictators.

For holding essentially the same views as Scheuer, Hitchens's leftist opponents were labeled apologists, rationalizers, and eager excusers of terror. A few moments' reflection or a few grains of knowledge would have saved Hitchens from indulging in these slurs, so damaging to his reputation for fairness and decency (insofar, that is, as anyone cares about slanders against leftists). But although his prose has retained its poise since 9/11, his thinking has not.

On and on Hitchens's polemics against the Left have raged, a tempest of inaccuracy, illogic, and malice. Naomi Klein opines that since most Iraqis agree with the insurgents at least in wanting an end to the occupation, the US should end it. Without disputing her premise, Hitchens condemns her "nasty, stupid" conclusion as an "endorsement of jihad," "applause for the holy warriors," "swooning support for theocratic fascism." He jeers repeatedly at the antiwar Left for having predicted that Saddam would use WMD against a US invasion, conveniently forgetting that what the Left actually said was: If, as the Administration insists without evidence, Saddam has WMD, then the most likely scenario for their use is against a US invasion. And that was true. Hitchens fiercely ridicules the antiwar argument that there was no contact and no sympathy between Saddam and Al Qaeda—only that wasn't the argument. The argument was that it was so unlikely Saddam would entrust WMDs to Al Qaeda or any other uncontrollable agent that the United States was not justified in invading Iraq in order to prevent it. And that was true, too. Hitchens continually deplores left-wing "isolationism," even though his opponents are, on the contrary, trying to remind Americans that the UN Charter is the most solemn international agreement ever made ("the first universal social contract," Hitchens's friend Erskine Childers once observed to him), embodying the deep, desperate hope of the weaker nations that the stronger ones will someday submit themselves consistently to the rule of law; while the Bush Administration is—not reluctantly but purposefully—undermining it. "The antiwar Left," Hitchens scoffs, "used to demand the lifting of sanctions without conditions, which would only have gratified Saddam Hussein and his sons and allowed them to rearm." Not quite true—all leftists agreed that import restrictions on military materials were justified. But more important, a gratified Saddam would not have been the "only" result of ending sanctions.

Besides killing hundreds of thousands, the sanctions left Iraqi society helpless, disorganized, and dependent on the state, thus blocking the most likely and legitimate path to regime change—the path followed in Romania, Haiti, Indonesia, South Korea, the Philippines, and other dictatorships, all of them more broadly based, and all (except South Korea) ruling poorer and less-educated societies, than pre-sanctions Iraq. Really, one could almost get the idea that Hitchens thinks the antiwar Left doesn't care every goddamned bit as much as he and the neocons about the sufferings of Iraqis.

About any sufferings that cannot serve as a pretext for American military intervention, moreover, Hitchens appears to have stopped caring. (Given how much he writes, and in how many places, if he hasn't mentioned something for several years it doesn't seem unfair to assume he's stopped caring about it.) He is "a single-issue person at present," he wrote in endorsing President Bush for re-election. This issue, compared with which everything else is "not even in second or third place," is "the tenacious and unapologetic defense of civilized societies against the intensifying menace of clerical barbarism." The invasion of Iraq was a justified act of self-defense against clerical bar-barism, and the Bush Administration is to be praised and supported for undertaking it.

A lot of suffering people would disagree, I think—and not just the perennial ones, betrayed by every US administration: the tens of millions who die annually for lack of clean water, cheap vaccines, mosquito nets, basic health care, or a thousand additional daily calo-ries while the US devotes 0.2 percent of its GDP (one-thirtieth of its military budget and less than one-tenth the cost so far of invading Iraq) to international aid. These unfortunates are mostly not part of a "civilized society under attack from clerical barbarism," so they're out of luck. No, I mean a new class of suffering people, specifically attributable to the new tenacious and unapologetic compassionate conservatism. From its first days in office, the Bush Administration has made clear its determination to reverse as much as possible of the modest progress made in the 20th century toward public provi-sion for the unfortunate; public encouragement of worker, consumer, and neighborhood self-organization; public influence on the daily operation of government and access to the record of its activities;

public protection of the commons; and public restraint of concentrated financial and corporate power—not only at home but also, to the (considerable, given American influence) extent feasible, abroad. And from the first weeks after 9/11, as Paul Krugman and many others have documented, the Administration has found ways to take advantage of that atrocity to achieve its fundamental goals. The results, now and in the future, of this return to unfettered, predatory capitalism have been and will be a vast amount of suffering. Enough, one would think, to be worth mentioning in the second or third place, after the dangers of clerical barbarism. Not a word from Hitchens, however, at least in print. Perhaps he is whispering a few words about these matters in the ear of the "bleeding heart" (Hitchens's description) Paul Wolfowitz and his other newly adopted neoconservative allies.

From Hitchens, this silence is peculiar. Another one is equally so. The South African critic and historian R. W. Johnson once alluded to George Orwell's "simple detestation of untruth." Hitchens—who has written very well about Orwell—was once thought (and not only by me) to feel the same way. *No One Left to Lie To*, his finely indignant critique of Bill Clinton's "contemptible evasions" about his sexual predations and even more contemptible efforts to intimidate potential accusers, convinced many of us that Clinton should have resigned and faced criminal prosecution or at least been served with a sealed indictment at the end of his second term. (Hitchens rightly didn't try to make a case that impeachment, properly limited to official malfeasance, was warranted.) It's a short book, though, pocket-size and with only 103 pages of text. You would need more than that just for a preface to an adequate critique of the lies of the Bush Administration. As the journalist Paul Waldman has remarked, "Bush tells more lies about policy in a week than Bill Clinton did in eight years." He has lied about taxes, budgets, and deficits; about employment statistics; about veterans' benefits; about the Social Security trust fund and the costs of privatization; about climate change; about environmental policy; about oil drilling in the Arctic; about the California electricity crisis; about stem-cell research; about Enron and Harken; about the Florida recount in November 2000; about his National Guard service and his record as governor of Texas; and about most of his political opponents. And then there are his lies about Iraq. The Bush Administration is the most ambitiously and skillfully dishonest pack of liars in American history, probably by a large margin. And since 9/11, Hitchens has never said a mumbling word about it.

Why? What accounts for Hitchens's astonishing loss of moral and intellectual balance? I think he had a plausible and even creditable reason. Anyone intelligent enough to understand that there are institutional and structural, not merely contingent, constraints on the behavior of states will also understand how difficult it is to budge those constraints and produce a fundamental change in policy. To make the United States an effective democracy—to shift control over the state from the centers of financial and industrial power, now global in reach, to broadly based, self-financed and self-governing groups of active citizens with only average resources—will take several generations, at least. This is a daunting prospect for just about anyone. For someone of Hitchens's generous and romantic temperament, it is potentially demoralizing. The temptation to believe that this long, slow process could be speeded up if only he could find and ally himself with a faction of sympathetic souls close to the seat of executive power who really understood—i.e., the neoconservatives, the only ones, Hitchens has written, willing to take "the radical risk of regime change"—must have been overpowering.

And why not? It is hardly dishonorable to try to influence even arbitrary, undemocratic power in a more humane direction. Hitchens has rebuked the American Left for its supposedly intransigent refusal to consider supporting the American government in any military undertaking "unless it had done everything right, and done it for everybody." He is mistaken. I was not, I am sure, the only leftist who at least tried to distinguish between intentions and consequences. It was as plain as day to me (and no matter what Hitchens may say, I can't help suspecting it was equally plain to him) that the Bush Administration's chief purposes in invading Iraq were: to establish a commanding military presence in the region where the most important natural resource in the world is located; to turn a large and potentially rich country into a virtually unregulated investors' paradise; to impress the rest of the world once again with America's insuperable lead in military technology; to exploit the near-universal hatred of Saddam to legitimize (by establishing a precedent for) the doctrine of unilateral American military intervention expounded in the National Security Strategy document of September 2002; and to unify the electorate behind an administration that was making a hash of the economy and the environment in order to reward its campaign contributors. Still, this is not why I opposed the war. If I had not also believed that the invasion would strike a sledgehammer blow to most of the world's fragile hopes for international order and the rule of law, I might have calculated that, whatever the government's motives, the potentially huge expenditure of lives and money it contemplated would be better employed in removing Saddam than in, say, providing clean water, cheap vaccines, mosquito nets, et cetera to the wretched invisibles, and so saving tens of millions of lives. Not likely, but it would have been a decision based on calculation rather than principle.

Even at their easiest, such calculations are excruciating. Weighing immediate costs and benefits is hard enough; figuring in the effects of setting a good or bad precedent, though often just as important, is devilishly hard. The conscientious have always struggled with these difficulties, and sometimes lost patience with them. Randolph Bourne, criticizing the *New Republic* liberals of his era for supporting America's entry into World War I, wondered whether

> realism is always a stern and intelligent grappling with realities. May it not sometimes be a mere surrender to the actual, an abdication of the ideal through a sheer fatigue from intellectual suspense? . . . With how many of the acceptors of war has it been mostly a dread of intellectual suspense? It is a mistake to suppose that intellectuality makes for suspended judgments. The intellect craves certitude. It takes effort to keep it supple and pliable. In a time of danger and disaster we jump desperately for some dogma to cling to. The time comes, if we try to hold out, when our nerves are sick with fatigue, and we seize in a great healing wave of release some doctrine that can be immediately translated into action.

Compare Hitchens's widely quoted response to 9/11: "I felt a kind of exhilaration . . . at last, a war of everything I loved against everything I hated." More recently, explaining to *Nation* readers last November "Why I'm (Slightly) for Bush," he testified again to the therapeutic value of his new commitment: "Myself, I have made my own escape from your self-imposed quandary. Believe me when I say . . . the relief is unbelievable." I believe him.

Will Hitchens ever regain his balance? Near the end of his Bush endorsement, Hitchens defiantly assures us that "once you have done it"—abandoned cowardly and equivocating left-wing "isolationism" and made common cause with Republicans in their "willingness to risk a dangerous confrontation with an untenable and indefensible status quo"—there is "no going back." Well, it wouldn't be easy. After heavy-handedly insulting so many political opponents, misrepresenting their positions and motives, and generally making an egregious ass of himself, it would require immense, almost inconceivable courage for Hitchens to acknowledge that he went too far; that his appreciation of the sources and dangers of Islamic terrorism was neither wholly accurate nor, to the extent it was accurate, exceptional; that he was mistaken about the purposes and likely effects of the strategy he associated himself with and preached so sulfurously; and that there is no honorable alternative to—no "relief" to be had from—the frustrations of always keeping the conventional wisdom at arm's length and speaking up instead for principles that have as yet no powerful constituencies. But it would be right.

Evatt Foundation News Letter (April/May 2005)

◄ 49 ►

The Passion of Christopher Hitchens

A Review of *Love, Poverty, and War* by Christopher Hitchens

MICHAEL KAZIN

Since the attacks of September 11, 2001, an unsettling matter has roiled certain precincts of the Left: Christopher Hitchens's zealous support of the Bush administration's foreign policy, in particular its war in Iraq. How could the once fearless radical polemicist have become a cheerleader for the neoconservative project to remake the world? Why must he revile former comrades as either traitors or slackers in the struggle against terrorists? Why, this June, did he join David Horowitz to conduct a ten-day tour of London, featuring private visits to the House of Lords and the estate of Winston Churchill?

Some believe Hitchens's apostasy began in 1989 when an Iranian *fatwa*—which still stands—demanded the murder of his close friend the novelist Salman Rushdie. A few connect his militant patriotism to his applying for American citizenship or even the discovery that he had Jewish ancestors. Others prefer to fault his personality instead of his politics. Hasn't Hitchens always been an arrogant individualist, eager to bash the illusions of the Left? Perhaps all that good whiskey and champagne finally curdled his synapses?

Turncoats can fascinate, particularly when they are such brilliant and prolific writers. For decades after the 1947 hearings of the House Un-American Activities Committee, left-wing commentators tried to psychoanalyze Whittaker Chambers; they alleged that spurned affection, perhaps even lust, for Alger Hiss drove the squat, anxious journalist to target the suave, handsome diplomat. Hitchens is certainly Chambers's intellectual equal, although the sum of his opinions will never match the historical significance of the former spy's testimony to Richard Nixon and his fellow red-hunters.

What tempers the furor over Hitchens is the recognition that he has not really become a soldier for the Right. Browsing through his ample writings during the first quarter of 2005, one finds, alongside support for the war in Iraq, a variety of opinions that many American leftists would applaud: a slap at the late Pope John Paul II for "saying that condoms are worse than AIDS," praise for John Brown as a prophet "who anticipated the Emancipation Proclamation and all that has ensued from it," and a tribute to Tom Paine as "our unacknowledged founding father . . . the moral and intellectual author of the Declaration of Independence." Hitchens also continues to oppose the death penalty and to advocate putting Henry Kissinger on trial as a war criminal.

He does seem perverse at times; why indeed would any non-disciple of David Horowitz choose to do business with that screeching bully? But Hitchens, who put in many years as an editor of *New Left Review* and a columnist for the *Nation*, has clearly stuck by many of the convictions that made him a radical back in the 1960s. And nearly everything he writes is full of sly observations and delicious prose—even when one finds something to disagree with on every page.

There is one constant in his torrent of publications since the end of the cold war—whether the topic is literature, politics, or history. Strange as it may sound, Hitchens is a romantic—and a particularly ardent one at that. His romanticism harks back to the beginnings of the Anglo-American Left and of modern literature—to Paine's and Mary Wollstonecraft's passionate engagement with the French Revolution but revulsion at the orgy of the guillotine, to the early socialists who imagined they could build a cooperative order that would do away with class distinctions, and to the writers and artists inspired by Wordsworth's maxim "that poetry is the spontaneous overflow of powerful feelings . . ."

For Hitchens, too, it is unforgivable to compromise one's principles, to flirt with lies, to heed the sirens of *realpolitik* over the call of the heart. His anger at such corruptions shouts, elegantly, from the brief introduction to this collection of his pieces written from the early 1990s to 2004: religion is "the most base and contemptible of the forms assumed by human egotism and stupidity"; Kissinger, Bill Clinton, and Mother Teresa are all "despicable" figures; American schools are "designed to bore" students "to death with second-rate and pseudo-uplifting tripe." "I wake up every day," Hitchens confesses with a certain glee, "to a sensation of pervading disgust and annoyance."

This style of moral outrage at wicked, mendacious authorities was stoked by the Enlightenment and burned on through countless manifestos, anthems, and the oratory of socialists and anarchists over the next two hundred years. Formidably well-read, perpetually self-confident men like Bakunin, Trotsky, and Max Shachtman were masters of the idiom. The counterpoint of such invective is a strong sympathy for those whom priests, presidents, and principals are fooling and pushing around. It is not surprising that, in his title, Hitchens chose to give "love" top billing. Although celebrated for his sardonic hauteur, he has always championed intellectuals he believes fought the good fight for ordinary people.

Elsewhere, Hitchens has revealed, in a doleful tone, that he no longer calls himself a socialist. But here, in a review published in 2004, he fairly gushes about Trotsky, from whom "a faint, saintly penumbra still emanates." Hitchens salutes the "Old Man" for predicting that Stalin would sign a pact with Hitler and for sternly admonishing leftists in the 1930s who saw little distinction between the Nazis and the older, aristocratic Right they toppled from power. Trotsky, he writes, set down "a moral warning against the crass mentality of moral equivalence."

Alas, a taste for romantic heroes often leads one to neglect their flaws. Hitchens says not a word about Trotsky's infamous crushing of the 1921 revolt at the Kronstadt naval base, which alienated many independent radicals from the Soviet cause. Nor does he mention that the Old Man remained, until the end, an Old Bolshevik, insisting he could pick up where Lenin left off, if only Stalin, the Oriental despot with a poor education, could somehow be whisked into the dustbin of history. But when Hitchens loves you, it's no good unless he loves you all the way.

That spirit also animates his essays on literary giants. Byron's poem "The Isles of Greece" "can still start a patriotic tear on a manly cheek" even though it "was originally composed and offered as a self-parody." Hitchens lauds Kingsley Amis for demonstrating in *Lucky Jim*, his satire of British academia, the "crucial human difference between the little guy and the small man." The novel's protagonist, "like his creator, was no clown but a man of feeling after all." Bellow, Borges, and Proust all get the same smart, adoring treatment. Hitchens makes no apology for writing solely about "the gold standard" in modern literature, with "the sort of words that hold their value." Romantic critics from Thomas Carlyle to Harold Bloom would warmly agree.

The longest essay in the collection describes a different sort of love, that between a tourist and the great, mostly late American West. One recent summer, Hitchens—outfitted, presumably, with a large expense account from *Vanity Fair*—cruised the length of Route 66 in a bright red Corvette convertible, the same model driven by two buddies in a not-quite-forgotten television show named after the highway. "It winds from Chicago to LA, more than two thousand miles," and Hitchens got as many kicks as he could on the journey. He praises the hamburgers and "terrific jukebox" at a St. Louis bar; marvels at the skills of the auto mechanics in Elk City, Oklahoma, who patch his tires; gapes at a huge meteor crater in the Arizona desert; and orders too much food from "a hauntingly beautiful Spanish waitress" before he heads into California.

But Hitchens is appalled to see how the crude and greedy are trashing what remains of this quaint and seductive cultural landscape. Drug dealers and prostitutes hassle him outside his motel, and Indians peddle "bogus beads and belts and boots" by the side of a mountain. "Surely," he laments, "a decent silence could be observed somewhere, instead of this incessant, raucous, but sentimental battering of the cash register." One can share his opinion yet be amused by his naiveté. Learned folks have been deploring the commerce in culture since the Renaissance, if not before. Hitchens is nostalgic for an America he never knew and that never existed.

That passion for an idealized homeland may help explain his unqualified fury at the antiwar Left. Hitchens has no patience with a politics of difficult choices. In the waning years of the 1990s, he and I held two debates about the merits of Bill Clinton and the Democrats—one at a *Dissent* meeting, the other in print. Hitchens, in high moral dudgeon, thought it "contemptible" to defend the president on strategic grounds, as a figure who had blocked the advance of the Gingrichite Right, even if he hadn't done enough to advance a progressive agenda. To him, Clinton was the vilest member of the political species, a man whose "mock-compassionate and pseudo-humanitarian bilge" concealed the raw ugliness of his egomania. Realists like me were cowards who did not want the knave to be humbled and driven from office.

The attacks of 9/11 roused Hitchens to a greater, and more justifiable, fury. True to character, it was mingled with righteous joy. "I felt a kind of exhilaration," he wrote a few days after the Twin Towers came down, "... at last, a war of everything I loved against everything I hated." Hitchens had not supported the first Gulf War. During one appearance on CNN, he dared Charlton Heston to name all the nations that bordered Iraq. When the aging conservative fumbled the attempt, his antagonist remarked that such ignorance was typical of Americans who believed their might gave them the ability to forge a new world order. Yet a year later, Hitchens was reporting on the valiant Kurds who, protected by US warplanes, had carved out a liberated enclave for themselves in northern Iraq. "They have powerful, impatient enemies," he wrote, "and a few rather easily bored friends." In Hitchens, the Kurds now had an ally as steadfast and articulate as they could desire.

The shock of 9/11 finally persuaded him to abandon his troubled romance with the Left and begin another. In war, he embraced the cause of a country he had always held at arm's length when it was at peace. Enraged by the coldly reflexive anti-imperialism of such figures as Noam Chomsky and Michael Moore, he abandoned his previous ambivalence about the perils of deploying the American military in the Islamic world. He hailed the United States for "bombing" Afghanistan "back out of the Stone Age" and reported happily that children in post-Saddam Iraq chanted "Boosh, Boosh!," while weeping men declared, "You're late. What took you so long?" To a right-wing interviewer, Hitchens complained, "Most of the leftists I know are hoping openly or secretly to leverage difficulty in Iraq in order to defeat George Bush. . . . this is a tactic and a mentality utterly damned by any standard of history or morality. What I mainly do is try to rub that in."

It's the stance of a man whose passion outruns his reason. Hitchens knows there are many liberals and some radicals who cheered the fall of Saddam Hussein yet also cursed Bush and British Prime Minister Tony Blair for lying their way into Iraq and then doing more to cover their tracks than to rebuild that devastated nation. Such ambivalence is the main reason no mass antiwar movement exists today, despite widespread aversion to the administration's conduct before and after the invasion. But the arrogance and brutality of empire are not repealed when they temporarily get deployed in a just cause.

What defines Hitchens's great talent also limits his political understanding. It is thrilling to read and argue with a gifted writer who evinces no doubt about which side is right and which wrong and who can bring a wealth of learning and experience to the fray. We judge public intellectuals partly on their performance, and few can hold an audience as well as he.

Still, the most romantic position is not often the most intelligent one. It is unheroic but necessary to explain how the Bush administration threw Americans into a bloody morass and might now get them out. A lover of absolutes would label this task an act of bad faith; I would call it common sense. In a luminous recent essay about successive translations of *Swann's Way,* Hitchens observed, "To be so perceptive and yet so innocent—that, in a phrase, is the achievement of Proust."

The author might also have been speaking about himself, a self-made patriot who has added to his love of fearless rebels a fierce apology for the neoconservative crusade.

Since Bush's reelection, some of Hitchens's old left-wing friends have urged him to come back home, to confine himself to the elegant slashing of powerful hypocrites on which he built his writerly reputation. But their wish is unlikely to be granted. Christopher Hitchens, you see, is already home.

Dissent (summer 2005)

⟨ 50 ⟩

Christopher Hitchens: Flickering Firebrand

GARY MALONE

Faith in Bush

His former illusion at least implied a positive ideal. His disillusionment is utterly negative. His role is therefore intellectually and politically barren. . . . He advances bravely in the front rank of every witch-hunt. His blind hatred of his former ideal is leaven to contemporary conservatism.[1]

In an offhand remark tucked away in a book review in the *Nation* many years ago, Christopher Hitchens once averred: "The real test of a radical or a revolutionary is not the willingness to confront the orthodoxy and arrogance of the rulers but the readiness to contest illusions and falsehoods among close friends and allies."[2] Years later, he was to famously leave the *Nation* over just such differences of opinion with the Left concerning every major political development that has flowed from the September 11 attacks.[3] In the immediate aftermath of the multi-story immolations in New York and Washington, Hitchens unsheathed his pen and with it gored such sacred oxen as Noam Chomksy, Sam Husseini, and later, Tariq Ali.[4] Whether it is acknowledged or not, the seed of an apostate had been slowly germinating in him for some time. (He has dated—or backdated—his first rethinking of the morality of intervention in Iraq to the end of the Gulf War.)[5] And the 9/11 cataclysm provided him with the necessary *Grenzsituation* in which to reveal his true credentials as a contrarian—specifically, that he would tolerate no nonsense even from fellow-travelers. Hitchens's apparent disgust that the Left had the nerve to continue to critique the "larger issues" of US policy in the Middle East throughout this period provided him with what might, in the world of David Horowitz, be called his Betty Van Patter[6] epiphany: in short, a moment of disenchantment (with the response to a violent attack) that quickly grew into a full-blown political apostasy.

If he is now (as the above citation seems to indicate) being true to himself, he is certainly not being false to no man. For in the years since, Hitchens, in attempting to excoriate the anti-war Left as essentially hypocritical, has himself contributed in no small measure to the bloated corpus of hypocrisy surrounding the "war on terror." In giving practical expression to his own definition of radicalism, he has done so only in the most lopsided way, abandoning serious scrutiny of the rulers with the worst possible timing, and stigmatizing as "soft on fascism"[7] friends and allies who critique them. When illusions and falsehoods (with very real geopolitical consequences) about WMDs and (now thoroughly discredited) Al Qaeda links to Iraq were being promulgated with breathtaking arrogance by Washington, Hitchens chose to go along with them against all evidence to the contrary, and was characteristically nettled by people who did not see matters his way. Is the Horowitz comparison deserved? Has Hitchens become, as he once described Paul Johnson (who also made a "much-advertised stagger from Left to Right")[8] a man who having lost his faith, believes he has found his reason? It's time to examine the apostate's progress.

Christopher Hitchens once possessed near-iconic status in the print media world. An Oxford-educated journalist who moved to the US more than twenty years ago, he quickly became the darling of the

Left, exhibiting a prodigious ability to skewer double standards and abuses of high office. Indeed, his pieces in the *Nation* and *Harper's* often exemplified Amira Hass's very definition of the purpose of journalism—to "monitor the centers of power." Whether writing on the deliquescence of communism in eastern Europe, the tragic fate of Cyprus, or the machinations of Washington power-mongers, he was insightful, learned, and a thoroughly entertaining literary pugilist. (He memorably described Norman Podhoretz as "a moral and intellectual hooligan";[9] and a reading of Nixon's memoirs gleaned the lesson that "the unlived life is not worth examining."[10]) For me, two works stand out: *No One Left to Lie To*, his superbly reasoned polemic on Bill Clinton; and *The Trial of Henry Kissinger*, in which, in one slim volume, he compiled a devastating indictment of a war-crimes celebrity and geopolitical gangster.

So the question arises: why now defend George W. Bush personally and his Iraq invasion politically?

From a goulash of wobbly rationales and flat assertions, three main arguments, roughly overlapping, can be distilled from Hitchens's post-9/11 writings. One: the US confrontation with Saddam Hussein was a welcome development, long-postponed and unavoidable. Two: the intervention in Iraq is an important humanitarian one that at least partially redeems the previous depredations of US *realpolitik*, especially with regard to the Kurdish population. Three: Iraq possessed WMDs.

As with even the most disingenuous apologias, a slender thread of veracity runs through at least Hitchens's first two reasons for supporting the dauphin's campaign in Mesopotamia. But this thread strains to support the weighty baubles of contradiction which he dangles from it. Moreover, the vitriol which Hitchens pours upon the anti-war movement seems somewhat out of court for someone who openly agrees with them on the irrefutable history of Western interference in Iraq. Note too that the anti-war faction agree with Hitchens on the turpitude of Al Qaeda and the Iraqi Baath regime. For them, it literally goes without saying. But because the obvious remains unsaid at the expense of broadcasting the rather more urgent message of putting a halt to the new imperialism, Hitchens has been able to score easy points by turning their silence against them, pretending that it is symptomatic of callous indifference to the fate of Iraqis (which the movement presumably signaled by turning out in unprecedented numbers to insist that Iraqis not be bombed).

During the course of this essay I will examine—*inter alia*—each of these arguments in turn, and their immanent contradictions. Firstly, however, it is necessary to briefly examine the contradictions that suffuse Hitchens's support for George W. Bush's administration.

One will note that this is not merely support, but *uncritical* support. The conspicuous controversies which envelop the President and his cohorts constitute the elephant in the room which Hitchens has to squeeze past virtually every time he defends the Washington hawks. Anyone familiar with Hitchens's previous incarnation as an archmuckraker will know that his full-throated support for George W. Bush (and coziness with Paul Wolfowitz *et al.*) is a true metamorphosis, and nothing beautiful has emerged from the chrysalis. The current occupant of the oval office, freshly placed back in power by the ballots of biblical literalists (the belief that the world was created yesterday seems to hold great appeal to those born at that time), is just the kind of incurious dullard and venal right-wing warmonger whom Hitchens has spent much of his career railing against. One might imagine that Bush and the kakistocracy that enthroned their philosopher-king would be an intolerable offense both to Hitchens's intellect and politics. Not so. In an election-year interview on C-SPAN, Hitchens freely admitted that he would vote for Bush if he had a vote. In an earlier C-SPAN interview, Hitchens also admitted that the President exhibited "that apparent lack of curiosity, that apparent inability to read for pleasure, that apparent want of intellectual weight" but then added that "maybe that would be a positive thing. . . . maybe that would prove that anyone really can be president. Never let us forget . . . it's supposed to be possible in this Republic for anyone to be the president." As everyone knows, the true nature of the American dream (which Hitchens here mangles) is that a highly capable person ought never to be impeded by limitations of class from achieving greatness—the hackneyed example being Abraham Lincoln's journey from log cabin to White House. Bush's ascendancy, on the other hand—whereby a moneyed dolt was hustled into high office by Dad's cronies and a fortuitously positioned brother—represents a kind of Presidential primogeniture, the triumph of class privilege over all strata of meritocracy, including grammar.[11] But even if all of what Hitchens said were true, that still wouldn't stop an educated fellow like him from at least *hoping* that the world's finest democracy could produce a leader who doesn't think that people from Greece are called Grecians and can name at least one President from a list of two of the world's nuclear-armed nations.[12]

Is it bravery or just embarrassment that induces Hitchens to defend George W. Bush on the weakest of issues and attack his detractors when the President is at his worst? Consider his apologia for a *faux pas*:

> The President is also captured in a well-worn TV news clip, making a boilerplate response to a question on terrorism and then asking the reporters to watch his drive. Well, that's what you get if you catch the President on a golf course. If Eisenhower had done this, as he often did, it would have been presented as calm statesmanship. If Clinton had done it, as he often did, it would have shown his charm.[13]

Note that this passage accidentally admits to Bush's *lack* of statesmanship and charm. Note also the author's betrayal of his own writings on Bill Clinton: having devoted an entire book to pillorying the former President as a war criminal and a rapist, Clinton now apparently has "charm"—and all this in defense of an even worse president. A pretty pass to arrive at.

Moreover, Hitchens attempts to portray his support for the Republican oligarchy as some sort of conscience-driven ideological sacrifice. "I decided some time ago that I was, brain and heart, on the side of the 'regime change' position," he wrote in March 2003.[14] Noting in the same paragraph that *New York Times* writer Thomas Friedman had "finally lost his nerve" and withdrawn his support for "this" removal of Saddam, he adds, "I am fighting to keep my nerve." Two things to note here. One: the putatively steely moral fiber that is required to side with the strong, with the militarily unstoppable, in preparing for their assault upon a disarmed and sanctions-ruined nation. Two: the contradiction. Hitchens admits that it takes an act of will to cling even to this position—so there's clearly some vestigial, left-wing pang of conscience still twitching in him. Not to worry though—he's fighting it.

My favorite Hitchens rationale, however, is perhaps his most oft-repeated one: that George W. Bush is the only US President to have used the word "Palestinian" and "state" in the same sentence (Hitchens's words).[15] It is a breathtaking defense of lip-service. And it is a sad end for a critique of great power to arrive at. From a myriad of hypocrisies, Hitchens could easily point to the endless US flow of arms to a state that openly uses this *matériel* to maintain an illegal thirty-seven year occupation, brutalize a defenseless civilian population, and effect a slow-motion, settlement-based colonization which—if allowed to continue *sine die*—will guarantee the final erasure of Palestine. For all his rhapsodizing about the tyrannical regimes in Iraq and Afghanistan, Bush has somehow never found the time to condemn the ravages of the despot in Jerusalem who, with tanks and US-supplied helicopter gunships, tyrannizes over millions of Palestinians. With the slaughter of 69 innocent civilians at the Jordanian village of Qibya in 1953, Ariel Sharon was the man who opened Israel's account of UN condemnations, and then went on to preside over greater massacres (of up to 2000 Palestinian refugees) in West Beirut in 1982. Does Hitchens really believe that a US President who describes such a person as a "man of peace" has a serious plan in mind to help the defenseless civilian population suffering under his jackboot? But Hitchens now seems content to accept the crumbs of verbiage brushed from the imperial table.

"Herd" Morality versus "Humanitarian" Intervention

With respect to the "long postponed" confrontation with the Baath regime in Iraq, there were plenty of signals early on that might have alerted Hitchens to having backed the wrong horse. A stream of pre-war UN weapons reports documenting no WMDs is difficult to willfully ignore, much less miss. The unprecedented millions who poured into the world's capitals on February 15, 2003 to protest the "war" necessitated by the "threat" would surely give anyone pause. Moreover, they raise a more fundamental point. If the mob the world over can spot a fabricated *casus belli* a mile off, and an educated journalist couldn't (and still refuses to—more on that later), why should anyone ever again read him for an enlightened opinion on the matter? (As early as March 18, 2003, he wrote: "there's reason to believe bin Laden may be dead,"[16] and just six days before bin Laden's pre-election reappearance Hitchens had the misfortune to write: "Even if he is still alive—which seems open to great doubt . . ."[17]) With regards to the millions who protested this war he had the following to say:

> I should like to say that the demonstrations I attended or witnessed in London, Washington, San Francisco and elsewhere were actually organized by people who do not think that Saddam Hussein was a bad guy at all. They were in fact organized by groups who either openly like Saddam, and Milosevic, and Mugabe, and Kim Jong-Il, or by those who think that Osama bin Laden represents a Muslim cry for help.[18]

Nietzsche once said that when we find ourselves on the side of the majority, it is time to stop and consider. Hitchens, the inveterate contrarian, seems appalled that his views have been adopted by popular elements, and his knee-jerk reaction seems to have been to swing the other way entirely. Any credible exponent of left-wing ideology would be delighted that the public at large had finally announced its recognition of the piratical nature of US foreign policy, and its rejection of Bush's overextended "preemption" doctrine. But the masses of people who expressed condemnations of US power entirely consonant with much of Hitchens's pre-9/11 writings seem to have left him in the lonely position of being unoriginal and uncontroversial. So before we knew it, he was on the other side, a contrarian once again. Note that Nietzsche—who was himself no lover of the morals of the masses— said stop and consider, not reflexively assume that your views are wrong *because* they are the majority opinion.

But is that all? Noam Chomksy once theorized that the post-1967 coziness of the American Left with Israel had its roots in the Vietnam war protests during the sixties. Intellectual elites appalled by the rabble gate-crashing the public arena to enact real political change took consolation in Israel's six-day pulverizing of nationalist third-world upstarts like Nasser.[19] This development essentially cauterized the wound suffered in Indochina. Something not dissimilar seems to have happened to Hitchens, who plainly cannot abide the presence of a demotic element in the debate over Iraq's future and the war on terror. Part of the explanation for Hitchens's turnaround may lie in his temperament—the impulse to express willfully invidious views has always been a strong trait—but that should not prevent us from recognizing the undisguised snobbery of his tone whenever he speaks of the "nihilistic antiwar faction,"[20] or "blithering ex-flower children"[21] and their "silly placards."[22] He has, in separate places, referred to the Iraqi resistance and the Iranian and Libyan regimes—all of whom are implacably opposed to US interference in the region—as "riff-raff,"[23] a choice of words which probably imparts more than he would wish it to.

There is also the chic doctrine of "liberal imperialism," to which Hitchens appears to have tacitly hitched his wagon. In this *Weltanschauung*, force can be used by Western civilization for "good," to topple autocratic regimes for the benefit of mankind in general, particularly when circumstances are sufficiently exigent to trump any considerations of sovereignty (a word increasingly appearing in scare quotes). Subsequent investigations in Iraq have shown, however, that circumstances *vis-à-vis* WMDs were *not* exigent. And "Orwellian" is too hackneyed a description for the "liberal imperialism" conceit, a neologism which would not look out of place in the colonial lexicon beside the "white man's burden" of the British (memorably shouldered at Amritsar); the "philanthropy" of Leopold II's piratical rule over the Belgian Congo (which is estimated to have claimed between five and seven million lives and inspired the world's first human rights movement);[24] and the "civilizing mission" of the French Empire.[25]

The "civilizing" of Algeria, to take just one example, involved the forced conversion of mosques to churches, the suppression of the native language, the expropriation of tribal lands, destruction of the environment, and (during one not atypical raid) the hacking off of women's hands for their jewelry.[26] In the recent furor over Iraq, there has been much knowing and ironic quoting of General Allenby's 1917 promise of liberation upon entering the conquered Ottoman *vilayet* of Baghdad. But it's also worth remembering today that when the French invaded Algeria in 1830, the false pretext was a threat of piracy that had long ceased to be a serious problem since Thomas Jefferson pacified the Barbary Coast in 1804. (The intervention was thus explained as a "defense" of the invading country, as with modern Iraq.) And as with Allenby and Bush, the pre-invasion rhetoric stated that it was not to be an occupation, but a liberation:

> We French, your friends, are leaving for Algiers. We are going to drive out your tyrants, the Turks who persecute you, who steal your goods, and never cease menacing your lives. . . . our presence on your territory is not to make war on you but on the person of your pasha. Abandon your pasha; follow our advice; it is good advice and can only make you happy.[27]

Following the "liberation," the French stayed for 132 years. When they were finally driven out in 1962, it was at the cost of war that claimed one million lives.

The evidence seems fairly clear. Virtually every Western colonial regime that ever existed has sought to justify its incursion into other countries by an appeal either to "defense" or "benevolence"—sometimes both at once. With this history in plain view, it is strange that Hitchens has never furnished his readers with an explanation of why the invasion of an oil-rich Iraq by an oil-hungry camarilla in Washington will be any different.[28] This concept of "liberal imperialism" is simply a dressed-up version of age-old colonial precepts; it thus has a chequered history to say the least; and those who are willing to take the risk of giving it moral currency today not only must accept the consequences of what may be done to a civilian population in its name, but must do so in the full knowledge that history has forewarned them. This, as we shall see, applies *a fortiori* to the people of Iraq and especially Iraqi Kurds.

But should we not cheer the toppling of a tyrant such as Saddam Hussein? This, after all, is the very best thing that can be said about the US intervention in Iraq, and yet, as the history shows, it is purely a side-benefit.[29] As I've stated before, Hitchens's main quarrel with the anti-war movement concerns their relative silence on this matter. In this blank space he has scribbled their imaginary support for a brutal regime—a self-supplied argument which he then easily refutes. Thus we learn that: "the anti-Bush/Blair 'Left' has, to its credit, been perfectly honest in identifying itself both with Saddam Hussein and with Islamic fundamentalism."[30] No examples provided.

In the course of advocating the downfall of a despot, Hitchens asseverates that the US, guilty of so much collaboration with Saddam Hussein, is therefore morally obliged to clean up the mess they helped to create. If we ponder the consensus that the Saddam regime would certainly have been toppled from within years before the invasion were it not for the US-enforced sanctions which crippled the country's economy and made the populace hopelessly dependent on the government, it becomes apparent that this confrontation was not unavoidable, but *rendered* unavoidable by the US. Nevertheless, Hitchens asks us to believe that the nation which kept in place a regime that tormented a defenseless population for years should now be allowed—nay, is *obliged*—to put in place the successor regime. By this rationale, communist China should have exclusively supervised the process of state-formation in Cambodia, following the ouster of the Beijing-supported Pol Pot regime which cast the country into unspeakable darkness for four years; Russia likewise becomes the most apposite candidate to reconstruct the Hungarian independence which it crushed during the 1956 invasion; and a Turkish "liberation" of Kurdish north-eastern Iraq would have been just fine with Hitchens on redemptive grounds. (We know that's not the case, of course, since he has described the regime in Ankara as "an ally we're better off without.")[31] His best shot at advancing this argument goes as follows:

> Some say that because the United States was wrong before, it cannot possibly be right now, or has not the right to be right. (The British Empire sent a fleet to Africa and the Caribbean to maintain the slave trade while the very same empire later sent another fleet to enforce abolition. I would not have opposed the second policy because of my objections to the first; rather it seems to me that the second policy was morally necessitated by its predecessor.)[32]

The analogy could hardly be more specious. In terms of its gestation, its motives, and its power relations, the abolition effort was the diametric opposite of the Iraq intervention. It began in 1787 as a tiny grass-roots movement with no political support[33] and continued to snowball until it could no longer be ignored by a reluctant British government which had all along indoctrinated the country into believing that the slave trade was vital to the economy. The Iraq invasion, by contrast, originated at the exact opposite end of the power spectrum: plotted by a tiny cabal at the apex of political power in Washington who had a declared interest in preserving a hydrocarbon economy, it was instantaneously opposed by perhaps the largest grass-roots movement the world has ever seen, and, far from ending in liberation, it has now degenerated into what unembedded journalists in Iraq are uniformly describing as "a bloody mess."[34]

WMDs

What else? Oh yes, Hitchens expounded the ill-fated WMD argument for invading Iraq from the very beginning, and incredibly, has continued to do so up until quite recently,[35] albeit in rather more muted tones. The last bleat we heard on this issue was that "most of the groaning and sniping about the missing WMDs comes from the hard right"[36]—this unsupported claim insinuates that a statement of fact somehow betokens sympathy with unsavory elements, reductively leaving aside the fact that the non-existent (not "missing") WMDs is now a global consensus, including among the US intelligence agencies which formerly posited their existence. During a more confident era, however, Hitchens wrote an article leveled squarely at Seattle's "peaceniks" in which he darkly forecast weapons sites galore, and added: "Just you wait."[37] Well, we've been waiting. Since March 2003. So for Hitchens's benefit, allow me to paraphrase what is now regarded as the dying gasp of this argument—specifically, the conclusion of the Duelfer report, the findings of the US government's own nine-month investigation into Iraqi WMDs, published in early October 2004: *Iraq possessed no weapons of mass destruction at the time of the invasion, nor is there any evidence that it had produced any since 1991.* It's tempting at moments like this to say a "told you so" on behalf of the much-lampooned peace camp, in much the same way as Hitchens has been dying to say it to them, and now will never be able to.

It's been interesting to track the apostate's progress, however. Or perhaps his regress. Because there's a parallel here. Like Blair and Bush, Hitchens also picked his moment to clear his throat and dilute his claims of "WMDs" to "WMD programmes" . . . except that retrenching to this position has not worked out either. (When the facts force you to euphemize your own arguments, it's really time to bail. But again, Hitchens's nerve has held up admirably against reality.) During a December 4, 2003 debate with Tariq Ali on the *Democracy Now* radio show, Hitchens brought up the issue of Iraqi plans to buy a missile system "off the shelf" from North Korea. (I can hardly think of a country that *isn't* armed with missiles.) The only other card he could play was that of the uranium-enrichment components placed in a barrel and buried in the garden of Iraqi scientist Mahdi Obeidi. This clearly high-tech and expertly concealed plot to launch an apocalypse from a flowerbed prompted Hitchens to confidently state: "Of course there was a weapons of mass destruction programme: it's just been interrupted and now terminated." Well, Hitchens is indeed scraping the bottom of this nuclear barrel for proof that the whole Iraqi fiasco was worthwhile. An average of 70 US servicemen per month now being killed in Iraq; estimates that bring the post-invasion Iraqi death toll to over 40,000; Iraqi civilians now 2.5 times more likely to die than under the Saddam Hussein regime;[38] open anarchy on the streets; near-daily bombings; a "government" (whose members are wisely absent from the country most of the time) headed from its inception by an old henchman of the former dictator's regime and a stooge of the occupiers (does the name Hun Sen ring a bell?) . . . apparently it was all worthwhile to learn for certain what UNSCOM inspector Scott Ritter and scores of others had been telling us all along:

> When I left Iraq in 1998, when the UN inspection program ended, the infrastructure and facilities had been 100% eliminated. There's no debate about that. All their instruments and facilities had been destroyed. The weapons design facility had been destroyed. The production equipment had been hunted down and destroyed. And we had in place means to monitor—both from vehicles and from the air—the gamma rays that accompany attempts to enrich uranium or plutonium. We never found anything. We can say un-

equivocally that the industrial infrastructure needed by Iraq to produce nuclear weapons had been eliminated.[39]

But Hitchens the tyro, of course, knew better than Ritter the expert who spent years in Iraq. And he insisted on an invasion so that we could be sure. Then, in an astonishing C-SPAN interview on February 20, 2004, he told viewers that "Saddam's possession of these weapons was overstated" . . . as though Hitchens had not been doing some of the loudest overstating himself. But of course, there's a fall-back rationale. A few minutes later we are being told: "We are now able to say that Iraq is disarmed . . . but we would not have been able to say that without regime change. Iraq has now been inspected. . . . we don't know where those weapons went yet." As any rational person will understand, it takes quite a feat of mental gymnastics to persuade oneself that the reason for invading a country was wrong but that we could only know this for certain by carrying out the invasion anyway. And then there's that tack-on throwaway at the end, the refrain of the luckless warmonger caught red-handed and fumbling for an explanation: we don't know where the weapons went ("yet"). One of the ironies that Hitchens seems to have forgotten is that no sooner had the US gotten themselves into the Iraqi quagmire in early 2003, they then began demanding the same amount of time to find the fugacious WMDs as they had refused to give the weapons inspectors *before* the attack in a measure that might have avoided war. To the pre-apostasy Hitchens this simple fact would have been too delicious not to write about at length. But now that the whole world can see the obvious, Hitchens—ignominiously—has to look the other way. (The remainder of the interview found him accusing humanitarians of having "penis envy" over George W. Bush's humanitarianism. No commentary required.)

Even now, he continues to dig up the bomb in the garden. One of his last articles on the WMD canard exhumes Mahdi Obeidi's story with the tagline "A new book shows that Saddam didn't have nuclear weapons—yet." (There's that word again.) Well, what a journey it has been to arrive at this place. To listen to the pre-war Hitchens one would think we were on the Eve of Destruction. Today the best evidence he can produce for this is the collection of spare parts abandoned in someone's back yard. The book, with spectacularly bad timing, was published almost at the same time as the Duelfer report. This meant that in writing about one, Hitchens could not ignore the other. He opens with cloying forthrightness:

> It's a good coincidence that the Duelfer report appears in the same week as *The Bomb In My Garden*, a memoir by Saddam Hussein's chief nuclear physicist. Between them, or taken together, the two bodies of evidence enable two quite different yet quite compatible conclusions. The first is that the Saddam regime was more disarmed than perhaps even its leadership knew. The second is that it would have been very unwise to proceed on any assumption except that of its latent danger.[40]

One can almost hear the deep breath drawn before the next sentence:

> This may seem like an attempt to have it both ways, but consider: We only know all of this, about the Baathist weapons programs and their erosion and collapse, because of regime change. Up until then, any assumption that all the fangs had been removed would have been a highly irresponsible one. It would have involved, quite simply, taking Saddam Hussein's word for it.[41]

A more wretched case made for fraudulent war (and in hindsight at that) I have never before read. (Recall: Hitchens is a self-professed disciple of Orwell.) "Taking Saddam's word for it"? It is as though he has persuaded himself that years of UNSCOM inspections consisted of little more than Q&A, entirely dependent on the honesty of the respondent. To return to the words of Scott Ritter:

> We have the United Nations record of Iraqi disarmament from 1991 to 1998. That record is without dispute. It's documented. We eliminated the nuclear program, and for Iraq to have reconstituted it would require undertaking activities eminently detectable by intelligence services.[42]

Some threat. The plain truth is rather more revealing. The UN's best chances of ensuring that Saddam Hussein remained defanged were torpedoed in 1998 when the US unilaterally violated the terms of in-spections that were working and sent the inspectors to an off-limits Baath party HQ in Baghdad. Once they were refused entry, the Americans then unilaterally withdrew the inspection teams. Both these developments occurred without sanction from the Security Council. This was basically Iraq's Tonkin incident. Ever since, it has been the policy of the US to blame Saddam for the "interruption" that "necessitated" the invasion.

Befriending the Kurds

Then there is the matter of the "protected" populations of Iraq. Hitchens informs us that "for twelve years, a "no fly" zone has protected the Kurdish and Shia populations from extermination."[43] He repeated this claim while condemning the insufferably demotic Michael Moore, telling us, in his own italics: "Iraqi forces fired, *every day, for 10 years*, on the aircraft that patrolled the no-fly zones and staved off further genocide in the north and south of the country."[44] Well, I'm afraid the level of protection given to the Kurds in the north of Iraq extended only as far as political convenience allowed. The ugly *realpolitik* in this case was the desire to keep Turkey (with its long and paranoid history of suppressing Kurdish independence)[45] "on side." As Nick Cohen noted years ago: "The no-fly zone is not policed to protect Kurds but RAF and USAF flights deeper into Iraq. Nor does it provide a safe haven. The Turks are allowed to enter the sanctuary and exterminate Kurdish guerrillas."[46] And not just guerillas, unfortunately. As reported by John Pilger:

> Since 1992, the zones have provided cover for Turkey's repeated invasions of Iraq. In 1995 and 1997, as many as 50,000 Turkish troops, backed by tanks, fighter-bombers and helicopter gunships, occupied swathes of the Kurds' "safe haven," allegedly attacking PKK bases. In December 2000 they were back, terrorizing Kurdish villages and murdering civilians. The US and Britain said nothing; the Security Council said nothing. Moreover, the British and Americans colluded in the invasions, suspending their flights to allow the Turks to get on with the killing. . . .

> In March 2001, RAF pilots patrolling the northern no fly zone
> publicly protested for the first time about their role in the bomb-
> ing of Iraq. Far from performing the "vital humanitarian task" de-
> scribed by Tony Blair, they complained that they were frequently
> ordered to return to their Turkish base to allow the Turkish air
> force to bomb the Kurds in Iraq. . . .[47]

Yes, you read that right. The fighter jets that were supposed to protect the Kurds were taking off from the same airbases as the fighter
jets that were pulverizing their villages. So let's not kid ourselves
about "staving off genocide." Hitchens's fabled "safe havens" did not
protect the Kurds—they merely had the effect of transferring bombing privileges from one mortal enemy to another. For someone who
has appeared on TV wearing the badge of the *peshmerga* on his lapel
and the cause of Kurdistan on his sleeve, it seems extraordinary that
Hitchens would now find himself supporting the same coalition that
allowed this slaughter to take place. Can it be that he simply doesn't
know? I think not. The only other alternative—that he knows full well
but chooses to pretend otherwise for fear of imperiling his own argument—is less than flattering. Silence on this matter, needless to say, is
far more sinister than the silence of the anti-war Left on the depredations of Saddam Hussein.

Besides, the sequence of events which led to the creation of the no-
fly zones in the first place reveals a great deal about the motives of
the "protectors" who had taken the Kurdish and Shiite populations
under their Exocet-laden wing. Following Saddam's Gulf War defeat
in Kuwait, rebellions broke out in the north and south of Iraq, and
when the rebels asked for US assistance, they were denied even the
use of captured Iraqi artillery. The US, quite simply, wanted the re-
volts to fail. Facing the prospect of annihilation by a dictator who had
not been squeamish about gassing whole villages in 1988, two million
Kurds poured over the Iraqi border into Iran and Turkey. It was *only*
when this mass exodus threatened "stability" in the region (always a
key concern, and the fulcrum around which a great deal of hypocrisy
turns) that the US acted to create the no-fly zones. In an article in
Harper's in January 1991, Hitchens himself described the horror of
Henry Kissinger's use of the restive Kurds as a bulwark against Sad-

dam Hussein and Hassan Al-Bakr's menacing maneuvers against the Shah of Iran in 1975.[48] The Kurds were given arms and encouraged to revolt, but again, the US did not want the rebellion to succeed, merely to grind the Baathist regime down to a more obliging position. Once the Iraqi threat had receded, the US cut off all support to the Kurds, the Shah ruthlessly closed the border, and the resulting slaughter was foreordained.[49] (The British, incidentally, performed the same maneuver in 1932 with the Assyrians in the north of Iraq in an effort to bring the nationalist King Ghazi into line—this rebellion suffered a similar fate.) Incredibly, with this history in full view, Hitchens today sees no hypocrisy in supporting a country that has repeatedly sold the Kurds down the river simply to further their own interests. One wonders how he has rationalized this. That it couldn't happen a *third* time?

Hitchens's "safe haven" argument forms part of a response to Michael Moore's assertion that Iraq had never attacked or even threatened America—the point is clearly made in the context of the argument that there was no legitimate *casus belli* for a US invasion of Iraq. But Hitchens has to whisk it out of this context and tack up a patchwork of points-on-the-side to attempt to discredit it. Among these: "Saddam boasted publicly of his financial sponsorship of suicide bombers in Israel. (Quite a few Americans of all denominations walk the streets of Jerusalem.)"[50] That's reaching, to say the least. Compensating the families of suicide bombers, who, in losing their husband/father, had lost their source of income is simply not the same as paying assassins. As for Hitchens's parenthetical point, Iraq's endorsement of a Palestinian attack on an Israeli target at which an American might (or might not) get killed is a thin thread of causality with which to argue a war provocation.[51] Ditto for the presence in Iraq of terrorists such as Abu Nidal, or even the murderer of Leon Klinghoffer—the United States, after all, is harboring Emmanuel Constant, executioner of thousands, and has repeatedly refused Haiti's extradition requests.[52] Likewise Hector Gramajo, who slaughtered thousands of native Indians in Guatemala, was a Harvard graduate. But again, Hitchens sees no double-standard in endorsing a terrorist-harboring US invading Iraq because Iraq is harboring terrorists. (As though that were the reason.) Nor can he plead ignorance. When asked about the US-run School of the Americas that trained thugs of this ilk, he feebly conceded that it was "regrettably true . . . that there was a manual on terror."[53] Hitchens may bring up the undeniable war crimes of the Baathist regime, but is he not at all concerned that this regime was toppled by a country that has not only refused to endorse the International Criminal Court for the *openly expressed* reason that its soldiers may one day appear before it, but has arm-twisted many small countries into going along with its refusal to be held accountable for war crimes?[54] Is there nothing to write about here?

The Payoff

Now the final test. Hitchens couldn't possibly stand by and defend the Cheney/Halliburton war profiteering, could he? Well, in a word, yes. He actually goes one better and turns his ire on *critics* of the cabal, describing as "oleaginous" "people who prefer Saddam Hussein to Halliburton."[55] And if you enjoyed that *non sequitur* as much as I did, you will certainly appreciate the manner in which it is unpacked:

> I can't open a bulletin from the reactionary right or the anti-war left without being told that Iraq is already worse off without Saddam Hussein. My suspicion—that these people never meant what they affected to say—is thereby materialized. And how can we tell that Iraq is worse off? Because contracts for its reconstruction are being awarded to American corporations. Can that be right? In other words, of the three feasible alternatives (that the contracts go to American capitalists, or to some unspecified non-American capitalists, or that Iraqi oil production stays as it was), the supposed radicals appear to prefer the last of the three.[56]

But the contract (an exclusive, no-bid one at that) didn't *have* to go to the US Vice-President's old chums, did it? Hitch isn't so silly that he'll say that outright, but he's certainly there in spirit, implying that *only* this company could do it. The *reductio ad Halliburton* is made by the following elision: "The number of real-world companies able to deliver such expertise is very limited. The chief one is American. . . ."[57]

So let's have a look at the Cheney/Halliburton chronicles. During the 1990s Halliburton violated federal law by selling dual-use drilling equipment to both Iraq and Libya. The sale of six pulse neutron generators to Libya (which can be used to detonate nuclear weapons) led to Halliburton pleading guilty to criminal charges in 1995 and having to pay a total of $3.81m in fines.[58] In May 2003 it was revealed that Halliburton subsidiary Kellogg, Brown and Root [KBR] paid $2.4m in bribes to a Nigerian official in order to secure favorable tax treatment.[59] KBR now has contracts in Iraq worth $18bn, including a two-year $7bn no-bid contract awarded exclusively to that company by the US government, whose Vice-President is still on the Halliburton payroll.[60] Other work given to KBR includes a $7m contract to build holding cells at Guantanamo Bay. In July 2002 Halliburton and Cheney were sued by Judicial Watch Inc. for accounting fraud. And in August 2004 Halliburton paid a $7.5m fine to settle an investigation by the Securities and Exchange Commission into its failure to disclose changes in its accounting practices. So, as Hitchens might ask, what's all the fuss about?

Hitchens's glibness in the face of all this might be bearable if he had not contemporaneously poured scorn on France for doing exactly the same thing—that is, trading with the enemy and supplying rogue regimes with weapons technology.[61] But when Cheney/Halliburton do it, it's their *critics* who get Hitchens's scorn. Why? It's not as though all of the above is deniable, after all. If Hitchens had simply remained silent on the issue, he had a chance of pretending ignorance. But he could not contain his disdain for the peace camp, and in an attempt to carve some hypocrisy from their quite reasonable questions, he has merely drawn attention to his own. But is sympathy for shady businessmen really so out of character? After all, Hitchens continues even today to back the fugitive embezzler Ahmad Chalabi (whom he named as one of his "comrades in a just struggle and friends for life")[62] even when the US had ditched him—amid accusations of intelligence-peddling to an Iranian regime Hitchens detests—as a nonentity in Iraq's future.[63]

So where will it all end? The retroactive damage done by Hitchens to his own *oeuvre* is a concern. I find myself gazing sadly at his great passages critiquing abuse of power in high places, for he endorsed those abuses just when the Right was at its most reactionary and when the Left needed his voice and perspicacity the most. By his own admission, even those who published his pieces thought he was writing "rash and dangerous nonsense."[64] And his current stance now makes many of his most cogent arguments from the past look profoundly insincere. At the start of his pro-war book Hitchens self-consciously confesses:

> At the evident risk of seeming ridiculous, I want to begin by saying that I have tried for much of my life to write as if I was composing my sentences to be read posthumously. I hope this isn't too melodramatic or self-centered a way of saying that I attempt to write as if I did not care what reviewers said, what peers thought, or what prevailing opinions may be.[65]

To this lapidary passage we may now add: ". . . or what the evidence compels me to admit, or what reasoning obliges me to say." Since Hitchens has opened the door to a review of his journalistic legacy with this objective look at his own bravery, I think I can offer a counter-reading of how his writings might be studied a few years down the line. It's plausible to envision a future in which, as in the case of the philosopher Wittgenstein, writers will find themselves having to make reference to two different people. One of them will be reified as "the later Hitchens." But Hitchens, unlike Wittgenstein, had it right first and *then* revised his position. And Wittgenstein needed no prompting to admit that he was wrong.

It's clear now from the increasing ferocity used to defend ever-weakening arguments that the pre-9/11 Hitchens is not coming back. We are already reading him posthumously.

Arena Journal, July 7, 2005

NOTES

1. Isaac Deutscher, quoted in Hitchens, *For the Sake of Argument: Essays and Minority Reports* (London: Verso, 1993), 114.

2. Hitchens, *For the Sake of Argument*, 325–26.

3. Hitchens completed the metamorphosis relatively recently by defecting to William Kristol's Murdoch-owned *Weekly Standard*, where he wrote a prolix attack on the anti-war British MP George Galloway (see this volume, chap. 31).

4. See Hitchens, "The Fascist Sympathies of the Soft Left," *Spectator*, September 29, 2001.

5. See *Democracy Now*, December 4, 2003. The moment came, according to Hitchens, while being driven around northern Iraq by Kurdish guerillas with a

picture of George H. W. Bush taped to the front of their jeep. He found that "I didn't have an answer" to their remark that were it not for the US President, they would all be dead. Hitchens did not take the trouble to correct their innocence: Bush took some time off for golfing during the height of their crisis, and was only impelled to act by considerations of "regional stability" and the decidedly unphotogenic TV imagery of millions of Kurds streaming out of Iraq.

6. *Editors' Note*: on Horowitz and Van Patter, see Hitchens, "Left-Leaving, Left-Leaning," this volume, 189.

7. Hitchens, "The Fascist Sympathies of the Soft Left."

8. Hitchens, *For the Sake of Argument*, 260.

9. Ibid., 264.

10. Ibid., 244.

11. To crown it all, Bush has distinguished himself by dodging both the Vietnam draft *and* the national guard service that allowed him to perform the first dodge. This hardly qualifies him as the kind of President you'd want during wartime.

12. I'm being unkind, of course: during a pre-presidency interview Mr. Bush managed to identify Pervez Musharaff as "General Something" (see David Corn, *The Lies of George W. Bush* (New York: Three Rivers Press, 2003), 14.

13. Hitchens, "Unfairenheit 9/11: The Lies of Michael Moore," *Slate*, June 21, 2004.

14. Hitchens, *A Long Short War: The Postponed Liberation of Iraq* (London: Penguin, 2003), 5.

15. Ibid., 19.

16. Ibid., 8.

17. Hitchens, "In Front of Your Nose," *Slate*, October 25, 2004.

18. Hitchens, *A Long Short War*, 10.

19. See Chomsky, "US Middle East Policy and the American Peace Movement," UC Berkeley, May 14, 1984.

20. Hitchens, *A Long Short War*, 102.

21. Ibid., 11.

22. A Debate with Mark Danner, UC Berkeley, November 4, 2003.

23. Hitchens, "Gaddafi Does a Deal," *Slate*, December 22, 2003.

24. See Adam Hochschild, *King Leopold's Ghost* (London: Macmillan, 1998).

25. See, for example, M.E. Chamberlain, *Decolonization*, 2nd edition (Cambridge, MA: Blackwell, 1999), 71.

26. See Peter Mansfield, *The Arabs* (London: Penguin, 1976), 115.

27. Ibid.

28. To place the matter in context: if the oil-producing world is divided into seven geographic regions, the second-richest of these is South America, with an estimated 95 billion barrels of "proven resources." Iraq *alone* is estimated to possess in the order 105 billion barrels.

29. At the Azores conference on the eve of the war, the coalition announced that they were going to invade anyway, even if Saddam stepped down.

30. Hitchens, "Long Live Labor," *Slate*, April 25, 2005.
31. Hitchens, *A Long Short War*, 73.
32. Ibid., 6.
33. Specifically, with twelve men meeting in a printer's shop in London. See Adam Hochschild, *Bury the Chains: Prophets and Rebels in the Fight to Free an Empire's Slaves* (New York: Houghton Mifflin, 2005).
34. Patrick Cockburn, *Independent*, June 28, 2005.
35. Hitchens, "This Was Not Looting," *Slate*, March 15, 2005.
36. Hitchens, "Long Live Labor."
37. Hitchens, *A Long Short War*, 55.
38. Report published late October 2004 in *The Lancet*. This figure's likelihood of accuracy is estimated to be 90% based on data taken from clustered sampling. Robert Fisk attests to the same complaint on the ground from ordinary Iraqis concerning their safety in a post-Saddam Iraq. Fisk, whom Hitchens himself described (C-SPAN interview, November 11, 2001) as "one of the best of the Middle East reporters, if not the best," was pithy in his summation: "We have gotten rid of a dictatorship and replaced it with total anarchy" (*Democracy Now* interview, October 1, 2004).
39. Scott Ritter and William Rivers Pitt, *War on Iraq* (New York: Context Books, 2002), 26.
40. Hitchens, "The Buried Truth," *Slate*, October 8, 2004.
41. Ibid.
42. Ritter and Rivers Pitt, *War on Iraq*, 28.
43. Hitchens, *A Long Short War*, 9.
44. Hitchens, "Unfairenheit 9/11."
45. Turkey abrogated the original post-Ottoman Kurdish state with the signing of the Treaty of Lausanne in 1923.
46. Nick Cohen, "Our Enormous Lie," *The Observer*, August 12, 2001.
47. John Pilger, *The New Rulers of the World* (London: Verso, 2003), 80. Cohen and Pilger have both cited the findings of Bristol University lecturer Eric Herring on the matter.
48. Hitchens, *For the Sake of Argument*, 77.
49. See Tariq Ali, *Bush in Babylon* (London: Verso, 2004), 119.
50. Hitchens, "Unfairenheit 9/11."
51. Perhaps the only analogue available from recent history is Israel's ludicrous rationale for the 1982 invasion of Lebanon and its assault on the PLO's base there. The *casus belli* was the shooting—in London—of the Israeli ambassador to Britain Shlomo Argov. The attack was carried out by Abu Nidal, a sworn enemy of the PLO.
52. With one exception: the 1995 extradition attempt, which Constant thwarted by threatening to reveal the CIA's involvement in his war crimes. He was rewarded with a Green Card. The Nazi Alois Brunner lived in Syria for years

under a similar blackmail arrangement with its government. See Robert Fisk, *Pity the Nation* (Oxford: Oxford University Press, 2001), 179.

53. C-SPAN, November 11, 2001.

54. Julian Borger, "Congress Threatens to Cut Aid in Fight over Criminal Court," *The Guardian*, November 27, 2004.

55. Hitchens, *A Long Short War*, 85.

56. Ibid.

57. Ibid., 87.

58. Much of the business dealings with Saddam's Iraq took place under Cheney's watch as CEO from 1995–2000. The Libyan connection is particularly interesting. In a remarkable memory lapse, Hitchens threw Ghaddafi's opportunistic capitulation in with the invasion of Afghanistan and Iraq and came up with the following: "Not to end on too festive or seasonal a note, but the disarming of three rogue regimes in under one year isn't bad" ("Gaddafi Does a Deal"). There's no mention of the country that *armed* all three regimes.

59. "Halliburton Firm Bribed Nigeria," *The Age*, May 10, 2003.

60. Cheney continues to receive "deferred payments" from Halliburton in the order of approximately $150,000 annually. Interestingly, Cheney's wife, Lynne, sat on the board of Lockheed-Martin, the US government's third-largest defense contractor. When her husband became Vice-President, she rejected conflict-of-interest arguments and remained on the board until January 2001.

61. He pilloried the French for their business dealings with Iraq and added: "Did not France also build a nuclear reactor for Saddam Hussein, knowing what he wanted it for?" (*A Long Short War*, 5).

62. Ibid., viii.

63. It was clear anyway—long before this development—that Chalabi, who has not lived in Iraq for decades, would be no less of a stranger to the Iraqis—imposed from without by imperial forces—than Faisal I, who was handed the throne of Iraq in 1921 by the British, in what amounted to a mollifying gesture to the loyal Hashemites for their loss of Damascus (to the French) and the Hejaz (to Ibn Saud). See Said K. Aburish, *A Brutal Friendship: The West and the Arab Elite* (New York: Thomas Dunne Books, 1997), 26.

64. Hitchens, *A Long Short War*, viii.

65. Ibid., 7.

◄{ 51 }►

Christopher Hitchens's Last Battle

JUAN COLE

Bush administration foot-dragging and ineptitude in handling the aftermath of Hurricane Katrina in New Orleans has profoundly demoralized his supporters on the Right. The hawkish intellectuals who gathered around George W. Bush to support his "War on Terror" once used language that suggested his machine-like omnicompetence. The Afghanistan War was to be "Operation Infinite Justice" until it was pointed out that Allah was the only one in that part of the world generally permitted to use that kind of language. The images of civilians abandoned to their fates and unchecked looting from New Orleans, however, reminded everyone of Bush's disastrous policies in Iraq, and suggested a pattern of criminal incompetence.

These bellicose intellectuals—a band of Wilsonian idealists, cutthroat imperial capitalists, Trotskyites bereft of a cause, and neo-patriots traumatized by September 11—are now increasingly divided and full of mutual recriminations. Among them all, the combative British essayist Christopher Hitchens continues most forcefully to uphold the case for the war, most recently in a piece for the *Weekly Standard*.[1]

In contrast, this week Francis Fukuyama, long since upbraided by History for his Hegelian fantasies concerning the end of History, openly castigated the Iraq war as an unfortunate detour in the War on Terror, in an opinion piece in the *New York Times*.[2] Hitchens, fighting a rear-guard battle against public disillusionment with the war, suggested 10 reasons why Americans should be proud of the Iraq war. His essay appeared the week after George W. Bush launched his own public relations crusade for "staying the course" in the face of the media attention given to Cindy Sheehan, the mother of a US soldier killed in the war. (Hitchens dismisses her campaign as "the sob-sister tripe pumped out by the Cindy Sheehan circus and its surrogates.") The campaign was a dud, derailed by dithering in Baghdad over a never-finished constitution and continued mayhem and US deaths. Bush's alarmed handlers are looking at polling numbers on his performance as president and on his handling of Iraq that are heading so far south that they'll soon be embedded in the wilting Antarctic ice shelf.

It is sad to see Hitchens reduced to publishing in the *Weekly Standard*, intellectually the weakest of the right-wing propaganda fronts for the new class of billionaires created by the excesses of corporate consolidation in recent decades (it is owned by Australian media mogul Rupert Murdoch). It is even sadder to see this grotesque, almost baroque, essay carom from one extravagant argument to another, miring itself in a series of gross fallacies and elementary errors in logic. I have read Hitchens for decades and usually admire his acute wit, his command of detail, his polemical gifts, and his contrarian sense of ethics, even when we disagree. He must surely know, however, that his argument for the Iraq misadventure is growing weaker every day, since he clearly does not any longer care to defend it rigorously.

The essay begins by arguing that cowardice and short-sightedness dominated the 1990s, during which democratic leaders declined to react, or reacted too late, to the dictators, genocides and failed states that emerged with the end of the Cold War. Rwanda, Serbia, Kosovo and Afghanistan stand in this view as monuments of shame. Once the West finally shed its cynical isolationism with the interventions in Bosnia and Kosovo, and once the dangers of inaction had been demonstrated by September 11, Hitchens argues, it was natural and proper for the United States and the United Kingdom to fix their sights on Iraq.

Hitchens lays out the familiar charges against the Baath regime in Iraq. It had invaded neighboring countries, committed genocide, given refuge to terrorists, and contravened the provisions of the Non-Proliferation Treaty. Hitchens's argument succeeds only by confusing the situation in Iraq in the 1980s with that in 2003. He mysteriously neglects to note that the Baath regime had in fact given up its WMDs in the 1990s, in perhaps the most thorough-going and successful UN-led disarmament in modern history. At the time of the 2003 war, Iraq was neither in contravention of UN resolutions on disarmament nor of the Non-Proliferation Treaty.

A further problem is that the same charges could be made against other states. For example, Israel has launched several wars of aggression, gave refuge to terrorists of the Jewish Defense League, defied a whole raft of UN resolutions, and thumbed its nose at the Non-Pro-liferation Treaty far more successfully than Saddam, producing hundreds of nuclear warheads where Iraq never produced a single bomb. Of course Israel cannot be compared to Saddam's Iraq in the numbers of persons killed by its wars and repression, but if the issue is crimes against international law, then the numbers are surely less important than the fact of an infraction.

Hitchens is, moreover, highly selective in his outrage. He is not disturbed by the brutal, scorched-earth tactics of the Russians in Chechnya or the heavy-handedness of India in Kashmir. The deaths of 3 million Congolese pass without mention. The terrorist threat posed by the Tamil Tigers and the weakened state in Sri Lanka does not attract his attention. Many more dangerous situations existed in the world than the one in Iraq, which turns out not to have been dangerous at all.

Hitchens castigates Iraq as having been both a rogue and a failed state, and offers this self-contradictory depiction as a legitimate cause for war. If we translate this Orwellian concept, it transpires that a warrant is being offered to superpowers to invade other countries at will, since all possible targets clearly will either be fairly strong states (rogues) or weak ones (failed).

The argument is most dishonest in leaping from alleging crimes to lauding unilateral action to punish them, outside any framework of international legality. The UN Security Council declined to authorize a war against Iraq. Iraq had not attacked the United States or the United Kingdom. Iraq had no nuclear weapons program and no unconventional military capabilities, and it posed no threat to anyone except its own people in 2003. Hitchens collects anecdotes about centrifuge plans and centrifuge parts being kept by Baath figures after the nuclear program was dismantled, as though a few buried rotting blueprints and rusting parts were something more than pitiful testaments to a decisively defeated dream. In essence, Hitchens is arguing for the legitimacy of a sort of hyperpower vigilantism, in which the sitting president of the United States decides which regimes may continue to exist, virtually by himself. The US Congress did not even have the moral fortitude to declare war. The UN charter forbids wars of aggression, and, indeed, forbids all wars not clearly defensive that are not explicitly authorized by the Security Council. The Security Council may be, as Hitchens implies, corrupt and yellow-bellied, but it represents most of humankind, while Bush did not even represent a majority of Americans.

After his general argument, Hitchens turns to his 10 specific reasons why the war on Iraq should be celebrated. Hitchens's first point is that Bush has overthrown Talibanism and Baathism, and has exposed "suggestive" links between the two, who he says had formed a "Hitler-Stalin pact." His attempt to tie these ideologies together is absurd, but he goes through the motions because he wants to hide the Iraq disaster under the US achievements in Afghanistan—which he overstates. In fact, the secular Arab nationalist Baath state had nothing whatsoever to do with any radical Islamist movements, including Talibanism. Talibanism is a variant of the Deobandi School of revivalist Sunnism deriving from British colonial India. The link Hitchens suggests is the Jordanian terrorist Ahmad Fadil al-Khala'ilah, known as Abu Musab al-Zarqawi, who went off as a teenager in 1989 to fight the Soviets in Afghanistan, but arrived only in time to wave goodbye to them. He later had a vigorous rivalry with Osama bin Laden and refused to share resources with him. It is not clear what his relationship was to "Talibanism"; he appears to be a radical "Salafi" in the Jordanian Sunni revivalist tradition.

Hitchens writes that Zarqawi "moved from Afghanistan to Iraq before the coalition intervention." In fact, Zarqawi moved to Iraqi Kurdistan, over which the Baath Party had no control after the United States imposed the no-fly zone. Hitchens wants to use Zarqawi's ties in Kurdistan with the tiny Ansar al-Islam terrorist group, which he asserts Saddam supported to fight his Kurdish enemies, to prove that there was some kind of connection between Saddam and Al Qaeda. But the allegation that Saddam supported Ansar has never been proved. In any case, Zarqawi was not even in Iraq before 9/11, so his presence there can't be used to prove that Saddam was involved in 9/11. Hitchens also claims (who knows if it is true?) that Zarqawi recently renamed his group "Al Qaeda in Mesopotamia." But that is no proof of a link between Talibanism and Baathism. This fallacy is known as anachronism: later events do not cause earlier ones.

The truth is, Bush squandered his victory over the Taliban by failing to follow through at the crucial moment, and by diverting needed military resources into a disastrous second front in Iraq. He allowed bin Laden and his key associate, the Egyptian Ayman al-Zawahiri, to escape, probably into the lawless mountain regions on the Pakistani border, from where they put out videotapes encouraging the later bombings in Sharm El Sheikh and London. He diverted the resources that could have been used to put war-torn Afghanistan back on its feet instead to a costly imbroglio on the Tigris. After the successes in fighting narcotics trafficking in the 1990s, nearly half of Afghanistan's gross domestic product now derives from the poppy trade, which shows up as heroin in Europe and raises the specter of Colombian-style narco-terrorism. Remaining Taliban are adapting to Afghanistan the techniques of roadside bombings and shaped charges honed by the guerrillas in Iraq, with whom they appear to have established tenuous links. Politicians with ties to the Taliban are likely to do well in the Pashtun regions in the forthcoming parliamentary elections.

Hitchens next lists as an achievement of the Iraq war the "capitulation" of Muammar Gaddafi's Libya over its WMD programs. But Hitchens offers no proof whatsoever that Libya's overture had anything at all to do with the Iraq war. Rather, it is quite clear that Libya is a case where the European and US economic sanctions placed on the country to punish it for its terrorist activities actually worked as designed. (European sanctions had already been lifted, in return for a change in Libyan behavior, in 1999. US sanctions had not.) Moreover, Al Qaeda leader Anas al-Libi had Gaddafi in his sights. Gaddafi, influenced by North African Sufism and millenarianism, is no fundamentalist. He saw an opportunity to end the US sanctions, which were harming Libya's economic development, and to form a common front against radical Islamism. All he had to do was give up his rather insignificant "weapons of mass destruction" programs.

Hitchens does not do us the favor of admitting that the tiny country of Libya, despite its past involvement in serious acts of terrorism, was not exactly a dire menace to Western civilization. Gaddafi no longer needed the chemical weapons he is alleged to have used in the Chad war, since it had wound down. His nuclear ambitions had never advanced from the drawing board. So he made a small concession and received huge rewards. There is no reason at all to believe that without the Iraq war this breakthrough, years in the making, would have been forestalled. This fallacy is known as *post hoc ergo propter hoc*, that is, "afterward, therefore because of." Not every event that occurs after another is caused by its predecessor.

Hitchens is correct in asserting that the Libyan breakthrough led to the unmasking of the A.Q. Khan network, which illegally transferred nuclear technological know-how from Pakistan to Iran, North Korea and Libya. But since the breakthrough itself was not a consequence of the Iraq war, the unmasking cannot be credited to the war.

Having committed the fallacies of anachronism and questionable cause, Hitchens now goes on to some other points that I think are too trite to spend much time on. He says that the Iraq war helped to identify a quasi-criminal network within the United Nations elite, referring to the oil-for-food scandal. But surely we did not need to send 140,000 young Americans to war in Iraq in order to carry out some basic investigations with regard to United Nations officials resident in New York? This fallacy is known as a lack of proportionality.

He then goes on to suggest that the Iraq war had caused President Jacques Chirac of France and Chancellor Gerhard Schröder of Germany to admit that nothing will alter their "neutralism." He suggests that their current alleged insouciance with regard to Iran is of a piece with this neutralism. This argument contains an *ad hominem* fallacy, since it seems to suggest that their political stances simply derive from their being craven men. Hitchens neglects to address the obvious rejoinder that the Bush administration failed to make a convincing case to them that Iraq posed an imminent danger to Europe or the United States. It might also be that no convincing case has been made about Iran as yet, either.

Hitchens then argues that the ability to certify Iraq as truly disarmed, rather than having to accept the representations of a "psychopathic autocrat," is a benefit of the Iraq war. Yet the American public spends over $30 billion a year on our intelligence agencies. Why should it have to be necessary to launch a costly and possibly disastrous war in order to find out something that a few spies should have been able to tell us? Moreover, if Hitchens were not so contemptuous of the UN weapons inspectors, he might acknowledge that they could have answered this question themselves from February 2003, if only Bush had given them the time to perform their mission, which he asked the UN Security Council to authorize. The CIA gave them a list of more than 600 suspect sites. Satellite photos of many of these sites showed "suspicious" activity, but it turned out that they were mostly just being looted, something easily certified when they were visited and found stripped. The UN inspectors had cleared some 100 of those before Bush pulled them out and just went to war.

The weapons inspectors were all along far more professional and far more capable than anyone gave them credit for. It was they who had dismantled Iraq's nuclear weapons program after the Gulf War. We did not need a war to discover whether Iraq was truly disarmed. Hitchens has here attempted to turn Bush's enormous blunder, of invading Iraq on suspicion of nonexistent WMDs, into a virtue. "Well," he says with a smirk, "now we know for sure, don't we?" This fallacy is called the "false dilemma," since Hitchens has left out the possibility of our knowing with fair certainty—by methods other than warfare—that Iraq was disarmed.

The seventh benefit of the Iraq war, Hitchens says, are the "immense gains" made by the Kurds. But the Kurds had already made their gains, under the US no-fly zone. Since the war, their situation has arguably worsened. They are faced with finding a way to reintegrate themselves with Baghdad, a process clearly painful for them (they keep threatening to secede at the drop of a turban). Their oil pipelines have been sabotaged, and they have been subjected to a wave of assassinations, kidnappings and bombings. And the petroleum city of Kirkuk, which they desperately covet, is still inhabited by Turkmens and Arabs who do not intend to go quietly. Turkey has threatened to invade to protect the Turkmens. Kurdistan is now a powder keg. These are not immense gains.

Hitchens then rehearses the argument, loudly made in conservative circles a few months ago, that the Iraq war encouraged democratic and civil society movements in Egypt, Syria and Lebanon. He argues that Lebanon, in particular, has "regained a version of its autonomy." As I argued in greater detail in March,[3] the argument that Bush's Iraq war has spread democracy in the Middle East is extremely weak. Let us look at his examples one at a time.

Hitchens has not shown that the Iraq war has encouraged democratic and civil society movements in Egypt. Bush's war did encourage 100,000 Muslim Brothers to come out to protest it, and it therefore reinvigorated the fortunes of political Islam in Egypt. The Mubarak government, however, refuses to recognize the Brotherhood as a legitimate political party, despite its popularity. Democratic and civil society movements in Egypt are of old standing, and they did not need an American imperial boot print in Iraq to jump-start them. Hosni Mubarak has agreed to allow a small number of officially recognized parties to field candidates against him in the presidential elections, but this change is window-dressing. Does Hitchens seriously believe Mubarak will lose?

As for Syria, it has not changed much. The Syrians had to leave Lebanon in part because their heavy-handedness had decisively alienated the Lebanese, including Sunni allies. In addition, the Saudis, who in the past have helped to fund the Syrian troop presence, withdrew their support for it.

The major change in Lebanon is that in the wake of the Syrian withdrawal of 14,000 troops, the Shiite fundamentalist Hezbollah Party and its militia seem to be filling in the security vacuum. These developments in Lebanon had almost nothing to do with Iraq. Lebanon has been having parliamentary elections since the 1940s (there were even some in the French colonial period). This entire argument is simply a form of the *post hoc ergo propter hoc* fallacy, which seems plausible to Americans only because they know so little about Egypt, Syria and Lebanon and the preexisting trajectories of those countries' political development.

Hitchens's last points are the most gruesome and heinous. As number 9, he argues that "thousands" of "bin Ladenist" infiltrators into Iraq have been killed. The studies done of the Muslim volunteers who have gone to Iraq indicate that the vast majority of them had never been involved in terrorism before. They went because they were angered by the US military occupation, as they see it, of a Muslim country. So Bush's Iraq is not a flytrap bringing in already-existing Al Qaeda operatives. It is actively *creating* terrorists out of perfectly normal young men who otherwise would be leading a humdrum existence. This argument is a form of begging the question, since it assumes facts not in evidence in order to force a foregone conclusion.

There are, by the way, probably not very many foreign fighters in Iraq. Only 6 percent of the fighters captured by the United States at

Fallujah were foreigners. At that rate, if estimates of 20,000 guerrilla fighters are accurate, there would be about 1,200 foreigners. It is also probably not the case that the United States has killed all that many of them, though hundreds have died as suicide bombers, helping kill thousands of Iraqis and hundreds of US troops. That the argument is heinous was recognized by one Iraqi observer, who asked Bush to please find some other country to which to attract terrorists and kill them, since rather a lot of innocent Iraqis were getting killed in the cross-fire.

Finally, Hitchens argues that a benefit of the war is the "training and hardening" of many thousands of American servicemen and women, which he says will be of use in "future combat." Large numbers of the servicemen and women in Iraq are in the National Guard or the Reserves, and very large numbers are not going to renew their service when they finally get out of Iraq, so their war experience is unlikely to do anyone much good later on. Many will suffer severe trauma, psychological problems and alcoholism as a result of horrific wartime experiences. Some number will end up on the street begging. Thousands of US troops have been "hardened" right into wheelchairs, with lost limbs, faces blown away, and little prospect of productive lives. We had a right to ask them to sacrifice themselves to defend our country against aggression. We did not have a right to ask them to give their bloody forearms, tattered eyeballs, shattered tibias, oozing brain mass, and crushed pelvises to achieve the petty foreign-policy aims that Hitchens lists in his article, even if the Iraq war had accomplished most of those aims, which it has not.

Christopher Hitchens has produced not a coherent picture of positive achievements clearly flowing from Bush's Iraq war but rather a farrago of innuendo, logical fallacies, begged questions, anachronisms, false dilemmas and questionable causes. Nor has he in any balanced manner addressed the negative foreign-policy consequences of the war. These include the diversion of resources from the fight against Al Qaeda to Iraq, the neglect of Afghanistan (itself a basket case and a proven threat to global security), the strengthening of the Iranian position when the Shiite religious parties came to power in the January 30 elections, the deep alienation of much of the Muslim world, the dangers to the world economy inherent in a destabilization of the Oil

Gulf, and the rendering of the American colossus as faintly ridiculous, given the false representations that the Bush administration made about the danger Iraq posed to Europe and the United States.

Even the ability of the US Embassy in Tashkent plausibly to lecture Uzbek strongman Islam Karimov about his use of torture has been effectively removed after revelations of US torture at Abu Ghraib. Hitchens says that the US practices at Abu Ghraib were much better than those of Saddam. But when you are reduced to defending yourself by pointing to your superiority over a genocidal psychopath, then you are suffering from severely low self-esteem and should enter a 12-step recovery program rather than invade other countries.

The Iraq war, like all foreign-policy quagmires, is a conundrum, not an unalloyed propaganda victory for any "side." There was a case to be made for removing Saddam Hussein, on the basis of the Genocide Convention. But that case required a UN Security Council resolution. As it was, the war was illegal, and I turned against it the moment the Bush administration tossed aside the United Nations, in March 2003. As undertaken, it contravened the United Nations charter. Worse than being merely illegal, it was impractical. It lacked the kind of international support that George H.W. Bush assembled for the Gulf War in 1990–91, and which would have been critical to its success.

Still, the war itself was short and need not have been a total disaster. It did after all accomplish the overthrow of one of the most odious dictators of the 20th century, a mass murderer. But the manner in which the Bush administration trumped up the *casus belli* was profoundly dishonest, and few good things follow from a dishonest policy. The subsequent period of American hegemony in Iraq has been a disaster, beset with ignorance, arrogance, cupidity, double-dealing and shadiness, not to mention a massive civilian death toll, vindictive military policies, and a sheer incompetence that dwarfs all the previous foreign-policy misadventures of the United States during the past 220 years.

It is not that no good has been done. Enormous good has been done, by devoted troops on the ground helping build community centers or restore schools, by campaign workers helping build a democratic ethos, by medical workers carrying out immunizations, by savvy commanders who have taken on and killed the serial murderers who call themselves by such names as "Monotheism and Holy War" or "The Army of Muhammad." The good that has been done, however, has been fatally poisoned by bad policy. The best-case scenario for Iraq is now to limp along as Lebanon did in the 1980s, in a desultory and shadowy set of revolving civil wars. Iraq may eventually emerge, as Lebanon did, from this medium-term instability. It is certainly the case that the sooner US ground troops are out of that country, the sooner its recovery can begin.

Salon, September 5, 2005

NOTES

1. *Editors' Note*: Cole is referring to "A War to Be Proud Of," this volume, chap. 33.
2. See Francis Fukuyama, "Invasion of the Isolationists," *New York Times*, August 31, 2005.
3. See Juan Cole, "Democracy—by George?" *Salon*, March 16, 2005.

◄(52)►

The Genocidal Imagination
of Christopher Hitchens

RICHARD SEYMOUR

The Lighter Side of Mass Murder

Picture a necrotic, sinister, burned-out wasteland—a vast, dull mound of rubble punctuated by moments of bleak emptiness and, occasionally, smoking. Those of you whose imaginations alighted instantly on the Late Christopher Hitchens have only yourselves to blame, for I was referring to Fallujah. The "city of mosques" was sacrificed in November 2004 during an all-American war movie: the MacGuffin, an obscure yet deadly figure known as Abu Musab al-Zarqawi who, predictably, "escaped" with his wily confederates into the deserts.[1]

Before the operation, the city was bombed to "encourage" its evac-
uation, and shortly thereafter sealed off—any male of fighting age (ten
years old and upwards by present occupation standards) was prevented from leaving. During that operation, white phosphorus was
used against civilians since, as one US soldier explained, anything that
walked or breathed was considered an enemy combatant. It is reasonable to suppose that some of the melted bodies discovered had suffered agonizing deaths as the material sizzled their flesh to the bone.
Others may have been more lucky—if they inhaled the substance, it
will have blistered their mouths, throats, and lungs, suffocating them
to death before they had to suffer the pain of flesh melting away both
inside and outside. It is indeed hard to overstate what was pitilessly
inflicted on Fallujah: a hospital deliberately bombed;[2] another occupied;[3] more than half of the houses damaged or destroyed;[4] 150,000
people obliged to flee to live in rough tents on the outskirts of the
city as they were bombed and their water and electricity cut off;[5]
those returning to the devastated city were to be subjected to forced
labor.[6] While the US military only admitted to having killed 1,200
insurgents,[7] initial civilian tolls were as high as 800.[8] Lately, Iraqi
NGOs and medical workers have estimated as many as 6,000 deaths,
mostly civilians.[9] In the face of all these facts, Christopher Hitchens
remarked: "the death toll is not nearly high enough. . . . too many [ji-
hadists] have escaped."[10]

You may have noticed this supererogatory relish in Hitchens's rhetoric before. Here is another sample, regarding cluster bombs:

> If you're actually certain that you're hitting only a concentration
> of enemy troops . . . then it's pretty good because those steel pel-
> lets will go straight through somebody and out the other side and
> through somebody else. And if they're bearing a Koran over their
> heart, it'll go straight through that, too. So they won't be able to
> say, "Ah, I was bearing a Koran over my heart and guess what, the
> missile stopped halfway through." No way, 'cause it'll go straight
> through that as well. They'll be dead, in other words.[11]

There is much more of this merriment. Here he is again: "Cluster
bombs are perhaps not good in themselves, but when they are dropped

on identifiable concentrations of Taliban troops, they do have a heartening effect."[12]

And on those jihadis who appear to occupy a special place in his imagination:

> We can't live on the same planet as them and I'm glad because I don't want to. I don't want to breathe the same air as these psychopaths and murderers and rapists and torturers and child abusers. It's them or me. I'm very happy about this because I know it will be them. It's a duty and a responsibility to defeat them. But it's also a pleasure. I don't regard it as a grim task at all.[13]

Something is decidedly up here. The formal disavowal involved in the unctuous recitation that one is only, ever, targeting the bad guys doesn't quite convince. There is too much joy involved in the murder of designated foes, just as there was too much liveliness in his celebration of bin Laden's "world-historical mistake" in attacking the twin towers.[14] Jacqueline Rose was perhaps the first to notice this. In May 2002, the psychoanalytic theorist found herself in a debate about the "war on terror" sponsored by the *London Review of Books* [LRB]. Christopher Hitchens was sitting next to her, and so she had ample opportunity to catch the flavor of his effluvia as they issued forth.

First, Rose noted the apocalyptic language that had been aroused by 9/11. By way of comparison with Hitchens, she offered to the audience some indistinguishable statements from Blair, Sharon, and bin Laden, all marked by their extraordinary millenarianism and Manichean tone. The "extraordinary proximity" of this language was alarming, as was the fact that such apocalyptic language provides, copiously, the agar on which fundamentalism breeds. Rooted in a fear, it "thrives on the possibility of annihilation." Second, she suggested that what Hitchens referred to as "civilization" (Western society) might well be problematized, given its extraordinary propensity for barbarism, past and present. Thirdly, she noted the decline of democratic possibilities within Western societies as a result of the "war on terror." Fourthly, and most importantly, she ventured that 9/11 had ripped apart the American fantasy of invulnerability and immortality. Freud famously said that it is very difficult to imagine one's own death, but this does not stop us from imagining that of others with extraordinary ruthlessness. Hence, a man might say to his wife, "When one of us dies, I think I shall move to Paris." This is a homicidal impulse, one that operates on the level of unconscious fantasy life. Because our fantasy of immortality has been torn asunder, someone else must die. For reasons of ideological coherence and public relations, those Others must always be the bad guys, but die they must.[15]

"Someone else" happened to be several thousand people in Afghanistan. Note that Hitchens immediately followed Rose's latter point by suggesting that a Human Rights Watch report would be released that would "mantle" the cheeks of those who believed the stories of massive civilian casualties with "a blush of shame." That report, as it happens, did not exonerate the US or say anything specifically exculpatory. What it in fact said was:

> The U.S. air strikes against Taliban military targets entailed an undetermined number of civilian casualties, at least some of which resulted from mistargeting. The air strikes also contributed to the humanitarian crisis, with thousands of Afghans fleeing their homes. Their flight swelled the ranks of hundreds of thousands who were already internally displaced because of drought, war, and conflict-related violence.[16]

There were such varied reports about the civilian death toll in Afghanistan that you could take your pick, of course, but why highlight a report to support your point when it doesn't say what you claim it does? Possibly, Hitchens doesn't expect to have his references checked. It would explain a lot.

However, when "someone else" became Iraq, Hitchens blinked. He was in favor of a conflict with the Hussein regime, although not necessarily an invasion, as he told *Salon* in late 2002.[17] And then, in short order, he was in favor of an invasion. There will be no war, he said, so "bring it on." And while he had angrily declaimed to Tariq Ali at the LRB debate that he did not classify the Iraqi regime as fascist for cheap points, he did in fact tell *Mirror* readers that Saddam was Hitler (and Stalin as well).[18] What have we been waiting for, he wondered? He has weapons and underground chambers—just you wait.[19] When "just you wait" became "never mind," Hitchens found other reasons to continue toward his doom.

Kurds, Imperialism, and Muslim-Baiting

Hitchens had a history of support for "humanitarian intervention" to fall back on, when all else failed. If the war wasn't about WMDs, it was about Saddam's links with bin Laden. And if it wasn't about that, it was about the Kurds. For Hitchens, the Kurds provide a crucial ideological quilting point in relation to Iraq, in which support for imperialism can be suffused with the drama of revolution. About this, a curious myth abounds, which appears to have been generated by Hitchens. The myth is that he was in a jeep with some Kurds in 1991 following the Gulf War, who allegedly evinced some warmth for George Bush Senior, and in the course of that exchange he changed his mind about the war on Iraq. Conflict with Saddam, from then on, was both inevitable and devoutly to be wished. That is hardly thrilling political fiction, but fiction it is. As noted before, he in fact opposed the invasion of Iraq as late as 2002, and he had criticized Clinton for bombing Iraq in 1998's Operation Desert Fox.[20] As Dennis Perrin, a friend of Hitchens, writes:

> He may have been in a Kurdish jeep, but the [story about his conversion therein] is a complete lie, and Hitchens knows this. I spent time with him in the period he mentions, and he never stopped criticizing Bush's "mad contest" with Saddam, much less opined that "co-existence" with Saddam was "no longer possible." I have a tape of him debating Ken Adelman on C-SPAN in 1993 where he's still critical of the Gulf War, and again no mention of wanting to overthrow Saddam. As late as 2002, when I asked him directly if he did indeed favor a US invasion, he waffled and said that W. would have to convince him on "about a zillion fronts" before he could sign on.[21]

It is tempting to conclude that the main function of the Kurds for Hitchens is to cover his guilt, and shame, and embarrassment about allowing himself to be made a conduit for lies in the service of mass murder—but it is a considerable stretch to believe that Hitchens is capable of guilt, shame, or embarrassment these days. However, if Hitchens did not come to support an invasion of Iraq until very late in 2002, he did begin to express a fondness for interventionism back in 1993.[22] He had supported Thatcher over the Falklands war, by his own account as a means of dislodging the Argentinian junta; and he became more and more in favor of intervention in the former Yugoslavia and also supported the restoration of Aristide in Haiti, something he supposes that the Clinton administration was forced into and subverted over. Hitchens also claims to have demanded that Britain intervene in Cyprus to defend it from an attempted partition by Greek and Turkish incursions. The argument bears a certain consistency—if imperialist governments are not moral agents, it is not too much to hope that they might be. We should "demand that the government acts according to its proclaimed principles."[23]

In Kosovo, he was less consistent than perhaps he would like to admit. While he was later to deploy the now familiar line that "if the counsel of the peaceniks had been followed" something dreadful would have happened, he was initially less sanguine about the American strikes. On ethnic cleansing by Serb forces, he said: "The cleansing interval . . . was both provoked and provided by the threat of air attacks on other parts of Yugoslavia." About the responsibility of the warmongers for the fate of Kosovars, he added:

> The "line of the day" among administration spokesmen, confronted by the masses of destitute and terrified refugees and solid reports of the mass execution of civilians, was to say that "we expected this to happen." . . . If they want to avoid being indicted for war crimes themselves, these "spokesmen" had better promise us they were lying when they said that.[24]

It was, he feared, another imperial carve-up. Later, he proceeded as if he had never said any of this, or at least never really thought it, even though it happens to be true: the NATO attack drastically worsened the situation of Kosovars. Needlessly so, since Western leaders had needlessly thwarted a deal that would have saved Kosovars from death and expulsion,[25] not to mention preventing quite a few Serbs from being pounded into pink mist. That much is empirically established, and yet it is precisely at this point that Hitchens begins to be immune to inconvenient facts. Prime Minister Blair was acting out of principle, he later supposed, while Clinton was a war criminal for having bombed Al-Shifa and sites in Afghanistan (something that Blair supported).[26]

Shortly thereafter, the oleaginous Clinton was replaced by the astonishingly inept Bush after a campaign in which the Democrat candidate could hardly find a word to say for himself, his sole simulation of passion and commitment being a bestial tongue exchange with his censorious wife in front of the television cameras. With Bush and his team of appointees from the Nixon and Reagan years in charge, Clinton would not be at the helm when the 9/11 bombers struck. Initially, those horrors inspired an uneasy response from Hitchens. He was at first critical of President Bush's instant war cry, and even dared in the worst climate to offer a bit of criticism of US foreign policy,[27] but it was not long before the torrent of bile was unleashed. If the Left couldn't drive Hitchens further to drink, it could at least set the fluid rushing in the opposite direction. They were guilty of "self hatred" and "fascist sympathies."[28] Rebuking those who thought that the root causes of the attacks included demonstrably baleful aspects of US foreign policy, Hitchens said:

> The grievance and animosity predate even the Balfour Declaration, let alone the occupation of the West Bank. They predate the creation of Iraq as a state. The gates of Vienna would have had to fall to the Ottoman jihad before any balm could begin to be applied to these psychic wounds.[29]

Aside from being extraordinary ahistorical babble, this inaugurated Hitchens's period as what Alex Cockburn calls "the hammer of Islam."[30] Let us pause only briefly to consider why. Only an intellectual midget or a racializing essentialist would suppose that modern political Islam has anything to do with traditional Islamic societies under the Caliphate. Hassan al-Banna may well have bemoaned the fall of the Ottoman Empire, but this was neither uncommon even in Egypt which had temporarily freed itself from that orbit before being occupied by Britain, nor did it signify ideological continuity with the traditionalist ulama. Nor was the Ottoman Empire governed particularly stringently according to theological propositions. Rather, military power was pre-eminent, as it was with coeval empires and polities, while the theorizing of Islamic scholars was largely its circumstantial by-product. You may as well compare Ariel Sharon with Moses as compare Al Qaeda with the armies of the sultanates and the caliphate. Yet, this is the kind of mindless distillation that arises when "understanding" and analysis are eschewed. Indeed, Hitchens showed exactly what he thought about Muslims, when, in reaction to the French uprising, he told right-wing radio host Laura Ingraham that "if you think that the intifada in France is about housing, go and try covering the story wearing a yarmulke."[31] He is happy for others to do his talking from time to time, as when he approvingly cited Abdulrahman al-Rashed claiming that "all the World Terrorists are Muslims."[32] This article went on to aver that "our terrorist sons are an end-product of our corrupted culture." Daniel Pipes was as delighted as Hitchens was, although those Muslims who have never committed a terrorist act and would never contemplate doing so would have had good grounds for feeling insulted. On the matter of empirical evidence, evoking Islam as an explanation for modern terrorism—particularly suicide bombing—must tickle the FARC or LTTE, but academic studies tend to suggest that Islam is far less important than geopolitical considerations.[33] That's the sort of fact that it pays to ignore if you don't want to be slandered by Hitchens as an apologist.

Coterminous with Hitchens's shift on imperialism was a definite move to the Right. He ceased, for instance, to call himself a socialist. He began to reminisce about his admiration for Margaret Thatcher, and expatiate on the virtues of capitalism. Capitalism was more revolutionary than its opponents, he suggested. In fact, Hitchens went so far as to say that he regretted not having voted for Margaret Thatcher in 1979 and that he had actually wanted her to win. Unemployment, union-bashing, homophobia, and nationalism are of little consequence in this equation, since the "radical, revolutionary forces" were led by the Right, who broke the "political consensus." This is a fairly consistent theme for Hitchens, inasmuch as he needs to believe that whatever his position is on a given topic on a given day, it is contrary to whatever the consensus is. Hence, opposing the Iraq war became "respectable," indeed "establishment"—to support this ridiculous claim, Hitchens hallucinated that Ariel Sharon may be against the war.[34] In *Letters to a Young Contrarian*, Hitchens urges his young reader to live "at a slight angle to society," which means to be idiosyncratic rather than tendentious. This contrarianism is a fetish, and it is one that encases in amber the burning polemical zeal of a former radical, a *soixante-huitard*. In the wake of a detumescent revolutionary fervor, and with the associated political vision largely gone, we are left with an opportunistic polemicizing in which no matter how much one's opinion alters, it remains permanently in opposition, permanently contrarian. And this delivers the hammering Hitchensian irony in which the most consummately bourgeois opinion acquires the mould and fashion of resistance.[35]

Tortuous Rhetoric

Indeed, something of that can be detected in the anfractuous rhetorical strategies Hitchens has deployed. On WMDs, he first channeled Cassandra and then rejoined the chorus and suggested that it wasn't about WMDs in the first place (only to bleat more about it when some new wafer-thin "evidence" emerged).[36] The torsions of posture and tone are, at times, astonishing. Hitchens terrified *Mirror* readers by advising them of all the nasty things that Saddam was getting up to—the mukhabarat were busying themselves destabilizing other countries and WMDs were being readied. Little of what Hitchens said in the run up to war was accurate, and what was accurate was rarely worth saying since it was widely acknowledged. Within a couple of years, he was telling the intellectual amoebas of the *Weekly Standard* that Bush and Blair had ruined a good case for war by trying to frighten people instead of enlightening them.[37] Enlightenment in Hitchens's hands, however, radiates disaster triumphant. Here is a man who dared to introduce a set of essays written during the war with a monograph entitled "Twenty-Twenty Foresight."[38] In what did this foresight consist? Well, for example, following a series of surgical strikes, "a massive landing will bring food, medicine and laptop computers to a surging crowd of thankful and relieved Iraqis and Kurds."[39]

Laptops. He actually said *laptops.* Similarly: "Will an Iraq war make our Al Qaeda problem worse? Not likely."[40] Further, "War requires that two countries pit their armies against one another for indefinite combat. I'm willing to bet you now that there will be no such engagement in Iraq."[41] There would be no war, so "bring it on." They brought it on alright. And I still wonder if the man who spent so much time slandering opponents as fascist sympathizers, who accused Naomi Klein of "swooning" for "theocratic fascists,"[42] and who said "Ha ha ha to the pacifists" really ever thought he would find himself begging others to "stop the taunting."[43]

To disarm critics of Bush's pre-war lies, particularly his claim to have been doing all possible to avoid a war when in fact he was readying one from very early on, Hitchens said that after all this was merely a continuation of the Iraqi Liberation Act, passed unanimously by the Senate in 1998, and of a post-9/11 policy of changing the balance of power in the region.[44] As it happens, the Iraq Liberation Act specifically precludes invasion,[45] and, although I happen to know Hitchens was made aware of and acknowledged this, he nevertheless repeated the claim during his "debate" with George Galloway in New York.[46] In a later article, he suggested that the Act had not mentioned invasion, whereas in fact it had mentioned it—to specifically preclude its use.[47]

Hitchens specializes in retailing myths about Zarqawi these days, too. I think his first mention of Zarqawi was in February 2003, when Colin Powell brought him up. He averred that the "presence of Al Qaeda under the Iraqi umbrella is suggested chiefly by Abu Mussab al-Zarqawi, a senior bin-Laden aide and an enthusiast for chemical and biological tactics," while "most US intelligence officials now agree that it is unlikely to be a coincidence that the pro–Al Qaeda gang, Ansar al-Islam, is fighting to destroy the independent Kurdish leadership in the northern part of Iraq that has been freed from Saddam Hussein's control."[48] The interesting thing about this is that Hitchens didn't even get it right in *hindsight.* He continues to insist on the Baghdad–bin Laden connection (via Baghdad and northern Iraq)[49] despite ample refutation, of which we might mention the fact that Zarqawi's supposed presence in Baghdad was speculation, an "inferential leap" in the first place; that both British and German intelligence cast doubt on the story at the time;[50] that even George Tenet, when testifying to a Senate Committee that Zarqawi had been in Baghdad, nevertheless said that he was neither under the control of Al Qaeda nor Saddam Hussein; that Zarqawi was an opponent of Al Qaeda at this time;[51] that Ansar al-Islam leader Mullah Krekar denied having ever met Zarqawi and that his group was opposed to Hussein and did not associate with Al Qaeda;[52] that, according to the International Crisis Group, the potency of Ansar al-Islam was drastically inflated by the PUK for its own reasons.[53] There is considerable doubt about whether Zarqawi is alive, has two functioning legs, and is really in Iraq.[54] Whether Zarqawi is a myth or a monster, the only story that obtains here is that there is no story. Saddam and Zarqawi never did have their Baghdad nuptials, however convenient the tale is for pro-war storytelling.[55]

On WMDs, Hitchens keeps trying. Of late, he has been amplifying claims made in the *New York Times* that Saddam's key weapons sites had been systematically "looted"—probably, Hitchens darkly intimates, by Saddam's goons. The curious thing to note about these claims is that Hitchens has either lost the capacity for skepticism or just doesn't care to apply it in this case. Saddam's best weapons plants are supposed to have been raided and stripped in a systematic fashion, perhaps by his cronies, unchecked by US soldiers. If the US had thought its evidence on WMDs was up to *anything*, it would have guarded those plants just as zealously as it guarded the Ministry of Oil.[56] These weapons were the primary justification for the war, and one would expect that the US military would be eager to ensure that whatever was there was recorded and displayed—if they really believed their intelligence to have been up to anything. Further, the story's backbone is composed of claims made by Dr. Sami al-Araji, presently operating as a minister under the US occupation. Not only are the claims not remotely credible, they come from a source with an obvious and declared interest in the matter.

Aside from WMDs, Hitchens's most cherished blind spot is that he cannot and will not stand for the notion that there is a resistance movement in Iraq which is domestic, grassroots, and increasingly popular among Iraqis. He would not be alone in this, since the very suggestion is generally obscured by moralizing cant. Of late, he tried saying, *inter* an awful lot of *alia*, that:

Where it is not augmented by depraved bin Ladenist imports, the leadership and structure of the Iraqi "insurgency" is formed from the elements of an already fallen regime, extensively discredited and detested in its own country and universally condemned.[57]

This happens to be entirely and exclusively nonsensical. The Iraqi resistance is notable for many things, and one of them is that there is not a leadership or indeed much of a structure to speak of. Intelligence reports suggest a movement that is cellular, decentralized, and disarticulated.[58] Moreover, it is composed not of Baathists and Zarqawi loyalists, who are "lesser elements," but rather of "newly radicalized Sunni Iraqis, nationalists offended by the occupying force, and others disenchanted by the economic turmoil and destruction caused by the fighting." For this and other reasons, the notion of a movement directed from above by an axis of bin Ladenists and Baathists simply isn't persuasive.[59]

Nor is it true to say, as Hitchens does, that the resistance is primarily composed of "gangsters" who "pump out toxic anti-Semitism, slaughter Nepalese and other Asian guest-workers on video and gloat over the death of Hindus, burn out and blow up the Iraqi Christian minority, kidnap any Westerner who catches their eye, and regularly inflict massacres and bombings on Shiite mosques, funerals, and assemblies."[60] Statistics from the most reputable sources suggest that, although there is certainly an element that behaves in an abominable fashion, the bulk of resistance attacks are overwhelmingly directed against US troops, not civilians.[61] According to figures from the Center for Strategic and International Studies, an independent Washington think-tank, attacks on US military forces account for 75% of attacks, while civilian targets comprise a mere 4.1% of attacks. The Department of Defense figures show a consistently similar trend. A lot of the demonization of the resistance is also related to unconscious fantasy life, with Iraq perhaps reduced in many minds to an imaginary menagerie, a hothouse full of savage, exotic animals leaking blood indiscriminately. If the resistance are like *that*, of course, so much the easier to enjoy a joke about mass murder, so much the easier to dream of their erasure from the face of the earth. But Iraqis, who have to live with the occupation, have a more positive attitude toward the resistance than they do toward the interlopers who have so far imprisoned, killed, tortured, beaten, and raped them, generally appropriating every vile method of Baathist dictatorship and making it their own. How many Iraqis support resistance attacks? According to a secret Ministry of Defense poll, 45% of them—that includes Kurds. How many Iraqis support the occupation? Close to zero, with 82% strongly opposed to it.[62] How many Iraqis reported an improved opinion of Moqtada al-Sadr after he fought the Americans in Najaf? 81 percent.[63] What we have in Iraq, in other words, is a grassroots guerrilla movement, one which has arisen because of the brutality of the occupation (rather than the other way round), and which is growing in number and support.

Yet if Hitchens cannot face easily accessible facts about the resistance to the occupation, he still insists on the stupid disavowal of what the occupation has done to Iraq. He advertises that he pays no attention to the casualty figures (is oblivious to the evidence in other words), yet becomes hysterical the second anyone mentions the *Lancet* report. When it was raised in New York, he described it as "politicized hack-work," a "crazed fabrication," whose conclusions had been "conclusively and absolutely shown to be false."[64] To justify this claim, he referred to a notoriously ill-informed piece by Fred Kaplan, that rested on a ridiculous misunderstanding about confidence intervals.[65] The least one can say is that the *Lancet* report is not hack work. It is an extensively peer-reviewed epidemiological study. Its method of cluster sampling and extrapolation have been used in other parts of the world, for instance in the Congo, and recently in Sudan.[66] Those figures were lauded as "reliable estimates"—by Christopher Hitchens.[67] It is obvious to me, as it should be to any passing insect, that this is as transparent an instance of self-deceit on Hitchens's part as one is ever likely to encounter. He doesn't care about the casualty numbers, but he would like *you* to understand that they aren't so very high, and can't be, and anyone who says otherwise is a fraud.

In Place of a Conclusion . . .

Norman Finkelstein was probably guilty of understatement when he wrote that Hitchens, while redoubtable as a left-wing polemicist, only invited doubt as a right-wing one. It's worth quoting some of what Finkelstein wrote:

> To prove that, after supporting dictatorial regimes in the Middle East for 70 years, the US has abruptly reversed itself and now wants to bring democracy there, he cites "conversations I have had on this subject in Washington." To demonstrate the "glaringly apparent" fact that Saddam "infiltrated, or suborned, or both" the UN inspection teams in Iraq, he adduces the "incontrovertible case" of an inspector offered a bribe by an Iraqi official: "the man in question refused the money, but perhaps not everybody did. . . ."
>
> Hitchens maintains that that "there is a close . . . fit between the democratically minded and the pro-American" in the Middle East—like "President for Life" Hosni Mubarak, King Abdullah of Jordan . . . ; that Washington finally grasped that "there *were* 'root causes' behind the murder-attacks" (emphasis in original)—but didn't Hitchens ridicule any allusion to "root causes" as totalitarian apologetics?; that "racism" is "anti-American as nearly as possible by definition"; that "evil" can be defined as "the surplus value of the psychopath"—is there a Bartlett's for worst quotations?; that the US's rejoining of UNESCO during the Iraq debate proved its commitment to the UN; that "empirical proofs have been unearthed" showing that Iraq didn't comply with UN resolutions to disarm; that since the UN solicits US support for multilateral missions, it's "idle chatter" to accuse the US of acting unilaterally in Iraq; that the likely killing of innocent civilians in "hospitals, schools, mosques and private homes" shouldn't deter the US from attacking Iraq because it is proof of Saddam's iniquity that he put civilians in harm's way; that those questioning billions of dollars in postwar contracts going to Bush administration cronies must prefer them going to "some windmill-power concern run by Naomi Klein"—is this dry or desiccated wit?[68]

Hitchens expended a great deal of energy responding to that particular essay precisely because it was so cutting (and so thoroughly deserved). I cite these passages because in them Hitchens's present absurdity is expertly encapsulated and because Hitchens, in his punch-drunk yet extensive reply, could not dream up a word to say about them.[69]

Yet it is not just that Hitchens has slyly detached himself from those aspects of reality that he cannot bring himself to accept. It is not merely that he has moved so far to the right that he has internalized the virtues of aggressive American militarism and rapacious American capitalism. Or that he has become a calumniator, a ridiculous liar, and a back-stabber. It is not even the unpleasant confluence of the way in which his literary flair has declined in proportion to his political nous. On the strength of the evidence, his left-wing convictions weren't all that invulnerable from the start, while he has never been terribly shy of supporting gunboat diplomacy. This is not a noble mind overthrown, although there may have been some kind of regime change post-9/11. What is most alarming is that Hitchens has a new audience: he purveys his deranged fantasies about killing more and more evil-doers for the mass ranks of Republican twenty-somethings. Malodorous macho assholes who nevertheless like to think that their myopic nationalism and sociopathy has something to do with liberation and freedom—or just, indeed, *something*. This is his audience today—a collection of barely post-pubescent neophytic imperialists, and bumpkin billionaires who read the *Weekly Standard*. The sort of degraded, hallucinatory nonsense that this poetaster of genocide exudes these days ought not to be exposed to daylight, never mind offered up as intellectual sustenance for a class of powerful men. Hitchens can't change, of course, and he will just have to live with the thought of what a hideous figure he has become. Or, more probably, die with it, perhaps suffocating on the impacted faecal matter that is perpetually welling up inside him. Let's just say that when that tumescent cadaver finally explodes, the Left should be grateful to think of what new friends he will surprise.

Monthly Review, November 26, 2005

NOTES

1. News reports later announced that locals were in fact the core of the Fallujah insurgency: Associated Press, "Two Locals Were Core of Fallujah Insurgency," November 24, 2004. There is no clear evidence that Zarqawi was ever in Fallujah: BBC, "Inside Besieged Fallujah," October 18, 2004. Major General Richard Natonski never expected Zarqawi to be there, as he explained: "We're not after Zarqawi. We're after insurgents in general" (Associated Press, "General Praises Assault's Speed," November 14, 2004).

2. BBC, "US Strikes Raze Fallujah Hospital," November 6, 2004.

3. See Richard A. Oppel Jr., "Early Target of Offensive Is a Hospital," *New York Times*, November 8, 2004.

4. Ann Scott Tyson, "Increased Security in Fallujah Slows Efforts to Rebuild," *Washington Post*, April 19, 2005.

5. Jim McDermott and Richard Rapport, "Investigate Alleged Violations of Law in Fallujah Attack," *Seattle Post-Intelligencer*, January 11, 2005.

6. Anne Barnard, "Returning Fallujans Will Face Clampdown," *Boston Globe*, December 5, 2004.

7. Sgt. 1st Class Doug Sample, "Fallujah Secure, But Not Yet Safe, Marine Commander Says," American Forces Press Service, November 18, 2004.

8. Early estimates from the Red Cross were that 800 civilians had been killed: Dahr Jamail, "800 Civilians Feared Dead in Fallujah," Inter Press Service, November 16, 2004.

9. Cited in Mike Marqusee, "A Name That Lives in Infamy," *Guardian*, November 10, 2005.

10. Mike Ludders, "Columnist Hitchens Lectures on Political Dissent," *Kenyon Collegian*, November 18, 2004.

11. Cited in Adam Shatz, "The Left and 9/11," *Nation*, September 23, 2002.

12. Cited in Edward Herman, "Christopher Hitchens and the Uses of Demagoguery," *Z Net*, September 22, 2002.

13. "An Interview with Christopher Hitchens," *WashingtonPrism.org*, June 16, 2005.

14. Hitchens, "A War to Be Proud Of," this volume, chap. 33, 154.

15. "The War on Terror: Is There an Alternative?" *London Review of Books* debate, Logan Hall, Institute of Education, London, May 15, 2002.

16. "Human Rights Watch World Report, 2002: Afghanistan."

17. See Edward W. Lempinen, "How the Left Became Irrelevant," *Salon*, October 29, 2002.

18. Brian Reade, "Two Out-of-Control Despots," *Mirror*, March 21, 2003.

19. Hitchens, "Chew on This," *Stranger*, January 16–22, 2003.

20. Hitchens, *No One Left to Lie To* (London: Verso, 1999).

21. Dennis Perrin, "Punchy," Red State Son, June 2, 2005.

22. Hitchens, "Never Trust Imperialists: Especially When They Turn Pacifist," *Boston Review* (December 1993/January 1994).

23. Sasha Abramsky, "Christopher Hitchens," interview in *Progressive*, February 1, 1997.

24. Hitchens, "Bloody Blundering: Clinton's Cluelessness Is Selling Out Kosovo," *Salon*, April 5, 1999.

25. John Pilger, "What Really Happened at Rambouillet? And What Else Is Being Kept under Wraps by Our Selective Media," May 31, 1999. John Pilger was notoriously attacked by a *Guardian* journalist named Ian Black for saying that the Rambouillet text included the demand that Serbia a) become a free market economy and b) that the entire territory of the FRY become subject to NATO occupation (see Ian Black, "Bad News," *Guardian*, May 19, 1999). Pilger was correct.

26. BBC, "Hitchens: Clinton Could Sell Out Blair," June 3, 1999; Hitchens, "Close, but No Cigar," *Nation*, October 5, 1998.

27. Hitchens, "So Is This War?" *Guardian*, September 13, 2001.

28. Hitchens, "The Fascist Sympathies of the Soft Left," *Spectator*, September 29, 2001.

29. Hitchens, "Of Sin, the Left, and Islamic Fascism," this volume, 47.

30. Alexander Cockburn, "Hitchens Backs Down," *Counter Punch*, August 24, 2005.

31. It was so difficult to believe that this was an accurate quotation that I had to contact Hitchens himself and ask if it was correct. He confirmed that it was, which I then duly recorded: see "Christopher Hitchens's Bad Language," Lenin's Tomb, November 10, 2005.

32. Hitchens, "Murder by Any Other Name," this volume, 79.

33. See Diego Gambetta (ed.), *Making Sense of Suicide Missions* (Oxford: Oxford University Press, 2005); Jacqueline Rose, "Deadly Embrace," *London Review of Books*, November 4, 2005; and Robert Pape, *Dying to Win: The Strategic Logic of Suicide Terrorism* (New York: Random House, 2005).

34. Hitchens, "Hawks in the Dovecote," *Observer*, August 25, 2002.

35. See Rhys Southan, "Free Radical," *Reason Online* (November 2001); reprinted in this volume as "An Interview with Christopher Hitchens, Part I: Radicalism, Liberty, and the Post-Socialist World," chap. 35.

36. Hitchens, "This Was Not Looting," *Slate*, March 15, 2005.

37. Hitchens, "A War to Be Proud Of."

38. Hitchens, *A Long Short War: The Postponed Liberation of Iraq* (New York: Plume, 2003).

39. Hitchens, "What Happens Next in Iraq," *Mirror*, February 26, 2003.

40. Hitchens, *A Long Short War*, 60–62.

41. A Debate on Iraq between Christopher Hitchens and Mark Danner, Zellerbach Hall, University of California at Berkeley, January 28, 2003.

42. Hitchens, "Murder by Any Other Name," this volume, 79.

43. Hitchens, "Nowhere to Go," *Slate*, November 22, 2005.

44. Hitchens, "Conspiracy Theories," *Slate*, June 21, 2005.

45. See Section 8 of the Act.

46. Debate at Baruch College, New York, hosted by Amy Goodman, September 14, 2005.

47. Hitchens, "Believe It or Not," *Slate*, November 14, 2005.

48. Hitchens, "Powell Is Showing His Hand," *Mirror*, February 5, 2003.

49. Hitchens, "In Front of Your Nose," *Slate*, October 25, 2005.

50. Don Van Natta Jr., "Portrait of a Terror Suspect: Is He the Al Qaeda Link to Iraq?" *International Herald Tribune*, February 10, 2003.

51. Cam Simpson and Stevenson Swanson, "Prisoner Casts Doubt on Iraq Tie to Al Qaeda," *Chicago Tribune*, February 11, 2003.

52. "Mullah Krekar Interview," Insight TV.

53. International Crisis Group, "Radical Islam in Iraqi Kurdistan: The Mouse That Roared?" Middle East Briefing, No. 4, February 7, 2003. Indeed, much of the "evidence" linking Ansar al-Islam to Al Qaeda appears to come from PUK sources, or their prisoners: Catherine Taylor, "Taliban-Style Group Grows in Iraq," *Christian Science Monitor*, March 15, 2002.

54. *Editors' Note*: Zarqawi was killed in Iraq on June 7, 2006.

55. For more on the Al Qaeda–Zarqawi disputes, see Jason Burke, *Al Qaeda: The True Story of Radical Islam* (London: I. B. Tauris, 2004). For more on the Zarqawi myth, see Loretta Napoleoni, *Insurgent Iraq: Al-Zarqawi and the New Generation* (New York: Seven Stories Press, 2005). Suffice to note that like every other bogey man of the US imperialist imaginary, Zarqawi is Hitler: "Rumsfeld: Zarqawi Like Hitler," CBS, May 26, 2005. This, according to Donald Rumsfeld, who, unlike Zarqawi, did meet Saddam and did exchange WMDs in the process.

56. Charles Clover, "Confusion over Who Controls Iraq's Oil Ministry," *Financial Times*, April 20, 2003.

57. Hitchens, "Beating a Dead Parrot," *Slate*, January 31, 2005.

58. Walter Pincus, "CIA Studies Provide Glimpse of Insurgents in Iraq," *Washington Post*, February 6, 2005.

59. See Michael Schwartz's excellent analysis here: "Schwartz on Why the Military Is Failing in Iraq," *TomDispatch*, March 5, 2005.

60. Hitchens, "History and Mystery," this volume, 137.

61. See M. Junaid Alam, "Does the Resistance Target Civilians? According to US Intel, Not Really," *LeftHook*, April 16, 2005.

62. Sean Rayment, "Secret MoD Poll: Iraqis Support Attacks on British Troops," *Telegraph*, October 23, 2005.

63. "Iraqis' Opinions on US 'Grim,'" *Washington Times*, June 17, 2004.

64. Debate at Baruch College.

65. Fred Kaplan, "100,000 Dead—or 8,000," *Slate*, October 29, 2004. The reply: "Reply from Author of *Lancet* Report," Lenin's Tomb, October 31, 2004. Not only had Kaplan misunderstood confidence intervals (a poisson-curve

distribution of values is not a dart-board) but he had failed to understand that there was information not contained in the confidence interval, vital information at that, which suggested that the median figure was conservative. Further, he relied upon some unusually high pre-war infant mortality figures to suggest that the report had underestimated these, thus providing an inaccurate figure for excess deaths: Jack Kelly, "Estimates of Deaths in First War Still in Dispute," *Pittsburgh Post-Gazette*, February 16, 2003. What is more, the UNDP Iraq Living Conditions Survey figures for pre-war infant mortality are much closer to those provided by the *Lancet* authors than those provided by Beth Daponte. That is not the only way in which the ILCS corroborates the *Lancet* report: "Bringing Out the Dead," Lenin's Tomb, September 27, 2005.

66. E. Depoortere, F. Checchi, F. Broillet, S. Gerstl, A. Minetti, O. Gayraud, V. Briet, J. Pahl, I. Defourny, M. Tatay, and V. Brown, "Violence and Mortality in West Darfur, Sudan (2003–04): Epidemiological Evidence from Four Surveys," *Lancet*, October 1, 2004.

67. Hitchens, "Realism in Darfur," *Slate*, November 7, 2005.

68. Norman Finkelstein, "Hitchens as Model Apostate," this volume, 242.

69. Christopher Hitchens, "A Few Words of Fraternal Admonition to 'Norm' Finkelstein," Christopher Hitchens Web, 2004; reprinted in this volume, chap. 46.

Afterword

CHRISTOPHER HITCHENS

"Have you seen that book of interviews with Raymond Williams by the *New Left Review*," inquired James Fenton one spring morning in 1979, when *Politics and Letters* had first fallen stillborn from the press. I responded that I had managed thus far to avoid it. "Well, take a look. They talk to him as if he was *a category*."

The decades proceed; I deliver the Raymond Williams memorial lecture in such a way as to give a normally unsentimental professor like Stefan Collini the sense that I have abused some kind of hospitality;[1] history is not kind to those at the *New Left Review* who had predicted to Williams (in 1979!) that "*Nineteen Eighty Four* will be a curio in 1984"; the years after the implosion of the Soviet Union in 1989 are marked by the recrudescence of danger from different forms of absolutism in Serbia, Iraq, Afghanistan, Iran, Darfur, and North Korea, and, once again, a huge number of "intellectuals" will not agree that the totalitarian principle, whether secular or religious, is the main enemy. There is, apparently, always some reason why this is either not true or is a distraction from some more pressing business or is perhaps a mere excuse for "empire."

It is now almost five years since I joined battle with some of those who think this, or who think this way, and did I do so in the expectation of becoming a "category" myself? I can sincerely disavow having had any such ambition. Byron is supposed to have woken one morning to find himself famous: I woke one morning on 11 September 2001 to find that further discussion of my new book on Henry Kissinger was likely to be indefinitely postponed, but also to find that the global situation had taken itself into a new shape. Whether I welcomed the change of subject is as irrelevant as anything could be. The point was not so much to interpret it as to recognize the fact that it *had* changed. (One of the New Left's outstanding members, Mike Davis, was shortly to write that it was ironic that I, the supposed master of irony, could see nothing ironic in the wreckage of the World Trade Center. Well, no I couldn't and no I still cannot, and I maintain that any irony involved is strictly at the expense of Comrade Davis.) Accused by so many people of being solely responsible for an unconditional defense of democracy, however *bourgeois*, against tyranny however messianic, the only Byronic feeling I have is the one the poet expressed on another occasion: that such a lyre should "degenerate into hands like mine."

Fortunately, the excessive concentration on my own writing (which I further and perhaps "ironically" indulge by agreeing to write a response to the foregoing) is of third-order importance. The defense of liberal values has not at all been left in my feeble hands. Tens of thousands of young soldiers—all of them volunteers—have stood in baking sun to guard the places where voters have first registered and then cast their ballots. I have been privileged to see some of this, and also some of the work done by civilian volunteers in opening clinics and schools, exhuming mass graves, and preparing the trials of those who committed crimes against humanity. To have played even the smallest part in this is satisfaction enough for me.

A minor corollary of this observation would be the following. If everything that my critics have to say about me is true, it makes absolutely no difference. These defeats for the common enemy, and exemplary actions by volunteers, would have occurred whatever I said or wrote or argued. Thus I take the hysterical and *ad hominem* assaults upon me (of which the editors have selected only the mildest examples) as being a citation of the impotence of their authors. And I would be in a poor position to complain in any case, since I was the one who issued the first barrage of insults, and did not always resist the chance to be *ad hominem* myself. Yes I did say "hah, hah, hah to the pacifists" when the Taliban ran away, and should have been much harsher. Yes I did refer to the so-called Dixie Chicks as "fat sluts" (having not the least idea of what any of them looked like). In both instances I was trying to don borrowed and superior plumes: Michael Kinsley had done very well in 1987 with a "hah, hah, hah" headline about the Iran-contra arms-for-hostages racket, and a British dirty-humor mag called *Viz* has a highly amusing cartoon about "Fat Slags," but in one case the allusion was too obscure and in the other I was out of temper and exhausted and my memory cast up a "slut" line from

Flashman instead. Thus I have to concede that Scott Lucas is probably right when he talks about "the pressure of newspapers clamoring for answers." This—along with radio and TV chat-shows and campus debates—is the permanent temptation for a *deformation professionel*, of instant or improvised answers (and not just on this subject). I hereby swear to try and reform. However, I am sure that my enemies do not live simply for the moments when I speak clumsily. And in one case, namely my growing conviction at a certain point that Osama bin Laden might be dead (or at least badly disabled: a thought that has not entirely left me), I was not reasoning under any pressure but my own. The prediction that Saddam Hussein's regime would buckle swiftly and easily once hostilities began, which is often quoted against me in a "Mission Accomplished" sort of way, was at least better than the much more common view that a move against his regime would trigger everything from a mass exodus of refugees to the unleashing of the WMDs that he was otherwise supposed not to possess.

I suppose that, before I move on, I ought to say a few words about the other shortcomings of prescience. Contrary to what the editors say here, I did not in fact believe that Saddam Hussein had an arsenal of WMD. I did believe that he was concealing some of what he had earlier unarguably amassed, and I did believe (and still do) that he should be treated as one who might well be concealing more. I further believed (and still do believe) that he intended to remain a latent WMD power until such time as the UN "sanctions" system—which was much more corrupt than anyone had even known how to allege—had eroded. The one direct allegation that I did make in print—of the concealment of weapons-lab equipment under a mosque in Baghdad—came to me on good evidence and was later confirmed, with photographs, by the David Kay report. (I had thought that such a juxtaposition of mosque and weapons, once established, would sway the opinion of some people. I can certainly say that I was mistaken about *that*.)

On a matter that has occasioned immense controversy—the assertion that Saddam Hussein sought uranium from Niger—I think I can claim to have shown that the Bush administration's original claim was well-founded. An immense quantity of half-baked propaganda to the contrary, it remains the case that in February 1999, just after the UN inspectors had been barred from Iraq, Saddam Hussein sent his senior envoy for nuclear matters, Ambassador Wissam al-Zahawie, to Niger. No other plausible reason for this trip has ever been adduced, and the claim by Zahawie himself (that having attended several IAEA and NPT meetings as the Iraqi envoy, he was unaware that Niger exported uranium "yellow cake") can safely be discounted. Ambassador Joseph Wilson failed to mention the Zahawie visit—since reconfirmed by two independent inquiries into British intelligence—and has also wasted an enormous amount of time on his now-disproven assertion that members of the Bush administration approached Robert Novak (a strong opponent of the war and admirer of Wilson's) in order to "expose" his wife Valerie Plame. To clarify this much-distorted episode, it was only necessary to perform a few lowly feats of elementary inquisitive journalism—a task from which the majority of reporters in the case have simply excused themselves. (*Time* magazine, for example, reprinted Zahawie's absurd claim, under the byline of Hassan Fattah—now of the *New York Times*—without even challenging it.) We now know that A. Q. Khan, whose nuclear black market was not exposed until after the capitulation of Colonel Gaddafi's Libya (itself not unconnected to the fall of Saddam Hussein), was also visiting Niger at precisely the same time.

As to the charge that the Bush and Blair governments exaggerated or invented the ties between the Baath Party and transnational Islamic terrorist organizations, a large tranche of evidence now exists to suggest that the "connection" was if anything understated. A whole series of filiations between Baghdad and bin Ladenist groups as far away as the Philippines has been unearthed since the translation of captured Iraqi documents began. The obstinate reluctance of the CIA to declassify more of these may seem bewildering to some people, but the hesitation becomes less baffling when one remembers that the CIA did not just deny the existence of such an alliance in practice. It denied that it was possible *in theory*, maintaining that it was *ipso facto* unthinkable for a "secular" regime like that of Saddam Hussein to collude with a theocratic gang. Doubts about the "secular" nature of Saddam's increasingly Islamized regime to one side, it has been proved repeatedly since—by the policy and actions of the Syrian Baath party in particular—that collaboration with Iran and Hezbollah and Hamas is the rule in this case rather than the exception. There may be those who also believe that the late Abu Musab al-Zarqawi, who was able to hit important targets in Iraq with explosives of military grade, was no more than an extremely talented Jordanian freelance operator who was able to lay hands on Baathist arsenals within weeks of arriving in the country. Those who wish to believe this are free to do so. It seems to me quite obvious that collaboration between "Al Qaeda in Mesopotamia" (as Zarqawi conveniently titled his group, having sought permission from bin Laden and Zawahiri to do so) and the former regime was latent if not blatant. One of Zarqawi's deputies, Hamad Jumaa Faris Juri al-Saeidi, who was responsible for the destruction of the Golden Dome at Samarra, was a former Baathist intelligence officer. The atrocity he committed against a holy site, as part of the chosen tactic of incitement to sectarian bloodshed, may yet be remembered as the hideously brilliant choice that it was, and as the means by which regime change in Iraq was ultimately defeated. If this awful premonition turns out to have been right, then it will not just be the Bush administration that was brought low. Generations yet unborn in the region will have reason to curse the confessional killers, and the much-mocked word "evil" will appear as an understated description of the work that they did.

Many of the articles and exchanges reprinted here have a flavor of antiquity to them (at least to me). Did I ever really have to argue that bin Ladenism was not a *product* of poverty and misery and repression but a *producer* of same? The years fall away, and I feel young again. . . . Indeed, for a while, there were those who pretended that they opposed an intervention in Iraq only because it would detract from the war—against the Taliban and Al Qaeda—that they now claimed to support even if they had opposed it at the time. But now, the same mentality breaks to the surface again. It is said even by senior members of the Democratic Senatorial leadership—Harry Reid himself being one of the most prominent—that there would be no sadistic saboteurs and Islamist death squads in Iraq if it were not for the presence of the Coalition. The implied corollary—that a withdrawal would lead to the evaporation of suicidal death-squad activity—is often not stated confidently. (I believe I can guess why that is.) Instead, a resort to the passive voice is made. Iraq, we are often told, has become a "magnet" for jihadists. Yes, that must be right. They were just loose iron filings until we activated their innate ironlike properties. In the same passive voice, we are told that "the war" in Iraq has killed tens of thousands of civilians—when it is in fact the alliance of Baathists and Islamists that has murdered them.

A similarly passive and masochistic argument, again partly borrowed from the school that felt that the World Trade Center was somehow connected to events on the West Bank, has become known as the "Pottery Barn" theory. On the basis of this annexation from the cheap language of American mass-marketing, if you break it, you own it. I used to be irritated by this flippant analogy, offered by practitioners of statecraft as varied as Colin Powell and Maureen Dowd, until I realized that it possessed a core of truth. Iraq and Afghanistan, before 2001, *were* both broken. And—because we had contributed to "breaking" them—they were both to some extent "owned" by us.

Indeed, I think that the true division of opinion is between those who recognize that Iraq is a serious historical responsibility, and those who do not. Even if the "antiwar" forces had been right instead of wrong about WMDs and terrorism, they would still have been chiefly concerned, as they still are, with dissociating the United States from any of these obligations. To summarize briefly: if the CIA did not help to bring about the Baathist coup in 1969 (as its agents have boasted), it certainly did nothing to oppose it. The presidency of Jimmy Carter ought to be better remembered than it is, for inciting Saddam Hussein to invade Iran in 1980 and thus to start a long and sanguinary war which wreaked incalculable damage to both societies. The successor Reagan and Bush administrations continued to furnish Saddam with the sinews of war: armaments that were employed in the genocidal *Anfal* campaign in Iraqi Kurdistan, which was begun (be it noted) *after* hostilities with Iran had ended. Highly suggestive evidence exists to support the contention that the first Bush administration colluded with what it thought would be an Iraqi incursion into Kuwait in 1990, only switching gear when Saddam's megalomania impelled him instead to annex the entire country. (This unbelievable rashness, incidentally, makes fools of all those who have since maintained that he was a "rational actor," capable of understanding deterrence and of weighing his own self-interest.) The end of the war, or perhaps better say of that phase of it, was marked by the decision to leave Saddam Hussein in power, a decision which in practice involved something more than neutrality. It actually meant *collusion* with his restoration, and passivity in the face of his renewed attempt to extirpate the Kurdish and Shia populations. The subsequent "no-fly" zones over northern and southern Iraq, imposed after much public outrage, were an acknowledgment that the "First Gulf War" had actually ended in a truce or armistice, with the real outcome not yet decided.

The ensuing twelve years of sanctions-plus-Saddam, during which ordinary Iraqis suffered great privation and during which a very large number of children and older and infirm Iraqis actually died for want of supplies, remains a huge reproach to our statecraft and to the stewardship of the United Nations, whose "oil-for-food" program has since become a byword for the most cynical kind of corruption. It has to be said in passing that this interlude reflects very badly on the anti-interventionist forces. Not only did many of their best-known political leaders, in several countries, become actual beneficiaries of Saddam Hussein's ill-gotten largesse, but in general they used the civilian deaths as a moral weapon only against the United States. It was obvious from Saddam's palace-building program and continuing exorbitant military expenditure that Iraq could afford to feed its people better, so that the problem was not sanctions per se but sanctions plus Saddam. One or the other variable in this ghastly equation had to go—and the Left said that it should be the sanctions. This was bad faith, since Iraq would clearly have been better off with the removal of Saddam, which would have meant (and has meant) the removal of sanctions by definition.

The incessant and largely bogus fuss over the ostensible pretexts for the war, then, seems to me little more than a ruse. It is designed to avoid the central question of historical responsibility. At a minimum, the United States was under some obligation to make up for its past crimes and mistakes, to repair the damage done by the sanctions, to compensate the country's population (most particularly its Kurds and Shiites) for the harm done to them, to disarm the tyranny and prevent it offering safe haven to Al Qaeda and others, and to put the war criminals and torturers on trial.

Every partisan of regime change in Iraq has his or her story of greatest disappointment at the way in which this program was ultimately implemented. I shall mention one of the lesser-known ones. In Britain during the late 1990s there was established an organization known as INDICT. Founded by Ann Clwyd, a leading member of Labour's parliamentary Left, it called for the attorney-general of the United Kingdom to prepare the legal warrant for the indictment of Saddam Hussein on a range of charges from genocide to kidnapping. That Britain had jurisdiction in this cannot be doubted: British citizens had been taken hostage in Kuwait, for example, and used as "human shields." The Blair government, however, declined to adopt this course, which meant that we missed the opportunity to enter Iraq to serve a proper warrant. These and many other shortcomings of the planning—many of them known very well to me—still cannot be used to negate the responsibility that we did have, and are discharging.

There is something Berkeleyean about the mainstream opposition to the war. (I speak not of the university campus, where this opinion is common, but of the bishop who gave the campus its name.) It is argued that somehow, if the Coalition was not in Iraq, the effects of violence and disorder would not be felt by us. In other words, that a country that was already on the verge of breakdown and implosion and civil war would have been best left to its own devices. Apart from its callousness, this view could only with extreme charity be called myopic. The collapse of a large and important state, its infrastructure already damaged by our sanctions and botched previous interventions, would not only have created a Rwanda or Somalia on the Gulf in humanitarian terms. It would have drawn opportunistic interventions from Iran, Saudi Arabia, and Turkey—as it has to some extent already—and created a post-Yugoslavia on a grand scale right on a chokepoint of the world economy.

Thus, matters of principle and matters of "realism" intersect and coincide. In a criticism of me that is not reprinted here, Harold Meyerson of the *American Prospect* wrote that I had gone astray because of my old allegiance to the Iraqi and Kurdish leftists and secularists who had fought for so long to depose Saddam. It was generous (and correct) of him to point this out. Those who incessantly write to me and urge me to join the ranks of the "second thoughts" contingent do so in vain. I am never going to write an open letter to my Mesopotamian comrades, all of whom face death every day in a death-grapple with fascism, and say, "sorry, brothers and sisters, but the heat has become too great and I must bid your lost cause farewell." What a disgraceful thought. But it also seems obvious to me that there is a general interest in preventing the breakdown of Iraq and in ensuring that even if it does decide to separate into its component parts—as Peter Galbraith so powerfully argues that it both has and should—that this adjustment is made as peacefully and democratically as possible and is not left to the sectarians and tribalists.

Leafing through these *madeleines*, I note an old friend here and there. Susan Sontag, I am proud to say, somewhat amended her remarks about 11 September in a later interview with *Salon*, stated her firm opposition to "Islamic fascism," and partly credited me with having persuaded her. My old Oxford tutor Steven Lukes warns me that the United States will betray the Kurds—one predicted outcome that has definitely not occurred[2]—and my old colleague Katha Pollitt corrects me on the bedfellow question.[3] (That Steven and Katha have since got married is a source of nothing but delight to me.) Stefan Collini gives a hostage to fortune by saying that he doesn't understand the phrase "premature antifascist" but rightly upbraids me for underlining my cheap shot at Louis Althusser.[4] Dennis Perrin continues to franchise his brief acquaintance with me into a career path, in which I wish him all the luck in the world. Noam Chomsky, Edward Herman, and Tariq Ali continue to refuse to let their attacks on me be reprinted, thus deliberately making this volume harder to produce. George Scialabba, a master of the "more-in-sorrow-than-in-anger" style, has recently asked me for—and received—a dust-jacket endorsement of his book of essays. Is it possible that he regrets his near-total reliance on the work of the eccentric CIA hack Michael Scheuer, whose opinion of Osama bin Laden borders on almost idolatrous admiration? Is it not weird in general, as also evidenced by the Left's adulation of Joseph Wilson and Valerie Plame, that radicals should have teamed up with, of all agencies of the US government, the venal and incompetent CIA? Meanwhile Mr. Richard Clarke—a hero to many critics of the Bush administration—has not retracted his view that Clinton's Al Shifa bombing in Sudan *was* justified, in that the factory was being used by Osama bin Laden to mix chemicals for Saddam Hussein. Even if this was not true for that factory,

it might have been true of other Sudanese ones. Why are the Clintonoids not demanding that the relevant proofs be declassified?

Out of all these, I find I do want to return to my argument with
Katha. Of course one must never judge a position by the bedfellows it
involves. But some of the conduct of the Left has been unconscionable.
I debate George Galloway, for example, who is by no means marginal
in the "antiwar" movement, and find that I am dealing with a man who
openly praises Saddam Hussein, the "martyrs" in Iraq and the death-
squad regime of Bashar al-Asad in Syria. Ramsey Clark turns up on
Saddam Hussein's defense team—no bad thing in itself—and publicly
says not that he did not commit the massacres of which he stands accused but that he would have been justified in doing so! Matters are
not much better on the Right, where Scott Ritter—for example—told
me three times in a public exchange that Iraq was better off under
its deposed despot. The "realist" Henry Kissinger delivers himself of
the opinion that Iraq is a majority-Sunni society. Professor Juan Cole
writes that he believes the late Abu-Musab al-Zarqawi to be a ficti-
tious character. And people think that it is I who owe the explanation.

My main regret is, and remains, that I have done so little. But of that
little, I am reasonably proud. In an average week, my wife and I have
usually welcomed at least one Iraqi or Kurdish or Afghan democrat
into our home or been able to offer hospitality to some of the extraordinary young men and women who are about to ship out to (or have
returned from) their volunteer service on the front line. I am in regular contact with secular activists who risk their lives every single day
in an effort to save their societies from barbarism. Sometimes I have
been able to publicize a good cause or some useful work. I did manage to make the reunion in Baghdad that I promised on page 108. I did
see the women lining up to register to vote in Kabul. I was invited to
be the only non-Iraqi on a live television linkup during that country's
first-ever election. I have not been an uncritical supporter of the Bush
administration (I was, for example, asked by the ACLU to be a named
plaintiff in the lawsuit against the NSA for warrantless wiretapping,
and I was happy to join the suit), but I have never engaged in that foolish, empty casuistry which says that Abu Ghraib or Guantánamo are
the moral equivalents of the Gulag. It has for me been a privilege and
an education to take part in this necessary struggle, and I hope it may

have helped me acquire some of the sinew that will be necessary to participate in future ones.

NOTES

1. *Editors' Note*: This is a reference to Collini's suggestion that it was indecorous of Hitchens to use the Raymond Williams Memorial Lecture as a platform for inveighing against, as Hitchens put it in *Orwell's Victory*, "the overrated doyen of cultural studies and Cambridge English" (see Stefan Collini, "'No Bullshit' Bullshit," *London Review of Books*, January 23, 2003).

2. See Steven Lukes, "Sorry, Hitchens, This Time It Should Be 'No' to War," *Open Democracy*, January 27, 2003.

3. See "The Hitchens-Pollitt Papers," in the *Nation*, December 16, 2002.

4. *Editors' Note*: See Collini, "'No Bullshit' Bullshit." Collini rebukes Hitchens for his "schoolboyish," "blimpish" reference to Althusser's "application for the Electric Chair of philosophy at the Ecole Abnormale." The above references to, respectively, Lukes, Pollitt, and Collini were made before all three authors decided to withhold permission to reprint their articles for this volume. Naively, we—the editors—assumed that they would happily grant permission, and the manuscript Hitchens received included their pieces.

ABOUT THE CONTRIBUTORS

Juan Cole is Professor of Modern Middle East and South Asian History at the University of Michigan. He has written extensively on modern Islamic movements in Egypt, the Persian Gulf, and South Asia. His books include *Shiism and Social Protest* (Yale University Press, 1986), *Roots of North Indian Shiism in Iran and Iraq* (University of California Press, 1989), *Comparing Muslim Societies* (University of Michigan Press, 1992), *Colonialism and Revolution in the Middle East: Social and Cultural Origins of Egypt's Urabi Movement* (Princeton University Press, 1993), *Modernity and the Millennium: The Genesis of the Baha'i Faith in the Nineteenth-Century Middle East* (Columbia University Press, 1998), *Sacred Space and Holy War* (I. B. Tauris, 2002), and, most recently, *Napoleon's Egypt: Invading the Middle East* (Palgrave Macmillan, 2007).

Simon Cottee was educated at Cambridge University, the London School of Economics, and Keele University, where he took a Ph.D. in criminology. He has taught at the University of London, the University of the West Indies at Trinidad, and the University of Wales at Bangor, where he is currently a Lecturer in Criminology and Criminal Justice. His areas of specialization are social control, deviance, political violence, and terrorism. His Ph.D. dissertation was a history of socialist/ radical thinking on crime, and he is currently working on a book on the vilification of apostates. He has published extensively in the *Journal of Human Rights*, *Theoretical Criminology*, and the *International Journal of the Sociology of Law*.

Thomas Cushman is Professor of Sociology at Wellesley College and the founder and former editor in chief of the *Journal of Human Rights*.

He has written or edited numerous books, including *Notes from Underground: Rock Music Counterculture in Russia* (State University of New York Press, 1995), *This Time We Knew: Western Responses to Genocide in Bosnia* (New York University Press, 1996), *George Orwell: Into the Twenty-first Century* (Paradigm, 2004), and *A Matter of Principle: Humanitarian Arguments for War in Iraq* (University of California Press, 2005). He is the editor of two book series: Post-Communist Cultural Studies and Essays in Human Rights—both published by Penn State University Press. He was a Mellon Foundation New Directions Fellow for 2002, a Fellow of the Salzburg Seminar Academic Core Session on International Law and Human Rights chaired by Lloyd Cutler and Richard Goldstone, and a former visiting scholar at the Carr Center for Human Rights Policy at Harvard University. He is currently a faculty associate at the Center for Cultural Sociology, Yale University.

Norman Finkelstein has held faculty positions at Brooklyn College, Hunter College, New York University, and, most recently, DePaul University, where he has been an assistant professor since 2003. His books include *Image and Reality of the Israel-Palestine Conflict* (Verso, 1995), *The Rise and Fall of Palestine* (University of Minnesota, 1996), *A Nation on Trial: The Goldhagen Thesis and Historical Truth* (Henry Holt, 1998), *The Holocaust Industry: Reflections on the Exploitation of Jewish Suffering* (Verso, 2000), *Beyond Chutzpah: On the Misuse of Anti-Semitism and the Abuse of History* (University of California Press, 2005), and *Ariel Sharon* (Lerner, 2005).

Christopher Hitchens is Christopher Hitchens.

Michael Kazin is a professor in the Department of History at Georgetown University. An expert on contemporary US politics and social movements, his books include *Barons of Labor: The San Francisco Building Trades and Union Power in the Progressive Era* (University of Illinois Press, 1987), *The Populist Persuasion: An American History* (Basic Books, 1995), *America Divided: The Civil War of the 1960s* (Oxford University Press, 1999), and *Godly Hero: The Life of William Jennings Bryan* (Knopf, 2006). He is currently working on a history of the American Left, to be published by Knopf.

Scott Lucas is Professor of American Studies at the University of Birmingham. He specializes in US politics, international relations, and diplomatic history. His books include *Postwar Britain: Themes and Perspectives, 1945–1964* (Pinter, 1989), *Contemporary Britain: Continuity and Change, 1931–1961* (Pinter, 1991), *Divided We Stand: Britain, the US, and the Suez Crisis* (Hodder and Stoughton, 1991), *The Lion's Last War: Britain and the Suez Crisis* (Manchester University Press, 1996), *Freedom's War: The US Crusade against the Soviet Union, 1945–1956* (New York University Press, 1999), *George Orwell* (Manly Press, 2001), and *The Betrayal of Dissent: Beyond Orwell, Hitchens, and the New American Century* (Pluto, 2004).

Gary Malone is a columnist and blogger. His blog is called the Self Made Pundit, available at http://selfmadepundit.blogspot.com/.

Dennis Perrin is a writer and blogger. His books include *Mr. Mike: The Life and Work of Michael O'Donoghue, the Man Who Made Comedy Dangerous* (Spike, 1999), and *American Fan: Sports Mania and the Culture That Feeds It* (Spike, 2000). He blogs at Red State Son, http://redstateson.blogspot.com/.

George Scialabba writes regularly for the *Boston Globe, Boston Review, Dissent,* the *Nation,* and the *American Prospect.* In 1991, he won the National Book Critics Circle's Nona Balakian Award for Excellence in Reviewing.

Richard Seymour is a political activist who lives, works, studies, and writes in London. He maintains a weblog called Lenin's Tomb: http://leninology.blogspot.com.

Studs Terkel describes himself as a "guerrilla journalist with a tape recorder." He is the author of numerous books, including *Division Street: America* (New Press, 1967), *Hard Times* (Norton, 1970), *Working* (New Press, 1974), *American Dreams: Lost and Found* (New Press, 1980), *The Good War* (Weidenfeld and Nicolson, 1985), *The Great Divide* (Random House, 1988), *Race* (New Press, 1992), *Coming of Age* (New Press, 1995), and *Will the Circle Be Unbroken?* (Ballantine, 2001).

INDEX

Abdullah II (King of Jordan), 247

Abizaid, John, 116, 124

Absolutism: of Hitchens, 2–3; theocratic, 103, 114 (*see also* Al Qaeda; Islam, reactionary; Jihadists/jihadism; Taliban, the)

Abu Gheith, Suleiman, 65

Abu Ghraib, 134–36, 152, 311

Abu Nidal group, 73. *See also* Nidal, Abu

Afghanistan: Buddhas at Bamiyan, desecration of, 41; civil society, efforts to rebuild, 163; Hitchens's overstatement of US achievements in, 305; misery of Taliban rule imposed on, 64. *See also* Taliban, the

Afghanistan War: Bush's squandering of victory in, 305–6; civilian lives lost in, 15, 66–67, 228–29, 315; Hitchens's support for/scorn for critics of, 14–15, 52–54, 66–67, 197, 226–27, 229–30; the left's criticism of, 228–29

Al-Ani, Ahmed, 102

Albright, Madeleine, 13, 104–5, 126

Alcohol, Hitchens's consumption of, 240–41

Alexander, Jeffrey, 32n45

Algeria: the "civilizing" of, 286; French invasion of 1830, 286–87; fundamentalist gangs in, 64; Islamic-fascist wave, fight against, 51, 124–25; the revolution in, Iraq's current situation compared to, 123–24

Ali, Tariq: debate with Hitchens on the *Democracy Now* radio show, 290; on Hitchens, 22; Hitchens as critic of, 81, 280; at the *London Review of Books* debate, 232, 315; refusal of permission to reprint work by, 29, 339

Allenby, Edmund, 286–87

Al Qaeda: assassination attempt of Kurdish leader, links to, 100; description of, 60; evidence against, 103; hosts after Afghanistan War, prediction regarding, 67; intentions on September 11, 11, 49–50; Islamic mafia, characterization as, 71–73; Madrid bombing attributed to, 77, 86; Neve Shalom synagogue, bombing of, 74; in Pakistan, 70–71; program/goals of, 137–38; Saddam and, 102–3, 109–10, 113, 120, 122, 305, 321–22, 334–35; Saudi Arabia, operations in, 113; US national security view of before September 11, 65; Vieira de Mello's death, communique celebrating, 95, 139; Wahhabism and, 49. *See also* bin Laden, Osama; Islam, reactionary; Jihadists/jihadism

portraits of in Nigeria, 59; Saddam and, 102–3, 118, 120, 126, 321–22, 334–35 (see also Jihadists/jihadism, Saddam and); service performed in mistaken assault on the US, 154; the Sudanese regime and, 225; Zarqawi and, 137–38, 305. See also Al Qaeda; Jihadists/jihadism
Black, Conrad, 236
Black, Ian, 328n25
Black Panther Party, 192
Blair, Tony: confrontation with Saddam, attention drawn to, 154, 160; the former Yugoslavia, position regarding, 203, 318; Galloway electoral victory and, 149; London bombings, alliance with Bush and, 89; McCarthy's mention of, 189
Blanco, Carrero, 77
Bloom, Harold, 276
Blumenthal, Sidney, 205, 242, 259, 261
Borges, Jorge Luis, 276
Bosnia. See Balkans, the
Bossi, Umberto, 188
Botero, Fernando, 134, 136
Bourne, Randolph, 272
Bousakla, Mimount, 87
Bouyeri, Mohammed, 85–86
Brahimi, Lakhdar, 131
Bremer, Paul, 131
Brezhnez, Leonid, 180
Britain: abolition effort to end slavery, 288–89; terrorist bombings in, 87–93. See also London
British Charity Commissioners, 147
Brown, John, 274
Brown, Tina, 191
Brunner, Alois, 300n52
Buchanan, Patrick, 209
Buckley, William, 172

Burke, Edmund, 207
Burnett, Thomas, 48
Bush, George H. W.: Gulf War, coalition assembled for, 311; Khomeini fatwa against Rushdie, reaction to, 63; Kurdish guerillas' beliefs regarding, 298–99n5, 316; prudence, counsel of, 114–16, 119; Saddam, indulgent attitude towards, 99, 209; Saddam's attempted assassination of, 116
Bush, George W.: ascendancy and characteristics of, 282–83; attempted assassination of his father as motivation for, 116; "axis of evil" speech, 68; case for the Iraq War, mishandling of, 156–57, 160, 320; Hitchens's support for, 261–62, 269, 272–73, 281–84; Hitchens's unflattering characterization of, 233; Israel and the Palestinians, actions regarding, 215, 284; London bombings, alliance with Blair and, 89; Madrid bombing, blamed for, 86; military service record of, 299n11; "nation building," original opposition to, 209; regime change in Iraq, readiness for, 19; Saddam regime as evil, reference to, 104; secularism, contribution to, 84; September 11 attacks, reaction to, 40, 75, 184–85, 234; "staying the course," crusade for, 302–3; Taliban, recollection of in casual conversation, 41; Taliban, squandering of victory over, 305–6; UN inspections and, 307–8; as "wanton boy," 237–38
Bush (the elder) administration: Hitchens on, 260; Khomeini fatwa against Rushdie, reaction to, 63, 203; Saddam in power after the Gulf War, decision to leave, 153, 209

Hitchens vs. the left (*Continued*)
Horowitz's movement from left to right, 190–92; the Iraq War as issue between, 26–28 (see also Iraq; Iraq War)

Hobhouse, L. T., 228–29

Holland. See Netherlands, the

hooks, bell, 54–55

Horowitz, David: apostasy and idiocy of, 260; Cold War, changing opinion regarding, 265; Hitchens and, 274, 280; from left to right, movement of, 190–92, 243

Huntington, Samuel, 11

Hurricane Katrina, 302

Hussein, Qusai, 117, 122, 125, 156

Hussein, Saddam: Abu Ghraib, use of, 135; Abu Nidal group and, 74, 102; Al Qaeda/jihadists and, 109–10, 113, 116, 118, 120, 122, 126, 305, 321–22, 334–35; the Al Shifa chemical plant and, 339; as chair of the UN Conference on Disarmament, 155; crime family/mafia, regime characterized as, 71–72; current fate of, 212; French support for, 80; Galloway's view of, 142, 144–45; gassing of the Kurds by, 100; Hitchens's view of, 16–18, 101–3; Iran, US and British support in war with, 76; Kuwait, reason for invading, 153; the Left's perspective on, 20–21, 105–11; missiles from Korea, attempt to purchase, 120–22; 1993 bombing of the World Trade Center and, 116, 126; Palestinians, lack of real concern for, 57; revenge for defeat in 1991, personal need for, 116; Simpson's meeting with, 99; successor to, 117; unfinished business with, 93; US, longstanding foe

of, 125–27; US obligation to topple, 287–88; US support of, 51, 76, 145, 288, 336–37; weapons deployable by, decline of, 112–13; weapons of mass destruction held by (see Weapons of mass destruction)

Hussein, Uday, 117, 125

Husseini, Sam, 47–49, 52, 234, 280

Ibrahim, Saadedin, 197

Idris, Saleh, 223

Imaan, 92

INDICT, 338

Indonesia: absolutist Islamic republic promoted in, 60; bombings in, 93–96, 113; East Timor, independence of, 94–95

Ingersoll, Robert, 84

Ingraham, Laura, 319

International Action Center, 105

International ANSWER, 161

International Criminal Court, 296

International Crisis Group, 322

International Socialists, 179

Iran: Kurds, use of in 1975, 295; neutralism of France and Germany regarding, 159; relations with, positive impact of the Iraq War on, 119; relations with and the "axis of evil" speech, 68. See also Khomeini, Ayatollah

Iran-Iraq war, pro-Saddam tilt of Britain and the US in, 76

Iraq: Algeria, compared to, 123–25; Bremer administration, mistakes by, 130; Bush administration competence to rebuild, assumption regarding, 27–28; Canal Hotel bombing, 94–95; civil society, efforts to rebuild, 163; de-Baathification

Left, the (*Continued*)
 rhetorical style of (see Rhetorical
 style of the left); Said, Hitchens on,
 193–97; September 11 attacks and
 (see September 11 attacks); Sontag
 (see Sontag, Susan); Stalin/Stalinist
 terror, reaction to, 180–82; war on
 terror and (see War on terror). See
 also Peace movement
Left criticism of Hitchens: Afghanistan,
 civilian casualties in, 15, 66–67,
 228–29, 315; the Bush administration, Hitchens's uncritical support
 of, 24–25, 27–28, 261–62, 269,
 272–73, 281–84; from Chomsky, 221
 (see also Chomsky, Noam); from
 Cole, 302–12; costs of the Iraq War,
 inattention to, 26–27, 324; from
 Finkelstein, 242–50; from Herman,
 228–29 (see also Herman, Edward
 S.); from Kazin, 273–79; from Lucas,
 230–36; from Malone, 279–301;
 movement away from the Left,
 charge of, 21–22 (see also Hitchens
 vs. the Left, Hitchens's movement
 from left to right); from Perrin,
 259–63; from Scialabba, 264–73;
 from Seymour, 312–30; from Terkel,
 237–38
Left Illusions (Horowitz), 190–92
Leopold II (King of Belgium), 286
Le Pen, Jean-Marie, 125
Levi, Primo, 185–86, 188
Levin, Carl, 142
Lévy, Bernard-Henri, 70–73
Lewinsky, Monica, 223
Liberal imperialism, 286–87
Libertarianism, 167–69, 174
Libi, Anas al-, 306
Libya, 159, 301n58, 306–7

Liebknecht, Karl, 161
Lieven, Anatole, 232
Lincoln, Abraham, 282
Lindbergh, Charles, 207
"Live 8," 152
Livingstone, Ken, 92
London: terrorist bombings in, 87–93;
 "The Battle of Cable Street," 149. See
 also Britain
London, Jack, 198
London Review of Books, debate spon-
 sored by, 235, 314–15
Lott, Trent, 207
L'Ouverture, Toussaint, 192
Love, Poverty, and War (Hitchens),
 review of, 273–79
Lucas, Scott, 230–36, 333
Lukes, Steven, 29, 339
Luxemburg, Rosa, 4, 161, 181

Macdonald, Dwight, 265
Macmillan, Harold, 188
Makiya, Kanan, 18–19, 196, 203, 249,
 254
Malaysia, 60
Malone, Gary, 22, 27, 279–301
Mandela, Nelson, 153, 179, 263
Maniatis, Gregory, 82
Mann, James, 127
Mann, Thomas, 198, 243
Mariam Appeal, 146–47
Marx, Karl: as anti-statist, 169–70; on
 capitalism, 175–76; "common ruin of
 the contending classes," prediction
 of, 216; conflict as the life force of
 social change, 4; on people learn-
 ing a new language, 10, 55; revolu-
 tion from above, 174; truth as a tool
 against domination, belief in, 2
Massu, Jacques, 123–24